and the
COPPER SKYROCKET

C. L. Sonnichsen

The Spectacular Rise and Fall
of William Cornell Greene:
Copper King, Cattle Baron,
and Promoter Extraordinary
in Mexico, the American Southwest,
and the New York Financial District

THE UNIVERSITY OF ARIZONA PRESS
Tucson   Arizona

About the Author . . .

C. L. Sonnichsen has been investigating and writing about his major interests — the history, literature, and folklore of the Southwest — since his arrival in the area in 1931 to teach English at what has since become the University of Texas at El Paso. In order to express the attitudes and assumptions of his fellow Americans in their thinking about the Western experience, he later extended his writing interests to Southwestern fiction. His published works include *Cowboys and Cattle Kings, Ten Texas Feuds, Billy King's Tombstone,* and *Alias Billy the Kid.* The present volume, authentic Southwestern history, is his fifteenth published book.

Holder of the Ph.D. degree from Harvard University and recipient of numerous awards for scholarship and writing, on June 1, 1972, author Sonnichsen retired from his university duties. Three days later he went to work as editor of the *Journal of Arizona History* and director of publications for the Arizona Historical Society, meantime continuing his research and writing.

THE UNIVERSITY OF ARIZONA PRESS

Copyright © 1974
The Arizona Board of Regents
All Rights Reserved
Manufactured in the U.S.A.

I.S.B.N.–0–8165–0429–6 cloth
I.S.B.N.–0–8165–0465–2 paper
L.C. No. 74–77205

Contents

ILLUSTRATIONS

The Copper Skyrocket

WILLIAM CORNELL GREENE, like all the other copper millionaires, owed his prosperity to Thomas A. Edison. When the great inventor finally made his electric lamp work on October 21, 1879, he opened the door to a new age, the Age of Electricity. As his lights winked on all over the country and copper power lines sprouted along the highways, American industry began to be copper oriented and copper hungry. The great production centers — in Michigan, in Montana, in Arizona — which had often been hard put to it to stay in business during the lean years of the 1880s and 1890s — now commenced to pile up profits for their stockholders, and prospectors combed the mountains for new ore bodies. Providence, or luck, saw to it that there was always "a supply of new copper mines at the right time to meet the rapidly multiplying demand."[1] As the excitement grew, investors of all grades scrambled to lay their money on the line, and before long the journalists found a phrase to describe the situation. "Copper," they said, "is King!"

After the depression of the early and middle 1890s, the industry took off like a great metal skyrocket and carried a whole generation of copper kings to unheard-of financial heights. Some, like William E. Dodge of Anaconda, or Hearst and Haggin of the Butte complex, were rich already. Many, like James Douglas of Bisbee and Marcus Daly of Butte, began in the most moderate of circumstances and rode the Copper Rocket to fortune and power. They all belonged to a generation which accepted and admired the self-made millionaire as the hero of an "industrial saga." His human qualities, they believed, were "identical with the elements that were woven into the fabric of American democracy."[2]

This enthusiasm for the man who could make it and keep it was not unnatural. The country was young then, and its riches seemed inexhaustible. A promoter who could put the mines and the forests and the grasslands to profitable use could still consider himself a public benefactor. If, like Andrew Carnegie, he could believe that he was God's trustee for the wealth of the world, he could feel almost religious about his gift for accumulation. In an era of explosive expansion when the rules of the great game of business were changing every day and failures far outnumbered successes,[3] a man who could survive and found an empire was considered a genius, and people enjoyed watching him spend his money. He enjoyed spending it himself. As naturally as he put on his pants in the morning, he adopted the life style of other rich men. It was expected of him, and his peers reminded him that his conspicuous consumption put people to work. It would have been impossible for him to believe that two generations later historians would find him guilty of selfishness, greed, and callousness toward his fellow man.

One man who seemed to be a tremendous success to his own generation and was assessed as a soulless adventurer by the next is William Cornell Greene — a Quaker boy from New York state who settled in Arizona, developed the rich copper mines at Cananea in the Mexican state of Sonora, achieved fame, and became the subject of a remarkable series of legends in Mexico and the American Southwest. His career was spectacular but brief. He was forty-six years old when he began his ride on the Copper Skyrocket. He was only fifty-three when he came down.

Human beings are always interested in stories of extraordinary success and failure, but Colonel Greene's career is worth rehearsing for other reasons. One is the fact that he was a special human being, a man of great charm and ability, superlatively well equipped to make friends and money. Another is his involvement, unwillingly and fatally, in an enormous human movement which he could neither understand nor accept as a fact — the Mexican Revolution. South of the border he became, without deserving to be, a prime example of the greedy foreigner raping the country, a symbol of capitalistic exploitation of the working classes. He continues to be so presented by the revolution-minded historians in Mexico and by specialists in business history in the United States.

When the Colonel died in 1911 at the age of fifty-eight, a continuously developing legend had already started about him and has since almost obscured the truth. This book is an attempt to set the record straight and tell the facts about what happened to Will Greene before, during, and after his remarkable ride on the Copper Skyrocket.

C. L. S.

With a Sound of Trumpets

IN SPITE OF A GREAT SNOWSTORM which had paralyzed New Mexico and West Texas, February 17, 1905, was a great day for El Paso, Texas. Rock Island train no. 29, a day late because of heavy snow above Alamogordo, rolled into the muddy yards at the Union Passenger Depot at 8:30 in the morning.[1] In the position of honor at the end of the train was the private car *Starlight,* occupied by multimillionaire Colonel W. C. Greene, promoter of mining, lumber, and ranching enterprises in Arizona and northern Mexico, a man whom the Southwest delighted to honor. El Paso was expecting him. El Paso was eager to welcome him. He was the answer to some, at least, of El Paso's prayers.

Other important people were on the ground, but they hardly mattered. John W. "Bet-a-Million" Gates, filthy rich from selling barbed wire to reluctant Texas cattlemen, was there in his private car, the *President,* marooned by the storm. Madame Nellie Melba, the pride of Australia and "the world's premier singer," was spending the day in majestic seclusion in her own rolling palace.[2] The reporters who moved moistly from car to car looking for interviews tried without much enthusiasm or success to get something out of these celebrities, but their real interest was in Colonel Greene.

Here was a man who created excitement wherever he went. When the train pulled into Tucson or New Orleans or Chihuahua with his private car in tow, invisible trumpets blew and the pulse of life picked up. There

[1]

was always hurrying and scurrying, changing and arranging, and the news spread like waves in all directions: "Colonel Greene is here!" Affable, genial, generous, radiating confidence and good will, he was the American Dream come true.

The Colonel enjoyed the excitement. Although he was a quiet man and conducted his business with considerable dignity, he knew the uses of publicity, was a master at arousing interest and getting attention, and played his role as Millionaire-in-Action with enjoyment and even with gusto. He injected drama into everything he touched.

The basic reason for this situation was the fifty million dollars he was said to be worth. His habit of spending money freely was also part of it. He tipped high, took excellent care of those who worked with him or served him, and was popularly supposed to carry ten-thousand-dollar bills in his vest pocket. Even his lawsuits (he was always engaged in million-dollar litigation with somebody) added to his aura of power and wealth, and the vast enterprises in which he was always involved contributed still more. But there was more to the Greene image than dollar signs. It was a matter of contagious confidence. He had no doubts himself about the solid foundation of his concerns and corporations, and he made it almost impossible for other people to doubt. His copper mines were the greatest in the world. His new Gold-Silver company, which was buying up old Spanish mines in Chihuahua, was the most promising in the Western Hemisphere. His stockholders could not avoid growing rich, and his schemes were destined to redeem the wildernesses of northern Mexico from barrenness and isolation and make the deserts bloom.

Time and again he had proved that he could make his dreams come true. His town of Cananea, forty miles below the international boundary, had grown from nothing to a city of 20,000 people, the largest in the state of Sonora. His new town of Dedrick was rising beside his railroad right-of-way in Chihuahua, and other new communities were projected. He had put together almost a million acres of ranch property in Arizona and Sonora, and his breeding stock was the best in the Southwest. Almost everything he touched was successful. Almost every investment was a potential moneymaker.

Now he was going to pour some of his wealth into the lap of El Paso. He liked the place and was about to spend hard cash to prove it. He was planning to build a railroad from Cananea to Juarez, just across the border from El Paso — a railroad which would bring the products of his mines and forests and grasslands to the twin cities for processing and distribution. The businessmen of El Paso could hardly wait to show him how much they esteemed and valued him, and the Chamber of Commerce appointed a committee to call on him as he passed through and to ask if he would be the guest of honor at a public function.

The great snowstorm upset the committee's plans, and the members were caught by surprise when the *Starlight* pulled in. Three of them — A. P. Coles (real estate and insurance), C. R. Morehead (banker and mayor), and Captain Charles Davis (capitalist and politician)[3] — assembled hastily and presented themselves, a little before 9:00 A.M., out of breath and not quite organized, on the platform of the Colonel's car. Greene acted as if he had been expecting them, and invited them inside.

They saw a big handsome man of fifty-two with a fine head of auburn hair, an opulent mustache, and the beginnings of a portly stomach. He was neatly and expensively dressed and carried himself with dignified geniality. Journalists and magazine writers liked to call him "Bill" Greene, but nobody called him that to his face. He was always "Colonel Greene" or "Mr. Greene." In his youth, his family and friends had called him "Will."[4]

He put the men at ease at once. Although he was usually portrayed as a poor unlettered cowboy who had risen from rags to riches, Greene had had a good, if brief, education in his native New York state, and was at home in both his worlds. He could be a tough frontiersman or a complete gentleman, whichever was called for. After an exchange of compliments and presentation of a key to the city, Mr. Coles suggested that El Paso would like to honor Greene at a public dinner some time in the near future. The Colonel graciously replied that he would like nothing better. At 9:45 A.M. he was on his way to Cananea, leaving the sullen Gates and the aloof Melba lurking in their steel-and-mahogany retreats.

A week later — on Washington's birthday — Greene was back, and the committee was ready for him. A sumptuous dinner had been arranged at the Hotel Orndorff, El Paso's premier hostelry and banquet head-quarters. Every detail, from decor to dessert, had been carefully worked out in shades of green (green candles with green shades; green ices with the coffee). Among the important guests were C. B. Eddy, president of the Northeastern Railroad; James Douglas ("Professor" to his friends), president of the Southwestern Railroad and top man in the American Smelting and Refining Company; and A. B. Fall, Greene's lawyer and second-in-command in Mexico. The menu was elegant, from the Manhattan cocktails all the way through to cigarettes and Egyptian delights. French wines and short speeches were interspersed between courses.[5]

The colonel seemed deeply moved by the attention of the crowd.

He rose to speak:

There is nothing we appreciate so much as the friendship of the men with whom we live, and I certainly appreciate your good will. For years I have experienced the vicissitudes on the ragged edge of civilization, and have known what it is to go hungry, and I am in a position to appreciate fully the friendship extended to me here.

Highlight of the program of speeches was Judge A. B. Fall's dissertation on "The Sierra Madre," the great mountain range in western Mexico where the Colonel's newest enterprises were concentrated. Following Fall's "intensely interesting" description of this vast region, Greene replied:

The section I propose to develop is the richest undeveloped section in the West, and I believe it will greatly benefit the West and El Paso. I am satisfied that the Sierra Madre is the richest mineral country in the world today. I have started out to build a railroad and I can assure the people of El Paso that I will run it to the Pacific Ocean.

The applause was tremendous, and when Captain Davis proposed a final toast, "Colonel W. C. Greene, the Cecil Rhodes of America," every man present came to his feet and cheered madly.[6]

On that February evening Greene was at the climax of his spectacular career, and it seemed that there was no limit to what he could accomplish. Newspaper stories paid tribute every day to his resourcefulness, his foresight, his great dream of opening the Mexican wilds to industry and agriculture, his energy, his success. When writers contemplated his millions — past, present, and to come — the style rose toward poetry. Their favorite adjectives were *vast, enormous, rich,* and *great,* shifting often to *richest, greatest, finest,* and *most promising.* Greene seemed to call forth the superlative.

A newspaper dispatch from Chihuahua, written on the day of Greene's arrival in the *Starlight,* was typical:

The very latest news that is taking the breath of every mining man in this state is that he has supplemented his purchase of the Santa Juliana in Jesus Maria in western Chihuahua and that he has closed a deal . . . for another famous old mine, the Santa Eduviges in the same camp. . . . The Greene Gold-Silver Company is expected to do for Chihuahua what the Greene Consolidated Copper Company has done for Sonora. . . . These purchases at Jesus Maria mean that Greene will build a railroad into it, when it is destined to become one of the greatest gold camps of the world.[7]

That was how they talked about W. C. Greene during the time of his success. For eight years, from 1899 to 1907, he dominated much of the capital and conversation of the border region.

Nothing that good could last, and trouble and frustration were waiting, but while he was in full flight, Greene rode far, fast, and high.

The Making of a Westerner

ON THE EIGHTEENTH OF JUNE 1880 a man named E. H. Cook went from house to house in the log-cabin community of Tiger, Arizona, high up in the mountains south of Prescott, collecting information for the census. On the single page listing the names, ages, and occupations of the fifty inhabitants appears the record of Greene, W. C., age 27, occupation miner. Greene was single and was sharing a dwelling with Frank Millen, another hard-rock miner born in Italy of Italian parents. The cabin next door was occupied by Lizzie Flynn, twenty-eight, prostitute.[1] Tiger was a real Western community.

The Bradshaw district had been known as a potentially rich gold and silver area since the early 1860s,[2] but it was located in up-and-down country where the trails were not far from vertical, and it took two days to get there from Prescott, only thirty miles away. Water was scarce, and until 1874, when the Indians were moved out, no white man's scalp was secure.

The big strike at Tiger was made in 1871, and at the head of Humbug Creek, Bradshaw City sprang up — first a tent town, then a collection of log cabins. There were plenty of saloons and dance halls, but no churches.

Within a year or so the rush was over, and most of the boomers moved. Bradshaw City lost much of its population, but the Tiger mine continued to produce good ore, and a hard core of hammer-and-steel men clung to the mountainside, working hard, living hard, and amusing themselves as best they could with the opportunities at hand. Thanks to them, the place kept its reputation for toughness. An observer in 1879 described it as follows:

Bradshaw is one of those God-forsaken places where none but those who are barred from the place of civilization should live. It is the headquarters of the Tiger Mine, and it has been appropriately named the Tiger as many former residents who packed their blankets out of camp can testify.[3]

The men who blasted out the ore at the Tiger were suitable to their time and place. They had considerable *esprit de corps* and formed friendships which in some cases lasted a lifetime, but they didn't ask questions and didn't volunteer much information. Greene's friend and associate A. B. Fall once declared that so few of them went by their right names that when Greene and an acquaintance from those times met in southern Arizona later on, they did not know how to address each other. Each supposed that the other had adopted a new name when he left the camp.[4]

The last person one would expect to find at a place like Tiger would be a New-York-state boy with old-line Quaker ancestry on both sides and three years experience as a clerk in O. H. Angevine's tea business at 689 Eighth Avenue, New York city — but that was W. C. Greene's background. By the time he reached Arizona he was long out of the tenderfoot class, and when he reached Tombstone a year later he was quite familiar with the three basic elements of Western culture: whiskey, women, and poker.

Some elements of his Quaker upbringing stayed with him. He didn't swear. He was not a drunk. And he always behaved respectfully toward women, no matter what their class. At first glance you would have thought of him as just another husky good-looking young American in rough clothes with the marks of wind and weather on his face. On closer acquaintance you would have noted that he had better manners than his companions and was more than usually agreeable and likable — that he was quiet and often a little abstracted.[5]

When you got to know him well, you learned that his outer calm covered an inner tension which could find an outlet in long hours of hard physical effort, in cheerful social intercourse, or in volcanic discharges of wrath. He hardly ever lost his temper, but when he did, there was something doing.

By the spring of 1880 he was as much at home in an uncurried Western mining camp as he had ever been in New York state. How he came to be at Tiger, equipped to survive on the frontier, cannot be set down in detail at this late date, but the outlines of his transition to the West and its ways can be pieced together.

*   *   *

William Cornell Greene, the second child of Townsend and Eleanor Cornell Greene, was born at Duck Creek, Wisconsin, near Green Bay, on August 26, 1853. An older brother, Charles Henry, was born on April 11, 1852; two sisters, Mary Ann and Phoebe T., arrived on April 11, 1855, and May 26, 1857.[6]

The Greenes, both Quakers, came west like other Easterners to take up land and start a new life tilling their own soil. Some of their relatives already had taken the long step from the East to Wisconsin. Eleanor's brother Cornelius, for instance, was a member of the Third Wisconsin Regiment, and was killed at the siege of Atlanta in 1864.[7]

Will Greene's family on both sides reached far back into the history of the United States and Europe.[8] The Greenes and the Cornells were of Quaker stock[9] — sturdy, hard-working, prolific; people of modest means and of strict, even rigid, morality; farmers and businessmen who worked hard, saved their money, brought up their children with a firm hand, and behaved like civilized people. Some of them attained distinction. General Nathanael Greene, the Revolutionary War hero, was related to the Orange County Greenes. The Cornell ancestry went back to Thomas Cornell, a friend and business associate of Roger Williams, the founder of Rhode Island. Eleanor Cornell's father, Haydock Hunt Cornell, was a cousin of Ezra Cornell who founded Western Union and Cornell University.[10]

Far from the green hills of their native New York state, Townsend and Eleanor Greene made a home in Wisconsin. Their new life lasted for eight years and ended when Townsend, driving his horse and buggy through a violent winter storm, was killed by a falling tree. When he was laid to rest under leaden skies in the Green Bay cemetery, his young wife and four children looking on with Quaker reserve and dignity, a new chapter began for all of them. After a time Eleanor left Wisconsin and went back to New York state to her people. Still later, for reasons unknown, she moved to Kasson, a town in southern Minnesota, to live with relatives, taking her son Charles and her daughter Phoebe with her. She died there in 1876.[11]

The other two children stayed with their eastern relatives: Mary Ann with her grandfather Haydock Hunt Cornell, a sash-and-door manufacturer in the village of Chappaqua, New York,[12] William with his great-aunt Phoebe Hunt. Phoebe's daughter Charlotte conducted a small private school where Will and possibly Mary Ann formed a close acquaintance with McGuffey's readers and the Blue Back Speller.[13] A Quaker academy was founded in Chappaqua village in 1870, and there is a possibility that Will attended it, but if he did, it was for a short time only. By the end of 1870 he was far away in New York city.[14]

Will was devoted to Charlotte Hunt, and she must have been a good teacher, for he came out of her school with a good command of language, a feeling for words, and a facility in composition which he put to use later in his life when he had to compose letters to stockholders and investors. He had read the Bible, and had some acquaintance with the English poets. When he became a man of affairs, he insisted that his stenographers write his letters exactly as he dictated them.[15]

He was seventeen when he left school for a job in New York. He became a clerk in Mr. Onderdonk Angevine's tea store on Eighth Avenue and found living quarters on the same street a short distance away.[16] He stayed for over two years and learned what it was like to work for wages. The experience was useful to him, but he was not an indoor type, and the daily round grew more and more dull and frustrating for him.

The time came when he had to make a decision: Should he stay or should he go? It was a Sunday morning and he was free for the moment from Mr. Angevine's supervision. He went out for a morning walk, his thoughts moving in the old familiar circles. After an hour or so he came to the East River where work was just beginning on the Brooklyn Bridge. As he stopped to watch the shipping, the gulls, and the water, he took a penny from his pocket and pitched it over the railing. His mind seemed clearer as a result. He pitched another one. He felt a hand on his shoulder and looked to see an elderly gentleman standing beside him.

"My boy," said the stranger, "you will never amount to anything if you throw your money away like that."[17]

In that instant his mind was made up. He said goodbye to Mr. Angevine, shook the dust of Eighth Avenue from his feet, and went back to Westchester County for a final visit with his relatives. "I'm going West," he told them. "If I don't make a fortune, you'll never see me again."[18]

The goodbyes over, Will Greene vanishes into the realm of contradiction and uncertainty. The most persistent story says that he joined a surveying crew running the line of the Northern Pacific Railroad through North Dakota and Montana; that he found dragging a surveyor's chain over the monotonous miles of the northern plains a good deal less than thrilling; that he struck out on his own as a surveyor and laid out the townsite of Fargo, North Dakota.[19]

The timing was right for such activities. The Northern Pacific built

to Brainerd, Minnesota, in 1870 — to the Red River in 1871 — and
"surveys were prosecuted in Dakota and Montana."[20] Greene may have
been a part of this activity, but no records have been found to prove it.[21]
Neither has anything turned up to confirm statements that he was "a
government contractor in Kansas and then in Colorado," or that he
"teamed along the Santa Fe Trail and then took an army contract to
freight supplies to the Powder River outposts."[22] The only real certainty
is that in the spring of 1874 Will Greene was living in Texas.

He had rented a farm in the midst of Texas-style civilization in
Grayson County, directly north of Dallas near a post office, now vanished,
called Little Mineral.[23] At first he liked Texas, and when it appeared
that the opportunities were going to be good, he sent for his brother
Charles to come and join him. In the spring of 1874 he was looking
forward to working with Charles "this year," implying that he had worked
alone during the preceding year. This establishes a probability that he
reached Texas in the spring of 1873. A letter to a cousin, probably one
of the Romers of Tarrytown, New York, gives us our first authentic
glimpse of Will Greene as a young man:[24]

Little Mineral, Texas
Feb. 13 74

Dear Friend
    Your letter of Dec. 15th reached me last Tuesday and I need not say
it was most welcome. The P. M. said it had been taken to Fort Sill in the
Nation by mistake and that accounted for the long delay. I received the
papers George sent over a month ago and I have been looking for a letter
ever since. I suppose that you have learned from Mother's letters of Charley's
arrival here. He took my place and I hired another place adjoining and we will
work together this year. We are getting along very well and shall commence
planting next week. We have had splendid weather all winter broken only by
occasional rain. The River Bottom here is mostly filled with birds of all kinds.
They have commenced to migrate and Robins, larks jays Ducks geese &c are
all flying north. The grass begins to look green Buds to swell and everything
looks like Spring although the old settlers say that we will probably have frost
after this. We have had one little snow this winter, just enough to make me
shiver as I thought of the frozen wastes that I had traveled over a twelve month
before. And of the days when I have lain in a little "storm house" waiting for
the storm to go down and wondering whether we should ever see civilization
again. I may not live in Texas, but if I ever try another place it will be south
of this. But I think that Texas is the "garden of the earth" as the old settlers
term it.

Will's mention of the "frozen wastes" over which he had traveled
a year before adds plausibility to the report that he had spent some time

on the northern plains working as a surveyor or freighter or both. His letter continues:

I will try to give you some general idea of what I have seen of the State. Although you have no doubt read so many descriptions from abler heads and pens than mine that it will fail to interest you.

With this apology he goes on to describe the state — its geographical divisions, its timber, soil, grasslands and minerals; its glorious future. In conclusion he throws out some hints of his interests and activities before leaving home:

Your letters gave me much interesting news in regard to matters and things at Chappaqua. I suppose that by this Lottie Griffith is married. Please give her my compliments when you see her again, also to Florence if your surmises were correct. Lottie, I have blown out that "flame" and shall buy a bottle of Spalding's glue to bind up my broken heart and try to survive the shock. Remembering "That ever thus from childhood's day I've seen my fondest hopes decay." And now please pick me out another nice girl, for I think that there is nothing like the good old Oriental custom of having those things fixed without any trouble to the parties concerned. I have been looking for a letter from Mary for the last two months. Tell her to write when you see her. Hoping that this will find you all enjoying good health, I remain with many thanks for your interesting letters and with much love to all.

Your nephew and cousin
Will

George I wish you could be out here a few days and hunt with me. We have a fine pack of hounds and the woods are filled with deer, wild cubs, fox, wolf and smaller game. I will send a Texas paper with this.

This letter, written in the early spring, has youth and hope in it. The tone changed nine months later when Will wrote to his mother in her exile at Kasson in southern Minnesota, tubercular and close to her death:

Arrived in Dallas this morning and found two letters waiting for me. Was glad to hear that you were better as well as sorry to hear that you had been so sick. . . . I enclose a money order for twenty dollars. I shall probably go to Fort Worth tomorrow and shall be back in about a week. I am anxious to hear from Charley as to whether he takes the Bunker place or not. I do not approve of Mary's trying to fit herself for a teacher. It will take her two years and then perhaps the necessity of her doing anything of that kind will be past although the education would not be lost. But you who are there know best. If I had the money to spare I should send it at once but I have not got but about sixty dollars and have nothing to do. I shall buy a wild horse and will try to sell him when broke at enough advance to pay me for my time and risk. I think I can make more at that than I can on a farm. Hoping this will find you much better I remain with much love,

W. C. Greene

What had happened between February 13 and November 9? The answer, as the story has come down in the family, is Outlaws. "Everything was stolen from him there by Indians and white badmen."[25]

Discouraged, defeated, and looking for a place to start over, Greene could go only one way, and that was west, into newer and more dangerous country. A biographical sketch printed many years later, presumably with his cooperation, says that his next stop was a ranch on the Clear Fork of the Brazos River a hundred miles west of Grayson County:

The Indians stole his horses and cattle-rustlers inflicted such heavy losses on the cattle herds that Mr. Greene was obliged to retire for a time from independent operations and hired out to one of his neighbors at $15.00 a month.[26]

He drifted farther and farther west. By 1877 he had reached the Bradshaw Mountains of central Arizona,[27] where he did some prospecting with a friend named George Burbank[28] — the beginning of a lifelong friendship. He may have hauled firewood on burro-back to Prescott when other jobs failed.[29] However he managed to survive, every day toughened his muscles and his mind and made him more of a Westerner.

By the fall of 1880 he was ready to leave Tiger. News had come of rich strikes in southern Arizona. Tombstone, in particular, was booming. The boys from Tiger talked it over and agreed to try their luck. A complete list of the emigrants is not available, but some familiar names were enrolled. Besides W. C. Greene, the party included Jim Kirk (later Greene's right-hand man at Cananea); George Burbank, who also worked for him; John Behan, soon to be sheriff of Cochise County and chief opponent of the Earp brothers; and John Brickwood, later a mayor of Nogales and owner of a famous saloon on the "line" (the United States-Mexican border). The legend says that the men from Tiger hit Tombstone first, went on to Harshaw near present-day Patagonia, which was in the midst of a boom,[30] and ended in Nogales.[31]

For the next nineteen years Greene lived in the Tombstone-Bisbee region. He was little known outside his own corner of Arizona; his circumstances were no more than moderate; and before those nineteen years were finished, he had to endure trouble and tragedy. But it was a time of preparation which opened the door for his fantastic success later.

FAMILY ALBUM

Grandmother:
Phoebe Townsend Greene.

Charles H. Greene

Charles H. Greene
Father: Townsend Greene.

Charles H. Greene
Mother: Eleanor Cornell Greene.

The four children: Phoebe,
Mary Ann, Charles, William.

Charles H. Greene

Charles H. Greene
Will Greene at seventeen.

Charles H. Greene
W. C. Greene, age thirty-five.

Mrs. F. L. Culin
Ella Roberts Moson:
the first Mrs. Greene.

Frank T. Greene
W. C. Greene and daughter Eva, about 1899.

FAMILY ALBUM
Volume II

Arizona Historical Society
Mary Proctor, 1896.

Mary Proctor Greene,
with children Virginia and William.

Charles H. Greene

At the big house, 1910:
William, Frank, Virginia.

Robert W. Jesson

Growing family: William, Virginia,
Frank, Charles, Florence, Kirk.

Charles H. Greene

The big house after
the trees had grown.

Charles H. Greene

Tombstone Days

WILL GREENE came to Tombstone before it was tamed. Three years after Ed Schieffelin's great silver strike,[1] the population was close to 2,000 and the community was on the way to civilization, but it still had a long way to go.[2] The Citizen's Safety Committee (a vigilante organization) took the place of law and order.[3] The red-light district at the east end of town was going full blast. Raucous throngs crowded the sandy thoroughfares day and night, and when a preacher found a place to hold services, he needed brass-bound lungs to make himself heard above the din of the dance hall next door.[4]

Young men who experienced Tombstone in its uncurried era were likely to be permanently and radically changed. They laid aside many of the old taboos and learned to be broad-minded about other people's manners and morals.[5] They took their fun where they found it, and most of the time they found it in the saloons, the theaters where Dutch Annie and May Davenport were hostesses and entertainers, or in the assignation houses run by Blonde Marie or Crazy Horse Lil.[6] They accepted the Western conviction that it was up to every man to right his own wrongs. A few months of this and even a young man of Quaker background from New York state found his life falling into new patterns which he could not have imagined a few years earlier and two thousand miles eastward.

Greene was twenty-seven years old in 1880. He was big and powerfully built, his body toughened by his years in the Bradshaw mines, his knowledge of men and manners much deepened by his Western exposure. He was quiet and self-contained, but he could and did talk well and was already becoming known for the persuasiveness which contributed to his success later on. "He could talk anybody into anything," the old-timers say.[7] It all added up to a genius for making and keeping friends. Almost a century after Greene's advent on the Tombstone scene, the legend of his personal charm and the loyalty it generated still persists.[8] Everybody was his friend.

He had his weaknesses, including a hot temper and a fondness for gambling. He was a good gambler and a persistent one, though the stories of his spending every penny he could raise at the gambling tables are exaggerated. He put in most of his time out in the hills away from those gambling tables, for one thing. For another, he had horses and gear which cost money. He could not have lost it all.

It is true that he was not a member of the Reverend Endicott Peabody's Episcopal congregation and that he did not try out for a part in *Pinafore* when it was presented early in 1882.[9] The fact is he was "wild" in his early Tombstone days, according to the second or third-hand testimony which is still available.[10] He always liked women and probably knew his way around in the Tombstone tenderloin, like other young men of that time and place. But he was too busy to spend much time in those frontier hotspots. Dissipation and prospecting did not mix.

At first everybody who came to Tombstone intended to get rich in the mining business. The "Cousin Jacks" — the professional miners from England — might be contented with their four dollars a day for an eight-hour shift in the Contention or the Vizina or the Lucky Cuss, but it seemed that every American arrival wanted a mine of his own. So the prospectors fanned out into the Dragoons, the Whetstones, the Huachucas, the Dos Cabezas, the Mules. Their chances for fame and fortune were just about nil. Their only hope was to find a valuable prospect and sell it to one of the big companies. They never had money enough to develop a mine themselves, but they kept on looking, thinking of Ed Schieffelin's find and hoping for a break for themselves. According to one historian, three thousand claims were located in and around Tombstone,[11] and the records in the courthouse at Bisbee show that hundreds more were located in the outlying areas.

W. C. Greene was one of the seekers. He was in Mexico in 1881,[12] but he did most of his prospecting in the country east of Tombstone.

To finance his forays, he may have worked in the Tombstone mines at intervals. Some interesting stories say that he already had "polished a drill" in the diggings around Prescott and wasted most of what he earned at the gambling tables. He built up a rivalry with another gambling man named Tribolet. When either of them took the other's last dollar, he would advise the loser, "Go out and polish a drill." Both of them reached

Tombstone in 1880, Tribolet with enough cash to become the owner of a gambling casino.

> One day while Tribolet was asleep upstairs — he worked all night in the games — he heard a big voice that he knew.
>
> "Come up," it shouted. "The drinks are on me! I've broke the faro bank!"
>
> Tribolet crawled out and looked down the stairs. Then he went back and got $400, slipped the roll to the faro dealer, and between them they broke Bill Greene.
>
> "Go out and polish a drill!" advised Tribolet. And that was Bill's start in Tombstone.[13]

Dane Coolidge, who tells this story along with other improvisations, adds that Greene would not work for wages but preferred to take contracts on drilling jobs. "He would take a contract at so much a foot and earn three days' pay in one."

Joe Chisholm, a Bisbee old-timer, carries the legend a little farther. Jim Kirk, he says, got a contract to drive a drift in the Grand Central Mine for himself and Greene, but Greene could not stop gambling long enough to get the job done and somebody else had to handle it.[14] Even such a reputable historian as John Myers Myers believes that "all Bill Greene wanted when he spent half his time in the Tombstone mines swinging a sledge to make a stake was to be able to wear the richly sober clothes which marked the established dealer."[15]

It may be that Greene never worked in the mines at all. The few men left who know anything about Greene's Tombstone days doubt that he did.[16] When he and Jim Kirk left the Bradshaws, they agreed that the miner's life was not for them. No more working by the day for wages. Prospecting? Yes! Mining? No! So Jim went off to make his fortune in Mexico, and Greene began combing the rocky hills around Tombstone for silver and gold. He acquired an outfit and struck out on his own. That he did so is certain, because in the fall of 1881 the Apaches raided his camp and took everything he had — cleaned him out completely. Ten years later (on June 8, 1891) he filed a bill of damages with the U. S. Court of Claims stating that on December 21, 1881, he lost four horses, one mule, one burro, two saddles, one pistol and belt, two rifles (a Winchester and a Sharps), a complete assaying outfit (burned), a tent (burned), plus provisions, blankets and clothing — the whole worth, by his calculations, $1,275.[17] Just how the crafty natives got all this booty without getting the owner must remain a mystery, but the fact that he lost his belt and pistol indicates that he was caught completely off guard.

One lesson was not enough. On March 23, 1883, the same thing happened to him again. At the very beginning of the raid through New Mexico and Arizona staged by the Apache leaders Chato and Mangus (the latter a son of Mangus Colorado), Greene was caught for the second time. He survived, but he lost six horses. A month later, on April 26, he lost two more, possibly to the same band on their way to Mexico. Both horses were shot and killed. One was a "bay gelding saddle horse thoroughbred, out of Hooker's Gold Dust" (Colonel Hooker's Bonito Ranch above Willcox was famous for fine horses) and was worth $400. The other was a gray gelding valued at $125.[18]

Six more of his horses disappeared in a fourth and final attack on December 26, 1886.[19] By now Greene was a farmer on the upper San Pedro, his prospecting days over. A horse was still worth money, however, and these he valued at $570. His losses in all four raids amounted to $2,785. He never pressed the claim and never collected any money, probably because within a few years he was too rich and too busy to think about it.

In the light of all this activity, it is strange that Greene's name never appears in the records of Indian trouble in southern Arizona. The official reports do not mention him. Unofficially, however, he gets plenty of credit. Many stories, some printed during his lifetime, insist that he was in the middle of Indian excitement time and again. He "once killed two Apaches single handed in a half-mile running fight on horseback."[20] He "fought as many engagements as any man alive, and has been shot five times."[21] When Juh and his band of renegade Apaches were out, Greene "mounted his horse and rode — night and day . . . warning the miners and ranchers of their impending peril and assisting them to places of safety and security," gaining in the process the title of "Colonel Bill."[22] Actually his title was a product of his financial activities; he carried it back from New York with him in 1899.

His narrowest escape, the stories say, came in 1883 when he and five other frontiersmen ran into an Apache ambush in a rocky canyon. Joe Watson, in the lead, fell dead at the first volley, and Greene's thoroughbred was shot through the heart. It ran a hundred yards before it fell, however, and Greene got off unhurt. He made a run for Watson's now riderless horse, caught it, and joined his remaining companions in charging the Indians. He picked up two wounds during the engagement, killed two Apaches, and got out alive.[23]

A biographical sketch published in 1905, almost certainly with his knowledge and encouragement, added the final touch: "He commanded several expeditions against the Apaches. Four times he was seriously wounded and thrice his horse was shot from under him." With his friend Jim Kirk, he "finally aided directly in the capture of that bloodthirsty old savage Geronimo."[24]

Greene's old cowboy Mack Axford remembered hearing the Colonel tell about that episode. Greene and Jim Kirk were traveling in a buggy a few miles south of the Mexican boundary when they ran into an ambush staged by Geronimo and his warriors. One of their horses was shot, and their only hope was to reach some rocks between them and the Indians. They charged straight for the enemy and made it to temporary safety. To their surprise, the ambushers stopped shooting and slithered away.

A few months later Greene happened to be in the border community of La Morita when Geronimo was brought in under guard. Greene asked the chief in Spanish why he had called off the attack. Geronimo replied, "You were too brave to be killed. You ran straight toward us."[25]

With all this anecdotal evidence, there must be some truth in the stories of Greene's Indian-fighting exploits, but his adventures cannot be documented. His children heard, however, that he visited the St. Louis Exposition in 1905 when Geronimo, as inscrutable as ever but now willing to shake hands with any white-eye, was one of the attractions. Somebody suggested to the Colonel that he might be interested in meeting the chief. "No," he replied. "I have suffered too much from that old devil. I wouldn't shake hands with him under any circumstances."[26]

In Greene's prospecting activities the Apaches were the greatest obstacle, but he had other problems — including food, transportation, and tools. For help he turned to his white friends. One of these was S. M. Barrow, a Tombstone merchant who grubstaked him.[27] Barrow's son Sam describes their relationship:

My father S. M. Barrow and W. C. Greene were the best of friends. Mr. Greene come to Tombstone prospecting and asked my father to credit him for provisions so he could prospect. For several years he prospected around Middlemarch in the Dragoons and Gleeson. He sold some mining claims to give him his start to expand and went to Mexico. . . . He did have some gold mining claims that started him to financial security.[28]

Greene never forgot a friend, and when his millions came in, he tried repeatedly to do something for Mr. Barrow. More than once when he was in Tombstone he came by the store to invite the whole Barrow family to ride to New York as his guests in his private car. Unsuccessful in these attempts, he sent his friend a gold-headed ebony cane inscribed, "A Friend in Need Is a Friend Indeed."[29]

No claims in the name of W.C. Greene had turned up in the records of Cochise County by 1973, but there is reason to believe that he owned several somewhere in southern Arizona and that he still owned them in

1897. On July 8 of that year, according to the *Prospector,* he left Tombstone for Nogales to "perfect the transfer of the mining property recently sold to California parties by him."

From such scraps as these, Will Greene's years as prospector and Indian fighter have to be reconstructed. About the only surviving relic of those difficult times is his gold pan, rusted and battered but still serviceable, preserved by his daughter Florence Greene Sharp at her ranch home near Patagonia, Arizona.[30]

After the Indian adventures of 1883, Greene looked around in Tombstone for something less hazardous to do. Some time before the end of 1883 — there are no dates — he formed a partnership with a recent arrival named Ed Roberts, who was thinking of opening a butcher shop. They agreed to work together, Roberts in the store, Greene responsible for the meat supply.[31] The association was to have far-reaching effects.

Ed J. Roberts belonged to a well-to-do California family owning cattle and timber in Tulare County. John G. Roberts, his father, died at San José in 1878, leaving an estate of nearly $200,000 for his son Return Roberts to administer and divide among eight heirs, fifty percent going to their mother.[32]

Ed Roberts' sister Ella, born in 1858, had married William Montgomery Moson in California in 1876. After presenting him with two children, Frank and Virginia, she divorced him in 1880. In that year Ed was living in Oregon with his family, and Ella joined him there. By this time a sort of reverse migration was going on as the mines and cattle ranges of Arizona drew more and more people from the West Coast. In 1882 the Moson and Roberts families joined it. Ed was hunting for a place to start a cattle ranch, and Tombstone looked to him like a good prospect.

Shortly after his arrival, he met W. C. Greene and they became partners. Their first joint venture was an expedition into Mexico to buy cattle and start the Roberts ranch. Part of the herd was to belong to Ella, who had money from her father's estate to invest. Greene went along to help.[33]

Will Greene and Ella Moson met when Ed brought his new friend home for dinner one evening. An attachment developed between them, and on June 9, 1884, they were married by the Episcopal rector in Tombstone and began a new life together.[34]

Ella Roberts Moson Greene was not the usual type of frontier woman. She was convent educated, unused to rough living. Her descendants credit her with "culture, good family and money,"[35] but not with business experience. She let her husband handle her affairs. "I think my mother understood that he was sincere about all his investments," Ella's daughter Virginia once said. "He was rather reckless at times, but he usually proved himself right."[36]

Anxious to protect Ella's interests and those of her children, Greene established her cattle herd. On June 30, three weeks after their marriage, she recorded the OR brand (her father's) at the courthouse in Tombstone. Greene's only known comment on this transaction was made to his daughter Eva in 1909: "At the time of her marriage to me, she had $8,400, which I invested for her in cattle. After her death, Frank and Jennie [Frank and Virginia Moson] valued the cattle, the proceeds of that investment, at $30,000."[37]

In the years that followed, Greene continued to protect his wife's interests. On November 10, 1894, Ella filed affidavits in the Cochise County courthouse describing herself as "the head of a family having minor children to support" and claiming the Greene dwelling as her homestead.[38] Her son Frank summed up the family situation many years later: In 1894 "the first bunch of my mother's OR branded cattle and horses were taken to Mexico . . . and later returned to the United States. . . . They were moved to Mexico at Wm. C. Greene's instructions to me, and all with our mother's knowledge and consent, and our mother sent me down to Mexico to look after the cattle."[39] Greene was afraid something might happen to him in Mexico, or that the cattle might be seized if his activities there should fail, and he wanted her title to be clear and unmistakable.

To make Greene's position entirely clear, it should be added that he had his own herd of cattle. In 1899 he owned 300 head, valued at $1,000.[40] He also owned, or thought he owned, a homestead near the village of Hereford in the San Pedro Valley seven miles north of the Mexican boundary and almost due west from Bisbee.

In later years it developed that he had no legal right to this homestead, which lay within the boundaries of a Spanish grant known as San Rafael del Valle. It was owned by a number of heirs of the Camou family, whose title had been confirmed by the United States after considerable litigation in 1879.[41] Greene thought the land was open to location, but he learned later, to his dismay, that he was actually a squatter on those fertile acres.[42] When he grew rich it became a matter of great personal importance to him to own that land, and since it was involved in the San Rafael del Valle grant, he decided to buy up the whole Camou estate. It took years, a battery of lawyers, and much money to satisfy every possible heir, but eventually San Rafael del Valle was all his — a year before his death.[43]

In 1884, when Will and Ella stood up before the rector and plighted their troth, all that was far in the future. His marriage was the beginning of the quietest period of W. C. Greene's Western experience. He had a house on his San Pedro claim, and he moved his new family into it. Three other human beings now depended on him, and the scramble for a living began. Primarily he was a farmer. There was plenty of water in the San

Pedro, and his crops flourished. Beans were one of his specialties; he used to bring in his annual crop to the Copper Queen store in Bisbee, where W. H. Brophy, a genial Irishman, was busily engaged in building good will and founding a fortune. Greene's beans made them lifelong friends.[44] He raised hay and delivered it on contract to Fort Huachuca twenty-five miles west of his home,[45] and he picked up an honest dollar wherever he could find one.

Above everything else, he was careful of his water rights, in that country more precious than gold and silver. In February 1886 he registered a claim to "the Old Tanner Ditch on the East side of the San Pedro River about one mile below Hereford, being the same as taken out by me in Feb. 1885 and flowing about one thousand miners inches. . . ."[46] Some uneasiness about the situation must have prompted this action, but he was willing to share with another man, as he showed on April 5, 1889, when he deeded to Peter Moore a one-third interest in the same dam and ditch. The price was "one dollar and other considerations."[47]

His concern for his water supply was finally expressed on November 18, 1892, when he recorded at Tombstone the construction of eight reservoirs on his property with ditches to serve them. Total capacity was 11,430 acre feet.[48] He was not going to be dependent on the caprices of the river if he could help it. Flood waters would not go to waste, and he would have enough for all his needs, barring trouble with neighbors who might feel that he was getting more than his share. In a dry country, that could easily happen.

Until the late 1890s, he got along well enough with his fellow citizens. He was in court at intervals, suing and being sued. Allen English, the Tombstone lawyer, sued him for debt in 1895. Greene paid the $431 he owed, and he and English remained friends.[49] He sued Samuel Howell for libel in 1898 and lost his case (the records have been lost).[50] There were a few other personal difficulties, impossible to explore now, which could hardly have been avoided by a man of Greene's hot temper. On the whole, his life was placid and normal. His wife bore him two daughters — Ella in 1887; Eva in 1890. Will and Ella were fond parents. For a few years they were content.

All this time, however, an outside influence was gripping Greene and his life more and more firmly. From the date of his arrival in Tombstone he had felt the pull of Mexico. In his prospecting days he had gained a foothold in northern Sonora. After his copper-mining venture was well under way at Cananea, he wrote to General Manager George Mitchell about water rights at the Ojo de Agua, the source of the Sonora River and of the town's water supply: "The main fall immediately below Secres was denounced [registered] as a claim by me twenty years ago and has the prior water right. . . ."[51] This was written in 1901 and would date his first Mexican venture in 1880, shortly after his arrival in southern Arizona. In 1904, when he organized the Greene Consolidated Gold Company to exploit the Santo Domingo mine thirty miles below the southern point of the Cananea Mountains, he wrote: "I last actually worked the property in 1893."[52]

The Mexican border in those days, of course, existed only in theory. People living close to it, like W.C. Greene, passed and repassed it without giving a thought to international implications. Jeff Milton, the famous lawman, used to tell as a great joke how he arrested a Mexican for moonshining near San José Peak, sent him to the penitentiary, and then found that he had captured him in Mexico.[53] Cattle, like people, often crossed the line and had to be pursued and brought back. Greene was as much at home in the vast pasture lands south of the border as he was in Arizona. By the middle 1890s he was spending "most of his time" there.[54] His wife knew what he was doing and helped him do it.[55] Already he was dreaming his great dream. On his trips to the Cananea area he used to camp on the mesa east of the mountains — the mesa which became his new town of Cananea — and declared that on a particular spot overlooking the villages of Ronquillo and Cananea Vieja (Old Cananea) he would one day build his house. And that was exactly where he did build it, when the time came.[56]

Greene, it is true, was not the only American with an eye cocked toward Mexico. The Tombstone *Weekly Epitaph* reported as early as January 16, 1882, that "the Sonora mines were much in the news." A stage ran at irregular intervals between Tombstone and Arizpe in Sonora, where the mines were going full blast. Traffic back and forth across the border never stopped in spite of Apache bands on the loose who were stealing horses and murdering anyone they could catch. With characteristic American condescension, the *Epitaph* rhapsodized: "What an awakening to the quiet old land of *mañana!* This great influx of Americans into Sonora will ultimately work its complete regeneration."[57]

The currents and cross-currents of life on the San Pedro are beyond comprehension now, but Mack Axford tells a story which, if true, would explain Greene's final commitment to his Mexican venture. As the man in charge of Ella Greene's multiplying herds, Greene was responsible for getting the livestock to market. Often he shipped to San Francisco, where cattle brokers handled the sales and collected fat commissions. He decided that he might as well be collecting that money himself and took a trainload of cattle to the West Coast, intending to act as his own broker. The regular dealers heard that he was coming and combined against him. When he arrived, nobody would make him an offer. He had to rent pasture and buy feed for his livestock until he could find a taker, and he lost all his profit.

Knowing his reputation as a gambler, Mrs. Greene thought he had lost her money bucking the tiger, and she could not be convinced to the contrary. She told him to get out and hustle and pay back what he had lost. So he leased the Cananea mines.[58]

The picture of Greene, rejected and gloomy, wandering into Mexico and striking it rich, is good feature-story material, but his interest in the Cananea region went back so far the tale can't be entirely true.

Trouble on the San Pedro

A MILE AND A HALF below Greene's place on the San Pedro, Jim Burnett had his combination farm and ranch. Jim was the justice of the peace at Charleston, a few miles downriver, and a man to be reckoned with. He was the roughest citizen of the roughest town in southern Arizona. Everybody, with the exception of W.C. Greene, got out of his way. Greene never backed off from anybody.

Charleston was a byproduct of Tombstone, founded in 1878 because a water supply was necessary for processing the Tombstone ores. For seven years the great wagons rolled down the eight-mile slope to the Charleston stamp mills in the San Pedro valley, and a village sprang into being which was wilder than the parent community. "On Charleston," says Hal Mitchell, "all of the rebels, malcontents and adventurers of the time in the inland Southwest seem by tacit understanding to have converged."[1] The Wild Bunch made themselves at home there, Curly Bill Brocius and John Ringo among them. Burt Alvord and Billie Stiles, holdup artists who masqueraded as peace officers, came often along with many a minor badman. All historians agree that "the town had a bad reputation as a hangout of cattle thieves and outlaws."[2]

One thing could be said for Charleston: In Jim Burnett it had a justice of the peace quite capable of handling the meanest desperado in the territory. Like W. C. Greene, he was a native of New York state,[3] but he had shed whatever Eastern refinement he may have brought West with him and had made a complete adjustment to his new environment. He had hair to his shoulders, a beard right out of the Old Testament, and an eye as hard as a ball bearing.

While Charleston flourished, Jim Burnett did too. He owned a butcher shop and a livery stable in town and also the ranch on the San Pedro which he used as a headquarters for a rapidly expanding cattle business. When his justice court was in session, he liked to impose fines in terms of so many head of cattle, thereby providing livestock for his ranch and steaks for his butcher shop. His methods were a little crude, but they worked fine for Jim Burnett.

Fred Walker, once a timekeeper in Colonel Greene's office at Cananea and an avid collector of Western lore, recorded in 1908 the sort of tale that was circulating in southern Arizona eleven years after Burnett's death:

Well, old Judge Burnett he goes and runs his little old one hoss court just about to suit himself. . . . He ups and fines Mr. Mexican say ten or fifty dollars. Mexican man has no dinero to pay the fine with. "All right, my brown brother," says old Judge Burnett, "you get out in them hills with your burros and pack in wood until I say enough!" So the old Judge always has a Mexican or two a-packing in wood to his big corral. This wood the Judge sells to the mines around about for fuel for their hoist engines.

It seems the county commissioners in calling on all judges of Cochise County to make a report on their bi-annual income found they had for years overlooked Charleston, or never knew there was a court in that desolate desert. Well, one fine day comes a legal notice telling our Judge Burnett to make a report up to date. . . . Old Burnett had held that court job so long that he had got to feel that it was his own private business. . . . So he wrote them commissioners "that he didn't have to make a report to them or no one else; that his was a self-sustaining court which he had built up slowly by his own hard efforts and that it could take care of itself without any outside assistance." [4]

Burnett didn't bother much with courtrooms and legal formalities. Carrying a shotgun draped over his forearm, he made his arrests and imposed his fines wherever the suspect (or victim) might be found. Since he usually had the element of surprise on his side, he didn't get much back talk and made his collections with amazing ease.

He proved his efficiency one Sunday when Curly Bill and his rustlers took over a church service in Charleston, just for laughs. The regular churchgoers left in haste, but the preacher stayed, after some urging, and gave the boys a lecture on sin, in which he pulled no punches. The sermon over, the "congregation" passed the hat with excellent results and joined vigorously in the closing hymn.

Next morning as Curly Bill was sitting relaxed in front of a Charleston saloon, Burnett and the shotgun took him by surprise. The judge announced that court was in session and that Bill was fined twenty-five dollars for disturbing the church service the day before. Bill handed over the money and "declared that he would attend church no more as it was too expensive."[5]

On another occasion Burnett fined a drunken desperado twenty head of three-year-old steers.[6] Livestock acquired by fine or confiscation supplied most of his needs, but it was common knowledge that he had other sources for his beef supply. In the fall of 1882 the *Weekly Citizen* accused him of paying ten dollars apiece, about half the market price, for thirteen head of cattle in five different brands. "They had the proper brands on, which had not been vented, and there was no trouble in identifying them when the owners found out where they were."[7]

No doubt Jim sometimes accomplished what better men could not in dealing with the hard cases of his town, but he soon made himself as much feared as the desperados he was supposed to control. In fact, says one historian, he became "the actual dictator of the whole area."[8]

When the Tombstone mines declined, Charleston fell upon hard times and by the end of the 1880s was becoming a ghost town.[9] Burnett saw what was coming and moved to the little mining town of Pearce, east of the Dragoons and twenty or thirty miles from Tombstone, depending on the route taken. He carried on there as justice of the peace — considering this his true vocation — but he kept his property on the San Pedro. Since his butcher shop and his livery stable were no more, and the pickings in his justice business had declined, he fell back on serious farming as the best cure for his anemic income. To raise more and better crops, he needed more water. Greene had it. Burnett wanted it. Trouble was bound to result.[10]

Bad feeling between the two men went back a long time. It may have begun in 1892 when Greene recorded his intention to store water in reservoirs on his farm. By 1894 the two men were threatening to kill each other. "As far back as three years ago," the Tombstone *Prospector* reported in 1897, Burnett had threatened to shoot Greene.[11] According to B. A. Packard, banker, ranchman, and future partner of Greene, Burnett said, "The country is not big enough to hold him and me. Greene and I can't both live, and I'm going to live."[12] Others heard Burnett say he meant to end Greene's life the first chance he got.[13] A couple of sources credit Greene with making threats of his own, and he may very well have done so when his blood was up.[14] The *Prospector* summed it up: ". . . the relations of the two men have not been of the most friendly character for a long time past, Greene accusing Burnett of having tried to injure him in different ways."[15]

Burnett made himself unpopular toward the end of the 1890s by leasing his land to a group of six Chinese farmers who were carrying on

Arizona Historical Society
Frontier Justice: Jim Burnett.

a rather intensive cooperative enterprise in the valley.[16] These men were aliens and strangers, regarded with suspicion by their white neighbors, and a citizen who dealt with them lost some of his standing in the community. By the summer of 1897 Burnett was meeting disapproval with his usual hot-eyed defiance, and his relations with Greene deteriorated still further.

The water situation brought the trouble into the open. Hoping to capture a little more for himself, Burnett built a dam of his own, but since Greene's dam and reservoirs were above Burnett's, not much trickled down. Jim's tenants complained that they needed more. Jim said they were going to get it. With that the stage was set for the most tragic events of Greene's life.

Half a mile below Greene's dam and only a short distance from his house, his children had found a swimming hole in the river. The shore was sandy. The water was never more than waist deep. On hot days they liked to splash and pretend they were swimming. Ella and Eva were now nine and seven and very dear to their father. He would never have let them take chances in the water, but how could there be any danger in that shallow placid stream? He went off to Mexico in June without any forebodings. On June 24, while he was doing business in Nogales, somebody blew up his dam.

That day the Greene girls had company — Katie Corcoran from Tombstone. In the afternoon they asked their mother if they could go swimming. Mrs. Greene said they could if they would be careful.

There are two stories about what happened. One says that when the dam went out the girls were caught in the resulting flood. As the other tells it, the dam was blown out the night before. The flood had subsided, but it had washed out a deep hole where there had been shallow water before.[17] Katie beat the other girls in a race to the river, jumped in first and disappeared. Ella knew Katie could not swim. She could not swim either, but she plunged in and tried to save her friend. Eva almost followed her, but Ella called out, "Eva, go back, go back!" Eva ran to the house for help, but by the time help came, it was too late.

Greene came back to this tragic situation, summoned by telegraph. He was crushed. The whole countryside was horrified by what had happened, and the funeral of the two girls was attended by sympathizers from far and near.[18] Greene was deeply touched by the kindness of his friends and neighbors, but more than any other emotion he felt a cold anger at the man or men responsible for this senseless and unforgivable tragedy. As soon as he could get away from the funeral in Bisbee, he went to work to find out who was guilty.

At the dam site he found an exploded cap and a piece of fuse, and the thought passed through his mind that somebody might have dynamited the reservoir to kill fish.[19] In his heart, however, he was convinced that the dynamiters were after his water supply. He decided to see if an offer of reward might bring in some information. On June 28 he came to the *Prospector* office in Tombstone and arranged to have the following notice inserted in the paper:

$1000 REWARD

I WILL PAY $1000 REWARD FOR PROOFS
OF THE PARTY OR PARTIES, WHO BLEW
OUT MY DAM AT MY RANCH ON THE NIGHT
OF JUNE 24, THEREBY CAUSING THE DEATH
OF MY LITTLE DAUGHTER AND KATIE CORCORAN.

W. C. Greene

The editor commented:

Mr. Greene came into the Prospector Office on the 28th ult. and had a notice inserted in the paper offering a reward for proof of the identity of the person who destroyed his dam and thereby caused the death by drowning of his daughter and her little companion. He said very little at the time but seemed deeply affected and showed signs of grief.[20]

Either through his offer of reward or through his own investigations Greene found out, or thought he had found out, who was to blame. He told about it on the witness stand later:

The personal knowledge I have that Burnett caused the death of the little girls is this: I had hearsay evidence that the dam was blown up with giant powder. . . . When I returned from Mexico, my son-in-law, Ben Sneed, told me the dam had been blown up by the aid of Mexicans and Chinese. A Chinese who farmed on the Burnett place told me that Burnett had the dam blown out. The Chinaman's name is Ah On. I found out by their own words that the men had been told by Burnett that if they needed any water to blow my dam out and if I did anything, he would kill me.[21]

On July 1, three days after he published his offer of reward, Greene was back in Tombstone. As luck, or fate, would have it, Burnett was there too. There was no particular reason why he should have been there.[22] Naturally he came to Tombstone fairly often. It was the county seat, the trading center of the area, and the place where he would naturally stop on his way to his farm. In the normal course of things, however, he could have been in and out of Tombstone for a year without running into W. C. Greene. It was just bad luck that he picked July 1 as the date of his visit.

In sworn testimony delivered in a Tombstone courtroom almost six months later, Greene said he did not know Burnett was in town on that day, and it must be admitted that he did not act like a man in search of an enemy. He drove his team and buggy to John Montgomery's livery stable and corral — the famous O. K. Corral — and asked John to take care of his team. Then he handed over his pistol with the request that it be put away and kept for him. Something had happened to the handle of the gun, and he had wrapped it with rawhide to hold it together. Montgomery did as requested. Greene went about his business, whatever it was. Since he had checked his weapon, he would not seem to have been looking for trouble.

After an absence of about two hours, just before one o'clock in the afternoon, he reappeared and asked for his pistol. Later that day Montgomery told what happened:

. . . he asked me if there was anyone working in Hart's old shop. I told him there was. He intimated to me his pistol needed repairs and he wanted to have it repaired. I started to get it for him as the room was occupied at that time. And I told him he would have to wait a few minutes. He talked of the weather a few minutes, about rain; then I got a chair for him to sit down until I could get the pistol. He sat down. Perhaps five or ten minutes after he spoke about the pistol, I went in and got it for him.[23]

A little later in his statement Montgomery revealed the reason for keeping Greene on the outside of his "occupied" place of business. "Burnett had been sitting for some time in the inside of the office."

Neither Burnett nor Greene knew that the other was only a few feet away, though by this time each may have known that the other was in town.

A week later (on July 8), the *Prospector* reported that at some time during Greene's stay in the village "threats of violence toward petitioner was communicated to him." It could have happened. Many a shoot-out in frontier times might never have occurred if some of the "boys" had not gone back and forth between the principals reporting what each had said about the character and antecedents of the other. The two men may have been on guard, then, but in view of Montgomery's actions and the way things developed later, it is quite likely that each was ignorant of the other's presence at the O. K. Corral office.

Montgomery thus found himself in the middle of a fantastic situation. If Greene, his friend, went into the office unarmed, Burnett might kill him. If Montgomery went in himself and brought Greene's pistol out, as he started to do, Burnett might follow and cause trouble. If he smuggled the pistol out, unknown to Burnett, and gave it to Greene, Burnett might get killed and it would look to a jury as if Montgomery had provided the weapon. So he waited and did nothing until Burnett went out of the side door, which opened into the driveway at the entrance to the corral. Then Montgomery went inside and brought out Greene's pistol.

Probably he expected Burnett to keep moving — out of sight and out of range — but Burnett did no such thing. He paused just outside the door, where several of the town characters were gathered, sat down in a chair, and engaged them in conversation. As he did so, Greene, around the corner in front of the office, took his pistol and started for Hart's gun shop.

In 1897 the O. K. Corral occupied the same site as it does today, in the 1970s, with two entrances a block apart, one on Allen, the main street — the other on Fremont a block north. In later years the office was moved to the east side of the driveway, but at this time it was on the west side adjoining Hafford's saloon. To get to Hart's gun shop by the shortest route, a man leaving the O. K. office would naturally turn left at the corral entrance, walk the full length of the premises to the other entrance on

Fremont Street, turn right, and proceed half a block to Hart's place.[24] This was what Greene started to do. He was around the corner of the office before he had time to put the gun in his pocket. There was Jim Burnett, holding forth as usual, and the inevitable happened.

"You blew up that dam and killed my daughter," Greene said.

"No, I didn't," Burnett replied, and put his hands on the chair arms as he started to rise. The instant his hands moved downward, Greene fired three rapid shots. Burnett, badly hurt and confused, staggered up, went through the door and back inside the office, came out in front, stumbled a few steps farther, and collapsed in front of Hafford's saloon. As he lay on the ground, Greene shot him again, then turned to walk east on Allen. The shots had alarmed everybody within hearing, and men came running from every direction. Among them was Chief of Police Charley Wiser, and Greene handed him the pistol. Wiser told him he was under arrest and they headed west toward the courthouse, passing Burnett's body lying in a spreading pool of blood. At the courthouse Wiser turned his man over to Sheriff Scott White, who held him in nominal custody in the sheriff's office.

A *Prospector* reporter found him there and asked for a statement. Greene replied:

I have no statement to make other than that man was the cause of my child being drowned. I ascertained beyond the shadow of a doubt that he was the guilty man and when I thought of my little girl as she put her arms around my neck on the day she was drowned,[25] I could think of nothing but vengeance on the man that caused her death. I have lived in this territory twenty-five years and have always been a peaceable, law-abiding man. I held no animosity and have no regret for anything except the death of my little girl, and the little Corcoran girl and the grief of my poor wife.

Then he added, " 'Vengeance is mine, I will repay,' saith the Lord."[26]

The shooting occurred about one o'clock in the afternoon. As quickly as he could arrange it, Coroner James Duncan assembled a seven-man jury who listened to half a dozen witnesses. John Montgomery told his story. W. A. Gilman testified that Burnett had just sat down when Greene turned the corner. Robert McCarty swore that Greene shot Burnett after he fell. Gilman and Samuel Moore stated that Burnett was unarmed.[27]

The jury ruled that Burnett "came to his death by gunshot wounds inflicted by W. C. Greene."

The official records are not clear about what happened next, but every old-timer in Arizona can tell you about it. Sheriff Scott White was a close personal friend of Greene's. The day before the shooting they had left Tombstone together and gone to the Greene ranch to spend the night, returning the next morning. The legend says that White declared Greene would never go to jail as long as Scott White was sheriff, and he never did.[28] Scott stayed with him, however, and let it be known that he was taking full responsibility.

Less than a week later, on July 6, the preliminary examination was held. It was a strange proceeding. The prosecuting official was Allen English, district attorney, a member of the Tombstone bar famous for conviviality and eloquence — the eloquence rising as the conviviality increased. At first he felt obliged to do Greene a disservice. He pointed out that when a possible conviction for murder in the first degree was involved, all precedents insisted that the defendant must be denied bail. As the *Prospector* reported his argument:

He expressed himself that while it was a painful duty to prosecute one whom he had known on terms of friendship, yet duty, the sublimest word in our language, impelled him to urge that the defendant be denied bail. It was so ordered.[29]

Then Attorney English had a change of heart. He asked to be replaced as prosecuting attorney because of his long friendship for the defendant and because he was Greene's legal advisor. Judge James F. Duncan granted his plea. William Barnes of Tucson joined English for the defense, and Colonel William Herring came over from Tucson to represent the Territory.[30]

On July 8 the court reversed itself and Greene was admitted to bail in the sum of $30,000. There was no difficulty about the money. More was available than was needed. The *Prospector* noted that S. M. Barrow (Greene's backer in his prospecting days) qualified for $10,000. B. A. Packard qualified for the same sum. And Ed Roberts, Greene's brother-in-law, put up the whole $30,000. Trial was set for the winter term of the district court, and Greene was released without further ado.

It has been said that the five months between Greene's examination and his trial were spent in "fence mending" — in other words, bribery, and payoffs.[31] There are two good reasons why this need not be true. In the first place Greene was still in modest circumstances and couldn't, by himself, have paid off to any great extent. In the second place, he didn't have to spend money to win friends. He had them already.

The truth is, Greene was a very popular man in southern Arizona. His geniality, generosity, and genuine concern for his fellow man had been at work since 1880, and now, when he needed to reap what he had sowed, a bumper crop came in. William Barnes, "the eloquent attorney of Tucson," is said to have volunteered to assist without pay in the defense.[32] Frank M. King[33] of the *Border Vidette* went overboard to make out a good case for him. On July 17 King published a piece declaring that

Burnett was armed at the time of his death and stating that his pistol with one chamber fired had been placed in evidence. On December 11 King remarked, "There is not much doubt that Mr. Greene will be cleared as he did what any man under the circumstances would have done and the man he killed was a mighty good man to be dead."

With or without "fence mending," Greene was ready for the show-down when the time came. The grand jury indicted him on December 9 for murder in the second degree. He was arraigned and pleaded Not Guilty. On the sixteenth, twelve Arizonans, good and true, qualified for the jury; and on the seventeenth the trial got under way.

It was one of the great trials of early Arizona. Greene's friends were on hand in force to give him aid and comfort. Ella Roberts Greene, his wife, was "ever present." Visitors from all over the territory crowded into the second-floor courtroom in Tombstone. Affable attorney Barnes, in his black clothes and spotless linen, came over from Tucson to join the elegant English for the defense. Colonel Herring gave stately presence to the prosecution. All were magnificent orators, and they gave their distin-guished best. It took nearly a week to finish the proceedings, but Greene was never in apparent trouble.

He was, as a later historian puts it, "his own best witness."[34] He took the stand on the first day of the trial and told his own story — how he had brought his gun to town for repairs — had anticipated no trouble — had come upon Burnett in the driveway of the O. K. Corral.

I heard him ask if one of the men had a rifle in the wagon. I heard him say, "It makes no difference. I've got a gun myself and I'll kill that — — — before night." I knew he had threatened my life; knew he was a desperate man. I saw him attempt to rise with his hand at his hip. I fired two or three shots as quick as I could. I then started to walk up the street, met Charley Wiser, gave him my pistol and he said, "You have done old Jim up." I said, "I had to do it." Burnett told me with regard to land on the San Pedro, "If you don't get off that land, I'll kill you." B. A. Packard told me to look out for Burnett; that he was a bad man and might kill me.

Cross-examined, Greene added, "The minute he threw his hand behind him I fired as fast as I could. I saw him have a pistol in the waist-band of his overalls when he arose from the chair."[35]

Finally he explained what he meant by quoting from the Bible:

I meant by saying " 'Vengeance is mine, I will repay,' saith the Lord," that he had tried to kill me and had met the same fate himself. I felt that the Lord had made me the instrument of the Lord's vengeance.

It was enough. His own story, reinforced by the testimony of other witnesses and bolstered by the frontier principle that if a man threatens your life you are justified in shooting him on sight, Greene's case went to the jury at 8:40 in the evening on December 20. Ten minutes after retiring, the jury was back with a verdict of Not Guilty.

There was great rejoicing in the courtroom. Mrs. Greene was "overcome with joy," and Greene himself was deeply affected by the "protestations of friendship and congratulations immediately after the decision."[36]

He was a free man, but the long-range consequences of the affair at the O. K. Corral followed him down through the years. Even some of his friends were never quite sure he did not come to Tombstone with the intention of killing Burnett. People believed on the basis of their instincts that he had bought his acquittal. There was nothing he could do to change these things, and he seems to have thought it best not to try. He never discussed the case himself, and nobody talked to him about it, either. It is worth noting, however, that he would not carry a pistol after that, and was heard to say on one occasion that he disapproved of pistol-toting on principle. "If you carry a gun," he remarked, "you might use it."[37]

After he became famous, journalists and magazine writers who wanted to believe that Greene was a fire-eating, trigger-happy Westerner, a "buckaroo of Wall Street," always went back to the Burnett affair and "Vengeance is mine, saith the Lord." In the long run, those stories, which Greene never answered or contradicted, were probably the most unfortunate consequence of his feud with Burnett.

Cananea

WHEN W. C. GREENE left his Hereford farm in his horse and buggy and headed for Bisbee, he could see the Cananea Mountains fifty miles away, a blue shadow on the southwestern horizon. To get to them he had only to follow an ancient highway up the San Pedro Valley — a highway that had been trodden for centuries by Indians, Spanish explorers, priests, traders, and cattlemen. In Greene's time, men who found themselves in trouble in Tombstone or Charleston dropped into the old trail and headed for Mexico and safety.[1] Greene himself followed it often, pursuing his mining and cattle ventures.

From the time of his arrival in the Southwest, Greene loved the Cananea country — and it was a country easy to love. The land east of the mountains is an enormous rolling plain, five thousand feet above sea level, undulating to far horizons. Clumps of mountains rise here and there — the Cananeas and the Mariquitas to the west, the Manzanzals to the south, San José to the northeast, the southern point of the Huachucas rising tall to the north on the American side of the border. Water flows in the arroyos, and colonies of small oak trees flourish on the hillsides. It is grama-grass country, green in summer and a rich palomino tan in winter. When the Apaches were quiet, it was a ranchman's heaven. From the earliest times it was also a potential paradise for miners, but the Indians made it almost impossible for them to work successfully.

In the 1890s Mexico was much as it had been for centuries, unaware of the changes that twenty years would bring. It was a world still close to Spanish times in many ways, with memories of black-robed Jesuits and their missions; of presidios lost in the vastness of *Apachería;* of dreams of wealth beneath Sonora's earth. The pace of life was slower. The price of life was lower. The clutch of ancient ways was stronger. Just before the turn of the century, Sonora seemed to the restless American outsiders a country where time stood still and change was impossible.

All things went back to the Conquistadores, sometimes so far back as to be beyond explanation. Even the origin of the name Cananea is uncertain. It has no connection, apparently, with the Biblical Canaan but is probably a corruption of a name left on the land by the Andebe Indians, a branch of the Pimas, who lived there until the Apaches drove them out.[2]

Cananea existed as a Pima Indian village when Father Eusebio Kino passed that way, and the name appears on his map of 1696–97.[3] Coronado saw it in 1540, and Juan Bautista de Anza likewise visited it on his journeys from Arizpe to Sante Fe, New Mexico, in the eighteenth century.[4] The Spaniards knew it as a potentially rich mining region, and from time to time attempts were made to develop its resources. In the mid-eighteenth century Father Ignaz Pfefferkorn, a German Jesuit who worked among the natives, called Sonora "altogether a blessed country," but he found it in "the most pitiful condition" on account of attacks by hostile natives. In his time the mines at Cananea were worked by a Spanish lieutenant who did well for a time but lost all when the surface deposits of gold and silver were exhausted.[5] Between 1763 and 1765 Governor Tienda of Sonora had dreams of making a *real,* or royal grant, of the Cananea district, but again exhaustion of ore bodies, along with mounting pressure from the Indians, forced abandonment of the works.[6] About the turn of the century an important Chihuahua firm headed by Don Francisco Manuel de Elguea began an energetic program of development, but the enterprise was abandoned after several years of effort.[7]

Twenty years later another soldier, José Pérez of Arizpe, became interested. In 1820 the great San Bernardino ranch came into his hands, and he reopened the mines shortly thereafter, combining with his relatives the Arvayos of the Bacanuchi ranch south of Cananea. The Pérez-Arvayo combination set up a smelter near the old village of Cananea on the San Pedro Creek (sometimes called the Rillito) which flowed down out of the canyons to the west. They worked the mines for silver and gold, sometimes for lead. About the copper with which the region abounded, they neither knew nor cared.[8]

In time, when the Apaches renewed their attacks, the workings were abandoned again. The buildings fell into ruins and the machinery was blanketed with weeds and vines. Some activity continued, however. Sylvester Mowry in 1858 spoke of Cananea as "a famous mining district,"[9] and in 1860 Engineer Robert D'Aumaille, official assayer of the State of

Compañía Minera de Cananea

Pesqueira's Fort: Built about 1865; picture taken about 1900.

Sonora, described nine mines in the vicinity and indicated that there were others.[10]

By this time one of the great men of Sonora had become active in the region — General Ignacio Pesqueira, a leader in the struggle for Mexican Independence, governor of the state, and for many years its first citizen.[11] He acquired the abandoned Bacanuchi ranch and took his turn at the mines.

Pesqueira was a complicated character of great personal charm, considerable ability, and unbounded acquisitiveness, who inspired enthusiastic loyalty or intense loathing in the breasts of his fellow citizens, depending on which side the citizens happened to be.

Educated in Spain, he came back to Mexico with polished manners and a liberal philosophy which he professed for the rest of his life, though he was always much more interested in promoting his own fortunes than in improving the lot of the common man in Mexico.[12] He took his part in the Indian fighting, civil strife, and political feuding which characterized his harried state in the middle decades of the nineteenth century. From 1856 to 1876 he was governor of Sonora most of the time. When in 1876 the tide turned completely against him, he retired to his haciendas, one of which was Bacanuchi, stronghold of the Pérez and Arvayo families who once owned the Cananea mines.[13] A Cananea historian says he received an interest in the Arvayo grant as an inducement to reopen the old shafts.[14] He died at Las Delicias, a mill and orchard near Banamichi on the Sonora River, on January 4, 1884.[15]

Since General Pesqueira had become a very rich man by the time he retired from public life, he was able to move vigorously toward development of the mines. He erected an adobe fort beside the San Pedro Creek to protect his investment from Indian raiders and kept as many as five hundred soldiers in quarters there. He rebuilt the Pérez-Arvayo smelter and enlarged it considerably. Some of his machinery was imported from England, coming by ship around Cape Horn to Guaymas. As many as twelve vaso-type furnaces went into operation, built in a quadrangle around a central patio for ore reception. They were connected by a horizontal flue with a smokestack at one corner. A steam engine turned a rotary blower. In this elaborate (for that time and place) facility, and in two smaller ones at Ojo de Agua and at Puertecitos, the latter ten miles farther back in the mountains, Pesqueira treated the product of all the mines in the neighborhood, turning out matte (partially refined copper) which undoubtedly contained good percentages of gold and silver, for after sending the matte to Guaymas by ox team, shipping it to Swansea in Wales around the Horn, and paying for transportation and refining, he still emerged with a profit.[16]

Pesqueira's operation continued for some fifteen years,[17] but after his death it fell into disuse. By this time, however, many outsiders had come into the region, and they remained active from the early 1880s onward. George Kitt of Arizona, for instance, located the Qué Esperanzas mine west of Cananea in the Puertecitos district in 1881.[18] He sold it to Charles Benham, who in turn leased it to two Americans, A. Bennett of California and Ben Williams of Bisbee. They built the Puertecitos smelter and shipped their matte to Fairbank, Arizona, for final treatment.[19] Bennett did not know how to get along with Mexican labor, however, and was killed when he tried high-handed methods on one of his employees. When R. F. Morton came down from Indiana to carry on the work, he suffered the same fate as his predecessor and was finished off by a Chinese cook.[20]

Through the eighties and into the nineties the mines lay idle, but there was always talk of bringing them back into production. In 1888 General Pesqueira's widow, Doña Elena, sold the Elenita and the Alfredeña (named by Pesqueira for her and one of their sons) to a lawyer named Hilario Santiago Gabilondo. He added the Juarez (abandoned by its American owners in 1887), the Qué Esperanzas (abandoned in 1886 after the deaths of Benham and Morton), the Unión Mexicana (a group of five mines), and the Mina Quintera (likewise abandoned) to round out the holdings of a company which he called Compañía Minera de la Cananea. Gabilondo said he was interested only in exploration — not in mining or smelting — which probably means that he hoped to sell his holdings at a profit to somebody better able than he was to do the developing.[21]

This set the stage for the invasion of northern Mexico in the 1890s and early 1900s by important American capital. For ten or fifteen years Sonora was a magnet for American investors, big and little. There was a law on the statute books forbidding a foreigner to own land for any purpose within one hundred kilometers of the border, but exceptions could be and were made on all sides. American cattlemen owned or occupied many of the ranches, and prospectors and miners invaded Sonora in force. The government of Mexico until the time of the Revolution did everything it could to encourage the mining industry. Mineral rights did not go with surface rights, and anyone could "denounce" (register) a claim anywhere he found, or hoped to find, valuable minerals, and he could keep his claim as long as he paid the annual tax on it. Big operators (like Colonel Greene) could, with the consent of the government, preempt large areas for a certain number of years and carry on development work at reduced rates.

As a result the Mexican mining business became in some ways an extension of the American mining complex. Mexican mining news was followed as eagerly as local coverage in the Arizona newspapers. Mamie Donahue's Montezuma Hotel in Nogales was headquarters for men interested in Sonoran mines.[22] Colonel Greene was at home there and made Nogales his base of operations when he was getting under way.

Obviously Greene did not "discover" the Cananea copper mines. The standard version of his life story pictures him as a man of vision who, "reading aright the mute evidence of the Cananea rocks, grasped the immense possibilities of the locality"[23] and suspected that millions were there for the taking. The suspicion was born long before Greene was. What his predecessors lacked was the ability to think big enough and the know-how to organize an effective mining enterprise.

The slogan "Mexico for the Mexicans" had not yet been heard. Porfirio Díaz operated on the theory that the only way to develop Mexico's resources was to encourage foreign investment. The result was a benevolent attitude toward outsiders with money. They got the red-carpet treatment in the provincial capitals as well as in Mexico City. The common people, who remembered the Mexican War and the invasion of the forty-niners, did not love the foreigners; however these outsiders were welcomed and cultivated by Mexicans who hoped to make a profit from them. In Nogales, Sonora, for instance, the firm of P. Sandoval and Company, bankers and brokers, issued a circular on August 15, 1890, announcing the foundation of the Sonora Legal Consulting Bureau for the purpose of giving free advice to would-be investors. "The investment of foreign capital in Mexican business," the circular began, "is the topic of the day."[24]

It did not occur to the American prospectors, investors, and developers that they were "exploiting" Mexico. If they stopped thinking for a moment about the money they hoped to make and considered their historical function in opening up the Mexican mines, they tended to regard themselves as benefactors of Mexico. From the financial point of view, their attitude was correct. The gringos who did not make it (and they were far in the majority) left their money in the country and went home broke. Thus the exploiter was in fact the Mexican government — a fact which has usually been lost sight of in later discussions of the subject.

The first really successful American mine operator in the Cananea district carried the unlikely name of Lycurgus Lindsay. He was a promoter whose native shrewdness and ability made him wealthy and famous in his day. His path and W. C. Greene's crossed and recrossed as long as the Colonel was in business, not always with happy results.

Born in Missouri but an adopted son of California, Lindsay had been a cattleman, miller, grain broker, and numerous other things before he moved to Mexico.[25] His involvement at Cananea began when his brother-in-law Gus Harmes of New York asked him to see what he could do about the Mina Mexicana of which Harmes was president and leading stockholder.[26] The mine, which Harmes had never seen, was not making any money, and there had to be a reason. Lindsay took charge in 1895, sent for his wife and two daughters, and started getting out the rich lead and zinc ore. In his spare time he prospected on horseback and acquired several good mining properties of his own, including the Democrata, later an important producer.[27]

Greene was not far behind Lindsay on the Cananea scene, but it took him a long time to get a real foothold in the area. He schemed and finagled for years trying to get a start. He knew that two things were necessary: possession of mining property, as much as he could get hold of, and capital for development.

Possession had to come first, and he began working on the acquisition of titles as early as 1889.[28] His first recorded success came in 1896. By this time the Widow Pesqueira had become Mrs. Henry T. Caraway, and both she and her husband were anxious to make something out of Ignacio Pesqueira's legacy. Newspaperman Albert Des Saulles in his later years used to tell how Mrs. Caraway came to Bisbee with samples of ore from her mines and tried to find a buyer. Des Saulles went down to Cananea and saw for himself that the possibilities for someone with a little money were great indeed — but he didn't have the cash.[29] Greene didn't have the money either — not yet — but he thought he could get it.[30] On December 3, 1896, he leased from the Caraways for a term of ninety-nine years four important mines — the San Ignacio, the Chivatera, the Ronquillo, and the Cobre Grande.[31] The consideration mentioned was one dollar. Title was to be transferred "immediately after said person, company, or corporation have acquired the right to hold said interests from the Mexican Government."[32]

Five months before, another group of American investors had closed a deal with the Caraways for another group of Cananea mining properties known as La Unión Mexicana consisting of five other important mines, the Juarez, the Qué Esperanzas, the Elenita, the Alfredeña, and the Quintera. On July 23, 1896, Ignacio Pesqueira, son of the deceased general, deeded these five mines to J. B. Storman and Tadeo Iruretagoyena. A merger obviously was called for, and on December 3, 1896, the day he acquired his own leases, Greene organized his first corporation. It was called the Cananea Copper Company (the Cananea Consolidated Copper Company came later), and articles of incorporation were filed in the Pima County Courthouse at Tucson. The incorporators were Greene, Caraway, William S. Cranz of Nogales, and Tadeo Iruretagoyena of Hermosillo. Greene, Caraway, and Cranz owned an undivided half of the combined properties; Storman and Iruretagoyena owned the other half.[33] All the legal arrangements were not completed until the following May,[34] but the corporation existed with a capital stock of 200 shares valued at $20,000.

Greene's associates were local men with interests in Mexico — well to do but not at all in the capitalist class. Storman was a merchant living in Magdalena, Sonora, who bought and sold mining properties and was looking for a chance to get rich. Later on he tried to take advantage of Greene and received for his efforts an eloquent denunciation in Greene's best prose. Iruretagoyena operated a flour mill in Hermosillo for ex-Governor Izábal[35] and was no doubt included for political reasons. Cranz was Greene's lifelong friend and associate. They visited back and forth on a family basis and were often in business deals together. Caraway and Iruretagoyena dropped out of the picture almost at once and left few traces behind.

Word soon got around that Greene was up to something. The Nogales *Oasis* noted on July 17, 1897, that "Sunday Mr. W. C. Greene was over from Tombstone," and revealed in another column what was going on:

Messrs. J. B. Storman, W. C. Greene, W. S. Cranz and H. L. Caraway are closing a deal on the Cananea Copper mines by which those valuable properties will be shortly transferred to a heavy Eastern financial syndicate who will start operations on an extensive scale.

That was what Greene had in mind, even at this early date, but he was still two years away from realization. One obstacle was the Burnett affair, which came to an issue just as he was getting ready to go ahead at full speed. The emotional trauma, not to mention the legal entanglements and court appearances, distracted him and sapped his energy. And of course, between July and December of 1897, there was some doubt that he would stay out of prison or, indeed, remain alive.

When the jury brought in its verdict of Not Guilty, he was free to take up the threads of his former occupations, but he found himself enmeshed in other difficulties. One was the failing health of his wife, a victim of cancer, who was increasingly depressed and debilitated. Neither of them could shake off the gloom that resulted from the Burnett affair. Finally, in 1898, Ella went to California for treatment and perhaps to get away from the scene of so much grief.[36] On December 24, 1899, she died at the Good Samaritan Hospital in Los Angeles.[37]

Through most of 1898 Greene gave less than his full attention to business, but by the end of the year he was himself again. In October he recorded title to three new and promising properties which he named Cananea No. 2, Ronquillo No. 2, and Chivatera No. 2, all in the Cananea field and adjacent to claims already in his control.[38] In 1898 he was consolidating his holdings. The big push, the beginning of his rocketlike rise into the upper regions of high finance, came a year later after the organization of his first big-time corporation, the once-famous Cobre Grande.

Cobre Grande

"GEORGE, I TELL YOU it's a big thing. It can make us both rich." Greene gripped George Mitchell's arm as he spoke.

"Yes, I know there's mineral all through those Cananea mountains. But the mines have been worked for two hundred years, and nobody has got rich yet. What makes you think we could do better, Mr. Greene?"

"Two reasons. The Spaniards and the Mexicans were looking for gold and silver. The copper just got in their way. It all went into the slag heaps. We could make money just working those dumps for copper, and if you go with me, we will. The other thing is the size of the operation. Everything up to now has been small-scale, pick-and-shovel stuff. If somebody would move in there with machinery and the know-how to operate it, he could clean up. It would take capital and organization — and a few investors who were willing to take chances. If we don't do it, somebody else will. And the time to move is now."

Nobody was on hand to record this conversation between Greene and George Mitchell, but such a conversation undoubtedly took place. The result was the Cobre Grande Copper Company, which made headlines in Arizona in 1899 and 1900 and kept on popping up in the news until 1906. It was Will Greene's first real promotional venture; it nearly blew up in his face; and it taught him a great deal about survival in the world of high finance.

Without George Mitchell nothing like the Cobre Grande venture could have happened. Greene had the imagination to create the Cananea enterprise, but Mitchell had the technical know-how. Between them they put the fabulous mining camp together.

George and his brother Robert, also involved in the Mexican project, were Welshmen, natives of the old seaport town of Swansea, "smelting capital of the world."[1] In their teens they went to work for Vivian and Sons, copper refiners. An uncle was manager, and he saw to it that the boys learned the business well. In the 1880s they came to America. George worked his way west and became superintendent and metallurgist of the Boston and Montana Smelters at Great Falls, Montana. In the mid-1890s he came to Arizona and held the same position in Senator William A. Clark's great copper enterprise at Jerome. Robert made stops in Baltimore, Maryland, and Natrona, Pennsylvania, before he too heard about Jerome and came west. He soon rose to the headship of the Reduction Division in Clark's mining venture.

Both men were exceptionally able, but George had a turn for invention and was good at organization and development. His great contribution to the science of metallurgy was the Mitchell Economic Hot-blast Furnace, the most advanced thing of its kind in 1898. It was in great demand and was making George a good deal of money.

His personality was an asset also. He was a broad-faced, black-haired, firm-jawed Celt with a thick brush of mustache, heavy arching eyebrows that gave him a somewhat quizzical look, sad eyes, and a strong nose. Like Greene, he inspired confidence and deserved it. "Always approachable, always kindly," one description runs, "George Mitchell is one who is truly rich in the esteem of his fellow men."[2]

In those days everybody in Arizona knew everybody else, and the miners in particular developed bonds that were not much less than fraternal. Greene's old haunt at Tiger in the Bradshaw Mountains was not far from Jerome, and he was well acquainted there.

The confidence which these two mighty men developed in each other must have been the result of long friendship and close association. They probably made more than one trip to Cananea to look and sample. They no doubt talked about the great variety of copper ores, even in the same mine, and the ways of treating them. They watched the fluctuations of the copper market, which was moving upward as the demand for copper increased. Whether they knew it or not, the new Age of Electricity was beginning, and copper was the essential ingredient. They sensed that they had a chance to get in on the ground floor of something, and on November 28, 1898, they joined forces in a rather unusual partnership.

At this stage of his career, Will Greene was dreaming only small dreams. He had his hands on valuable property in Mexico, and he knew

George Mitchell,
General Manager, Cobre
Grande Copper Company.

Cananea Herald

he could get more, but he wasn't thinking of exploiting his holdings himself. He wanted George Mitchell to take charge and pay him a percentage. He agreed to deed two groups of mines, fifteen in all, to Mitchell. The deeds were to be placed in escrow in the Phoenix National Bank. Mitchell would erect a smelter and other improvements at Cananea, and as he completed these improvements, the bank would release the deeds to him. In three years, if all went according to plan, Mitchell would own all the mines covered by the contract. Greene would collect half of the earnings, month by month, and would receive four cash payments: $12,500 down payment; $37,500 on November 26, 1899; $100,000 on November 26, 1900, and a final $100,000 on November 26, 1901.[3]

Mitchell's obligations under the agreement were clearly spelled out. He was to erect a water-jacket smelting furnace (his own patent) within six months and start getting out the ore. Greene's contribution was not set down in black and white, but subsequent events show that his primary responsibility was to take care of the Mexican end of the business. Already he enjoyed the confidence of the *políticos* in Sonora, from the governor on down, but he had to have official approval from the Mexican government to own property and do business in Mexico within 100 kilometers of the border. Some time within the first year of the Greene-Mitchell association, if not earlier, Greene made a trip to Mexico City and presented his case, possibly going as high as President Porfirio Díaz himself. From then on he considered Díaz his friend, and the president justified this confidence by giving Greene just about everything he asked for.

As soon as the agreement with Greene was signed,[4] Mitchell seems to have gone with all possible speed to Cananea and started operations there. According to some reports, his first job was to send slag from earlier operations to the smelter at Fairbank, Arizona, there to be reprocessed to extract the copper.[5] It was obvious from the beginning, however, that money — a lot of money — would be needed to get the mining operation on its feet. Mitchell had some, but his resources were not by any means unlimited, and Greene had comparatively little. The partners agreed that they would have to find backers, and in the spring of 1899, backers were found. On April 25 the Cobre Grande Copper Company was organized.

Greene's salesmanship was no doubt brought into play, but at this stage of the proceedings, Mitchell had more monied friends than Greene did. The organizers were mostly northern Arizona men, or men interested in the mines in northern Arizona, and they came in because they trusted Mitchell. To his judgment, said a report in 1903, "coupled with his reports on the mines, much of the success in interesting capital in these now world-famous copper producers is due."[6]

The incorporators were Greene, Mitchell, George A. Treadwell, J. Dallas Dort, and O. O. Saxhang. Treadwell, sometimes called "Professor" Treadwell, was a mining engineer and promoter who made his headquarters in Phoenix, but was equally at home in San Francisco, Mexico, and New York. He was a part of Greene's organization for several years, during and after the Cobre Grande affair. Dort was president of the Durant-Dort Carriage Company in Flint, Michigan, and was a friend of Mitchell's. Saxhang was probably brought in as a friend of Mitchell's also.

The articles of incorporation authorized 200,000 shares of stock with a par value of $2.50 per share. Of these, 195,000 belonged to Mitchell. According to Mitchell's own statement, a large proportion of the shares went to people who had given him money to carry on "development and operations." The rest were put on the market, and many of them were sold.[7]

The major asset possessed by the corporation was the Mitchell-Greene agreement, which Mitchell assigned to it on the day of incorpora-

Cobre Grande, Greene's first mine.

tion. As owner of the agreement, Cobre Grande took over all Mitchell's obligations to Greene and any other obligations incurred by the partnership. The sums due and owing amounted to $20,000, and other bills would be coming in every day. The long-term prospects were fine, but the short-term obligations could not wait. On July 1 there was no money to take care of the June payroll at the mines, and something had to be done. After considering all possibilities and probably sweating a little blood, Greene and Mitchell decided to see if they could get some help from an immigrant capitalist named J. H. Costello.

This strange genius, a resident of Buffalo, New York, had inherited a great deal of money from a father who had grown rich as a tanner.[8] The son made more in the lumber business and then came to Arizona to try his luck in the mines. He owned the Trilby Mine in the Castle

Creek district in Northern Arizona and was on the lookout for new opportunities.[9] Although he was described as "one of the finest-looking men in the city" of Buffalo — a silver-haired fashion plate with a turned up mustache[10] — his judgment seems to have been much less impressive than his personal appearance.

After listening to Greene's account of the wonders of Cananea, he agreed to advance $10,000 in exchange for an option to acquire 75 percent of the Cobre Grande stock.[11] With a little more persuasion he undertook to buy outright a block of 31,000 shares at par — $2.50 a share — and signed the papers on July 22. The shareholders, including Greene, had to contribute from their own holdings in order to provide the 31,000 shares.[12] They agreed that $37,500 of Costello's money would go to the purchase of machinery and equipment. The remainder, $40,000, was to be used to pay off the Company's debts.[13]

As a result of this deal, Costello took over the corporation. On July 22, 1899, the day of decision, he became president of Cobre Grande; his secretary, J. Henry Wood, became secretary. Their general manager was an Irishman named Cornelius (Con) O'Keefe, a prosperous storekeeper from the mining town of Jerome, a remarkable character in the great Western tradition. "He readily makes friends," said his hometown newspaper, "and with his push and energy, there is no such thing as fail."[14]

Costello and Wood took charge at once and were in Nogales in July on their way to Cananea to begin operations. George Mitchell came up from the mines about the same time and announced that the smelter was in operation and "turning out all the bullion possible under a limited supply of water. A four-mile pipe line to the Cananea mountains will be built, when an adequate supply will be had."[15] Getting and paying for the pipe, incidentally, was a major headache during the short, unhappy administration of J. H. Costello, J. Henry Wood, and Con O'Keefe.[16]

By this time a good deal of stock had found its way into the hands of investors. W. H. Brophy of Bisbee, Greene's friend who ran the Copper Queen Store and operated a bank, owned 500 shares and left among his papers a list of his fellow stockholders — nineteen of them besides Greene and Mitchell, some from the East, most from Arizona. The smallest investment was 100 shares; the largest (Costello's), 31,000.[17]

While this was going on, Greene never stopped accumulating more mines. On June 2 he acquired the important Elisa mine from Jesús Martínez, and at the meeting on July 22, when so much happened, he sold it to the Cobre Grande for $100,000 on condition that Costello would take up his option on 75 percent of the stock. For some reason this deal was cancelled on October 6,[18] but the Cobre Grande contract included other rich mines which Greene was in process of acquiring — for instance the Esperanza, on which he owed a great deal of money. A payment of $27,000 was due that fall to one Joseph Muheim.[19] Cobre Grande was expected to pick up all such tabs, according to the Mitchell-Greene agreement. Greene hoped and prayed that it would work out to his advantage.

His final contribution, on July 22, was a turn-over of six more mines to Cobre Grande (El Rey, El Campo, La Bonita, La Pinita, San Pedro, and Los Chivos). The deeds were placed in escrow, with the others. The sellers were identified as W. C. and Ella Greene, but Mrs. Greene was far away in California, dying, and her signature was not recorded. This was the only time her name appeared in any of Greene's transactions.[20]

Greene was uneasy about Costello's management from the beginning. He, Greene, was in Nogales late in July of 1899 but probably did not visit the mines. Rumors came to him that Costello was working fast and getting ready to ship out a good deal of copper matte.[21] Greene was anxious to learn what was going on, but he couldn't wait to find out. About the first of August he left for New York, taking "Professor" Treadwell with him.[22] During his absence, and undoubtedly by his instructions, his attorney, Norton Chase, went to Cananea, tried to get a look at the books, and was apparently frustrated also.[23] His reports must have confirmed Greene in his resolve to find a better way if Cobre Grande got out of hand. This time he was going after the big money. If, as he firmly believed, he had his hands on the richest copper property in the world, he had something for the big investors, and he was going to make them see it.

This was Greene's first foray into the jungles of Wall Street, and a good deal of folklore has grown up about it. Dane Coolidge, who tells the tallest tales about him, has him borrowing money from banker B. A. Packard, ostensibly to get out some ore from the mines, then taking off for New York:

> Greene grabbed the money and disappeared as usual, only this time he headed north. At Benson, where the branch line joined the Southern Pacific Railroad, he talked the old hotel-keeper out of a thousand dollars more and took the train to New York. There at the Waldorf Astoria he registered as Colonel William C. Greene, Cananea, Mexico, and set out on his hunt for capital. But first he hired a dress suit, a top hat and some diamonds in order to put up a front.
>
> William H. Brophy, the manager of the Bank of Bisbee, happened to be in New York on business when, glancing at the register in the ornate Waldorf, he beheld the name of Colonel William Greene. It was the first time he had heard that Bill was a Colonel, but Brophy was not a spoil sport. He sent up his

card and Colonel Greene came down — plug hat, dress suit and all. He was tickled to death to see a man from home and Brophy addressed him as Colonel. Then he turned around and introduced him to various magnates who happened to be present, and always as Colonel Greene.

It was just the boost that Bill Greene needed and he sold enough stock to get a stake.[24]

As usual in dealing with folklore we find a few grains of truth among the inventions. Greene did adopt the title of Colonel. "He couldn't go up there and be just plain Mr. Greene," says a pioneer Arizonan.[25] He probably did dress like the people he dealt with. He did meet some of the top men in Wall Street and persuaded them that he had the greatest copper prospects in the world in his possession. With his imposing physique and his quiet and assured manner he commanded attention and confidence. He was not, of course, selling stock. He had no stock to sell. He was talking about the corporation he intended to set up if the Cobre Grande Copper Company folded. "It was not definitely known," said the *Republican* two months later, "that one was actually formed at that time, but the organization of one was under consideration in the event of the breaking up of the Cobre Grande Company."[26] When J. H. Costello went before Judge Webster Street in a Phoenix courtroom on October 21 to ask for an injunction to prevent Greene from removing him as president, he asserted that the organization in New York had already been formed. It was capitalized, he said, at $5,000,000 "to take up the Cobre Grande property in the event of its forfeiture by the failure of Costello to make the payment on November 26 of $37,500 under the Greene-Mitchell contract."[27] Just who Greene's New York contacts were can only be guessed at today, but later writers mention Thomas W. Lawson, whose name still echoes down the corridors of high finance, and "such Wall Street leaders as Gates, Hawley, Huntington, and Weir."[28]

It is unthinkable that he would have gone about New York knocking on the doors of such men as these. He had to have introductions, and he got them through a firm of New York lawyers: Logan, Demond and Harby, of 27 William Street. Members included Walter S. Logan (senior member), Charles M. Demond, Marx E. Harby, Norton Chase and Fred C. Hanford. Chase is said to have been a Greene relative.[29] The firm was already reaching for business in Arizona, and at some time before September of 1899, Chase had set up offices in Phoenix in the Adams Hotel, headquarters for miners and promoters of mines.[30] He may have come at Greene's suggestion, though he did business with miners other than Greene.[31] Logan became the secretary-treasurer of Greene's great copper company, when it was organized, and the connection between Greene and the legal firm was very close.[32]

George Treadwell's presence was useful also, for he was known and respected from San Francisco to New York by all mining men.

Not that Greene needed much help after he got past the office door. He was forty-six years old when he registered at the old Waldorf (he turned forty-seven while he was in New York) and was beginning to be a little portly. Some grey was showing in his thick auburn hair. These signs of maturity did him no disservice as he shook hands with potential investors, and his disarming smile and confident manner always got him a hearing. The confident manner, of course, was based on honest conviction. He *knew* his copper mines were fabulous; he *knew* they had unlimited possibilities. When he was through talking, his new friends also knew.

The trip cost money, and there has been speculation about where he got it.[33] Greene was playing in a league now where home-grown funds would not go far. From the beginning he traveled first class. He was not yet in a position to afford a private railroad car, but he had to impress a group of hard-eyed New York capitalists, which meant acting as rich as they did. And of course more and more money was required for operations at the mines. The $12,500 paid over by Mitchell to bind their bargain was enough for expenses, but he may have felt that he needed more. J. Edward Addicks gave him the margin that he wanted.

This Delaware millionaire had come West looking for investment opportunities. He had purchased 1,200,000 acres of ranch land, according to reports, from the Santa Fe Railway. Greene is said to have met him on a train between Benson and Tucson,[34] and as a result Addicks bought 5,000 shares of Cobre Grande stock and lent Greene a considerable sum of money. Several of Greene's mining claims were "assigned" to Addicks for security. The papers were signed in New York on August 14, 1899.[35] Nine months later, on May 29, 1900, Addicks in his turn assigned four mines to Greene, which must mean that the mortgage was paid off at that time.

Addicks was already famous in the East as the "Boston Gas King" who had locked horns with Standard Oil in 1896 and come out loser.[36] He probably thought (mistakenly, as it turned out) that he would find easier pickings among the simple citizens of the West. Addicks' money helped to finance Greene in New York, pay for his suite at the Waldorf, and provide his striped pants and top hat. One can discount an often-heard story which says that Greene had lived up almost everything he had with no results and, in deep discouragement, drifted over to Canfield's famous gambling establishment. He laid his last hundred-dollar bill on the line and walked out with $20,000. The next day (the story says) the tide turned in his favor.[37] Greene was a gambler and may have been lucky, but he was not that close to broke during his New York excursion.

He was back in Nogales on September 4 after "about a month in the East,"[38] and he did not like what he came back to. It should be said at once that not all his financial eggs were in the Cobre Grande basket. The Cananea mine was one that he had held back. The Nogales *Oasis* commented on August 19.

W. C. Greene, the owner of the Cananea Mine, says his property is not on the market. It is likely that in time the Cobre Grande and the Cananea will consolidate. The two mines cover a strip of land about six miles long and in some places a mile wide.

On September 1, about the time of his return from New York, the Mexican government patented the Capote and Picacho mines to him.[39] His activities were expanding outside the corporation, but his mind misgave him about the way things were going at the Cobre Grande shafts. Costello was selling matte, but he was not taking care of expenses. Greene's agents had not been able to learn much about what was going on, and that in itself was suspicious.

Everybody on the outside assumed that all was well with the Costello management. The Nogales *Oasis* reported enthusiastically on August 19, while Greene was in New York, that the Cobre Grande was more valuable than had been thought; that the smelter was turning out 100 tons a day; that the "immense slag pile" left by previous owners carried "a good percent of copper" and would be worked first; and that a railroad was planned from Cananea to Naco to transport all the potential wealth to smelters in the United States.

It seemed to Greene when he set foot on Arizona soil again after his pioneer foray eastward that all this hope and confidence was highly misleading; that in little more than a month Costello had taken the Cobre Grande a long way down the road to ruin; and that unless he did something about it in a hurry, he was likely to lose everything. In the long-drawn-out litigation which followed, his lawyers stated his case clearly more than once.

They said that Costello took his 31,000 shares of stock but never paid for them; that he contributed about $18,000 to the conduct of the business but remained $50,500 short of the money he had pledged; that at the same time he had gone in debt $60,000 for work and materials in Sonora, and under Mexican law this indebtedness constituted a lien on the property, making it liable to seizure and forfeiture; that he had refused to pay taxes; that he was "stripping" the property — taking out the best ore and not mining systematically, thereby endangering "future operations"; that he was exploiting previously established ore dumps that did not belong to him; that he had "wholly failed" to pay any portion

of the proceeds of the operation to Greene, though two monthly account-
ings were due and had been asked for; that matte worth $150,000 had
been shipped out; and that the books had been removed "out of the
jurisdiction of the courts" — in fact, out of Mexico.[40] Costello, of course,
vigorously denied these accusations. He was sure Greene intended to
keep him from paying the $37,500 due on November 26 so that the
property would revert to him and Mitchell, and that Greene had his new
corporation tuned up and ready to go as soon as Cobre Grande was on
the scrap heap. Greene, in his turn, was certain that Costello meant to
gouge all the profit he could out of the mines and get out as fast as he
came in, leaving the directors and stockholders of Cobre Grande holding
the bag.

Greene and Mitchell were so sure that Costello meant to swindle
them that they determined to take the company away from him. Ordinarily a quiet and collected sort of fellow, Greene could talk fast enough
when he was indignant, and this time he was really alarmed and outraged.
Costello's operations, he said, were "fraudulent and illegal" and the man
was going to ruin the whole enterprise if he were not stopped. Greene
let it be known that he intended to stop him.

Walter S. Logan of the New York law firm is said to have shown
him how to go about it. He suggested that the Cobre Grande Corporation
had not bothered to clear its operations with the Mexican courts or
register its holdings in Mexico and was therefore operating illegally.[41]
The Greene-Mitchell agreement, for the same reason, was invalid, and
they repudiated that. The plan of campaign was to organize a legal corporation and register it in Arizpe, Sonora, Mexico; then physically take
over the properties registered in Greene's name; and finally transfer everything to a new corporation to be organized in the United States, the
holding company which would be the actual owner and operator of
the mines.

This plan was promptly put into operation. The opening moves
went smoothly enough in spite of frantic opposition from Costello and
his henchmen. The first step was a meeting of the dissatisfied directors of
Cobre Grande — Greene, Mitchell, and Treadwell — at Bisbee on September 23. Costello heard that it was going to happen and went before
Judge Street in Phoenix to ask for an injunction, complaining that if the
meeting took place and Costello and Wood were removed from their
offices as president and secretary, Costello would lose the money he had
already invested and would not be able to pay the $37,500 which Greene
was to collect on November 26.

Judge Street granted the restraining order, but Greene *et al* met
anyway and did what they had planned to do.[42] The new president of

Cobre Grande was W. C. Greene. Scott White was secretary-treasurer. The new directors were Greene, White, Mitchell, Treadwell, and William Wylie. So for a while there were two sets of officers claiming to control the corporation.

By this time Greene had abandoned the idea, if he ever had it, of letting somebody else run the business while he collected a percentage. As one of his lawyers expressed it, he "immediately devoted himself and his energies to the raising of money so unexpectedly thrust upon him by the emergency to pay the said obligations,"[43] and he stayed in control of his copper mines for the next seven years.

The Bisbee meeting over, Greene and Mitchell hurried down to Arizpe to regain possession at Cananea — legally. They presented their case before the Court of the First Instance (comparable to our District Court), declaring that the Cobre Grande had "forfeited all rights" since no instruments had been filed in the Mexican courts and no permission had been granted the corporation to own property in the forbidden zone along the border. The court confirmed Greene's title to the mines; armed with this authorization, Greene and Mitchell hastened to Cananea. On the way they picked up a force of fourteen armed men, possibly a detachment of Colonel Emilio Kosterlitzky's famous ranger force, the *rurales*.

Con O'Keefe refused at first to be dispossessed. Greene went to the local court and got a summons which was served on O'Keefe on October 12. On the thirteenth O'Keefe moved out and Greene moved in.[44] His armed men probably had something to do with Con's decision to step down.

During this period of uncertainty, telegrams flew back and forth between Cananea and Tucson. Con was out. Con was still in possession. Con was finally dislodged.[45] Once in command, Greene and Mitchell kept the mines under guard and stood ready to defend their property.

They may have been put to the test. Frank M. King, well known Western chronicler and a close friend of Greene, tells how his brother Sam was called in when word came to Cananea that a hundred Mexican soldiers were on their way to take possession. Sam, a man of few words and positive action, was once well known in the West. Mitchell asked him, "How many men will you need?"

"I'll have to have about ten," was Sam's answer.

He actually had seven — Steve Aguirre, Scott White, Sam himself, and four others. He put up a breastwork of logs in front of the office, and when the officer in charge of the troops approached under a flag of truce and asked how many men he had, Sam replied, "I have plenty."

It seemed to the Mexican officer that he had better draw off and send for reinforcements, but before they arrived, the Governor of Sonora, quite naturally a friend of Greene's, heard what was happening and put a stop to it.[46]

Even before the O'Keefe ouster, Greene had gone into rapid action. On October 7 he announced that he was suing J. H. Costello in New York for "default and misconduct" in the matter of the $78,000 which he had pledged for his Cobre Grande stock and had not paid.[47] On October 9, he took a deed from Luis Echeverria to La Ventura mine,[48] and on the same day in Nogales he incorporated the Cananea Consolidated Copper Company, S.A., as a Mexican organization. The capital stock was $20,000, U.S. money, divided into 200 shares, of which Greene owned 190. The reason for the low valuation was a prudent desire to hold down Mexican taxes.

Likewise on the ninth he sent Scott White to Phoenix to arrest J. H. Wood on a charge of grand larceny for withholding the Cobre Grande books. White created a flurry of excitement and was in some danger of being arrested himself, but Wood went with him to Bisbee to undergo a hearing in order to put himself in the clear for future action. White did not get the books,[49] and apparently Wood endured nothing worse than annoyance and loss of time. Greene's action against Costello seems not to have been pursued either,[50] but he did succeed in keeping his opposition off balance.

On October 11, two days after Greene had organized the Cananea Consolidated Copper Company at Nogales, he turned up in Arizpe and took his second decisive step, deeding his Mexican holdings, consisting of twenty-four mines or groups of mines, to the new Company — the Four C's. Attorney Norton Chase accepted the deeds for the Company. On October 17, with Chase in tow, he left for New York "to meet the eastern men interested in the Company."[51]

This was the critical stage of Greene's great venture, and he couldn't hurry it. There must have been many conferences in Wall Street offices, many luncheons at the Waldorf, where the capitalists liked to meet each other, many strategy sessions with Walter Logan. When the loose ends were all gathered up, Greene and his friends had organized the Greene Consolidated Copper Company under the laws of West Virginia, issuing 500,000 shares of stock at par value of $10. The papers were signed on February 10, 1900.[52] To this holding company Greene turned over the capital stock of his Mexican corporation, and it was put on the market.

Offices at first were at 27 William Street, New York, the address of Logan, Demond, and Harby. Directors were Greene, Mitchell, Treadwell, Logan, and W. C. Barnes, the Tucson lawyer, a friend of Greene's since the Jim Burnett affair in 1897.

While these arrangements were going forward, the Costello forces were hacking away desperately at Greene and his enterprise both in Arizona and Mexico. They tried hard to win support from the stockholders, who were never quite sure what was going on, or which side they ought to support. The *Arizona Republican* observed:

Outsiders have never been able to see very far into the workings of the company, though its officers and principal stockholders have talked very freely at all times. Even many of the smaller stockholders here, with aggregate holdings amounting to something less than $50,000, have been unable to learn in which particular faction their interests lie. This prevailing uncertainty, not to say ignorance, is not the product of over-much secrecy, but of over-much and conflicting talking by those supposed to be on the inside.[53]

Just before the first annual meeting in November, the Costello headquarters issued a long circular letter to the stockholders explaining what the company had accomplished in spite of the defection of Greene and his fellow malcontents:

... the "Costello management" restored the Company's credit, reduced its expenses, improved its operating plant, constructed a much-needed pipeline, accumulated three hundred tons of coke and several months supply of fuel, constructed many buildings, increased the stock of merchandise in the amount of $10,000, inaugurated businesslike methods in all branches of the management, secured the legalization of the company in Mexico, opened up larger bodies of ore, and, in short, changed the company from an insolvent corporation to a selfsustaining concern. All this was done in the short space of ten weeks during the time the management was obliged to contend with shortage of coke and water, and was able to run the smelter only ten days in the month of August and seven days in the month of September.[54]

Contrary to Greene's assertion, the letter went on, the company had not yet made any money, so there were no profits to divide. It was on its way, however, to big returns if it had not been "interfered with."

George Mitchell countered the Costello letter with one of his own to the stockholders two days after the first one went out:

In the past you have with all other stockholders taken my advice in Cobre Grande Company matters, and with one and the same point of view — that is, I have tried to be honest with everyone and my advice to you is to keep away from Costello and Woods, who will by the course they are pursuing knock us out of the Cobre Grande Copper Company mines.

If you cannot be present in Phoenix at the stockholders meeting November 14th, please sign and return proxy.[55]

The meeting was held as planned, and it was definitely anti-Greene. E. B. Gage of Prescott and Tombstone, banker and mining entrepreneur, was elected president of the corporation, and five Costello men were named to the Board of Directors. Resolutions were passed against Greene and his seizure of the mines, and lawyer Aurelio Melgarejo, vice-president of the Cobre Grande and a very angry man, hurried down to Arizpe where, on November 25, 1899, he instituted criminal proceedings against Greene. The judge of the Court of First Instance, before whom Greene had appeared in October and secured confirmation of his titles, now reversed himself and ruled that Greene's seizure of the mines was unlawful. On December 5 he followed up this decision and ordered that Greene, for his "unlawful acts" should be "apprehended and detained." Greene was not around to be jailed or he would have seen the inside of a Mexican *carcel*.

The courts in both Arizpe and Nogales, Mexico, were now against Greene, and on December 9 a warrant actually went out for his arrest. By now, however, his own lawyers were on the firing line, and on the twelfth they got a suspension of the order.[56]

Meanwhile an appeal by Greene's lawyers from the decision of the Judge of the First Instance in Arizpe was on its way to Mexico City, and while the appeal was pending Greene's men remained in charge at the mines. Greene had full confidence, and so did everyone on his side, that the ultimate decision would be in their favor, and they went ahead with their plans for making Cananea the Copper Capital of the World. Their confidence was justified a year later, on October 9, 1900, when the Mexican Supreme Court decided for Greene.[57]

By now lawsuits were beginning to spring up around Greene like mushrooms after a rain, but at this stage of his affairs, everything went his way. Costello's suit to keep him from taking his deeds out of escrow in the Phoenix National Bank, where he had placed them at the time of his contract with Mitchell, failed on October 23, 1900,[58] and the dispositions which Greene had already made of his mining property were now legal.

His success discouraged a majority of the Cobre Grande stockholders. Their stock was in danger of becoming worthless. This was the moment for Greene to reassure them that he was ready to help them out of their difficulties. From the beginning of the trouble he had let it be known that if he had his way, the stockholders would not lose.[59] He was prepared to buy them out at the par value of $2.50 per share or exchange their stock for equivalent value in the paper of his new company.[60] President Gage and his directors held out as long as they could, hoping to get a better deal from somebody else. Their pride was also involved. At the meeting on November 15, they passed a resolution condemning Greene for "fraudulent misrepresentation" and resolved on legal action.

It was at this time that Vice-president Melgarejo undertook his mission to have Greene declared a fugitive from justice.

Nothing came of these gestures. The company was going farther into debt every day. In desperation the stockholders decided to pool their holdings, turn them over to President E. B. Gage, and let him try to market them at $2.50 per share. Gage did his best, but his best was not good enough. He had over 115,000 shares on his hands, and it was hard to find a customer for that much stock. Four times he came close to making the sale, and four times the customer reneged. The stockholders began to grumble. They knew that Greene was willing to buy them out, and they talked about breaking the pool, recalling their stock, and selling to him individually if Gage did not do something, and fast. Before the end of the year Gage gave in and opened negotiations with Greene. On December 12 a contract was signed and ratified by the directors. Greene's terms were "better than anybody else had ever offered."[61]

Greene's genius for making friends out of enemies now appeared for the first time. He handled the arrangements with the utmost frankness and generosity. Gage got $50,000 as reimbursement for his services in arranging the deal and for money he had spent while it was pending. Quite naturally, he became Greene's friend and ally thenceforward. The law firms — Baker and Bennett, Herndon and Morris, L. H. Chalmers — divided another $50,000, and Chalmers became one of Greene's stable of attorneys. $55,000 went to pay off the indebtedness of the corporation. A note for $23,000, which Costello owed the company, was returned to him. Almost everybody was happy. Almost everybody said kind things about W. C. Greene. The whole episode should have closed in a concert of peace and good will.

There were some sour notes, however. Two New Yorkers, James Shirley and Axel Hallenborg, were unreconciled. Shirley thought Greene and Mitchell owed him a commission for a stock sale which did not go through and he instituted at least one suit.[62] Hallenborg, a stockholder, would not accept the fifty cents a share which Greene paid down to bind his bargain, and would have nothing to do with the contract. As time went on, his desire to get even with Greene became an obsession. He never won a case, but he never stopped trying, and he kept it up for years. Immediately after the majority of the stockholders sold their shares, he sued in Yavapai County, Arizona, to upset the agreement, carried his suit to the Arizona Supreme Court, and when he lost there, went all the way to the Supreme Court of the United States. Decision was rendered against him in Washington on January 8, 1906.

Meanwhile he was conducting separate suits in El Paso and Buffalo, New York. The groundwork for the El Paso case was laid when the

Consolidated National Bank of Tucson shipped two carloads of matte to the Kansas City Smelting and Refining Company's smelter at El Paso. The bank had advanced $24,000 to the mining company for expenses, and the matte was part of the payment. Hallenborg sued to keep the smelter from paying $9,660 to the bank, claiming the money for the Cobre Grande Corporation.[63] The decision went against him, as usual.

The New York suit was to recover money allegedly lent to Cobre Grande. It dragged on for years, ending in November, 1906, in a negative decision by the Supreme Court of the State of New York. By the time of the final appeal, profits from the Cananea mines had run into the millions and stock worth $9,000,000 (Hallenborg's figures) had been sold. Hallenborg felt that he was entitled to a share in all this wealth, and went all out to get it. Greene, through his lawyers, accused Hallenborg of accumulating as much Cobre Grande stock as he could in hopes of getting a juicy settlement, and he was probably right, since by 1906 Hallenborg could hardly have hoped to win his suit.[64]

Since Greene's activity as a mining promoter was just about over in 1906, it follows that the Cobre Grande octopus had its tentacles out for him from the beginning to the end of his career. There was never a time in those years that his lawyers were not campaigning somehow in the Cobre Grande matter. Greene never had any doubt that he could beat his opposition, but he was always having to spend money and time to make his point. On July 8, 1902, he wrote to E. B. Gage at Tombstone, Arizona:

I had a long conversation with Costello in New York, and he is getting very anxious about his $80,000 in Phoenix. He has made several propositions for settlement, the last one on the basis of $100,000 for all claims. I wired Harby yesterday that if he would relinquish all claims the Cobre Grande would relinquish all suit against him and he could take his money.[65]

A letter from J. D. Dort, one of the incorporators, to L. H. Chalmers[66] shows what was going on:

Good Lord! haven't you got Cobre Grande quiet yet? Why boy, do you know that I got a little taste of it the other day. Friend Shirley offered me $100,000 if I would bring suit against Greene for my Cobre Grande stock which I sold him and he would tender the money for the stock to the Court, or Greene, or somebody, and pay all the expenses of the suit, but as I had no particular use just at the time for $100,000 I passed it up.[67]

With very little excuse for living, the Cobre Grande Copper Company resolutely refused to die. Greene was a director until August 27, 1901, when he resigned because of a suit threatening in New York.[68]

Arizona Historical Society

George Young, Secretary and General Auditor,
Cananea Consolidated Copper Company.

Again in 1901 when litigation was impending and depositions were being taken, it cost Greene $5,000 to obtain from J. Henry Wood, then an accountant living in Los Angeles, the correspondence and papers of the Cobre Grande Company.[69] When George Young, perennial secretary of the Four C's and its successors, wrote his thumbnail sketch of its history in 1920, he noted that the company was "still existent and in litigation."

By this time Greene was long past worrying about Cobre Grande or any other corporation, but his experience with this financial hedgehog had set the pattern for the rest of his career. Litigation became a way of life for him. He kept more lawyers busy than any other man in the history of Arizona or perhaps of the whole United States. It would be hard to guess how many of them he had on retainers or doing special jobs — in California, in Arizona, in New York, and even in Texas. But then, as Colonel Kosterlitzky once wrote to him, he was "fighting the whole world," and that takes time, money, and lawyers.[70]

The Ascent Begins

THE COPPER SKYROCKET, which was now carrying W. C. Greene heavenward, was actually divided into two stages, and his performance was a sort of Roman riding act. He had one foot in Cananea, where everything was happening at once in 1900 and 1901, and the other in New York, where all the financial action centered. In his mind and in his day-to-day activity, of course, the two operations meshed and interlocked, but they make better sense today if they are considered separately.

Although he assumed primary responsibility for the New York horizon, Greene felt most at home in the mining department. He once remarked in a communication to his stockholders: "I have never claimed to be a businessman. I do claim to be a miner. I do claim to know what to do down there to work the property successfully and economically."[1]

After his failure, when the chorus of praise turned to a chorus of criticism, nobody gave him credit for any mining know-how whatever. The *Engineering and Mining Journal* remarked in 1911:

Colonel Greene was not a miner, and under his charge a large amount of money was spent much of which was wasted on unsystematic mining and expensive and unsuitable machinery. It was not until later, when a competent management was substituted, that success was really attained.[2]

Greene was probably a better judge of his own abilities than was the editor of the mining journal. He had been a miner himself. He had been in close touch with the Copper Queen enterprise at Bisbee for years. He had Kirk and Mitchell and other experts to advise him, and he was always learning.

It was not news to him that copper production is a chancy business, complicated and full of uncertainties. He knew that the metal occurs in a wide variety of situations and combinations and that several types of ore, each requiring a variation in treatment, may occur in the same mine. He was aware that the smaller the percentage of copper, the more attention the ore has to have. After it is crushed in a mill, low-grade ore has to be "concentrated" — that is, a large percentage of the waste rock has to be eliminated. Like all copper producers, Greene had to worry about concentration.

At first the Cananea ore was very rich — so high in its copper percentages that a crusher and a blast furnace were about all that were needed for production. Stories got back to New York that there was so much rich mineral near the surface that it was not necessary to sink shafts.[3] This, of course, was a slight exaggeration, but Greene was fortunate at the beginning of his activities in being able to produce a great deal of copper at a minimum of expense.

As a practical mining man, however, Greene knew that eventually the rich ore would peter out and there would be lower-grade ore or nothing. That day had to be prepared for. In August of 1901 he wrote to George Mitchell:

If the grade of our ore should run down, it would be necessary to smelt more stuff in order to keep the converters to their full six million pounds blister copper per month and this is one of the things that we want to do. If we can get to seven million per month, it would be still better.[4]

In order to operate efficiently, Greene also had to think about installing converters. The product of the first trip through the furnace, called matte, consists of copper and other metals. In the converters, the matte is melted down again and brought closer to purity. It emerges in bars or "pigs" weighing approximately 450 pounds called blister copper. The final step, which separates the copper from the other metals (including silver and gold) requires the kind of sophisticated machinery that can usually be found only at a major copper refinery.

As soon as he could, Greene began to make plans for installing converters. Specifications were authorized in December of 1900.[5] Almost a year later they were still among the things hoped for but not seen. In August 1901 Greene wrote to Mitchell:

When you write again, please let me know how the new furnace is getting on, as to whether all of your material has arrived from the Union Iron Works as yet; also what the prospects are of our getting out our converters. Do you not think that you should have another stack outside of the ones you have ordered in order that one can be under repair while the others are running? . . .

Hope you are getting your concentrating plans defined. . . . It strikes me that there should be a thoroughly competent man to devote his attention strictly to concentrating as we shall have to handle a large amount of stuff. Of course you know about this and will use your own judgment.[6]

As Greene conceived his prospects — and he was a great dreamer — the Cananea enterprise was to be the largest copper producer in the world. Quite naturally he had to think in millions. And there was considerably more to plan for than the exploitation of the mines he owned. Just as important as production was development — exploration for and discovery of new ore bodies so that steady production could be maintained. Jim Kirk, Greene's old friend from the Bradshaw Mountains, and Ed Massey, another practical miner whom Greene had known for a long time, did most of the exploration. Kirk was superintendent under George Mitchell, the general manager, and was in actual charge of the mining operation. Massey, whose title was foreman, ran the underground operations. They both worked hard and successfully in locating new ore bodies. In December of 1900 the word went back to New York that they had found an important new source of supply. Walter Logan congratulated Mitchell from the New York office:

I am glad to hear of the new strikes you are making in the mines and that the smelter is so near completion. I know that you are doing everything that can be done to make the enterprise a great success and I am doing everything that can be done here to the same end.[7]

The story of the strike in the Oversight and Bonanza mines has been told and retold with much colorful embroidery. The now-standard version seems to have been started by James McClintock in his gossipy *Arizona* (1916):

Foreman Massey in his loyalty even disobeyed orders and insisted on sinking on the Capote property long after he had been ordered to quit and thus ran into the greatest body of copper ore ever encountered in the Cananea Mountains. . . .[8]

After fifty years of development the story has acquired a good many new features. It begins with a little scene between Greene and Mitchell. The mines have begun to play out, and Greene announces that he is going to New York.

"What for?"

"Money."

"You can't find investors if you have no ore."

Jim Kirk, Mine Superintendent
and old friend of Greene's.

Arizona Historical Society

"I'm going to tell everyone we have plenty of ore. Get busy and find some while I'm away."

On the train, the story says, Greene worked up a plan of the Cananea mining district, locating ore bodies in the places where he thought they ought to be. He showed it to various people in New York, including Hetty Greene (the legendary female multimillionaire who is sometimes mistakenly identified as the Colonel's kinswoman) and convinced them that his prospects had enormous possibilities. They yearned to see for themselves, and with his usual assurance he invited them to come along with him to Mexico. A number of them accepted. He wired ahead to Mitchell, instructing him to have the furnaces roaring when the group arrived. He thought there might be enough good ore left to give a green tinge to the smoke. Sure enough, the smelters were operating at full blast when the Colonel and his guests reached Cananea. Greene took his partner aside.

"Give me the worst news first. Have we any ore?"

"A whole mountain of it. . . . We struck another rich vein 250 feet from the point where the old one petered out," Mitchell said.

The only thing the camp ran short of during the next few days was blank stock certificates.[9]

The realities at Cananea were much less colorful than the stories which have been invented about Colonel Greene and his town, but the suspense and uncertainty and precariousness of the situation during those early days were real enough.

Everything had to be done at once. Mining, reduction, and exploration were only a small part of it. A town with all public services had to be organized. A system of transportation had to be devised, and enormous quantities of supplies of all kinds had to be hauled in. The plant had to be enlarged, which meant drawing up specifications, placing orders, and installing equipment. Government regulations had to be carried out. Visiting dignitaries, both Mexican and American, had to be entertained. There was no end to it, and Greene felt responsible for almost every detail. He was in New York or on the road most of the time after the fall of 1900, but his hands were always on the controls.

His first problem was to get title to the land surrounding his mines. Under Mexican law the mine workings were his, no matter who owned the surface rights, but a mine can't operate without people, and people have to have places to live and eat and amuse themselves. So Greene went to work on Senator George C. Perkins of Oakland, California.

In 1885 Perkins, with W. T. Garrett (a brass founder), H. L. Drew (a banker), and Richard Gird (a sugar-beet king) bought 3,000,000 acres of ranch land in Mexico with Cananea sitting in the midst of it. They intended to stock it with cattle but never got around to doing it. Gird's brother became a Mexican citizen in order to make sure everything was legal. Then along came W. C. Greene. Cananea began to boom, and in the early weeks of 1901 Greene approached Perkins with an offer for part of his land. Interviewed in his Oakland home in April of 1901, the Senator told how it was:

Why did we sell? Well, it was either sell at the figure which Greene offered . . . or stand a lawsuit which the mining people could not have helped winning. We sold at a nominal figure, getting rid of the entire property at a price which about returns our investment to us with about 4 per cent interest.[10]

Perkins did not say how much land was involved or what price was paid, but his story explains how the Four C's came to own some range land.

With his townsite firmly in hand, Greene's next big problem was taking care of the people who came to work for the Company. After the initial advertisement in the Arizona newspapers calling for two hundred American workers,[11] the influx started, and the people kept on coming. Only a very few of the newcomers could be accommodated in the two local villages of Ronquillo and Cananea Vieja, and quarters had to be built or improvised. The result was a shack-and-tent city — the tents and shacks gradually yielding to Company enterprises — boarding houses for miners, cottages for the men in charge, a Company store — then a bank, a hospital, a school, a slaughterhouse, a laundry, an ice plant — later an adequate water supply (pumped in from the great wells at Ojo de Agua), a newspaper, a church, and the Cananea Club for gentlemen and their guests.[12]

Future growth was taken care of by laying out a townsite on the mesa — the high ground east of the smelters. It was a pleasant spot dotted with tall oak trees, ideal for residences. Greene had picked out his own homesite years before, partly on account of the trees. There was such a demand for wood however, in the days before coke and coal were imported, that any sort of tree led a precarious existence. Greene's trees were no exception. They were there in flourishing condition when he left on one of his trips to New York. They were gone when he came back.[13] The townsite was laid out, however, and the Sonora legislature gave it the status of a municipality on October 13, 1901.[14] It belonged to the Company — that is, to Greene — and he saw to it that land was available for public use. He donated the lots and put up part of the money for a park, a cemetery, the school, the jail, and the city offices.[15] It was his town, and he took care of it.

Ronquillo, the old town in the valley between the mesa and the reduction works, grew without much supervision. The Mexican miners and other workers continued to live there in shacks and hovels. They clung to their inadequate housing and refused to move when the Colonel tried to improve conditions for them, and their plight helped to bring on serious trouble.

Since nothing was produced locally, housing and everything else depended on the Company's transportation system which operated between Cananea and Naco, the railhead on the border. At first the system had to be improvised. There was a stage (unsatisfactory) for people. Everything else came and went in horse-drawn wagons. Every ounce of material brought in and every ounce of copper shipped out had to be pulled over inadequate roads by Company teams. By the end of 1900 about 1,800 horses were traveling back and forth between Cananea and Naco,[16] forty-five miles to the northeast and only a few miles from Bisbee.

Frank T. Greene

Early Transportation: The Naco-Cananea Stage.

The system was cumbersome and expensive, and Greene soon thought of a better way. He decided to use steam traction engines to pull the supply and ore wagons. In the summer of 1900 he opened negotiations with the O. O. Kelly Company of Springfield, Ohio, placing orders for three engines and the wagons to go with them. This was heavy equipment — too heavy for the existing roads, which would have to be rebuilt and improved. George Mitchell took on the road project in addition to his other duties. At the close of the year 1900, he reported to Greene, who was temporarily at Naco:

I am pushing the roads as fast as possible with the men we have and expect we shall have everything in shape before the traction engines get there. In their last letter the Kelly people advised that they are building wagons of ten tons capacity instead of seven and a half tons, stating that they would recommend us to handle three wagons of ten tons each in a train instead of four wagons of seven and a half tons each, and that they will send 12 of these larger wagons, and if we find by experimenting that we can run four as easily as we can three, with thirty tons on, why we can do so.[17]

Ronquillo in 1902, (above) looking eastward toward San José Mountain, with no houses yet on the mesa, and (below) looking westward toward the smelter and the Cananea Mountains.

A. Blake Brophy

Narrow-gauge railroad to Puertecitos.

The engines and wagons arrived in due time and were used until railroad connections made them unnecessary. They were not entirely satisfactory, since Mitchell's roads were sometimes too soft and sandy for easy pulling,[18] but they were the best thing to be had at the time and performed their endless journeys at three miles an hour for over a year.

Greene knew at the start that there had to be a railroad. In fact, he planned and built two of them — a narrow-gauge line to connect the Puertecitos group of mines on the west side of the Cananea range with the smelter on the eastern slope, and a standard-gauge road from Cananea to Naco which would be the main artery of transportation. The folklore says that he tried to get E. H. Harriman of the Southern Pacific to build it, and when Harriman laughed at him, he built it himself.

Greene called his railroad the Cananea, Yaqui River, and Pacific, and he undoubtedly meant ultimately to extend it eastward across the Sierra Madre and then southwest to the Gulf of California. The Mexican mountains are about as rugged as they come, however, and they were not conquered for another half century.

Construction on the Cananea-Naco line was pushed vigorously through 1901, and service was formally inaugurated on January 7, 1902. Convinced at last that he had missed a bet, Harriman opened negotiations and in July of 1903 the Cananea, Yaqui River, and Pacific became part of the Southern Pacific system.[19]

George Mitchell, of course, could not wait for the railroad to bring the materials he needed for building his plant. The traction engines had to do the job, and piece by piece they brought his blowers and engines and stacks and flues. Only one furnace was operating when Greene took the mines away from Cobre Grande. It was a good one for its day — Mitchell had designed it[20] — but it had to be supplemented, and Greene immediately ordered another and larger one from the Union Iron Works in San Francisco. The equipment was almost ready to ship in August,

Compañía Minera de Cananea
Traction Engine in Action: Hauling ore and supplies, 1901–1902.

George Mitchell's Economic Hot-blast Furnaces.

1900, and Carl Clausen, a construction man working for the Copper Queen of Bisbee, went off to San Francisco to supervise the operation. Greene was on the point of leaving for Mexico City to do some fence mending there, but he placed an order for another furnace with the Union people before he left.[21]

Mitchell did all he could to get action. "Please wire them to hurry with all possible haste," he wrote to Clausen. "We have certain obligations to meet and promises to fulfill, and it is my desire to do so."[22]

His desire was constantly frustrated. New problems and delays cropped up almost every day. The blowers for the new furnace were to come from a firm at Connersville, Indiana. A fire in their factory put them off schedule. "I suppose we shall have to stand it," George wrote.[23] Greene's drafts did not reach the Union Iron works, and they grew uneasy about their pay.[24] There was always something. By the closing months of 1900, however, the foundations were pretty well laid and much of the suspense was over.

"The first Cananea blower has been shipped today," Clausen wired from San Francisco on December 1. The winter months of 1901 saw more and more shipments arriving. The electric plant and the electric locomotive were on their way early in March.[25] On March 13 the new smelter was in operation.

Greene, always optimistic, began to look forward to really important production, his hopes far outdistancing those of his top officers. A letter to Treasurer Scott White of the Four C's from Philip Berolzheimer, treasurer of Greene Consolidated, tells how matters stood in the early spring of 1901:

I note from your letter that you have had rainy weather in March but the telegram of later date tells us that it did not interfere with the hauling, of which I am very glad, because Mr. Greene figures that we should take in some $240,000 each month beginning March 1st, with a net profit of $200,000 per month, and we expect to pay dividends according to the result which the matte will bring us during the next few months to come.

I cannot quite agree with Mr. Greene as regards the result, but I hope that he is right and that I am wrong. . . . The telephone connection to the mines, electric light plant, the traction engines, and narrow as well as broad gauge roads, will be a revelation to me when I come to see you next time, which I hope will be next winter. . . .[26]

It should be said here that although Greene's head may have been in or near the clouds, his feet were always on the ground. He was infinitely careful about all the details of his business. People who could not solve their difficulties any other way did not hesitate to apply to him, and he was never too busy to give them thoughtful answers or refer them to Company officers who could help. A case in point arose in July and August of 1901 when a minor feud broke out between C. F. Von Petersdorff, who ran the Company store in Cananea, and S. M. Aguirre, who performed a similar service at Naco. Aguirre called himself General Manager in his letterhead, and Petersdorff objected furiously. In a typical paragraph he complained that he was getting Aguirre's merchandise by mistake since he — Petersdorff — was actually the General Manager.

Some time ago we received a shipment of Horse Collars from the El Paso Saddlery Co., ordered likewise by your concern, and sent to us by mistake. These Horse Collars are practically a drug on our hands on account of the high custom duties on them. In order to prevent similar mistakes and confusions in the future, it might be advisable to correct your letter heads.[27]

The horse-collar imbroglio was laid on Greene's lap. Aguirre complained, "I can't get along with this man."

At first Greene tended to favor Von Petersdorff, who had been appointed on his recommendation, and he wrote a sharp reply to Aguirre:

"It seems to me very childish for Von Petersdorff and yourself to be continually squabbling about these petty matters."[28] As Petersdorff continued to stir up trouble, however, Greene reversed himself, exonerating Aguirre ("I find that I did him an injustice and that I was wrong") and recommending that Von Petersdorff be "relieved."[29] He even suggested that Aguirre take Petersdorff's place since he already knew the business. His final observation is worth noting:

> As we have talked of several times, we are not playing favorites or anything of that kind. We want the man who does the work and does it best — it doesn't make any difference whether his name is Tom, Dick, or Richard Roe. The good of the Company is what we are working for.[30]

Several generations of historians and journalists have stated confidently that Greene always filled such vacancies with his "cronies." Undoubtedly he sometimes did so, but he did not do it as a matter of principle.

The Colonel did not often let himself get bogged down in these petty involvements. He knew how to delegate responsibility, and he seldom gave orders to his top men. He merely advised them. When he found a man overdoing or underdoing his job, however, he never hesitated to "relieve" him.

The bulk of his time and attention was devoted to policy making, building good will, and acquiring more property. He was always acquisitive and never missed a chance to pick up anything which might be profitable or would fill out his holdings. It was this quirk of character which brought him into collision with Lycurgus Lindsay, who entered the Cananea field in 1896, about the time Greene began his own operations.

Lindsay had developed several good mines, including the Indiana-Sonora complex and the Democrata,[31] and he too was on the lookout for desirable claims, particularly if they were near mines which had already proved profitable. This sort of coziness made other mine owners nervous and often involved Lindsay in controversy.[32] He was a fighter, however, "on the Greene model,"[33] and probably enjoyed these encounters.

In 1901 Lindsay picked up two claims, the Libertad and the Ultimatum, adjacent to Greene's holdings at Puertecitos. "These two claims," wrote George Young some years later, "are located right at Puertecito, and I believe, in the line of the long tunnel."[34]

This was the sort of situation which could lead to heavy skirmishing, and Lindsay fired the opening shots in January 1902 when he got out a four-page prospectus offering a great opportunity to the public. His name did not appear, but he included a map identifying the claims involved as the Ultimatum and the Libertad and showing their proximity to the Cananea, Juarez, Ventura and Pinal mines of the Greene organization.

The pitch obviously was: If Greene can make it, and we are right next to Greene, we can make it too. The first page read as follows:

What do you think of laying blistered Copper down in New York for four cents per pound?
Our prosperous neighbor, the
GREENE CONSOLIDATED COPPER COMPANY
claims to be able to do so

We offer you an opportunity to buy into a Copper Company in the same Zone,
THE LA CANANEAS COPPER COMPANY
(organized under Arizona laws)
Capital Stock - - - - - - - - - - - $5,000,000
1,000,000 shares par value $5.00 each, fully paid, non-assessable
and free from individual liability
Hon. Frederick A. Tritle, of Arizona, President.
Charles D. Cramp of Philadelphia, Vice-President
E. A. Darling, Secretary and Treasurer

A FEW WORDS IN GENERAL THAT MAY RESULT IN PROFIT TO THOSE WISE ENOUGH TO GRASP OPPORTUNITIES.
It has only been within the past two years that the wonderful Cananea deposits were brought to the attention of the Copper marts of the world, through the daily increasing product of the Greene Consolidated Copper Company which, had the Amalgamated Copper Company been under good advice, would have been acquired at a time when the entire Cananea zone could have been bought for $2,000,000. Now it is doubtful whether $30,-000,000 could control the wonderful copper area, for the mines have now the influence of railroad transportation, great smelters have been established, and their product is now astonishing the metallic world by its magnitude.
The LA CANANEAS COPPER COMPANY gives you an opportunity to obtain an interest in this rich Copper region at a reasonable price for its shares.
In this Cananea zone the copper deposits are among the richest ever discovered, and of great volume, besides labor is obtained at $1.00 per day gold, as against $4.00 per day gold in Montana, yet the copper produced by this cheap labor receives the same market figure as that produced by our high American labor. It is now predicted that the Cananea Mines will supply the world with copper, it being claimed that copper can be made in Cananea and laid down in New York City at 5 cents per pound.

It was Lindsay's hard luck that in 1902 an engineer named Roberto Servín was employed by the Mexican government to make a new survey of all the Cananea locations and revise the boundaries. As a result Lindsay's claims were drastically reduced. Ten years later George Young explained to J. S. Douglas how it happened:

I believe that the property which you have in mind at Puertecito is covered by the claims "La Ultimatum" and "La Libertad." This last was a fraction thrown out from our Cananea claim when the latter was consolidated under Servin's survey for the rectification of titles in 1902. Lindsay had title to this property covering 78 and a fraction pertenencias. Servin's survey gave us all but 16 and a fraction. Lindsay continued to pay taxes on the titled area, and for years kept threatening suit against us, but did not bring it to trial. The matter was settled in 1912 by the purchase of Lindsay's rights.[35]

Greene could not have helped being irritated by Lindsay's tactics, but his reactions did not become violent until he let Lindsay sell him the America[36] mine. What happened cannot be documented, but long-time employees of the Company have heard the story that for once Greene was outsmarted. He bought a salted mine.[37]

This means that somebody had brought in rich ore and planted it in such a way as to make the mine look like a great potential producer. The America, in spite of some very fancy advertising by Lindsay,[38] was never important. Greene should have known what it was worth, and knew he should have known, and he was scandalized when he found out what had been done to him. Lindsay got his mine back, and it did not become a part of the Greene complex until 1906, when the Colonel was about out of the management.

There is no way of knowing, after seventy years, all that went on between these two mighty mining men, but Greene's descendants say that the Colonel never trusted Lindsay, and Lindsay's descendants remember that he went in fear of his life from the Colonel for a while.[39]

Their difficulties threatened only once to be aired in public. In the fall of 1906 Lindsay brought suit against Greene in the superior court at Los Angeles. His complaint was that he had paid Greene $50,000 in cash on August 10 for 10,000 shares in the newly organized Central Cananea Copper Company. Greene was supposed to turn the money over to the Company, and the Company was to deliver the stock. The money had not been turned over; the stock had not been delivered; and Lindsay was angry. He declared that the stock had appreciated since he made the deal and that he had lost $175,000 through the delay. This pound of flesh he wanted the Colonel to give up out of his own financial hide.[40]

The suit was settled out of court — no details available — and there was probably no break in their communications. People like Greene and Lindsay instituted lawsuits the way other people write protesting letters. Probably they did not take their altercations too seriously. The game they played was a rough one, and the professionals lived by the unwritten rule: "All's fair in love, war, and mining." It is worth noting that Chief Surgeon Galbraith of the Four C's wrote to Secretary George Young in 1904: ". . . will state that at the instance of Mr. Greene last fall I telephoned the Indiana & Sonora and the Democrata Co. that if they desired, we could furnish them hospital accommodations."[41] It is worth noting also that Greene's children and Lindsay's children liked each other and visited each other in later years.

In 1901 their long duel had barely begun and was not giving Greene any concern. In fact, everything seemed to be going his way. Until late in the year, when prices slumped, copper stocks were booming. Thanks to Greene's talents as a promoter, the officers and stockholders of Greene Consolidated were bubbling with confidence and enthusiasm, and the mining operation was ready to go into high gear. It might have been said appropriately that all went merry as a marriage bell, for on February 16, Greene got married.

Enter Mary

NEAR THE END OF THE 1890s a severe drought struck the cattle ranges of southern Arizona. The rain refused to fall. The grass shriveled and died. The cattle grew thin and wandered restlessly in search of food. The price of beef went farther and farther down, and the ranchers were badly hurt. Some of them lost all they had.

Among those who suffered severely was Frank Proctor of Sahuarita, twenty miles south of Tucson. Frank, of Vermont stock, was a rugged Westerner, a long-time sheriff of Pima County who was serving as cattle inspector at Nogales when the bad times began. Everybody knew him; everybody liked him; and among his close friends was W. C. Greene.

They were actually connected by marriage, Mrs. Proctor's sister having married Return Roberts, Mrs. Greene's brother. Mrs. Proctor and Mrs. Greene were good friends and saw each other often.[1]

When Frank found himself in serious difficulties as a result of the drought, he decided to move to Cananea. Greene encouraged him to come and arranged for him to take over the wholesale meat concession. Later he was given the liquor concession.[2] When the Cananea Cattle Company was organized in 1901, Proctor became the manager. He was an important figure in Cananea for ten years — until he had a paralytic stroke and went with his wife to live in Santa Monica, California, where he died in April 1929. His personality and influence were such that he came to be called Colonel Proctor, as Greene had rated the same title a year or two before.

The Proctors had no children of their own, but in 1885 they had adopted a daughter, a nine-year-old orphan named Maria Benedict, only daughter and fifth child of Albert Case Benedict, one of Arizona's true pioneers.

Benedict belonged to an old New England family whose adventurous members heard the call of the West and got as far as Michigan. Albert himself heard the call loud and clear before he was twenty and in 1849 joined the stampede to the California gold fields. At the outbreak of the Civil War he marched with Carleton's California Column to the Rio Grande and in 1863 joined a prospecting party led by the famous Mountain Man Joseph Reddeford Walker. They invaded the dangerous Indian country near the future site of Prescott, Arizona — as W. C. Greene was to do some years later. Albert's cousin Kirby Benedict, then Chief Justice of the Territory of New Mexico, was interested in the venture, as were General Carleton and other important men.[3]

In the late 1860s Benedict left the northern mountains and settled next to Pete Kitchen's famous ranch in the Santa Cruz Valley between Tucson and Nogales as a farmer and cattle raiser. He and Pete are said to have been partners.[4] In 1868 or 1869 he married a local girl named Gregoria Alvarez.

Gregoria has not left many traces, but she belonged to a substantial ranching family with roots in Sonora. Benedict was very proud of her and wrote letters home telling what a lucky man he was. His cousin Gertrude M. Case wrote to him on May 28, 1873:

We were all greatly pleased on the receipt of your kind letter a week ago. . . . We were also pleased to hear that your home associations were so pleasant. We had not heard of your marriage. Pa and Ma were happy to know of their niece, and I am proud to claim my new cousin. We shall wait anxiously for the promised pictures, and for the *promised visitors* for *all* say you must bring your family when you come.[5]

The promised visit probably never materialized, for the Benedicts had their hands full with a rapidly growing family and the need for making ends meet. In 1870 they were living at Cerro Colorado, a mine west of the Nogales-Tucson highway in the direction of Arivaca. The census of that year gives his age as forty; his occupation as machinist; his wife's age as twenty-six. Their son John was one year old.

A year later, in the spring of 1871, an Indian war party attacked Benedict while he was plowing. He killed three of them and was just mounting one of his horses to ride for his life when a ball struck him in the ankle, crippling him permanently. Since his general health, as well as his ankle, was shattered, he moved his family to Tucson, where the living was not quite so strenuous. He had many friends and was easily elected county treasurer. In 1875 he was made territorial auditor. To supplement their income Gregoria opened a store in Tucson in 1873. She advertised in the *Citizen* on April 5 that she was a "sole trader" in general merchandise, real and personal property, "responsible in my own name for all debts contracted by me."[6] By 1878 Albert was able to move back to his ranch and manage affairs there, acquiring "a handsome competence in stock and improved farm." He died of typhoid fever, complicated by pneumonia, on March 31, 1880, at the home of his old friend and partner Pete Kitchen.[7] A mountain peak near his ranch is named in his memory.

Gregoria later married an ex-Army surgeon, an Englishman named Edward Chamberlain, by whom she had two children before he died of tuberculosis. In 1884 Gregoria contracted "galloping consumption" herself and laid her own burden down, leaving four orphaned sons and one daughter. Pete Kitchen undertook to raise the boys. The little girl was turned over to a Mexican family, but when Benedict's good friend Frank Proctor heard that she was being neglected, he took her into his own home.[8]

Named for her grandmother Maria (Ma-rye-ah) Benedict, she could hardly be called anything in Arizona but Maria (Ma-ree-ah) since every other girl of Spanish ancestry carried the name. This the Proctor's did not want, so the child was called Mary, sometimes Marie. She was a bright, attractive little girl, and she gladdened the childless Proctor home. With Frank she was always affectionate and close. Mrs. Proctor was a good if somewhat exacting mother and tried to bring Mary up in the way she should go. One of her precepts was, "Familiarity breeds contempt," and Mary remembered the lesson. There must have been some affection in the relationship, but on one count Mrs. Proctor did her foster daughter some harm. She made her ashamed of her Mexican blood — a feeling which she never lost. When Mary's brothers came to see her, Mrs. Proctor sent them away.

The Proctors formally adopted Mary in 1885.[9] Some years later the Michigan Benedicts decided that she ought to come to them, but she did not want to go. She wanted to be loyal to the Proctors.[10]

She did go to school, to the sisters of St. Joseph's Academy, and made an excellent record. She won awards for music and painting and developed considerable skill as a pianist. The friends she made during her school days remained her friends through life.[11]

There was a substratum of shyness and reserve in Mary's nature, but at the same time she was fun-loving and liked to be gay with people she trusted and knew well. Once when her mother had taken her to San Francisco, she and a teen-age friend were walking together down a city street surrounded by strangers. On a sudden impulse Mary announced, "I am going to speak to the next man I see, I don't care who he is." Immediately panic seized her, but by a miracle the next man turned out to be someone she knew and she was spared the consequences of her rash resolve.[12] As she grew older, she acquired a dignity suitable to her years, and the responsibilities which came with marriage changed her into a really stately lady.

After her graduation from St. Joseph's, Mary went job hunting. This was a rather unusual and daring thing for a girl to do in those times, but Mary was an unusual person, and she wanted to be independent. She went to George Smalley, editor of the Tucson *Citizen,* and asked if he had anything for her to do. As a result she become the first, and perhaps the only, lady typesetter in Arizona. In time she added a little reporting to her duties.

When Frank Proctor became a resident of Cananea, Mary often went down to visit him, perhaps to send back stories to the *Citizen* about what went on in the camp. She was there when the showdown occurred between Greene and Con O'Keefe in the days when the Cobre Grande feud was just getting started and her foster father was still living in a tent. "The Siege at Cananea," one account called it.[13]

Greene, of course, had known her casually since she was a baby, but in 1900 she was twenty-four years old and a beauty. Greene was not the only one who noticed it. At least one of his old friends was attracted to her and used to entertain her with stories and jokes, some of which were too much for a product of St. Joseph's Academy.[14] In the end Greene's charm and real affection awakened a response in her. He was twenty-five years older than she was and on his way to fame and riches, but she thought he needed her — and he did!

The *Daily Citizen,* her newspaper, carried the story on February 18, 1901:

REPORTED WEDDING OF A TUCSON LADY

The friends of Miss Mary Proctor and W. C. Greene in Tucson were surprised to learn this morning that this estimable couple had joined their lives in matrimony at Phoenix Friday night. The report received here says that the wedding was celebrated quietly and only a few of the intimate friends were present. Miss Proctor is the accomplished daughter of Frank Proctor, who is the wholesale meat dealer at La Cananea, and one of the best known cattlemen in Southern Arizona. The bride lived in Tucson the most of her life and has many warm friends here who thoroughly appreciate her worth, her cheery disposition which brings sunshine into any gathering and her strong womanly character. . . .

The marriage was kept secret and no news of it have been published in the Phoenix papers. Miss Proctor passed through Tucson last week on her way to Phoenix but left no word here of her coming marriage although there were rumors that the event was to take place soon.

What the reporter did not know, or did not choose to reveal, was Mrs. Proctor's bitter opposition to the marriage, possibly because of the difference in age. The result was an elopement and a wedding conducted by Greene's old friend Judge William Barnes of Tucson, who came to Phoenix to perform the ceremony. It should be added that Mrs. Proctor relented so far as to present to the newlyweds a pair of handsome silver boxes plus a diamond sunburst for Mary. They kept these gifts among their treasures and valued them highly.[15]

By now Greene's financial involvements had convinced him that he was going to have to spend most of his time in New York. He took a suite at the old Waldorf Hotel, and, shortly after the wedding, he and his bride left for their new home in the East. Before her departure, Mary came back for a farewell visit to Editor Smalley and her friends on the staff of the *Citizen*. Smalley's nose for news told him that here was a fine opportunity for a real-life Cinderella story. So he wrote up Mary's farewell visit from this angle and was pleased when the piece appeared in the Chicago *American* and the New York *Journal*.[16] To Smalley's surprise, the Greenes were embarassed and indignant. He tells about it in his reminiscences:

I told about Marie's return to Tucson after her marriage, and how she greeted all of her old pals in the *Citizen* office, even to the little "devil." Her white kid gloves were stained with ink after she had cordially shaken hands with the men and embraced the girls. It had been our practice to rush the growler for beer on Saturday evenings after the paper was out. In the stock room there was a tin pail, and during the week any member of the force who sold a newspaper after I had left the office placed the money in it; the contents were used to buy a can of beer and sandwiches. Marie at once called for the tin pail and after adding some coins, told the "devil" to run and get some beer. She was the same old Marie in spite of her finery.[17]

Smalley was at a loss to account for Mary's reaction to this gem of humor and speculated that it might have "lowered her position in the New York social set, the snobbish four hundred." The truth was, Mary was always embarrassed by any publicity which cheapened her or took away her dignity. From time to time during the years of her husband's fame and glory, journalists would pay their respects to the Greenes in ways which she resented. When the new piano arrived for their home in Cananea in 1903, a New York newspaper printed a cartoon showing her playing it in the midst of a howling desert, and she would not have the paper in the house after that.[18] The picture of Mary "rushing the growler" might have seemed sentimentally appealing to Mr. Smalley, but it was a real embarrassment to her. For some years there was considerable coolness between the Greenes and Smalley,[19] but eventually all was forgotten and they were friends again.

During most of their years in New York, they lived at the Waldorf, where two of their children, Virginia and William, were born.[20] Mary had time for some social diversions, but she never went in for "society." She was too busy. During her ten years with the Colonel, she had six children and was therefore pregnant much of the time — busy with her babies all of the time. Her great diversions were music and the theater. She went to concerts and was a regular attendant at the Metropolitan Opera House; Andrew Carnegie was one of the gentlemen who used to stop by her box to pay his respects. Toward the end of their second year in the city, they moved to the Ansonia apartment hotel, but in early 1903 their big house in Cananea was nearing completion, and eventually they moved back to the Southwest.[21]

For the rest of their life together the "big house" was home. It was, for that time and place, a stately mansion, a two-story clap-boarded house with wide verandas on three sides from which one could see the tall smokestacks of the Four C's to the west and the great open countryside to the north and east. Since both of the Greenes loved horses, the Colonel built extensive stables at the edge of the declivity overlooking Cananea Vieja behind and east of the house. He had separate quarters for the servants in the rear. Inside the Big House everything was fitted up with an eye to comfort and elegance — sixteen-foot ceilings, tremendous expanses of oak paneling, a stately reception hall, a great dining room with massive furniture, a library, finely appointed bedrooms upstairs and down, a fireplace in every downstairs room. It was the showplace of Cananea.

Greene's life became a good deal more regular after his marriage. He liked being at home. He got one, at most two, whiskeys before dinner. When his children came along, he loved them and tried to be with them as much as possible. It bothered him that he had to be away so much, and he always brought back presents for everybody when he had been absent on a specially long trip.

He could not have had a more faithful and devoted wife than Mary Greene. She was almost fanatical in her loyalty. She would never believe or even listen to any story which discredited him. She nursed him when his health broke, and she guarded his good name to the best of her ability after he was dead.

She told her children that he spoke sharply to her only once in his life. That was when they were coming back in a buggy from a trip to one of the mines near Cananea and the horses "spooked" at something. Greene held them back with some difficulty and told Mary to get out of the vehicle where she would be safe. Paralyzed, Mary did not move. Her husband said to her, "Mary, when I tell you to do something, you *do* it." It was the only time he ever took that tone with her.[22]

He never used strong language in her presence either, though he did slip once. It was when they were riding together on the *Verde,* his private car, and she wanted a window opened. It happened that the Colonel had a sensitive finger — acquired when he was trying to show somebody how to put a bridle on a mule in his early days. He got his finger in the mule's mouth, and the mule bit off the end of it. He hurt this finger when he tried to open the window and said, "Damn!" That, she said, was the extent of his rough talking in her presence. There are stories which indicate that he could do better in other environments, but he was ordinarily quiet and soft-spoken, and his Quaker training prevented him from taking the name of God in vain.[23]

Although she would not have exchanged places with any woman in the world, her responsibilities as the wife of a notable man were very real to her, and she was conscientious about living up to her position. Her manners were always gracious and often stately. She was always driven by a chauffeur when she went out, partly because she grew nervous about driving, but even more because she felt a sort of *noblesse oblige* about it. Her automobile, never an expensive one, was always immaculate.

People who did not know her well often failed to discover the warm nature beneath her reserve. She loved children and was always good to them. She wore simple clothes because she thought her money could be better spent than on personal finery, and she was a generous giver.

Her generosity was balanced by a strong sense of propriety. She never condoned what she considered questionable conduct, but she never turned her back on a friend or relative who made a bad mistake.

As one would expect, she was home oriented, looking inward rather than outward for fulfillment. She joined few organizations but she welcomed a great many people to her house and table — her husband's friends and her own. It was never necessary for her to prepare for guests. She was always prepared — and the guests always came. She loved people and enjoyed entertaining them, but she never forgot her station.

Neither did she forget the men who had stood by her husband. She looked out for them and their families while they lived and, if necessary, buried them when they died. Among those whom she so served were Scott White, once sheriff of Cochise County, and General Luis E. Torres, Colonel Greene's ally during the troubles of 1906.[24]

Her last will and testament begins: "I direct that my body be decently buried without undue ceremony or ostentation, but with proper regard to my station in life."[25]

She was a great lady to the end.

In 1901 that end was still far in the future. Her immediate concern was to be of some help to her husband while he was blazing a trail through the wilderness of Wall Street.

The Financial Stratosphere

THE NEW YORK HALF of the Copper Skyrocket was as different from the Mexican half as one world could be from another. In Sonora, Greene was comfortable and at home with his men, his mules, his mines, and the things of Mexico. Friendly and outgoing, he had exchanged small talk with hundreds of his fellow Westerners; a great many people who did not really know him at all spoke familiarly of Bill Greene, or even of Old Bill Greene, and retailed the folklore about him as if they knew what they were taking about. When Greene heard of their inventions, he smiled and said nothing.

In New York he was somebody else: Colonel W. C. Greene, the millionaire Western mining man, and he lived in a world of hotel flunkies, stockbrokers, newsmen eager for a story, investors looking for a sure thing, and stockholders praying that their stock would go up.

The investors and stockholders were his raw material. Their faith and money were essential to his survival. His limber tongue and facile pen kept them in line; his ability to support the price of his stock kept them from panic; and his personal contacts with them kept them convinced — hence his move to New York, where his talents could best be put to use.

Some of his work, it must be admitted, was already done for him — especially in the early years of the boom. Stories were current about people who had started small and had come out large. The itch to get rich was epidemic, and a man who did not take his chances was "lacking in grit."

In December of 1900, the editor of the Tombstone *Epitaph* remarked:

Twelve years ago $100 invested in the United Verde copper mine of Arizona cost $1 a share and was worth $100. Today that $100 worth of shares is worth $30,000 and the returns are $1,200 a year. . . . One hundred dollars invested in the Greene Consolidated, at $1 a share, two years ago, it is now worth $8,700.

The editor admitted his error.

Like many others we were "conservative" — and we are still poor, but the next time Fortune knocks at our door, we will get a strangle hold and hang on.[1]

The country seemed to be full of people like the *Epitaph* editor — "lawyers, grocers, physicians, waiters, clergymen and chorus singers," as one financial historian classifies them, who were just "learning to acquire wealth without labor."[2] They were nervous and timorous, but they were eager to believe. Greene's contagious confidence brought them into the fold.

It has been said that Greene was never an insider on Wall Street[3] — that he was an adventurer on the fringes of the fraternity of financial pro's. This is true, in the sense that he had to fight for his financial life during most of his years in the market, and that the professionals tried incessantly to ruin him. It is true also that his office at 24 Broad Street was in the midst of the outdoor securities market where a great deal of trading was done, literally, on the curb. He owned a seat on the New York Stock Exchange, but the big board indoors was not for Greene Consolidated. Bankers did not ordinarily lend money on stocks sold on the curb,[4] and the establishment — the aristocracy of Wall Street — did not rush out to welcome him as a member. It is to his credit, however, that he convinced some of the biggest operators on the Street not only that his mines were sound and solid but that the big operators themselves ought to be on his board of directors. And for six years he matched them at their own game.

His first encounter seems to have been with Thomas W. Lawson and Amalgamated Copper.

At the very time Greene was getting under way, the giants of the mining industry were organizing the greatest metals combination of all time. The purpose of Amalgamated was to combine all the mines of "the richest hill on earth" (Butte, Montana). William Rockefeller, Marcus Daly, and Henry H. Rogers were the prime movers. Rockefeller controlled Standard Oil. Daly was one of Butte's richest men. Rogers managed Standard Oil operations, was president of Anaconda, and was involved with the Boston companies which controlled important Montana mines. Tom Lawson, a satellite of Rogers and one of the financial world's most flamboyant characters, was in charge of stock flotation.

In 1904 Lawson turned against his overlords and began the publication of an exposé which he called *Frenzied Finance,* in which he accused Rogers and Rockefeller of fleecing their stockholders with complete cynicism.[5] He pictured himself as an innocent catspaw at first — then as a defiant accuser. Although his emotional outcries can hardly be taken with complete seriousness, they did stir up a great deal of ill feeling. Greene was one whom he offended. In 1900, however, Greene's persuasiveness and charm penetrated the defenses of even Tom Lawson, and they agreed to do business together.

There was plenty of money to do business with. At the time of its organization on April 27, 1899, Amalgamated was capitalized at $75,-000,000. In 1901 the capitalization was raised to $155,000,000.[6] With this almost unimaginable wealth behind him, Lawson readily agreed to back Greene to the extent of $1,000,000. The credit was to be made available in short-term notes which Greene would pay back from the sale of stock and the proceeds of the mining enterprise. In return, acting for Amalgamated, Lawson would have an option to buy "a controlling block of shares" in Greene's Cananea at a third of the par value.

Something went wrong. In spite of the sensitive conscience which Lawson exhibited to the world in *Frenzied Finance,* he may have seen an opportunity to get something valuable for next to nothing. If he did, he was behaving normally for a capitalist of the early 1900s. Greene told his friends that after $135,000 had been borrowed and expended under the terms of the agreement, Lawson refused to lend any more and called in the notes already signed. If his scheme had succeeded, Lawson could have taken over Cananea for an insignificant part of its value.[7]

The story cannot be verified from primary sources, but Isaac F. Marcosson in his book on the Anaconda Corporation gives it some support when he notes that Amalgamated owned 30,800 shares of Greene Consolidated Cananea.[8]

Somehow Greene found new backers to pull him out of the hole which Lawson had dug for him. John W. "Bet-a-Million" Gates, with his partners Hawley and Huntington, rescued the Colonel, and in time all three became directors of Greene Consolidated Copper.[9]

It was that way for the rest of his active career. The wolves of Wall Street were always after him. As an independent operator, not a member of any inside group, he found that unceasing vigilance was the price of mere survival. Safety was out of the question.

The regulars were always trying to push somebody to the wall, spreading rumors to force a given stock down or buoy another one up, buying cheap and selling dear. Greene played the game with what weapons he had. He bought and sold his own stock, for one thing. He bought it to keep the price up when the bears were after him. He sold it when prices were high to keep financial blood in his corporate body.

During the years of preparation for full production, 1900 and 1901, Greene had to play the game with all his might. There was "unprecedented excitement" in the stock market in the spring and summer of 1901, a "furore of buying."[10] Greene Consolidated boomed with the rest, and money came in by the barrelful, but there was so much to do to commence operations, build a town, and get everything going at once, that the people who handled Greene's money were frequently in a state of shock.

Much of his local business was done at the Bank of Bisbee, operated by his long-time acquaintance Billy Brophy. Billy's correspondence (which has survived) is revealing.

Brophy invested in Greene Cananea stock and watched it climb to over $40 a share in the spring of 1901. Meanwhile, Greene funds — and Greene overdrafts — kept coming in to the bank to the confusion and consternation of Cashier M. J. Cunningham. Brophy wrote to his friend James D. Douglas at Nacozari (he was in charge for Phelps Dodge there) on May 9, 1901:

> W. C. Greene came in yesterday and negotiated a loan for $25,000 for one year with privilege of taking it up sooner. Interest at 6% per annum. Security as collateral one certificate of Greene CCC stock for 29,004 shares issued to J. H. Kirk and by him endorsed in blank. This I consider good collateral without transfer on the C. Books as Kirk is not very liable to be sued. . . . The rate is low but I considered it as good policy for the cultivation of future business.[11]

This was the sort of arrangement Greene frequently had to make, and it was not the last time he borrowed stock from his friends in order to meet a payroll or settle an oversize bill. He paid eventually, but in those early days he was always a little behind. On July 5, 1901, he sent his personal check to the Bank of Bisbee for $30,000 for the account of the Four C's and another in the same amount for Greene Consolidated. "What have you done about the proposition of starting a bank at Naco?" he inquired. "The company's business is very large and it seems to me as though a bank at this point would be very profitable."[12]

That was one side of the picture. Cashier Cunningham revealed another the very next day in a letter to Brophy:

> Greene applied for a further loan (to tide over the Cananea and Greene accounts) $40,000.00 secured by stock now in his possession, to run 30 days, or until he could get to New York. I advised him that owing to the absence of

the Board of Directors a loan of that magnitude could not be considered, as a full Board would be necessary to pass on such a loan. Just where the trouble lies I do not know, probably treasury stock is getting low and bullion not being produced fast enough. At any rate I propose to keep our head above water regardless of the consequences. . . . The way things are going now, and I think under the present management, it will continue, we will be quite lucky to keep their gold account in black ink.

Over and over as the days and weeks went by, Cunningham complained that Greene Cananea and Cananea Consolidated were always overdrawn. "It is one continual grand round of telephoning and worry," he wailed. "Their accounts cause me no end of worry. I do not understand their methods."[13]

Actually Greene's method was very simple. It consisted in keeping one jump ahead of his creditors, moving heaven and earth to get out the payroll, dividing up the money as it came in so that everybody got something (the ones who made the most noise, got the most). Everybody got paid — eventually. But during those first two years, when the Company was really being born, severe birth pangs had be be endured, and Brophy's bank helped to endure them.

Greene did business with a good many banks — in Tucson, Phoenix, New York — and other cashiers besides M. J. Cunningham had their worries as a result. On at least one occasion, however, Greene saved the management of a Tucson bank the trouble of making a decision. The payroll was coming due at Cananea and he was short of cash. He rode his private car to Nogales, planning to ask for a loan of $25,000 from the Consolidated National Bank of Tucson. While he was waiting in the yards for a switch engine to pick up his car, several of his friends dropped in and a poker game got started. It lasted for two days, right there on the siding, and when it was over, Greene went back to Cananea with the payroll in his pocket.[14]

New York capitalists and an occasional run of luck may have helped to keep Greene in business, but in the long run his major resource was his talent for attracting buyers for his stock and building confidence in his clientele. Here his abilities came close to genius, and most of the historians, sensational or serious, who have commented on his career, have noted his gift for playing Pied Piper to a crowd of "small investors," and some not so small.

His methods are worth study and would make an interesting chapter in a textbook on upper-division salesmanship. His eyeball-to-eyeball persuasiveness was no small part of it. His ability to write glowing reports and prophecies counted heavily. His honest confidence in himself and his merchandise was a tremendous factor also. And in many smaller ways he added color and character to the image which he had created — the image

Frank T. Greene

The Colonel and Cobre Grande, his racehorse, on a New York track.

of a benevolent capitalist protecting the little people who believed in him.

For one thing, he took pains to blend with the scenery, assume protective coloring, and avoid alarming the game which he and his fellow promoters were always hunting — the Amateur American Investor. He lived at the Waldorf, which was the favorite gathering place of his adopted species. He donned the uniform (Prince Albert coat and striped trousers for formal meetings). He accepted their basic axiom: that the object of a business is to make money for stockholders. The only way in which he diverged from the stereotype was in the matter of pleasures and pastimes. He did not buy a yacht, build a mansion at Bar Harbor, or go to Scotland for grouse hunting. His money-making enterprises were his whole life.

In 1905 he was the subject of a sketch in an expensive book called *Fads and Fancies of Representative Americans,* and the architect of this effusion was shocked to learn that Greene had neither fads nor fancies.

With barely concealed incredulity he remarked that the Colonel seemed interested only in his business.[15]

Greene did love horses and had a racing stable in New York — later in Phoenix (one of his fast horses was called Cobre Grande)[16] — but his conspicuous spending was mostly part of his approach to his promotional schemes. When motor cars became available, he owned several, but they had to pay their way, carrying him and his guests over the Mexican mountains. On his long journeys he traveled by private railroad car — and not just because it was more comfortable. The prosperity which it indicated was good for business, and he could take as many people along as he wanted to without making reservations or arranging for tickets. En route or in town he had a place to confer and persuade and play poker.

His instinct for assuming the coloring of his surroundings came in handy in his dealings with his board of directors and his stockholders. He communicated with them frequently, and he was always bringing groups of them to Cananea to see for themselves what was going on. "It gives them a better idea of the magnitude of the property to look at it for a few minutes," he said, "than it would to talk about it for a month."[17]

He was more than likely right in his conviction that the money and time he spent on these pilgrimages were justified. They seemed to keep his people excited and happy. As an example, there was the committee appointed by the stockholders at the end of 1899 which came to Cananea in January 1901. They reported to the directors that they found Naco, the shipping point, and Cananea, the production center, humming with activity. About 3,500 people were living in the new town of Cananea, many of them in tents. Warehouse space had been provided. A Company store carried a stock of goods worth $40,000. Machine shops, a lumber yard, and offices were in operation. Two furnaces were running wide open, and 900 teams were hauling ore to Naco and bringing back supplies. An electric-light plant was functioning, telephones were in use, a medical department had been organized, and a school with 246 pupils had opened its doors. The committee could find little to criticize and much to admire.

"We were amazed," they declared, "at what has been accomplished, and we cannot comprehend how so much has been done with the money which has been furnished. It could not have been done without great push, great ability, and great skill behind it, and this we have found in a remarkable degree, both in the President, Mr. Greene, and Mr. Mitchell, the manager." As for the mines, they were "becoming richer and richer and more and more valuable with every day's work of the miners."[18]

Greene was a great salesman, but his stockholders beat him at his own game.

Occasionally he found ways of getting a little amusement out of what must have been at times a worrisome business — riding herd on these tourists from the East. His best opportunity came when lady stockholders asked to be taken into the shafts and tunnels so they could see a copper mine in actual operation. Greene knew, though he did not usually say so, that the temperatures ran high underground and the miners often stripped off everything and worked in the nude. He kept his face straight, of course, when a sensitive guest fled screaming at the sight of a naked miner, but his inward satisfaction made up for some of the worry she might have caused him.[19]

He was at his best in stockholders' meetings. He staged them with some pomp and circumstance, adding as much drama as possible. He exhibited a phenomenal memory for the details of the business, answering complicated questions off the cuff, and he had a fine flow of words. Lady stockholders found him irresistible. There was Mrs. Miranda B. Tulloch, for instance, a school trustee of the District of Columbia and obviously a woman of great force and insight. Greene made her a member of his board of directors in 1900. Another loyal Washington lady was Helen L. McL. Kimball, eighty-eight years old but still full of vinegar, who never wavered in her devotion and wrote, when Mr. Greene's stock was under attack:

I think Mr. Greene may be very proud of the Washington stockholders. They may have often felt anxious, but they have had only contempt for the promoter who was so anxious to sell the Greene stock as the most promising of any investment that could be made and then so suddenly find it worthless. . . .[20]

Between meetings Greene often issued reports and circular letters to his flock. They were, as we have said, a nervous lot, and they were always dropping by the office or writing in to ask what was going on and was he sure that everything was all right? Greene was sure, of course, but rather than answer all these inquiries individually, he answered them en masse.

Once, when he was preparing a report on the Four C's, he wrote:

It is not necessary to give the public the details of the business. The report will be made directly to the directors of the Greene Company from the Cananea Company, and will not be given to the public, as life is too short to answer all the questions that 3,000 stockholders can think up. What they want is dividends, and we will give them dividends.[21]

A typical communique went out on March 8, 1901 — encouraging, hopeful, full of good news. Delays in receiving and installing equipment, Greene confided, kept down production in January and February, net profits being only $7,000 per day. With the new installations complete,

Compañía Minera de Cananea

Ronquillo, after it had grown larger, the
smelter going full blast in the background.

net profits should soar toward $300,000 per month. By October he expected to have a new 600-ton smelter in operation, and production might be expected to rise to as much as four million pounds of blister copper per month.[22] He included a letter from C. B. Lewis, president of the National Metal Company of New York, who at the moment was handling all the matte shipments from Cananea: "Their matte output has thus far been the highest grade and the most desirable class of matte we have ever handled. . . . I cannot see how they can fail to produce immense values in copper, in future."[23]

After this sort of preparation, the next logical step was to issue a block of stock. On March 5 Greene offered 10,000 shares at $25, and on March 19 he brought out another 10,000 at $40 "for the purpose of constructing a Bessemer refining plant at the mines." The stock was his own and he expected the Company to repay him for this outlay. "This is the last opportunity," he admonished with typical Greene bravura, "which will be afforded to obtain stock at a low figure in what is today the *largest and richest copper mines in the world.*"[24]

Financial moves followed each other in rapid succession during the spring and summer of 1901. At a stockholders' meeting on February 25, half a million dollars' worth of ten-year gold railroad bonds were authorized to finance the building of the railroad from Cananea to Naco, and on April 1 the stockholders were notified that the bonds were available for those who wished to buy. This was one time that Greene's persuasive powers failed him, however, for the bonds did not sell and were a worry to the Company for the next year.

Construction was begun on the railroad shortly after the bonds were authorized, and by the middle of June half the roadbed had been graded and some rails had been laid.[25]

Another important move in the late spring and early summer of 1901 was the purchase of an enormous tract of timber land. The hills near the mines had been denuded in the early months of mining activity, and it had become necessary to import huge quantities of lumber. There was tall timber in Mexico but no way to process it. Every stick used in the construction of Company buildings was hauled in from the United States. Most of the mine timbers followed the same route. It was either go on spending vast sums of money or find a source of supply in Mexico.

Greene reported to his stockholders on June 19:

During the last sixty days, the Company has acquired 440,000 acres of land at a cost of $351,000 in gold, of which $151,000 has been paid, leaving a balance of $200,000 falling due on the 1st day of November, 1901. A large portion of this land is heavily timbered with pine. It was an absolute necessity that we should own the timber upon this land, thereby securing us our own timber for many years at a minimum cost.[26]

Some stories have survived about Greene's reasons for putting so much money into the purchase of this enormous tract of range and timber land. At first the Company was paying for stumpage — for the timber actually cut and used — but the price was high, and Jim Kirk suggested that it would be cheaper to buy the property than to go on as they were. Greene thought he might be right and went to a man named Acuña, one of the owners of the timber land, and asked him how much he would take for his holdings.

"Sixty-three thousand dollars."

"All right, here it is."

And Greene reached into his vest pocket and started pulling out thousand-dollar bills (the best stories say that he carried *ten*-thousand-dollar bills in his vest pocket).

"No, no, not that way!" said Acuña, all in a flutter. "I wouldn't get across the street with all that money. I will come by your office tomorrow. We will make out the papers and you will give me a check."

And that was the way they did it.[27]

The timber purchase was probably a good thing for the Four C's, but it was to cause Greene some trouble later.

One special way Greene had of keeping his stockholders excited about the mines was to issue periodic reports on production. Careful records were kept at Cananea, and daily summaries were made out for the Company of how much matte was on hand, how much had been shipped, and the number of each car used in shipping. When the 400-ton furnace went into operation in January, 1901, production figures jumped immediately. A report dated April 17 of that year, covering the period April 1 to April 12, showed a production of 617,000 pounds of copper. Value at fifteen cents a pound: $92,655.00. Cost of processing: $11,401.77. Net earnings for eleven days: $81,253.23.[28]

This, of course, was nowhere near enough to pay the Company's bills, and since the railroad bonds had not moved and $351,000.00 had been pledged for the newly acquired timber lands, the directors voted, at their meeting at the mines on July 3, to propose an increase of capitalization from 500,000 shares to 600,000 shares at the annual meeting of stockholders in New York on July 22. To prepare the voters for their responsibility, Greene got out a letter in which he outdid himself.

To those of our stockholders who have not had the opportunity to visit the property personally, it may appear strange that it would be necessary to increase the capital stock in order to provide working capital upon a property that is now and has been for some months producing over $300,000 in copper per month; but when the great extent of the Company's property is taken into consideration, embracing, as it does, more than twice the area of the entire productive mines of Butte, Montana . . . and that this property has reached, with a comparatively small expenditure of money, within the short period since active development started, an output far exceeding that which any other copper mine in this country has reached until after many years of development . . . and when we remember that during the past six months the stock of our Company has advanced in value from $10 to $40 per share without manipulation, but from the mere fact of values being proved and generally known, there remains not a doubt in my mind that with the increased betterments we will be enabled to immediately make . . . sound business judgment will lead you to agree with me that the proposed increase of capitalization is more than warranted by the property.

"We have laid the foundations broad and sure for what we have always known it to be," he concluded, fortissimo, "the largest copper mine in the world."[29]

The stockholders believed him (how could they have doubted?), and at the July meeting they approved the increase in capitalization. They went even farther. When 50,000 shares were offered to them at $40 a share, the issue was "very largely oversubscribed."[30] In August the public was given an opportunity to buy 10,000 shares with the warning: "This is the last block of Treasury Stock that will be offered for sale at present. Full amount must accompany each subscription."[31]

That annual meeting — July 22, 1901 — was an emotional, even an inspiring, experience for those in attendance. General T. H. Anderson of Washington, D. C., U. S. Attorney for the District of Columbia, world traveler, experienced businessman, and a firm believer in the genius of Colonel W. C. Greene, made an impromptu speech which warmed the hearts of his listeners:

> I speak, of course, as a layman, and yet I have visited the famous Koro-Koro mines of the upper Andes. I am pretty familiar with mining conditions in South America. . . . I was so impressed with the value of the property that I not only stand ready to largely increase, or substantially increase, my own investments, but to advise my own warm friends to invest in the stock of the company.

Greene was by no means speechless, even after this tribute. He rose to give detailed and statistical answers to a number of questions from the floor and finished by explaining some of his own procedures:

> There has been a great deal of concern manifested by some of our stockholders in regard to some money that is due me. . . . Whenever money was needed at the mines I have never called a stockholders' meeting, but when the company needed $100,000 or $200,000, I simply went down in my pocket and advanced the money and that stands as an open account.
> I have told the Executive Committee that I hold today $600,000 of notes of the Company, $300,000 of which draws 5 per cent interest, and $300,000 draws 6 per cent. Those notes are payable every six months. I have offered to take out of the increased issue an amount of stock corresponding to the amount of those notes at $40 per share, the price at which it is offered by the company to the stockholders of record. (Applause.)[32]

One inquisitive stockholder at this meeting asked, "How about listing the stock?" Greene said he thought "the stock should be listed." It continued to sell on the curb, however, as long as he controlled the Company.

The stock expansion temporarily solved Greene's financial problems, and he was able to report to Mitchell at the end of August, "All our bills are paid and we are entirely out of debt. We have between $80,000 and $100,000 worth of matte on hand and unpaid for and credit balances in Western banks between $30,000 and $40,000."

Always optimistic, he added, "I think we have made ample provision for all the needs of the Company."[33] He was probably right — at the moment!

A mood of something like rapture filtered downward from Greene through the strata of his organization. On August 2, Walter Logan, treasurer, took his turn at the organ and sent out an impassioned letter to the stockholders. "When our advertisement first appeared on February 10," he declared, "there were ten stockholders." Four months later there were 400. On the first date, there were seven directors. Now there were seventeen. Stock sold at first for $5.00 a share — then for $6.50, then for $8.00, and finally for $10 — par value. "We knew at the beginning that there were great profits awaiting the stockholders of whatever company could successfully launch this enterprise. We know now that ours is that company and that it is our stockholders who are to receive the rewards."[34]

What widow with a few hundred dollars on hand could resist joining the happy throng of Greene investors?

The question that always arose was: "When will the Company pay dividends?" Greene remarked in one of his letters to the stockholders that this was one of "the principal points upon which information is desired."[35] And he was as eager as anybody to share the Company's profits. He could have taken his time. Most mining companies took five — ten — twenty years to produce enough to justify a dividend, if indeed they ever were able to declare one. He would probably have been wise to plow all the profits back into the enterprise, since he was expanding so rapidly, but he didn't want to wait. In the fall of 1901 the first dividend — $220,000 — went to the stockholders.[36]

Having done his best for the shareholders, it was time for Greene to do something for himself. He had plenty of money now, and his instinct was to put it to work. Rather late in his career, he had found out what he did best — that he was a born promoter — and for the rest of his life he was on the lookout for projects that took capital and imagination. He found them — too many of them. His weakness was that he wanted to do everything. He tried to be the universal promoter.

He was also a cattleman, and as he looked at the vast rolling pastures, rich with grama grass, which surrounded his mining town, he knew that some of his new money would have to go into ranch property.

First he bought the Palominas ranch on the American side, just south of his "homestead" on the San Pedro. It reached all the way to the border and joined his range on the Mexican side. Next he organized the Greene Cattle Company as an Arizona corporation, signing the papers on April 21, 1901. On May 10 he set up his Mexican cattle enterprise, the Cananea Cattle Company, under the laws of his adopted country. The nucleus came from the great tract of mountain and range land he had recently bought from Senator Perkins and his partners. The Copper Company kept the rangeland immediately adjoining the town of Cananea as a sort of buffer zone between the mining and cattle enterprises. The rest was transferred to the Cattle Company.[37]

In 1902 Frank Proctor, Greene's father-in-law, was appointed *gerente,* or general manager. Greene retained the presidency. He registered the RO brand in Mexico and transferred the OR brand to the Greene Cattle Company on the American side.[38]

The ownership of the OR brand was to cause a world of trouble later, long after the Colonel was dead. Ella Greene, his first wife, was the original claimant in Arizona, as she had more than once made clear in affidavits in Cochise County. She had died intestate, however, and Greene had simply taken possession. He was mindful of the fact that Ella had left three children, two by her first husband Moson, and one by him. He was generous with all of them. When Frank Moson married Pearl Parker on New Year's Day, 1902, the papers reported that Greene had given them $5,000 for a wedding trip to Paris.[39] It was the sort of gesture he loved. He much preferred to take care of people's needs rather than settle obligations once and for all. When Clarence Chase, his nephew from Minnesota, went to work for him in 1902, he paid Clarence no regular salary. He authorized him to draw on the Greene bank account for whatever he required.[40] He liked to play the role of generous patriarch.

A few years later he was forced to do something about the claims of Frank and Virginia Moson and of his daughter Eva to the inheritance due from their mother, but in 1901 he went no farther than setting aside a block of Greene Cattle Company stock for each of them and finding a place for Frank Moson and Virginia's husband, Ben Sneed, in his cattle business.[41]

So all went according to his desire through the summer and early fall of 1901. But Greene was like ordinary men in one way — he was subject to the turn of Fortune's wheel, and as September drew to a close, the wheel turned against him.

First there was a decline in the copper market, Greene's shares dropping with the rest. Amalgamated Copper was supposed to be behind it. Tom Lawson, who was still doing his best for Amalgamated, admitted in a Market Letter, "I *know* that there is something of tremendous import to the holders of Amalgamated being worked out at the present time."[42] He didn't say what. But prices went down and down, and one New York paper commenting on "Copper's New Low Record," observed: "Policy is a mild and harmless game, relatively speaking, compared with the Amalgamated Copper."[43]

Greene knew what was going on. Early in October he wrote to George Mitchell:

> I am in hopes that the present copper panic will be over in a few days as there is really nothing to base it on. It is simply stock manipulation by the Standard Oil and other heavy copper interests having for its object stopping the flotation of copper companies. It strikes rather unexpectedly but we will work it out all right in a few days.[44]

It was not over in a few days. In December it was still going on, but Greene's stock was not yet in bad shape. It hovered around 30 that fall, once reaching a low of 28½.[45]

What was worse was a whispering campaign which got started in October and kept working underground. Production figures were wrong, the rumors said. The veins were petering out, and Greene was lying about ore resources. Too much limestone was going into the flux at the smelters. The narrow-gauge railroad to Puertecitos was useless and wasteful when there was plenty of ore in sight at Cananea proper. Greene was extravagant. The purchase of the timber lands was a foolhardy venture.

George Mitchell, far away in Mexico, was the one who did something about these subtle slanders. He hired a detective to see what he could find out. It was done with Greene's blessing, but Detective Harry Block made his reports to Mitchell. On November 15, 1901, he pointed an accusing finger at Greene's old friend and ally, George Treadwell. Posing as a potential investor who wanted information, he had spent an hour and a half with Treadwell; significantly, their meeting place was at the offices of Logan, Demond, and Harby at 27 William Street, first home of Greene Consolidated. Block led off by remarking that he had a few thousand dollars to invest and asking for an opinion of the Greene properties.

> He said at present he would not advise me to buy any of the stock which is at the present time down to 19. He says that Col. Greene has spent a lot of money and has run things on a too extravagant scale, that he has spent money in buying 300,000 acres of land when it was only necessary to buy about 3,000 acres, his excuse at the time was that it was best for the Company in regard to the lumber and timber lands which was on it; he told me that the Greene Consolidated Copper Company had very fine property but that when they could get Mr. Greene out then they could get it going on a paying basis as the price of the stock at present was very uncertain.[46]

Mrs. Helen L. McL. Kimball of Washington also knew what was going on and commented on it in the letter to George Robbins already quoted. Treadwell was now carrying the ball for the San Luis Mine at Tayoltita, Durango, and Logan was in it with him. Mrs. Kimball mentions a brochure on the Cananea mines and adds, with a toss of the head:

It may not be as classic literature as Mr. Logan's but it will be very acceptable. Our holdings here have evidently become too insignificant to be referred to in this latest testimony to the richness of the Durango and Treadwell mines.[47]

Logan's "classic literature" must have been the effusion of August 2, 1901, to the stockholders. He must have broken with Greene soon afterward, for in October or November he resigned his post as treasurer of the corporation and his stock was put up for sale. It would be a good bet that the break occurred because Greene insisted on running his own show his own way. An alliance between a conservative Easterner and a Westerner who liked to shoot the works was probably doomed from the start.

Greene apparently was not particularly upset over Logan's defection — at least there is nothing left in the files to indicate that he was — but neither was he anxious to help Logan make a profit from the sale of his stock. He wrote to Mitchell at the end of November, "Our treasury stock is all sold. As soon as the Logan stock is all sold, the market will go up; but we do not want to support it until he gets rid of his stock."[48]

It would seem that Treadwell also was allowed to go without bitterness. He was dropped from the Board of Directors and disappears after 1901 from the Greene chronicle.

New leadership was not hard for Greene to find. Philip Berolzheimer of the Eagle Pencil Company with offices in New York became the new treasurer, and George S. Robbins of the Wirt Fountain Pen Company, Bloomsburg, Pennsylvania, became secretary of the corporation.

Unfortunately the whispers against Greene, once set in motion, were hard to stop. The stockbrokers tuned in on them and passed them along to their clients. A member of the firm of Harrison and Wyckoff, for instance, wrote to W. H. Brophy of Bisbee in May of 1902:

The writer believes that it would be decidedly beneficial if anyone but Mr. Greene had control. He has made a horrible botch of the financiering thus far, but as one of our friends put it, the properties are so good that they offset any poor work in a financial way.[49]

The charge that Greene was a financial ignoramus and that his great enterprise survived in spite of his blundering has been picked up by the historians of business who like to smile at the Buckaroo of Wall Street.[50]

It would probably be accurate to say that he made mistakes like other men, particularly when he was new in the Street, but that he had to know what he was doing most of the time in order to survive as long as he did.

In spite of everything, he stayed calm and collected. A typical Greene letter, mild and serene, and, somehow above the tumult and the shouting, went off to William Brophy on December 20, 1901:

Dear Mr. Brophy:

Your kind favor of the 13th received and on behalf of Mrs. Greene and daughter, as well as myself, I thank you for your kind wishes — my daughter particularly being very emphatic in expressing her appreciation judging from the amount of noise occasionally.

I expect to leave for the mines about the 26th or 27th of the month. Will have party of very prominent men — among them the Assistant Secretary of the Treasury and Colonel Parker, of Washington — perhaps Russell Sage; don't know whether I can get the old man to move out of New York or not but I am making an effort.

The copper situation is pretty badly muddled, due altogether to artificial manipulation and big stock deals. Greene pursues the even tenor of his way. We keep sawing wood and don't "give a rap" whether the stock sells for $3 or $300. Our business is making copper and we are going to make the copper world realize that we have a copper mine. They are a little skeptical yet but not quite so much so as they were two years ago.

Sorry to hear of Mr. Cunningham's indisposition and hope that his vacation will set him right again.

With kindest regards to Mrs. Brophy and yourself and wishing you the compliments of the Season.

Yours sincerely,

W. C. Greene

The Short Busy Reign
of Anson W. Burchard

1902 WAS THE YEAR of Anson W. Burchard. This unusual and contro-
versial genius, although his title was only Second Vice-president and
Comptroller, became in effect the General Manager at Cananea. He
lasted just seven months, but the Cananea Consolidated Copper Company trembled at his coming and shook for a long time after he was gone.
His letters[1] open a window on the problems and activities of the copper
enterprise when it was just getting into full production.

Burchard was a native of Hoosic Falls, New York, a small town
near the Vermont border, much like Greene's home community of Chappaqua. He was a man of considerable background and was endowed with
a keen mind, a good technical education, and a fine stock of driving
energy. A graduate of Stevens Institute, he was by profession an electrical engineer,[2] but his real talent was for organization.

Nothing is on record to tell us what brought Greene and Burchard
together or how their acquaintance ripened. He may have been spon-
sored by important stockholders who thought the Colonel's affairs at
Cananea were in a mess and Burchard was the man who could straighten
them out. It is more than likely that Greene discovered Burchard on his
own, listened to his ideas, and thought, "This is the man who can see
that there is a place for everything at Cananea, and that everything is in
its place."

Burchard's name appears on the list of Greene's directors on January 4, 1902,[3] and in March he was in Cananea taking charge and issuing orders.[4]

Greene was unwearying in his efforts to improve the situation at the mines — to avoid waste, improve efficiency, save money. He was distressed by the reports of mismanagement and extravagance which pursued him throughout his active life, and he did what he could to counteract them. The trouble was that he could spend little of his time in Mexico, and he wanted somebody on the spot to be his eyes and ears. Burchard seemed to have been made for the job, and he came at a time when he was badly needed.

George Mitchell developed a serious illness about the first of the year and went off to California for treatment. Robert Mitchell, his brother, took his place, but Bob was a smelter man, not an executive, and he was not used to the responsibilities he had to assume. Things began to get out of hand. George was back in harness and handling his correspondence again on March 8, but he could not concentrate on the main issues. Manifests and invoices for the Supply Department were missing. There was trouble on the railroad — a customs inspector was complaining of mistreatment by one of the conductors.[5] The production statement for February was wrong and Mitchell had to ask Greene, in New York, not to release the figures until they were revised.[6] Mitchell, still not his old vigorous self, needed all his time to get the concentrator set up and operating, and these petty details of management were undoubtedly a trial to him. Burchard was sent to bring him relief, and George acted as if he were grateful.[7] In his heart, he may have regarded Burchard as a mixed blessing.

By this time Mitchell's ties with Greene were loosening. He continued to sign himself General Manager, but in statements issued from the New York office, he was referred to as Manager, Reduction Division. The change in title probably is significant.

Many things may have contributed to the disharmony — George's health; his outside interests; disapproval of Greene's policies — but the efficient cause seems to have been a rift with Jim Kirk.

Kirk, the Manager of the Mining Division, was Greene's most honest, most outspoken, most reliable old friend. At least Greene thought so, and he had reason to know. They had known and trusted each other since their Tombstone days, and before. Kirk was a man of no pretensions but of great strength of character and much practical sense. He had a rugged Scottish face distinguished by a fine pair of drooping mustaches, was most at home underground with his miners, and wrote his letters in pencil. He was fiercely devoted to Greene and gave him good blunt advice.

Dr. Louis D. Ricketts, genius in the background.

In January of 1902, for instance, Greene had an engineer looking into the possibility of building a railroad across very rough country to Imuris, west of Cananea, and on to Nogales. Kirk wrote him:

> If I were in your place I would quit Railroading for a while I think. It would be better to let him draw his salary without doing anything than allow him to continue on his present course. . . . Expecting my usual rounding up for interfering with your affairs, I am as ever
>
> yours very truly,
Jas. H. Kirk.[8]

A possible hint as to the nature of the trouble between Greene's two closest friends appears in one of Kirk's penciled letters:

Would also like to have you arrainge with George Mitchell so that the heads of the Smelter Dept. know when their authority begins and stops, so as to avoid friction. A word from you will do this and thereby save this Company many Dollars.[9]

The heads of the Smelter Department included George Mitchell and his brother Robert.

In the end Greene had to choose between them, and when matters came to a showdown, he chose Kirk. The story has been handed down in Kirk's family that George tried to have Jim ousted and was ousted himself.[10] Ostensibly he left the Company to pursue his other interests. He was president of the Mitchell Mining Company in the State of Guerrero; he was associated with his brother Robert in the management of the South Cananea Copper Company, whose property adjoined Greene's; and he was founder and president of the Bank of Douglas. He ranged as far afield as Alaska, but his major interests were in Mexico and the border country.[11]

He remained a believer in Greene's great copper enterprise and seems to have retained friendly feelings toward Greene himself, but he complained in 1904 that the Colonel had borrowed stock worth $2,000,-000 from him and had not paid it back.[12]

Greene tried to bring Dr. Louis Ricketts to Cananea to replace Mitchell. Ricketts was one of the top mining engineers in the country, a man of great sagacity and resourcefulness who left a permanent mark on the industry in Mexico and the American Southwest. He dressed in disreputable old clothes and is said to have had trouble occasionally with conductors who thought he was a bum and tried to put him off their trains, but his abilities were unquestioned. In fact, he became a legend long before he died. According to contemporary reports Greene offered him the post of chief metallurgist, which he turned down, but in May of the following year he agreed to act as consulting engineer for revamping the concentrator and the converter plant.[13]

Years later in an interview with the editor of the *Mining and Scientific Press,* Ricketts explained that he did not come into the Greene management because he was afraid the Company was not "properly financed." What he meant by that, it is not possible to know today. He may have heard the voices in the whispering campaign and noted that the price of stock was down to 19½ as a result of the anti-Greene activity in late 1901 and early 1902. He himself was never anti-Greene, however. He told the interviewer:

I admired the many good points of his [Greene's] character. He was always loyal and generous to his friends. . . . I owe to him my first real opportunity to make any considerable sum of money, as he let me have 5,000 shares in the America Mining Company of Cananea. Subsequently I disposed of this stock to pay its cost to me and invested the balance in Greene Cananea Copper Company.[14]

Into this complicated situation at Cananea stepped Anson Burchard, thirty-six years old, unmarried, an Easterner, a superior person, a man whose mission was to tell Greene's lieutenants what they were doing wrong. It is a marvel that he lasted seven months in an environment for which he was not prepared, and which certainly was not prepared for him.

Ten days after his arrival he wrote a revealing letter to George Robbins, the Company Secretary, in New York:

We arrived here on Sunday the 16th, and since that time I have been studying the situation diligently and carefully. There are a great many problems here and a great many difficult tasks to be accomplished. I have as yet given no attention to the question of accounting and management of the office and store departments, but have devoted my time to a study of the physical condition of the property and the requirements of the mines and reduction works to enable the proposed output of six million pounds of copper per month to be realized. This is, of course, the fundamental consideration, and all other questions subordinate to it. The elements necessary to success are all present although the requirements for funds to provide the necessary mining and reduction facilities are greater than have been estimated.

Many thanks for your cordial expressions of interest in the work and in the writer's welfare. You may be assured that my very best efforts will be exercised to bring about a successful outcome of the undertaking in which we are all interested.[15]

There was nothing wrong with the men Burchard had to work with. They were the best in the business. Ed Massey, responsible under Kirk for the underground activity, was another experienced miner who had known Greene since the 1880s and was as loyal to him as Kirk was. John A. Campbell had recently been appointed secretary. Ignacio Macmanus was cashier of the bank. George Young was the auditor. Scott White, ex-sheriff of Cochise County, was the local treasurer. Norton Chase, the lawyer, and Tomás Macmanus spent much of their time in Mexico City keeping in touch with the Mexican power structure. These men and the rest, on down the line, were devoted to Greene and good at their jobs.

If they had not been, Greene would not have been able to take up the roving role which characterized his leadership. It was amazing how he got around the country, coast to coast, cajoling, arranging, making friends. He passed perhaps half his time in New York where he could be close to the market and do what he could to keep the price of his stock

John A. Campbell, Secretary,
later Treasurer, of Cananea
Consolidated Copper Company.

Cananea Herald

Ignacio Macmanus,
cashier of the Cananea bank.

Cananea Herald

up. The rest of his days he spent on the road, always traveling in a private railroad car, leased by the company, until he arranged for the purchase of the *Verde,* his own name in Spanish, which became almost a part of his personality.

He traveled so fast that his mail could hardly catch up with him. To one disgruntled firm which was trying to locate him, Burchard wrote:

Mr. Greene left here about the 26th of April; he went to California, from there to New York, from there to Prescott, Arizona, and from there to California. During this time his letters have been forwarded from point to point with the view to overtaking him, but his stay at each place has been of such short duration that they have failed to reach him.[16]

Burchard added, "We are in receipt of a telegram from him dated May 21 advising that he has seen you and has adjusted the matter."

Several times a year Greene came to Cananea to see at first hand how things were going and to take part in the decisions being made daily there, but his time was so limited that Jim Kirk thought it necessary to send him ahead of time a list of important matters needing to be decided, leaving space between the items for his answer. "Have shut down work on Cobre Grande until such time as I get a pump capable of handling water. Is this right? . . . I would like to put a Detective in the Cananea Store. What do you think about it?"[17]

Burchard was there to handle such matters, and in an unbelievably short time he became the Man Who Did Everything. He was unceasingly vigilant in the Company's interest, saved every penny possible, kept after people who needed to be pursued, watched for the smallest sign of inefficiency, and seldom allowed himself to become exasperated.

At the beginning of 1902 the immediate problem was the desperate need to get the concentrator and the converters into operation. Low-grade ores had to be concentrated before smelting was feasible, and the concentrator had number-one priority. Mitchell wrote from his sick bed in California on February 2 to H. W. Hardinge, in charge of concentrator construction, begging him to "urge in every way possible, the erection of the concentrator."[18]

Only a professional mining man could have estimated the difficulties involved in erecting that vital concentrator, and even he could not have foreseen the accidents and delays that would occur. Nothing was simple. Prices were out of line. Specifications were wrong. The work got farther and farther behind schedule. And the cost was high — $200,000.[19]

The converter plant was an even bigger headache. Promised for September of 1901, it was still far from completed by the first of the year. Nobody would have suspected from Greene's letters, however, that anything was wrong.

Everything is running very well here; the mines are looking fine, and smelter is turning out about 160 tons per day matte. The Converters we hope to have running by about April 20, and we still think that God loves good people.[20]

Burchard's first troubles resulted from the delay in installing the converters. Until they were operational,[21] the Company had to ship matte to refineries in the East. It was a long and expensive haul which gave rise to unending difficulties.

Greene had contracts with two smelters — the Orford Copper Company with offices at 99 John Street, New York, and the Nichols Copper Company at 25 Broad Street. Between March 14 and April 30 Orford received shipments of 3,059,522 pounds of matte. The contract called for four million. Nichols got 7,514,968 pounds on a contract of ten million. Burchard was embarrassed over the deficiency and explained that it was due to "the necessity of shutting down some of our smelting furnaces while putting in the iron floor of our new smelter building. . . . If agreeable to you we will continue shipments during the present month as heretofore, until we shall have forwarded to you the entire quantity contracted for."[22]

That was brave talk, but Burchard admitted confidentially to Secretary Robbins, "We cannot definitely undertake at this writing to furnish them 1,000 tons additional between now and August 1st."[23]

Freight rates, of course, were of the utmost importance in shipping these millions of tons of matte, and Mr. Burchard was always trying to find a way to cut costs. The completion of the Company railroad from Naco to Cananea and the westward extension of the El Paso and Southwestern Railroad to connect with it — both in 1901 — helped immeasurably. Shipping by rail was a great improvement over hauling the matte out on mule back or in wagons. Most of the time the Company used the Southern Pacific route to New Orleans, where the sacks of matte were shipped by Morgan steamship to New York. The Santa Fe got some of the business, however, because it owned a fleet of forty-ton box cars. Since the Mexican customs duties were assessed on each car, regardless of size, the Company used these jumbo-size units whenever they were available.[24]

The whole business of transportation was complicated by the problem of rebates. Large-tonnage shipments provided so much business for the railroads that they were willing to kick back some of the cost, and this money was collected, sometimes following pretty stiff arguments, after delivery was made. Keeping up with this sort of thing could be abrasive to the nerves. "We think it desirable," Burchard wrote to Mr. Evans (later General Manager but in 1901 railroad auditor at Naco) "that you should install a system in your office for keeping an account of loaded cars moving outward, the rates on which are subject to rebate. In this way we will be able to determine whether or not we collect all the rebates due us."[25] Both diplomacy and firmness were called for in handling these negotiations, and Mr. Burchard was speaking the simple truth when he remarked that "the railroad situation is one of extreme delicacy."[26]

All sorts of accidents could happen once the matte was en route and out of Company control. Shipments went to the wrong smelter. Cars arrived without waybills. Occasionally equipment broke down and the cargo had to be shifted. Mr. Burchard was always steaming gently about one or another of these situations.[27] His biggest worries, however, were near home — at Naco, where shipments crossed the United States–Mexican border.

Naco, Arizona, was a Greene town. The Four C's had a forwarding agency there and maintained a Company store while the Cananea-Naco railroad was building. Naco, Sonora, was something else. Its main business was collecting duties on commodities going to or coming from Cananea. Mostly the Company paid in cash. It was fatal to issue drafts or checks and wait forever for clearance.

A good deal of the problem was summed up in one question: "To sack or not to sack?" Matte could be shipped in bulk if it went all the way by rail, but if it went to New Orleans for transfer to a steamship it had to be sacked. The problem was that Mexican law required an inspection of every tenth sack — twenty-five or thirty sacks per car at $2.50 Mexican money per sack. And the customs force was so small that only one car per day could be processed. Burchard thought of a way out. He had the sacking done on the American side.[28]

The converters, the matte shipments, and the fuel problem — these were the dragons that Mr. Burchard had to fight. And sometimes the greatest of these was fuel. All the coke and coal used to fire Greene's furnaces was imported from the United States. The major supplier was the Colorado Fuel and Iron Company with offices in Denver. When the Four C's was desperate, it sometimes placed orders with other firms, though this sort of desperation was rare. Most of the time however, Colorado Fuel and Iron had trouble in living up to its contracts, and Burchard was constantly sending high-pitched complaints to Mr. Cass, the vice-president.

Our available supply of fuel, in sight, is less than 30 days consumption, and it is therefore imperative that shipments be resumed in larger quantities. We require 120 tons coke and 80 tons coal daily. . . .[29]

Sometimes Colorado Fuel and Iron managed to live up to Burchard's expectations, and when that happened, Burchard found himself in trouble with the railroads for taking up too much space in their yards and on their sidings. Late in March the number of cars waiting to get through was 367, eighty percent of them loaded with fuel. He began to get indignant letters, especially from James Douglas, president of the El Paso and Southwestern Railroad. Burchard insisted that he was "making every effort"[30] and reminded Douglas that total charges owing the E. P. & S. W. amounted to $171,000, which was being paid out at the rate of $5,000 per day. The implication was, "The more congestion, the more money for the railroad."

This was in March. In April Burchard was embarrassed again, this time because new construction had interfered with smelter activities, lowering production and reducing the need for fuel. "We would therefore request you to suspend shipments of coal for two weeks."[31] Ten days later he was back in the original key: ". . . you must recognize that it is a matter of absolute necessity for us to maintain an ample supply of fuel."[32]

Construction, marketing the copper and keeping up the fuel supply were major problems, but Burchard could not give them his undivided attention. There were a thousand minor ones, new ones every day. All sorts of materials were needed to keep the enterprise going, and the price had to be right. Lumber, brick and fireclay were coming in all the time. Burchard estimated the timber consumption of the whole enterprise at 10,000 feet per day.[33] At first lumber was brought in from the United States at great expense, but before long Greene began to use his recently purchased forest land in Chihuahua. He set up sawmills in the mountains and operated a lumber yard at Cananea.

J. J. Cottrell signed a contract in Cananea on May 29, 1902, to produce 20,000 "first-class, sound, hard brick" per day.[34] The Company bought concrete in Kansas[35] and fireclay, fifteen carloads per month, from New Mexico.[36] Rails for the narrow-gauge railroad came from Belgium.[37] One by one the Company acquired a briquetting machine (to make flue dust usable), a telephone system, and an ice plant. A street railway and a brewery were planned but never materialized.

From the human point of view, the great need was for more and better housing. There was never enough. The Company built bunkhouses and eating houses for its employees and made every effort to stay abreast of the times. Burchard investigated prefabricated buildings, though there is no record that he bought any, and he was enthusiastic about mass construction of "cottages" for workingmen. He actually contracted with the firm of Trost and Rust of Tucson to design such dwellings with wainscoted walls in kitchen and bathroom.[38] Such luxurious quarters must have seemed like Burchard's Folly when so many were still living in tents, but the Company was certainly moving toward improved housing.

Those tents, incidentally, gave rise to all sorts of odd situations which Burchard or Robert Mitchell (when he was General Manager) had to handle:

We note that you are making certain improvements on a tent, which we understand you rent to other parties. Please note that in case it becomes necessary for any reason for this Company to dispossess you . . . no allowance or compensation can be made for any expenditure you may make on the property.[39]

Please let bearer have enough old sheet iron or old corrugated iron to cover tent No. 82 and charge to "Tent No. 82."[40]

The top brass at Cananea interested itself in even more fundamental matters than these:

June 7, 1902

Mr. Rolfe
    Architect, La Cananea
Dear Sir:
    As soon as possible, will you please build a five-compartment privy, with buckets, for the General Office and also one five-compartment privy for the General Manager's office. Please also build a privy for the smelter, and complete the installation of the bucket system in privies throughout the camp at the earliest possible date.

                Yours very truly
                Anson W. Burchard
                2nd V. P. & Comptroller[41]

A mining camp is, naturally, more than buildings and holes in the ground. Without people, there would be no camp, and human problems are always present. In April of 1902 the matter that had to be handled with most care at Cananea involved the use of *boletos,* or Company scrip, good for making purchases at the Company stores. The use of a money substitute redeemable only by the Company was ticklish business. It had been abused so often that the Mexican government had made it illegal. In April somebody complained about it, and Mr. Burchard had to add this thorny issue to his already heavy load. He explained the matter fully to A. C. Bernard, one of the Company lawyers who was then at Hermosillo. The *boleto* system, he said, was a necessity in a large camp because "a large percentage of the laborers employed are too poor to wait until pay day for payment of wages." Rigid enforcement of the law would work a hardship on them. The usual method of getting around the difficulty was to go on breaking the law until somebody complained; pay a small fine; and continue as before. "For a permanent solution," he concluded, "it will probably be advisable to have the matter properly presented to the Federal authorities at the City of Mexico, in which direction steps will be taken."[42]

Nobody in authority in Mexico City at this time wished to make trouble for the Four C's. The years of revolt against foreign exploiters were still in the future, and the government hastened to accommodate Colonel Greene. Mr. Bernard conferred with the district judge, who referred the matter to Mexico City, and instructions went off to Tomás Macmanus, the Company representative there, to follow it up.[43]

Two weeks later proofs of the *boletos,* as turned out by the American Bank Note Co., were ready for inspection by the New York Office, and presumably the miners continued to use them at the Company *tienda*.[44]

Thanks to Colonel Greene's cordial relations with President Porfirio Díaz and the governor of Sonora, the Company was never in any real trouble with the authorities, but the management was continuously involved in one fashion or another in the business of Keeping the Government Happy. Reports had to be sent periodically to various departments in Mexico City.[45] Mexican laws and regulations had to be observed, and Greene's Mexican lawyers were constantly occupied in making sure that he was not out of line. Mexican dignitaries had to be entertained or consulted. Mexican duties and taxes had to be paid. Greene and his lieutenants well knew that they were guests in Mexico and that they must behave accordingly. Greene gave his own view of the situation, writing from New York to George Mitchell in April of 1901, when the townsite matter was being threshed out:

As I have wired you, do not stir up friction. The few people scattered around on the West line of the town site, so that they keep out of our way, will not make very much difference, and remember we are foreigners and there is more or less race prejudice and we do not want to stir it up. The easiest and smoothest way is the best way in getting along with these people. It takes a little more time, but eventually we will get what we want.[46]

Mr. Burchard seems to have gone along with this philosophy. His letters even show some concern for the plight of the poor.[47] He was involved in so many areas, however, that he had no time to spare for special attention to any one of them, and his humanitarian instincts were never really brought into play. His concern for the poor workmen in the matter of the *boletos* seems genuine, though it may have been momentary.

A list of the things for which he felt responsible would take many pages. Nothing was too small for his attention. He mothered visiting dignitaries, including directors of the Company.[48] He issued railroad passes and was alarmed when it looked as if everybody was riding free.[49] He worried about the condition of the *arroyos* near camp where people dumped their junk, and he tried to get municipal prisoners to help keep things tidy.[50] He rode herd on the employees and got them fired if they proved to be lazy or inefficient, not hesitating to take on department heads like Fred Riley, the purchasing agent, who stayed out of town almost all the time and appeared to believe that "the Cananea Consolidated Copper Company is being run with the sole purpose of giving him a position as purchasing agent."[51] He never missed a chance to save money. He bought German glass instead of American if it was cheaper.[52] He insured buildings and made arrangements for garbage disposal.

In his few spare moments he appears to have prowled about the camp noticing things that had not been done, or that had been done wrong. After visiting the powerhouse, he went back to the office and wrote a note to Carl Clausen, in charge of construction, asking him to take care of parts for the Rand Blowing Engine "laying by the side of the road at the west end of the power house . . . exposed to the dust and dirt without any protection whatever."[53] He insisted that Four C's stationery should not be used by unauthorized persons, "even though the name be cancelled."[54] A typical note went off from him to the supervisors of coal storage on May 8:

Gentlemen: —
    In unloading coal you will please be particular to throw it back far enough from the track so it will clear the cars. . . . You have hitherto allowed the coal pile to extend so close to the track as to break the ladders of the cars and running boards of the engines passing. Any damage to the rolling stock resulting from your failure to observe these instructions will hereafter be charged to you.[55]

He even tackled public-health problems when smallpox visited the camp. Late in May he wrote to Dr. Van Dorn, chief surgeon in charge of the Company hospital, informing him that a Mr. Campbell was quarantined in the boarding-house corral with no attendant except his wife, who was "completely unequal to the task as Mr. Campbell is delerious. Mr. Wiggins, who is also in quarantine, has offered to take care of Mr. Campbell, if permission is given him to leave the premises where he is now staying to go to the Campbell quarters."[56]

Dr. Van Dorn apparently agreed to this arrangement, and Wiggins appeared on the street. The result was apparently one of Burchard's few defeats. Robert Mitchell, the general manager, wrote to Wiggins in horror and dismay: "If yourself or any of your family are found violating these instructions, the one so found will be immediately arrested and placed where instructions will be rigidly enforced."[57] Apparently giving up and washing his hands of the matter, Burchard had a deferential letter written in Spanish to Dr. Filiberto Barroso, in charge of the city hospital, asking him to investigate and take action.[58]

The news that there was smallpox in the camp somehow got around, and newspaper stories began to appear screaming EPIDEMIC. Burchard was appalled, as no doubt all the officials were, and fired off a barrage of letters and telegrams to newspapers in Los Angeles and El Paso: "These reports are absolutely without foundation and are directly traceable to certain former employees of the Company who strive by this means to create prejudice against this camp."[59] He telegraphed a report on the deaths in Cananea during the month preceding: seventeen due to respiratory troubles; five from fevers; five from alcoholism — thirty-four in all.[60] The five who died from "fevers" may have had smallpox, but there was no epidemic, and the outcry soon ceased.[61]

More serious was labor trouble which held up work on the converters, cost the Company a lot of money by the delay, and ran Mr. Burchard's blood pressure up to new heights.

Like all camps, Cananea had had some readjustments to make in handling its labor force, particularly in equalizing wages in the different departments. Wages at the concentrator, it appeared, were higher than at the smelter, and Burchard called for an investigation: "In the excavation gang at the concentrator are 14 men at $6.00 per day and 54 Mexicans at $2.50 per day. The stone masons at the smelter have 10 helpers at $2.50 a day whereas those at the concentrator have 10 helpers at $6.00 per day."[62]

It is worth noting that Burchard said nothing about the differential between the wages paid Mexican and American workmen. He took it for granted that it cost more to bring American workmen in and that Mexicans were getting superior wages as wages were paid in Mexico — that they really had no basis for complaint. Yet this was the reef on which Greene's ship nearly foundered four years later, in 1906.

The trouble broke out on April 21, 1902, among the mechanics who had been imported to work on the concentrator. They did not like their situation. Accommodations in the camp seemed primitive to them, and they wanted their wages raised from $4.50 to $5.00 for a ten-hour day. They announced that they were "On Strike."

The Company said the mechanics were not on strike — they had left their jobs and were no longer in the employ of the Four C's. There is no record of how the situation was handled, but it would be a good guess that the men were escorted to the railroad station by Company police and put on the next train north. Burchard wrote to A. B. Wadleigh, who had been sent to Colorado to try to get a little more action out of the Colorado Fuel and Iron Company, and asked him to pick up some replacements in Denver. "The customary rate among the mining camps in the Southwest," Burchard explained, "is 40¢ per hour. We have been paying 5¢ per hour more than these companies because of the somewhat inadequate living accommodations." He revealed that Robert Mitchell had gone to Los Angeles and signed up some more men, but the strikers had boarded the train at Tucson and Benson and talked the recruits out of going on.[63]

Wadleigh went to work in Denver and rounded up about forty men who were willing to face the unknown in Mexico for the wages the Company offered. Burchard wired Vice-president Paul Morton of the Santa Fe that it would be well to run through Deming without stopping, explaining in a letter that "the strikers are picketing the railroad junction points in this neighborhood."[64] Five days later he reported that the arrangements had been "entirely satisfactory" and asked for a memorandum of charges.[65]

Burchard's next step was to get up something resembling a blacklist. Writing to Walter Douglas at Bisbee, site of the great Copper Queen mines, he named fifty-one men who had "left our employ" and suggested that "operators of mining property in the Southwest should cooperate in the maintenance of a parallel wage scale, so far as practicable."[66]

The strikers made the next move. They went to C. C. Sroufe of Tucson, a friend of the Company, and asked to be reinstated. Sroufe listened to them and wrote to Burchard, who replied that he was willing to rehire the men but didn't want to fire anybody to make room for them.[67] Then he engaged eight Tucson boilermakers and three machinists, ignoring the repentant strikers.

The Tucson machinists ran into trouble at once. D. G. Belford, a striker, wrote to one of them named W. Dayhoff warning him to leave Cananea at once or "we will publish you in the Boiler Makers' Journal as a SCAB."[68]

So the matter rested for a few days, and then came a totally unexpected vindication. Burchard described it in a letter to Sroufe. A boilermaker named Barbarick had come in with the contingent from Colorado:

Mr. Barbarick became fully satisfied as to the intentions of this Company, and its position at the time the mechanics quit. He accordingly disclosed his identity to us as the President of the Boilermakers' Union, of Kansas City, and acknowledged that he had come here representing the labor interests for the purpose of investigating the labor situation. He accordingly telegraphed the representatives of the Unions in the principal cities of the Southwest, advising that "There is no labor trouble here and the conditions are good."

This is the first time in the writer's experience in labor matters in which the representative organization has publicly sustained the position of the employers without even suggesting a recognition of the Union in any way. Of course this is a very satisfactory conclusion to us.[69]

Vindicated Mr. Burchard may have been, but forgiving he was not. He learned early in June that one of the strikers had slipped back across the border and gone to work for the Railway Department. Noting that the man was in communication with "Mr. Cody, who was one of the most troublesome of the former employees," he gave orders to get rid of him. "You can probably arrange to dispense with his services without showing the real cause for his dismissal," he wrote to the superintendent.[70]

Quite naturally this meticulous and dedicated employee was a little fanatical about improving the business methods of the company. He loved memoranda, reports, and all signs of efficient organization. He set up a Purchasing Department and new accounting procedures in April[71] and introduced a system of work orders in June. As he described his method, "every operation of the Company's work will be carried on under a signed order bearing a number."[72] A new system of time keeping went into effect along with the work orders.[73]

Burchard had Greene's full backing in making all these changes and improvements. The Colonel even did a little upgrading himself. One thing that worried him was overemployment. His critics accused him of hiring so many men that they got in each other's way and said that he had a boss for every worker.[74] Although he loved to find jobs for his old friends and close relatives, his first thought was for efficiency, and he developed an extreme sensitivity to evidence that he had too many cooks in his kitchen. When S. M. Aguirre asked Burchard for some helpers to help his helpers and Burchard bucked the request to Greene, the Colonel wrote testily:

I see no necessity of having a collector, foreman of warehouse, assistant to Hamlet, helper to Webb, etc., etc., etc. as it seems to me in the present condition of affairs there, two men should be able to do all the business, and particularly as you are there yourself and being paid by the Company. . . . We want to get down to something like a business footing. Keeping people around simply for the purpose of having a picnic and signing the pay roll regularly, is getting monotonous.[75]

A few days later he complained to Felipe Barroso, the *Presidente,* or mayor, of the municipality, that thirteen policemen at Ronquillo were eight too many.[76] If people were getting in each other's way at Cananea, it would not be because he or Burchard approved.

If humanity was called for, they were humane. When George Masterson lost a foot in a mine accident at Capote No. 2, the Company took care of him. "Mr. Greene told him yesterday that the Company would get him an artificial foot and would pay the expenses of his sickness."[77] And when Dr. W. J. Galbraith decided that a little blind Mexican girl might get help from a specialist in San Francisco, a fund was raised at Cananea to send her.[78] J. T. Morrow, General Manager, was treasurer of the fund.

While these individual matters were being taken care of, many larger issues were moving forward during the Reign of Anson W. Burchard. The converters went into operation late in June. Announcement was made on July 18 that papers had been signed on May 1 transferring ownership of the Cananea-Naco Railroad to a new company, the Cananea, Yaqui River, and Pacific. Epes Randolph, Greene's friend and top man under Harriman in the Southern Pacific, was the president. The CYR&P was organized as a Mexican corporation with headquarters at Cananea, but the SP was the actual owner. A long-term agreement granting favorable freight rates to the Four C's was part of the contract.[79]

One of Burchard's acts had consequences which he could not foresee. He hired Charles E. Wiswall. In time Charlie Wiswall became Greene's second-in-command, took charge when Greene died, and inspired an almost religious devotion in everyone who knew him or worked for him. From his home in Aurora, Illinois, he came to Bisbee in 1900 in search of health, found a job in a livery stable, and spent his first months in the Southwest shoveling horse manure. One day when the bookkeeper was sick, the boss took him off the dunghill and put him to work in the office.[80] He was there, functioning efficiently, in February 1901, when somebody — perhaps S. M. Aguirre of Naco — offered him a job with the Four C's. In October 1902 just before Burchard left Cananea, he promoted Wiswall to Forwarding Agent, charged with the exasperating task of getting shipments into and out of Mexico.[81]

Burchard's last big job at Cananea was preparing the annual report for the stockholders' meeting in New York on October 10, 1902. Treasurer Philip Berolzheimer suggested in June that an elaborate brochure with plenty of pictures would be good for stockholder morale,[82] and Greene liked the idea. He wrote on July 8, "There is a very large amount of work involved and Mr. Burchard and myself have been working on it for the last month."[83] The result was a report to end all reports on a mining enterprise, and although the *Engineering and Mining Journal* sneered that it was "notably supplied with fine photographs" but "lamentably deficient in financial data concerning costs and earnings,"[84] Greene and Burchard were proud of it.

By October 5 Burchard was back in New York,[85] probably to arrange the big meeting, and although he returned to Cananea for a while in December, he never lived there again. He continued for over a year to work in the New York office, but his reign was ended.

The circumstances of his departure, as of his coming, remain somewhat mysterious, but it seems certain that he was involved — on the wrong side — in a Company feud which was beginning to simmer and which would give Greene the fight of his life when it came to a head in 1904.

In 1901, as we have seen, John W. Gates and Edwin Hawley were added to the Board of Directors. They were among the biggest names in high finance and they had invested heavily in Greene Consolidated stock. Like many other people in New York, they thought they could do a better job of running the Company than Greene was doing, and they started, or helped to start, the talk about waste, inefficiency, and extravagance which had pursued Greene almost from the beginning. Their object was to take his company away from him. Burchard, it turned out, was on their side and may even have been sent at their urging to Cananea to straighten things out. He had done his best to improve everything, to the discomfort of others besides Greene, but now the chapter was closed.

The curtain was actually rung down at an important stockholders' meeting at the Company offices in New York on February 10, 1904. Greene was fighting for existence against a divided board of directors and a group of rebellious stockholders. In the course of his address to the assembly he said:

The resignation of one director was asked some time ago. He had sold a lot of stock and we thought he should not be a director. He has not resigned, but I am heartily in favor of making the change.[86]

Six days later J. T. Morrow, the general manager at Cananea, issued a terse statement:

Mr. Anson W. Burchard has ceased to be Comptroller and Vice-President of the Greene Consolidated Copper Company or a member of the Executive Committee thereof.[87]

The Bisbee *Review* reported that Greene had "kicked Burchard off" the Executive Committee,[88] and this is undoubtedly what happened.

Greene's only surviving comment on the end of Burchard's reign was made in a letter to Secretary George Young three days after the announcement that the King was dead:

We have been endeavoring lately to get down to a working basis but under the regime as instituted by Gates, Hawley and Burchard, the policy appears to have been to exaggerate all expenses wherever possible and lay it on to the Greene management. We do not expect to have the books overhauled here-after every few days nor as much useless work done in the future as has been done in the past. Greater economy must be practiced in every branch of every department.[89]

Although Burchard was on the wrong side, from Greene's point of view, he was an enormously talented man and he did not lack for friends in high places. He went from Greene Consolidated to General Electric and carved out a notable career for himself in that great corporation. When he died in 1927 he was Vice-chairman of the Board of General Electric and Chairman of the Board of International General Electric. He had married a rich wife and owned a mansion worth half a million dollars on Park Avenue. He was having lunch with Mortimer Schiff in the latter's palatial establishment on Fifth Avenue when his heart failed on June 22, 1927.

Owen D. Young, Chairman of the Board of General Electric, said of him, "His loyalty to the company and his pride in it, his devotion to his associates and his wide interest in all good causes made him universally respected and loved."[90]

It would have been hard for W. C. Greene to say Amen to that, but the campaigns of 1903–1904 left him heavily scarred and with no reason whatever for loving his enemies.

Thunder and Lightning

THE SKYROCKET COULD CARRY a man no higher than the old Waldorf. Opened in 1893, it was a grand and glittering Mecca for travelers from all remote parts of the world, including Arizona, and when the Astoria was erected next door in 1897 with a "hyphen," or passageway, between the two structures, the combination seemed like a realization of all the inn-keepers' dreams of all the ages. "The linked hotels were a treasure house of paintings, tapestries, antique furniture, and sculpture."[1] They boasted a thousand bedrooms, a staff of 1,400 employees, a special basement for storing "segars," the Palm Court where only the super-elite could hope to dine, and Oscar, the magnificent maitre d'hotel, who had been a Great Person so long that he had almost forgotten his last name — Tschirky.

The Waldorf Men's Cafe was known as the Uptown Branch of Wall Street. The Stock Exchange closed at three in the afternoon, and the big operators were likely to show up in the Men's Cafe around four for informal meetings, gossip, and refreshments. The free lunch table was sumptuous, and the eight bartenders were masters of a repertory of nearly five hundred works of alcoholic art. Henry Clay Frick, Charles M. Schwab, Judge Elbert Gary — all the Movers and Shakers came there. John W. Gates lived in the hotel at incredible cost, and even J. P. Morgan made an occasional appearance.[2]

For a copper king on the rise, there could be no better address than the Waldorf. Greene was at home there and on familiar terms with the patrons of the Men's Cafe, though his manners were better than the crudities of Gates or the savage silences of Morgan.

[125]

The Company offices were at 24 Broad Street, next door to the Curb Market, where unlisted stocks, including Greene's, were bought and sold in the open air by frantic brokers who leaped and gesticulated as they signaled to clerks watching from office windows while a mob of money-worshipers swayed and jostled in what has been called "the outside market of Mammon."[3]

For five years the Greenes were part of this background. The routine of their daily life is lost in the cloud of years, but New York was their home. Four of their children were born there — Virginia, William, Frank, and Florence — the first two at the Waldorf.[4] They were swept along in the current of life in the great, noisy, unheeding city. They had breakfast every morning either in their apartment or in one of the many restaurants in the twin hotels. Then a carriage and two of Greene's fast horses sped him downtown to his office, where he read his mail from Cananea and dealt with the dozens of people who wanted a donation or a job or a payment on the bills the Company owed. Mary went shopping or took her children to Central Park when they were old enough, or listened to music somewhere. Who their close friends were, who entertained them of an evening, whether they ever got homesick for the barren mountains of southern Arizona or the sound of Spanish voices at Cananea — these things have passed from memory and can be reconstructed only in the imagination.

They were at the Waldorf on New Year's Eve, 1903, beginning their last year in the famous hotel. The birth of William Junior was only three weeks away, and they may have stayed quietly at home while the clerks and brokers on Wall Street staged a great celebration and 25,000 people crowded the downtown theatres. But Emma Eames sang Tosca at the Met that night, and Mary just may have heard her. They both listened to the "roar of the tin horns" as the New Year came in and got up in the morning to read in the *Times* that Pietro Mascagni, the great Italian composer, was anxious to get back to Italy and that Greene Consolidated was holding steady at 24⅞. Mary probably did not notice that Wanamaker's was advertising ladies' nightgowns at a dollar and muslin "drawers" at ten cents — only three to a customer — or that an Edison phonograph could be acquired for a dollar a week.[5]

The last three years of their stay — 1903, 1904, and 1905 — were the years of Greene's greatest glory and also of his bloodiest battles and narrowest escapes from ruin. To people on the outside, it seemed that he had attained prosperity, security, and serenity. His style of living said so. Newspaper interviews said so. His colleagues sometimes said so. George Robbins, the Company secretary, for instance, wrote to Anson W. Burchard at the beginning of the latter's reign:

Men of Mr. Greene's make-up and calibre are as scarce as the proverbial hen's teeth.... That he has been able to meet, defeat and override all opposition and all criticism and attain the success he has, is the wonder and surprise of all those who have been interested with him and also those who have been against him.[6]

Newspapers regularly paid tribute to his "persistent nerve and splendid courage."[7]

The men who believed in Greene had one point in their favor: the mines were indeed fabulously rich and made money from the beginning. The Colonel was not selling stock in a worthless prospect, and he was always willing to take important people to Cananea and let them see for themselves. "Mining development [is] a wonder," honest Jim Kirk wrote in March 1902.[8] A month later Walter Harvey Weed, a top geologist and mining man, went over the property at Cananea and sent an enthusiastic letter to George Robbins. "I availed myself of my proximity to your property while in Sonora a few weeks since on private 'expert' work to visit Cananea," he explained, "hoping to get a hasty view of its geological structure and to see if the extraordinary statements concerning the amount of ore there would be warranted by the facts."

My first impression of your property, railroad, townsite, smelting plant and mines was one of amazement that so much had been accomplished in so short a space of time, my second at the harmonious and systematic way in which the development of so large a district had been carried out.... The mining development is well planned and well executed.... The reduction works are well situated and well designed.... With the completion of improvements and development work now under way and which are I understand being paid for by profits from the mines, I see no reason why exceptionally large dividends should not be paid upon your present low capitalization. With your large bodies of high grade ore, model smelting plant, and well planned mine development you can and probably will produce copper at a lower cost than that of most copper mines of the world.

In conclusion permit me to express my appreciation of the ability, energy and perception shown by Mr. Greene in developing so great a property in so brief a time.[9]

Colonel Greene, of course, sounded the top note in the chorus of praise and thanksgiving. He knew what he had, and he knew what he could do with it. His report of October 10, 1902, told the stockholders that the plant was almost complete and that the entire issue of stock (100,000 shares) authorized on July 22, had been sold, bringing in well over three million dollars.

Upon the present basis of production of 5,000,000 pounds per month, the estimated net profits of operation at the present selling price of copper are $250,000 per month, which will be increased as production increases.

That was the bright side of the picture. There was a dark side, and in 1903 it grew darker, dividing the Company into two factions who jockeyed for advantage all through that year and lined up for battle and murder in 1904. It was the old story. Greene had a good thing and other people wanted it — the other people being Rogers and Rockefeller of Standard Oil and Amalgamated Copper. While the New Years' Eve celebrations of 1902–1903 were going on, they were getting ready for another assault on the Greene bastions. Greene told what happened in a letter to Billy Brophy back in Bisbee:

The cause of the present depression in the stock was short selling by people interested in the Amalgamated Copper Company and who were endeavoring to shake out Greene stockholders so that they could acquire a large interest. This is the third raid that they have made and they have again absolutely failed in their purpose. My friends and I have been able to take all the stock that they could borrow or obtain from any source off of the market at much lower prices than we otherwise could have got it. I personally have purchased in the last forty days 114,000 shares of the stock. It is a great big game we are playing as the Standard Oil millions are against us but we have the property and are making the money and don't owe anybody and I am praying that we are going to win out in spite of all the money that can be put up against us.

Always the salesman, Greene added:

Tell all our friends to hold what stock they have and buy every share that they can get the money to pay for. That is my advice. I may be wrong but I don't think I am and you had better go down in that old stocking and take up fifty or a hundred thousand dollars more of your loose change and buy some Greene and buy it quick.[10]

Up to this moment Greene had been able to withstand all attacks because they came from without. It was a different matter when his own directors and stockholders turned against him. A number of causes were at work behind the scenes — anti-Greene propaganda from Amalgamated's rumor factory; human ambition, greed, and suspicion; the price of copper; conditions at the mines — but they could all be summed up in one word: DIVIDENDS.

When shares were going at $40 and Greene expected them to go to $60, he could say confidently, "Dividends are what they want, and we will give them dividends." And he did give them dividends. In May and September of 1902 the Company declared a two percent return on investments.[11] Greene meant to declare a dividend every month, but he could not continue. In February of the following year he issued a statement from the New York office informing the stockholders that the Executive Committee had decided "that after the payment of Dividend No. 4,

February 2, dividends should be paid quarterly instead of monthly."[12]

For one thing, the price of copper had taken a nose dive in January and February of 1902, and it stayed down for a long time. The perennial "copper wars" on the street (like the one Greene survived early in 1903) were partly responsible,[13] and an oversupply of copper on the world market contributed also. Market analysts predicted that the price would not go above twelve for another year,[14] and copper stocks were depressed as a result. Greene was not yet in any real trouble. The stockholders authorized an increase of capital stock by another 120,000 shares on November 2, 1903, and the entire issue was bought up at $20 by the stockholders themselves. The money was used for "the extinguishment of the Company's indebtedness and improvements at Cananea."[15]

The trouble was that those debts were by no means "extinguished" and the "improvements" were never finished. The fact was, it had become necessary to work with a lower grade of ore at the mines, and Mr. Hardinge's concentrator had to be replaced.[16] It was at this stage that Dr. Ricketts was brought in to build a new concentrator and redesign the old one. He knew his business and his work was good, but it cost a lot of money. Greene had other plans also — he was full of plans — which would eventually bring greater efficiency to the operations, but they all had to be paid for, and money was always short.

A Los Angeles bank official told a worried Greene creditor:

The great trouble with them is that for the last few months they have been spending all their earnings in the enlargement of their plant, allowing their current bills to accumulate. They have about completed a new concentrator, changed the grade of their narrow-gauge railroad, enlarged their smelters, so that they now claim that they will be able to add 50% to their production without any additional cost over the present working. They have paid, as we understand, for nearly all of this additional expense and will now be in a position to meet their obligations which are outstanding.[17]

The letter was almost a thumbnail sketch of Greene's business life and a prediction of his future. He saw clearly and accurately what had to be done, but he tried to do too much too soon. It was on this rock that he nearly foundered, and the time of reckoning was at hand.

The thunder and lightning of the gathering storm, however, were manufactured by financial gods far from Cananea. The whispering campaign of 1902 was now becoming a chorus of accusing voices. They said that the Greene organization was near bankruptcy and that it would go into receivership.[18] They said that Greene was resigning and that Amalgamated was in charge. They quoted Boston "experts" who accused Greene of lying when he said he was producing copper for six to seven cents a pound (he made no such claims).[19] Every two or three months he had to deny rumors that he had sold out or had been forced out[20] — and the rumors kept on coming out of the factory.

The men who sat on the fence and watched this financial rodeo were well aware of what was going on. Editor Horace Stevens commented indignantly in the 1903 edition of the *Copper Handbook:*

> There is no other mining property in the world about which so many lies are told and none other against which such a systematic campaign of slander is in progress. Every effort is being made by parties closely affiliated with the Standard Oil and Amalgamated interests to oust Col. Wm. C. Greene from the management of the property, and rumors of his resignation, forced or otherwise, are put in circulation every month or two. The plan of campaign against the Greene Consolidated and its president includes the circulation of lies of every sort, ranging from financial lies, which, of course, do not count in high finance, down to personal slanders against Col. Greene . . . the property has been developed with unexampled rapidity, and never before in the history of the world has a copper mine been opened to a productive capacity of 4,000,000 lbs. monthly within two and a half years, as was the case with the Greene.[21]

The malcontents moved in whenever and wherever they could find an opening. The way it was done was illustrated by a signed article in the *Engineering and Mining Journal* in March of 1903 which retailed all the standard charges: exaggerated production figures, waste, irresponsibility in the management. It added the charge that the Company was cheating its American employees and was due for labor troubles, and concluded with a deliberate lie: "Greene has stepped out of the Cananea Company's problem by turning it over to Mr. Rockefeller."[22]

The editor ran into trouble over that one, and in the next issue he grudgingly admitted that he had been deceived and that the article was "untrustworthy." He showed, however, that he had been infected by the propaganda himself when he added that the mines had had a "chequered career" in which "suspicious methods, stock manipulation, extravagant management have all played their part."[23]

The stockholders could not withstand this barrage, and they reacted, according to plan, by becoming restless and suspicious. They gathered in worried little groups at such places as Syracuse, New York, to share their alarm. In New York city the bigger fish took action. A group of large stockholders, headed by Frank H. Ray of Continental Tobacco Company, a director of the Company, hired John A. Farish of Denver to go to Cananea and make an investigation. Farish's report, retailing the old charges of extravagance and mismanagement, was circulated among the stockholders and brought their uneasiness one notch closer to panic —which was just what the Gates-Hawley combination wanted.[24] When

Greene saw the report, he commented that it was a "fearful and wondrous thing," quite misleading "and in many respects wilfully so."[25]

Greene tried to go on making copper without replying to his critics, but even his silence was used against him. "There are all kinds of rumors current," said a Boston commentator, "as to floating debts, high costs of copper, extravagant management, exhaustion of orebodies, etc., but the management turns a deaf ear to inquirers, intimating that there is an ulterior motive behind the present attack on the stock."[26]

The "bear" campaign against the stock started in the fall of 1903. Gates, Hawley, and Company "went short" on their holdings, sold everything they owned, and bought back when the price was at the bottom. A stockholders' meeting was scheduled for February 10, at which time Greene was asking for approval of a new stock issue which would raise the capitalization from $7,200,000 to $8,640,000. They intended to control enough stock by the time of the meeting to vote Greene out of the management.

They came near succeeding. In December of 1903 the price was down to $12. In February 1904 it was down to $10 — the lowest it had ever been or ever would be. *The Wall Street Journal* watched the financial chess game and described the moves: the rumor campaign, the hammering down of the stock, the moving in for the kill:

It is a game well known by the particular interests who played it. It was the strength of their position, after this market campaign, that led the Gates-Hawley faction in the directorate to announce their plan for a large convertible bond issue in opposition to Colonel Greene's plan for an increase in stock. The bond issue, it was apparent, was for the purpose of lodging control of the property with the Rogers people.... They anticipated no difficulty in forcing the president's resignation and issuing the bonds.[27]

It looked like the end for the Colonel, and nobody knew it better than he, but he showed no signs of panic. Instead, he began looking for somebody who would step in and buy enough stock to swing the balance back to him, and he found his man in the person of Dr. James Douglas of Phelps Dodge. Dr. Ricketts, also of Phelps Dodge but friendly to Greene and very busy at the moment putting in the new Bessemer converters at Cananea, is said to have done the arranging. It was a good time to buy Greene stock, now that it had reached a historic low, and besides Greene was in a position to keep the great new reduction plant at Douglas, Arizona, working at full capacity with ore shipments from Cananea. Douglas sent Greene a check for a million dollars and told him to invest it in Greene Cananea for Phelps Dodge.

The big moment came in Greene's office when John W. Gates

stormed in to tell him it was all over for Greene Consolidated and its president.

> "You're helpless — you're broke!" Gates had roared. And Greene, saying, "Am I?" had reached into his desk and exhibited this million-dollar check.[28]

> "The Phelps Dodge people made Greene's fight their own," the *Wall Street Journal* summarized, and added that H. H. Rogers, front man for Standard Oil, had proved to be a good loser. He sent Greene a message after the coup: "I take off my hat to you."[29]

There was more drama when February 10 rolled around and the stockholders gathered in the offices at 24 Broad Street for another showdown. Greene took the chair and called the meeting to order at twelve o'clock. The first speech was made by a stockholder named Ogden, who went at once for Greene's jugular. "We regard it as the height of folly," he began, "to put $1,440,000 in the hands of the present management. If it is true that some directors will retire and that a new policy is to be inaugurated, I will vote for the motion. If it is not true, I will vote against it."

Greene rose to reply. Quietly, without any show of resentment, he began by admitting that the Company owed a lot of money — somewhere around a million dollars. Then he told them what the situation was. He had bought a year's supply of giant powder to avoid paying a Mexican duty of $261 a ton. A decline in the price of copper from 13½ to 11½ cents a pound had cost the Company $400,000. It was costing 10⅛ cents a pound to produce copper. Ore in sight was worth $17,000,000. The plant was almost finished, and this would be the last call on the stockholders.

To clinch his points, he called on Robert T. Hill, a geologist who had recently made a survey of the mines, to tell what he had seen. Hill answered the Farish report point by point and concluded: "I know of no three or four-year-old mine on earth with a similar or equal record."

When the vote was taken, Greene won 478,000 shares to 8,100.[30] It was a decisive vote, and there was nothing left for the schismatic directors to do but resign. Anson W. Burchard, Frank H. Ray, John W. Gates, Edwin Hawley and H. S. Black stepped out, much to Greene's satisfaction.[31]

He was not all the way out of the woods, however, for Mr. Ogden was not alone in demanding "some return on our investment." The stockholders gave Greene a sharp reminder before they left. They passed a resolution.

RESOLVED that it is the duty of the directors of said Company not to attempt any further enlargements of the plant for producing beyond what is now planned but it is their duty to devote the net earnings of the Company at the earliest practicable moment to the payment of dividends.[32]

Greene had no choice but to accept this resolution as a mandate and go to work as if his business life depended (as it did) upon it. The resolution was a clear note of warning that changes might be made at the annual meeting in October. Mine development had to go on, but Greene resolved that every activity that could be dispensed with or postponed had to go, and every employee who could be spared had to be dropped. He wrote to General Manager Dwight:

As you know, we have had quite a strenuous time and have had to run up against some pretty big men who still have a sharp knife out hunting for weak spots. There have been so many and such rank charges made of mismanagement, extravagance, etc., that we have got to get right down to good, solid bed rock and cut our expenditures in every line possible. Our mine development and smelter development work must be kept to a minimum. "Do the best we can with what we have" is our motto at present as we have positive instructions from the stockholders to make no new improvements this year.[33]

He was particularly concerned about the state of affairs in the clerical part of the business where, it seemed to him, a revolution was overdue. "That is one of the great sources of adverse comment by outsiders who visited the mines," he wrote to George Young, "that all around the offices of the Company appears to be a large number of men who appear to be busily engaged in killing time. I believe in paying good salaries but I also believe in getting good work for them." He suggested that if the men came to work on time and expected to put in a full day, "your work would be done with very much fewer men than it is done at present." In view of the charges of favoritism and "cronyism" which have followed Greene down through the years, his next observation is specially interesting:

It is not Mr. Young who is blamed for slackness in the accounting department, but Mr. Greene. . . . I look to you to take this matter up at once. . . . I trust that you . . . understand distinctly that in no department of the Company will any favoritism be allowed . . . that whether I have recommended a man for service or not makes no difference; that the only criterion by which he will be judged is as to whether he does his work properly or not. The mere fact of his being or not being a friend of mine cuts no ice.[34]

Everybody in the New York office seemed to be suffering from shell shock after the February 10 engagement, and reminders kept coming in that the battle might be resumed. George Robbins thought he really had

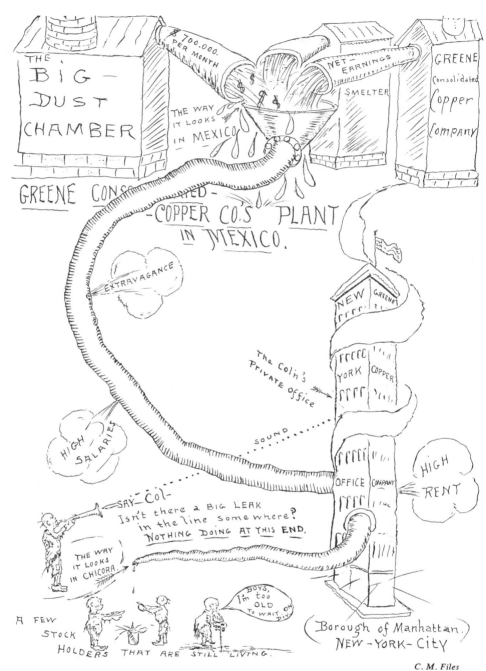

Greene Consolidated: earnings and leaks, as interpreted by a stockholder.

been blown up when somebody sent him a Rube-Goldberg-type cartoon showing net earnings going into a hopper at the top of the sheet and the profits leaking out all down the line. A few ragged stockholders at the bottom held out hats and tin cans for a dribble of reward while one disgusted graybeard walked off muttering, "Boys, I'm too old to wait on dividends."

Robbins had just received this shot in the breast when a letter from John A. Campbell of Cananea arrived, remarking casually: "We will require within the next ten days about $200,000 which will be drawn in installments of twenty thousand to twenty-five thousand per day." Robbins boiled over, and he fired back a letter which reveals the tension of the people at Greene headquarters:

Inasmuch as we assumed and arranged for payment of most of your overdue accounts up to November 1st, I am surprised to find that you will need $200,000 to pay an accumulation of overdue accounts within the next ten days. Will we ever, in your opinion, succeed in catching up? . . . To show you how our stockholders feel about this matter, I enclose you herewith a crude but pertinent pencil sketch I have received by mail. . . . I know that the large expenditures are responsible for your large requirements, yet at the same time the excessive expenditures must cease or there will be *something doing at this end about October 10.* . . . We have gone through deep waters and our escapes, as a former officer of the Company has truly said, seem almost Providential. I acknowledge that there were times when I — *even* I — was almost skeptical as to future success and that is acknowledging a great deal . . . it has at times been almost more than I could stand. . . . Is it any wonder that I was almost convinced that radical changes were necessary?[35]

By the first of April the missiles had ceased to fly and the weary warriors could, for the moment at least, afford to relax. Greene noted on April 4 that debts had been paid, leaving a surplus of $700,000 from the last stock issue. Copper was up from 11.87 to 12.87. Cost of copper laid down in New York was 9½ cents. And the directors had felt justified in voting a dividend of 3%.[36]

As a result of this combination of favorable circumstances the annual meeting went off without a harsh word. Greene had taken pains to collect proxies from practically everybody in the West who owned a share of his stock, and the reelection of the management, with himself at the head, was "a mere matter of form," according to news which reached the Southwest.

Colonel Greene is expected back from New York in a few days. . . . It is rumored that some of the heads of departments will be removed by Greene now that he has proven his ability to absolutely control the Cananea Consolidated which is selling for $18.[37]

In the life of W. C. Greene the moments of peace were few and of short duration, and the victory of October 1904 was only a prelude to an engagement more sensational than the confrontation of the preceding February. Thomas W. Lawson had already begun his no-holds-barred battle with Amalgamated and Standard Oil — a battle in which some of the blood shed was William Cornell Greene's.

The Lawson Comedy

AFTER THE VICTORY OF FEBRUARY 10, 1904, Greene had nine months of comparatively smooth sailing. In those months between February and December, the Copper Skyrocket gained considerable altitude and moved with a minimum of stress and strain. Stock prices continued to rise. Copper sold for fourteen and fifteen cents a pound. The Company turned out metal as never before and continued to pay dividends.[1] No disrespectful noises came from the stockholders, and Greene was able to cross the Atlantic on the *Mauritania* and visit London and Paris, probably in the interest of business.[2]

The Colonel's life was not without excitement, of course. It never was. In April a mild-mannered little man from Arizona named James P. Goodman came to New York with the intention of shooting him. He declared that Greene and lawyer Willis P. Harlow, formerly of Nogales, had "sold out his interest in some copper stock in violation of an agreement." He had filed suit in the New York courts demanding an accounting, but in a moment of impatience had stuck a pistol in Greene's ribs and threatened to pull the trigger.[3] He was by no means the only one who had expected to ride to riches on Greene's coattails and had blamed the Colonel for the failure of his schemes, but he was the only one in 1904 who came to New York to kill him. He was arrested and tried, but his sentence, whatever it was, was suspended while his civil suit against Greene was pending. He promised to get out of town but did not do so. Greene's friends kept an eye on Goodman, wondering if he intended to make further trouble. Eventually he did.

It was not Goodman, however, who shook Greene and his enterprises to their foundations in the fall of 1904. The great disturber was none other than Thomas W. Lawson, the Boston financial prestidigitator who had tried at the beginning of Greene's career to euchre him out of his copper mines, and was now ready to make more trouble. They apparently had been on friendly terms since those days in 1901, but Greene had his bitter memories.

The financial world had never seen anything quite like Lawson. He had been a financier and a spender from the age of fifteen, according to reports, and by 1904, at the age of forty-seven, he had made and lost several fortunes. He had also made, but not lost, a corps of distinguished enemies. "They are all thoroughbreds," he once boasted. "Every one of them would rise from a sound sleep to do me an injury. Long may they live. They put spice into life."

Lawson was personally impressive — tall, black-haired, ruddy faced, with a pair of piercing black eyes, unlimited energy and massive self-confidence. He verbalized easily and well and was master of an extremely colorful journalistic style. He loved to write books and articles about his experiences. A contemporary character sketch said:

When he loses a fight, he likes to write a book about his troubles and show up the inside workings of the financial world from his point of view, to illustrate what little chance the general public has to make money unless by blind luck.[4]

Lawson's pet hate in 1904 was Amalgamated Copper, which he had helped to organize in 1899 — in fact, he claimed credit for thinking of the merger in the first place and selling the idea to Henry H. Rogers and William Rockefeller. Later, as he told the story, he discovered that he had been deceived by these two unscrupulous men and had set out to reveal the truth to the public as an act of atonement. He contributed a series of sensational articles to *Everybody's Magazine* in 1904 and published them as a book in 1905. His indictment began:

Amalgamated Copper was begotten in 1898, born in 1899, and in the first five years of its existence plundered the public to the extent of over one hundred millions of dollars. . . . It has from its birth to present writing been responsible for more hell than any other trust or financial thing since the world began. Because of it the people have sustained incalculable losses and have suffered untold miseries.[5]

Rogers and Rockefeller were the villains of Lawson's melodrama, but behind them was Wall Street — "Wall Street, lined with huge money mills where hearts and souls are ground into gold dust, whose gutters run full to overflowing with strangled, mangled, and sand-bagged wrecks of human hopes."[6] And he went on to tell how the wicked financiers operated.

The professionals used tricks that the public never suspected. Amalgamated Copper, for instance, bought its mines at a cost of $39,000,000 and immediately capitalized at $75,000,000, giving the organizers an instantaneous profit of $36,000,000. Not satisfied with this modest sum, they found means to force the price of stock upward, inducing people to buy at the peak, then dumping their holdings on the market so the price would fall. Having "shaken out" those who had bought on margin and had to sell at a loss, as well as those who sold in panic when stocks began to slide, the manipulators would buy back at the bottom of the market, thereby sending prices up again and insuring enormous additional profits for themselves. The investors, who thought they were on their way to "dollar heaven," didn't have a chance in the world.

To show how the Wall Street operators reached into the pockets of every man in the United States, Lawson talked about the insurance companies who invested in inflated stocks, raising the price of their services when the stocks declined in value, and his charges caused something like a crisis in the insurance business.

Lawson played his role with such enthusiasm, screaming and accusing and prophesying, that many thoughtful people refused to take him seriously. Simpler citizens, people with an "agrarian" point of view, were already suspicious of Wall Street, however, and they listened with open mouths, believing every word he said. Since many of them were small investors, their fears and suspicions were bound to have serious repercussions in the business world. It was these repercussions which brought an end to Greene's nine months of peace and prosperity as the "Lawson Panic" took hold early in December of 1904.

It is only fair to add that modern business historians give Lawson credit for pointing out some basic truths about stock-market manipulations in the early years of the century,[7] the period when the "muckrakers" were searching for corruption in every corner and cranny of American life, and there was plenty of corruption to find.

Greene was an independent operator and had only casual relations with Rogers and Rockefeller, but as Lawson's attack on Amalgamated approached its climax, he suffered with the rest. Beginning on the sixth of December, Lawson began cranking out news stories and paid advertisements advising investors to sell Amalgamated — the price was going to break, and they would be left holding the bag unless they got out. On the eighth the stock began to slide, dropping ten points by noon. There were wild scenes on the floor of the Stock Exchange. "Every active stock on

New York Times

Lawson's Toys: Cartoonist Hy Mayer comments on the Lawson Affair.

the list" went down with Amalgamated[8] and the tension spread to the "outside" stocks, like Greene Consolidated.

"The Greene," as the papers called it, was steady around 34 when the drop came, and Greene determined to keep it there. He regarded it as a duty to his shareholders to support his stock, and he announced that he was going to "peg" the price — would buy at 34 all the stock that anybody wanted to sell. There was plenty for sale. He said later that he spent $4,300,000 in two days making good on his offer.[9]

The big excitement happened on Thursday and Friday, December 8 and 9. There was no trading on Saturday. Optimists during the week-end interlude began to hope that it was all over. But Lawson had no intention of reducing the pressure. The Boston and New York papers on Monday morning carried his "final warning" to the holders of Amalgamated stock:

Sell your stock now, before it is too late.
Bear in mind when Amalgamated sells at 33 that I have warned you.
And in the meantime watch for sharp breaks in Amalgamated. I will give no further warning on this stock, and under no circumstances will change my now advertised position on it.[10]

When Greene ran short of money and had to stop buying, his stock immediately slid from 34 to 18½. He was horrified and astonished and furious. He fumed and sweated all day. Late that night he called a stenographer into his office and, leaning back in his big chair, dictated an open letter to Lawson which appeared in the *Sun* and the *American* next day — Tuesday the thirteenth. His diatribe, in which he loosed all his thunderbolts, filled half a page.

THOMAS W. LAWSON — READ THIS PICTURE. For six months I have read with close attention your story of "Frenzied Finance," in *Everybody's Magazine,* and have paid close attention to the manner in which, by

Men of Affairs

W. C. Greene: Man of Affairs.

pandering to the worst prejudices of the American people, you have endeavored by misstatement of facts to distort the conditions actually existing through what you call the workings of the "System."

Nobody, Greene declared, had had more to do with the creation of the System than Lawson himself, and how could anybody believe a man who worked both sides of the street in this manner? Furthermore, he had no real acquaintance with the business he was trying to ruin.

Who are you, who should say in relation to a copper mine whether it is good or bad? Did you ever see a copper mine? Did you ever put a pick into ore? Did you ever reduce one ton of metal so that it would yield up its wealth for the benefit of mankind? Have you ever done anything except to act as a parasite upon honest labor, and, by chicanery and misrepresentation, endeavor to rob the people of their hard earnings?

.   .   .   .

Do you not know that your only motive is, by destroying confidence to endeavor to make a large profit for yourself, by the methods which you have pursued of advertising to the public? The men who do things, the men who created wealth, the men who are known throughout the world for integrity and for their business qualifications, will unanimously say that your motive is selfish from start to finish.

Do you remember the dealings that you had with me, how they were based on falsehood and misrepresentation from start to finish? How, by the use of names that are well known in the financial and business world, you endeavored to rob and convert to your own use what you thought was one of the greatest properties in the world? What has been the result of your advertisements of the last few days? Has it not been to destroy confidence, to create a panic among people who had invested their earnings in what they have considered as legitimate propositions?

.   .   .   .

Tomorrow, in Boston, I shall call upon you. . . . Tomorrow, at your office, I shall denounce you for what you are. The Master long ago said: "By your works ye shall be judged."

Personally I shall call upon you for your answer tomorrow.

W. C. Greene[11]

It was a wonderful moment for New Yorkers, in and out of the financial district. The ghost of Jim Burnett had followed Greene all the way to New York, and everybody knew that the Colonel had a record. He was going to hunt Lawson down and murder him. Lawson might fight back. It could come to a gun duel in the middle of Beacon Street in Boston. Word went off to Boston and Chicago and Denver and San Francisco and even on the cable to London. Joy was unconfined.

It made no difference that Greene had said nothing about blood and wounds and had only promised to tell Lawson what he thought of him.

People continued to believe what they wanted to. Greene was going to ride again, and there would be gore in the streets.

Lawson appreciated the potential drama of it all as well as the next man, and he lost no time in taking his turn in the public press. At first he spoke, like Hamlet's father, more in sorrow than in anger.

You say you know me. You are right, you do. You have said to me verbally and in writing, "Lawson, you are the only honest man I have ever found in the stock game." . . . My dear Colonel, I know you! I know you for one of the biggest hearted, squarest men I have ever met, and notwithstanding your attack upon me this morning, I have the fairness to repeat it. You are evidently crazed from some cause and have laid yourself open to be made the catspaw of people who have not your courage. I know if you had been in your right mind you would never have signed the document.

You say I attempted to rob you and your Greene Company. You brought me your Greene Consolidated Company and said, "Lawson, you are the only man on earth whom I would trust with it." I took it and for five months ran it and paid all its expenses to an amount, I think, of over $100,000. Then I had Mr. Rogers' best experts examine it, and when they reported it was no good, I went to you like a man and said: "I return it to you, and I take my loss." You told me I had made the mistake of my life, and I later found I had. . . .

Later, over a year after, you came to me and insisted upon my taking all I had lost with interest, and I said what I say now, notwithstanding the crazy wrong you do me this morning. You are one of the few white men I have ever met, and from that time until today I have gone out of my way to speak words for you and your enterprise.

Now for your threats, for I read clearly your meaning when you repeated three times you would come to my office. I know you to be a brave man. I know, not only because you have told me, but because I have verified it, that you have notches on your gun to mark where you went up against bad men in Arizona and Mexico, and I know you have made some of the leaders of the "System" in New York give over their schemes to ruin you simply by calling their attention to the fact that "you were going to call upon them at their office." But let me say to you that you have picked the wrong customer. You or any of those who have egged you on, or any of the people of the "System," may come to my office or any other place that is convenient or accessible, and when you come, I will be there to meet you.[12]

This set the stage for a battle which engaged the public interest more, perhaps, than any single combat since the days of Sir Launcelot and Sir Gawain. Newspaper articles pointed out that Greene had notches (the official count was three) on his gun and that Lawson kept pistols in his desk. "It is not an uncommon thing for Lawson to receive visitors in that office with his hand on a shooting iron."[13]

Almost before they had time to digest these interesting facts, the not-so-innocent bystanders learned that Lawson had received a telegram:

I will even matters with you in a very few days, and let me assure you not to your liking.

Two days later Greene denied indignantly that he had sent any such telegram and offered a thousand dollars to anyone who would reveal the author. "Someone has been stringing both of us," he said.[14]

Whoever sent the telegram, it did what it was intended to do. Lawson sent back an appropriate reply to Greene, supposedly already on the train:

Your wire you would be at my State Street office received. As you seem anxious to do your business out in public, I will meet you at the time named in State Street, front of old State House, and I herewith notify you that I will do all the denouncing that will be done.[15]

Both telegrams were printed shortly after they were sent and were soon public property. Word went off to London that Lawson had already been assassinated. When queried, Lawson wired back that he had not been completely killed.[16]

Supposing that Greene was on his way to the fatal encounter, people began to gather in front of the State House in Boston at an early hour on Thursday morning. "The crowd was so great," one paper reported, "the police had difficulty in keeping paths open for traffic." Sensational rumors came thick and fast. One said that a squad of detectives would meet Greene upon his arrival at South Station and disarm him. Another revealed that Lawson would go to the rendezvous accompanied by a heavily armed guard.[17]

Time wore on. Gradually it dawned on the crowd that there would be no fireworks that day. Greene was not coming. The letdown was very severe, and disappointment was followed by sneers. Obviously Greene had lost his nerve. Maybe the brave Colonel had been replaced by somebody else. "Colonel Bill Greene is the man of action. It is little Willie Greene that has been impersonating him and doing business in New York under the Arizona man's name."[18]

While all this was going on in Boston, Colonel Greene was sitting in the big leather chair behind his desk in New York, quite unaware that he was in such great demand in the land of the bean and the cod. A curious reporter called at the Greene Consolidated office to find out what was keeping him.

"You didn't go to Boston," the newsman said.

"That is correct," the Colonel replied.

"You voluntarily stated to the public through the columns of New York and Boston papers that you would go to Boston and have it out with Lawson."

"I was hot when I said it. It would make any man hot to lose $2,000,000. I never meant to make a gun play. I am getting too old to be going around with a cannon for everybody who disagrees with me. The episode is closed."[19]

It is hard to say now just what was going through the Colonel's mind, but some of his indignation had certainly vanished overnight and he wished he had not hurled all that rhetoric. Lawson's reminders of their former mutual respect may have influenced him also, and then there was Jim Goodman. It just happened that Goodman's civil suit had been thrown out of court on a technicality. He had called Greene up on the telephone and threatened again to take extreme measures if a settlement was not made. Three of Greene's friends, including John H. Martin, one of his lawyers, looked Goodman up at his hotel and in the course of the conversation learned that he had talked to Lawson and planned to go to Boston to observe, or participate in, the Greene-Lawson showdown. The three reported to Colonel Greene that this sounded to them like another threat, and they swore out a complaint which put Goodman back in jail. At the same time Greene asked for police protection, saying that he didn't like feeling each time he left home that "he might be perforated before he reached the office."[20]

Very much on Greene's mind also that Thursday were the rumors which went swirling through the financial district. A good many people were convinced that Greene had lost control of his company and that Amalgamated had enough shares to take command. Greene Consolidated had actually recovered after hitting bottom on Monday and had gone back to 25, but this sort of talk could send it down again. Greene issued a statement:

I hold 262,000 shares, of which amount I purchased 160,000 shares within the past two weeks. To the best of my knowledge, neither Mr. Rogers nor any of the Amalgamated Copper party have ever owned a share of Greene Consolidated. Together with my friends I control vastly more than a majority of the 864,000 shares.[21]

With all this on his mind, Greene did not feel like rushing down to the station and catching the next train for Boston. He growled to one of the newsmen who kept buzzing around him:

No doubt the boys in the Street would like to see a little dodging around the Treasury pillars and some pistol work, but this case does not require such methods. They're antiquated. As for fisticuffs, I'm a little rheumatic, and so I don't think I'll accept that invitation to go to Boston. Besides, I'm busy. Lawson can wait.[22]

But Lawson could not wait. He was enjoying the situation immensely and doing all he could to keep up the excitement. When he heard that the Colonel had declared the incident closed, he fired off another volley:

The genial Colonel from Arizona overlooked the fact that when a thing has been declared on it takes the consent of two to call it off, and that calling such episodes off is a branch of my education that has been neglected.[23]

Greene found this a bit much. He got up out of his office chair at last, took a cab to the station and caught the afternoon train for Boston. It was night when he arrived. He tried to locate Lawson at his office, failed to do so, and before he went to bed at the Touraine sent a message to the financier asking for a meeting in the morning. He refused to talk to anyone about his visit, but he did not need to. All the world knew he was there and all the world thought it knew why he had come. Word went out over the wires: GREENE NOW IN BOSTON. MAY BE TROUBLE TOMORROW.[24]

Anticlimax came with the dawn. Lawson was informed of Greene's arrival when he rose in the morning, and he came down to the Touraine, accompanied by John Adams Thayer, publisher of *Everybody's Magazine.* He asked the desk clerk to send his card to Colonel Greene, who was at that moment breakfasting with Major Charles Hayden and John T. Morrow, Boston bankers with whom Greene Consolidated did business. Greene sent back word that he would be out as soon as he finished eating.

At 9:15 he emerged from the dining room, and Lawson and Thayer met him in front of the elevators. They were well observed. The lobby was full of people, including a couple of police officers who just happened to be there, and of course the inevitable reporters.

The meeting was quite formal and polite. "How do you do, Colonel?" Lawson inquired in his high-pitched voice.

"Hello, Lawson," replied the Colonel, and they shook hands. "Suppose we go up to my room," he continued, and they took the elevator to the fifth floor, leaving their audience more than a little shaken.

Two policemen were already stationed at the doors of the Colonel's suite to keep out unauthorized callers, and when a newsman asked that the press be admitted, Lawson sent out word that he was willing but the Colonel wasn't. Consequently there was no official report of the proceedings. Nevertheless the Boston papers reported all that went on in the exact words of the speakers, and somebody had to tell them. Since the stories gave Lawson the best of it, it is a reasonable surmise that he was the one who leaked.

"Colonel," he began, when the party was seated, "I understood that you wanted to see me, that you had something you wanted to say to me, and I came down to hear what it was."

SATURDAY MORNING, DECEMBER 17, 1904 — FOURTEEN PAGES.

L. "BILL" GREENE WEARS A SATISFIED LOOK AS HE LEAVES THE CITY
AFTER FACING GAMELY THE LARGE CALIBER GUN OF A PHOTOGRAPHER

Boston Herald

As Boston saw him: Greene pays his respects to Lawson.

"Yes," Colonel Greene answered, "there are some things I want to say to you," and they went on from there. Lawson displayed the telegram of two days before, and Greene said he didn't send it. Greene displayed his cancelled checks for $4,300,000 and told Lawson he held him responsible for his losses. Lawson argued that the situation was Greene's own fault. "Your action was really an invitation to everybody to sell to you their Greene stock. That is why it was dumped on you in reams."

Greene did not press that point further, but brought up the Goodman matter. In the course of his last conversation with Greene two days before, Goodman had declared that Lawson was backing him. Lawson denied it. Then they turned to a discussion of the attack on Amalgamated, and by that time it was noon. Mr. Morrow sent out for lunch.

They stayed together until mid-afternoon talking over "general matters."[25] When they broke up, Major Hayden prepared a statement which both the principals were willing to endorse. As summarized by the *Wall Street Journal,* it declared that "After several hours conference each maintains his position but there is a better understanding as respects any direct connection between the Lawson attack and the slump in Greene shares."[26]

That should have ended it. Stone and Hayden convoyed the Colonel to South Station and put him on the train, where he retired, with two pillows, to his stateroom and told reporters he had nothing further to say. "Please go away and let me sleep," he begged. And the Massachusetts night swallowed him up. The storm was over, but there were some final rumblings of distant thunder. Lawson continued to lump Greene with Standard Oil and "The System." When *Frenzied Finance* was presented to the public in 1905, he reproduced Greene's first letter with the comment: "I am not going to enter into a defense of myself against Colonel Greene's charges. . . . I simply publish his vituperation to show how the 'System' sets about silencing those who dare protest against its villainous methods."[27]

Greene's comments were much milder. He told a reporter for the Los Angeles *Examiner* a few months later that he thought Lawson's articles were "an influence for good" by "bringing the public to realize the need of legislation to curb the evil of amassing of all wealth by a few."[28]

Probably the most sensible comment of all was made by the *Wall Street Journal,* even before the comedy reached its climax:

It is time to turn from frenzy to sobriety, from waiting for the latest telegram from Boston to consideration of the progress the nation is making toward renewed business activity and prosperity.[29]

Flying High

IN THE SPRING OF 1902 Colonel Greene was approached by Max Muller, the Hermosillo banker, about a mine called the Sierra Verde which looked like a good prospect. He wanted the Colonel to come and look at it. Greene was frantically busy at the moment and short of funds. On July 8 he wrote: "Our expenses here are still very heavy straightening up bills for machinery etc., and until we are out of debt at the Cananeas I do not want to take up any outside matters. By the first of September, however, I shall be in a position to talk to you in relation to it."[1]

It was probably the only time in his life he turned down a chance to at least look.

From the beginning of his career as a promoter, he was not merely open to propositions, he was out hunting for them. As soon as he had cash to invest, he was eager to put it to work.

His first object was to make money. His generation saw nothing wrong with that. His Quaker background had taught him to make the most of what he had, and he was doing just that, only on a much larger scale than had been possible for any of his ancestors. As a product of the American capitalistic system, he knew that big enterprises were financed by selling stock to investors who hoped to reap dividends and grow rich. Their proper symbol would have been the outstretched palm. Greene's primary purpose, then, was to show a profit as the prime requisite for staying in business, but the money itself was not the only thing. Attainment, realization, success were what he wanted — the ship launched, the mechanism in operation, the dream realized.

"Why do you want another million?" a friend demanded of James H. Keene, a successful market operator of Greene's day.

[149]

"Why does a dog chase another rabbit when he has just caught one?" Keene replied.[2]

As Greene himself once phrased it, "It is a great big game we are playing." And in 1905 the game got bigger. In that year, with some of his battles won and few indications that bigger ones were on the way, Greene was able to go ahead at full speed, accumulating projects and enterprises as he collected marbles in his school days.

His eagerness for new ventures was a passion which came close to being an obsession. He even went so far as to hire Tucson lawyer Frank Hereford at $5,000 a year to watch for desirable land acquisitions. When Hereford's performance displeased him, he "gave him cain" in the railroad yards at Tucson where the *Verde* was parked, and terminated his employment.[3] Hereford claimed two years later (in 1906) that the employment might have been terminated, but the financial arrangements had not; that Greene owed him $10,000. Suit was filed in Cochise County. Hereford lost the first round but won on appeal and collected the money.[4]

It would be impossible, more than half a century after the events, to list all the Colonel's promotional ventures — the mines, dams, railroads, ranches he thought about promoting, the schemes that died aborning, the projects that he actually attempted; but enough can be learned to give an idea of the range and fertility of his imagination.

He did a good deal of promoting in his town of Cananea. He organized the Cananea Realty Company, for instance, to handle townsite matters, set up the Cananea Cattle Company to control the wonderful virgin grazing land surrounding the community, and began construction of a slaughter house to process the beef grown on his cattle ranges for consumption in Cananea.[5]

Outside Cananea his fancy flew far and high. One of his earliest projects was the Greene Consolidated Gold Company which he began to develop in 1902. Actually he had begun to exploit the claims many years before — perhaps at the very start of his Mexican experience. "I last actively worked the property in 1893," he noted when he was ready to begin stock promotion, and added that "a portion of this property has been owned and worked by me on a small scale for many years."[6] Even before the Four C's was firmly on its feet, he sent Ed Massey, one of his best practical mining men, to the Santo Domingo field and put him to work getting it ready for development.

The property lay along the Santo Domingo River thirty miles south of Cananea at the tip of the Cananea Mountains, extending for nearly fifteen miles on both sides of the channel. The gold was mostly in the river sands, but Massey prospected the banks and ledges too.

As usual, somebody was trying to ride to riches on Greene's coat-tail. In this case it was his old associate J. B. Storman, the Magdalena storekeeper and mine developer, who had been a partner in the first corporation Greene organized back in 1899. Storman claimed a *hueco,* or unlocated area, in the middle of Greene's holdings, and the Colonel wrote him a real bombshell of a letter about it on June 9, 1902:

In regard to working the Santo Domingo, I shall do nothing there until the question of boundary etc. of the piece of ground which you denounced long ago and have done nothing with since, is settled. I shall not spend a dollar on any property of any kind as long as there is any question in regard to boundary or so-called "hueco." I do not think that the piece of ground that you claim will ever be worth a dollar except for the purpose of holding me up and endeavoring to get some money out of me in that way, and, as I have said before, until you have withdrawn your pretended claim on the piece of ground laying west of the Santo Domingo, I will not spend a dollar on the property. I believe there is a chance to make the property worth something by spending some money on it, but it is a gambling chance and I do not want to go ahead and do the work, and then have you come in and say you have a pretended claim to "hueco" and give me annoyance and trouble. The ground that you located is not worth a dollar to you nor to any other man except for what you can get out of me for it.[7]

In 1903 Storman was suing Greene in the local Mexican courts about his *hueco,* but by the fall of 1904 the problem had been solved[8] and Greene was ready to start getting out the gold. The river gravel, he declared, carried a value of two dollars per ton. He capitalized his company at $5,000,000 — "very low in proportion to the extent and value of the property. There is no indebtedness of any kind and no bonds or preferred stock." Directors and officers were mostly directors and officers of the Greene Consolidated Copper Company, and Greene himself was the president and chief stockholder.

In his first letter to prospective investors he observed that it should "not be deemed egotism" on his part to note that his mining experience, acquaintance with the great men in Mexico and familiarity with Mexican mining laws would be great assets to the enterprise. "Dividends should be paid in December, and, barring unforeseen contingencies, at least 15% on the par value of the stock should be paid during the year 1905."[9]

As might have been expected, the "unforeseen contingencies" were waiting in the wings and appeared on stage almost at once, the developments sounding a good deal like a replay of the history of Cobre Grande and Greene Consolidated. E. B. Tustin, treasurer of the copper company since the resignation of Philip Berolzheimer and at first one of Greene's most loyal supporters, became uneasy for some reason about Greene Consolidated Gold and sent an investigator to Mexico to take a look. Greene heard of it and sent his own investigator.

This went on until, according to newspaper reports in July of 1905, "Tustin now has seven reports against Colonel Greene's six."[10]

The villain of this little drama was apparently one James O. Glover, possibly one of Tustin's men, who published a report in the Los Angeles *Examiner* on June 14, 1905. His main contentions were that no work had been done on the Greene Consolidated Gold properties, that no gold had been mined, and that the works were seven miles distant from where Greene said they were.

Aroused and indignant, Greene sent six mining engineers and a number of prominent Mexicans and Americans to survey and report. He told the stockholders on July 6, 1905, that these men had gone over titles, checked boundaries, and even verified his estimate of the percentage of gold in the river sands; that Glover was being prosecuted for perjury; and that the resignation of E. B. Tustin as treasurer had been accepted.

There seems to have been plenty of gold in the sands of the Santo Domingo, but for some reason Greene was never able to get it out. When the tide turned against him, the property was disposed of at a sheriff's sale and the Colonel was out more than $68,000. Ed Massey, who owned a fourth of the company, was hurt even worse than Greene and in 1910 complained that he was nearly destitute.[11] According to talk in Cananea, however, the placers continued to be worked off and on for some time.

From 1902 onward, available records show that Greene was always looking over, trying out, or buying into one enterprise after another. He had dropped his option on the Pilares de Capteras gold mine in January 1903 and was said to be going into oil in California.[12] He tried to buy the great Babocomari ranch in southern Arizona and failed.[13] He attempted to buy out all the heirs to the Camou grant, succeeded, and became owner of the San Rafael del Valle Ranch in the San Pedro Valley, thereby acquiring clear title to the farm where he had lived for so many years.[14] He bought land near Yuma on a tip that the government was going to dam the Colorado River and start an irrigation project.[15] He organized the Yaqui River Gold and Silver Company[16] and the Bonanza Belt Copper Company.[17] He owned a copper mine at Patagonia, Arizona; 8,500 acres of coal land in Mexico; part of a Tucson newspaper; and (in 1907) a flock of 33,000 sheep to eat the grass of his timber lands.[18] A story about one of these projects was usually accompanied by some remarks about the Colonel's "vast enterprises," "enormous holdings," or "stupendous wealth." Even the cold type of a mining column on the third page generated a little of the excitement and anticipation which added the trumpet tone to the name of Colonel William Cornell Greene

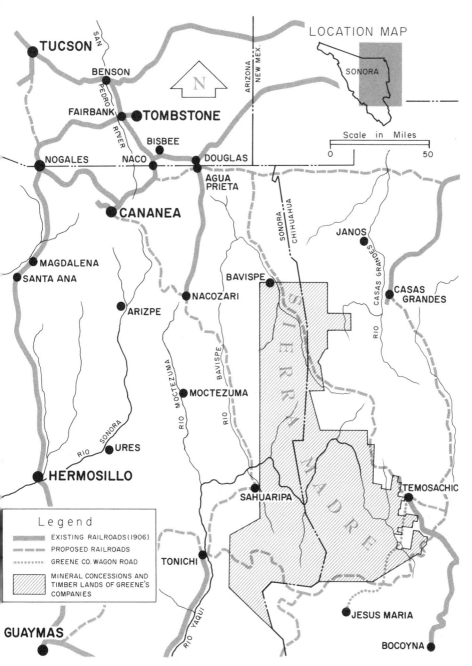

LOCATION MAP

SONORA

Scale in Miles

0   50

TUCSON

BENSON

FAIRBANK

TOMBSTONE

BISBEE

NOGALES   NACO   DOUGLAS

AGUA PRIETA

CANANEA

MAGDALENA

SANTA ANA

BAVISPE

NACOZARI

CASAS GRANDES

JANOS

ARIZPE

SIERRA MADRE

MOCTEZUMA

URES

HERMOSILLO

TEMOSACHIC

SAHUARIPA

Legend

EXISTING RAILROADS (1906)
PROPOSED RAILROADS
GREENE CO. WAGON ROAD
MINERAL CONCESSIONS AND TIMBER LANDS OF GREENE'S COMPANIES

TONICHI

JESUS MARIA

GUAYMAS

BOCOYNA

SAN PEDRO RIVER

ARIZONA / NEW MEX.

SONORA / CHIHUAHUA

RIO CASAS GRANDES

RIO BAVISPE

RIO MOCTEZUMA

RIO SONORA

RIO YAQUI

Greene's Mexican Empire

ITS FINAL EXPANSION

Don Bufkin

in the days of his glory. Nobody, least of all the Colonel himself, doubted that his magic touch would be with him always and that nothing could stop or defeat him.

He would consider anything if it looked like a moneymaker or a possibility for development, but he did not load himself with scattered or unrelated enterprises. He did have a master plan, though few of his friends and associates realized its sweep and magnitude. It amounted to a comprehensive blueprint for the development on all fronts of the resources of northern Mexico. It was a great dream, and it could have succeeded. Bits and pieces of it have become reality from time to time as Mexico has moved forward, but not everything he dreamed of will ever be accomplished.

His program started with a railroad. In the beginning, when he was getting ready to open up the Cananea mines, he realized that railroads were the key to development in the great virgin wilderness of northern Mexico, and he talked of building on past Cananea into the potentially rich country to the south. When he sold his line to the Southern Pacific, however, that enterprise passed out of his hands. It did not pass out of his mind. He had two reasons for keeping the idea alive. One was the Sierra Madre Land and Lumber Company. The other was the Greene Gold-Silver Company.

The Sierra Madre corporation originated in the Colonel's purchase of timber lands in Chihuahua to meet the demand for lumber and mine timbers at Cananea. This purchase was consummated in 1901. In 1904 his friend Governor Enrique Creel gave him timber concessions amounting to about 3,500,000 acres of forested mountainsides in the state of Chihuahua — magnificent country needing only a railroad to make it useful to mankind and profitable to Colonel Greene. He organized his Sierra Madre Land and Lumber Company as a Connecticut enterprise with a capitalization of $15,000,000. The management was almost the same as the management of Greene Consolidated Copper Company.[19]

Greene Gold-Silver was born in 1902 as a West Virginia corporation and was also capitalized at $15,000,000. Again Greene's friendly relations with the great men of Mexico paid off, and he began his activities with concessions said to have been "the most extensive and valuable that have ever been granted to any company in Mexico."[20] He controlled the mineral resources of a mountain region 600 miles long and 470 miles wide[21] — 2,500,000 acres of the richest mineral lands in the republic.

Along with the right to mine gold, silver, copper and lead, the concessions included use of the waters of the Aros and Yaqui Rivers for a power plant, the right to construct railroad and telegraph lines, exemption from taxation for twelve years.

President Porfirio Díaz followed a consistent policy of encouraging wealthy and able foreigners to do what Greene was doing. Díaz thought his country would benefit by the opening up of hitherto inaccessible regions and the development of Mexico's natural resources. Greene thought so too. The revolutionists of 1910 thought differently, regarding these concessions as a crime and a betrayal of Mexico. The question of whether Mexico was using Greene or Greene was using Mexico was resolved by rifles and machine guns, and the decision went against Greene and the other foreigners whom Díaz had encouraged to come in.

Gold and silver had been taken out of the rocky ribs of the Sonora and Chihuahua mountains since Spanish times, and there were many *viejas,* old workings — some producing, some abandoned — in every corner of the high country. The whole mountain area was mineralized, but much of it was inaccessible. Greene's idea was to do for Chihuahua gold and silver what he had done for the Cananea copper deposits: apply modern know-how to developing the mines and modern transportation to getting the minerals to market.

Some of his mines, like the ones at Ocampo (known to the Forty-niners as Jesús María and in existence since 1821) were too far from civilization to be really profitable. Some, like the Mulatos group in the mountains north of Ocampo which had produced $18,000,000 worth of gold,[22] were making money but could be operated more efficiently. They all had possibilities, Greene felt, if properly handled, and there was no doubt in his mind that he was the man to handle them.

The country itself was a joy to him. He loved the solitude of the high plateaus, the majesty of the soaring crests of the Sierra, the unbroken miles of virgin forest (waiting for a sawmill). He thought the climate was the best in the world. He even loved the mountain people and their little towns nestling in the deep valleys or clinging to the slopes high above them — towns with names like little Spanish songs — Ocampo and Concheño, Mulatos and Miñaca; towns whose names were a call to faith — Navidad and Trinidad, San Pablo and Santa María; towns with the smoke of Indian fires in their names — Tónichi and Guayanopa and Temosachic.[23] Whenever he could, he spent a few days in the back country hunting a little and thinking a great deal. He even took to inviting down his friends from Washington and Wall Street, particularly after the Gold-Silver Company got under way, to the astonishment of all concerned, natives and Easterners alike.

It never occurred to him that this wilderness should be preserved in its primitive, untouched condition. When he saw a river, he thought of water power and irrigation. When he saw a valley, he thought of a railroad. He visualized the whole country settled by happy and produc-

Emadair Chase Jones

Superintendent Pomeroy and miners
in the Matulera Mine, Ocampo District.

tive people, using the timber, working the mines, tilling the soil, doing business in new towns.

The first step was steam locomotives and steel rails. On November 4, 1904, Greene began what he hoped would be his great work. He bought the Rio Grande, Sierra Madre, and Pacific.

This unusual railroad, only 156 miles long when he acquired it, began at El Paso and meandered off to the southwest toward the Mormon colonies in the foothills of the Sierra Madre — Colonia Dublán, Nueva Casas Grandes, Colonia Juárez, Colonia García, Colonia Chuichupa, and several more. It ended abruptly at a small station called Terrazas, halted by the death of Solon Humphreys, who had begun construction in 1896 and intended to push his line southward to Chihuahua.[24]

This project, which served the Guerrero Valley west of the main line, brought the railroad into Chihuahua by the back door when the Casas Grandes–Madera link was completed in 1910, after Greene had given up control. In 1906, however, probably thanks to Greene's close friendship with Governor Enrique Creel of Chihuahua, the Chihuahua and Pacific railroad built a branch northward from Miñaca to Temosachic, opening up new country and providing railroad service to Greene's mining and lumber enterprises. The route was round-about — Cananea to El Paso to Chihuahua to Temosachic — but it was a great help to the Greene companies.[25]

From the beginning the trains on the Sierra Madre route were famous for their ruggedly individualistic attitude toward timetables and schedules. They traveled slowly and stopped often, enabling the travelers to take walks, pick flowers, and even shoot game. Raymond Reid, fresh from Chicago, traveled from Chihuahua to Temosachic in the summer of 1906 and found the tradition already established. "I had a blue serge suit," he says, "and a little flat-top straw hat with a colored band on it, and an umbrella."

We were crossing the Hearst ranch and I saw thousands and thousands of ducks out there. Mr. Weber, the conductor, told me that when they had important persons on the train they often stopped and had shotguns loaded up and they would go out and get some ducks. Well, I didn't happen to be an important person so they didn't stop that day.

Mr. Weber knew I was a greenhorn and a sucker, and he got people in behind me there to get in on the laugh, and he said,

"I suppose you have a gun?"

"Oh, yes," I said. "I got a revolver before I left."

"I would like to see it," he said.

So I fished my little twenty-two caliber revolver out of my vest pocket, and he looked at it and said, "Huh!" And he reached back and pulled out a forty-five — the biggest thing I had ever seen in my life. And he said, "Bring that thing over and let it suck."

So we had a lot of fun at my expense, and I took it all goodnaturedly.

In places the switchbacks were so sharp, Reid remembers, that he could have thrown his hat out on one side and picked it up on the other as the train came round the bend. But finally they reached the flat, and after a while somebody said, "There's the town."

"Why, I can't see any town," said Reid. He was looking for two-story or three-story buildings, American style. "All there was out there were adobe houses, nothing higher than one story and the same color as the soil. I just couldn't see any town."

Raymond's cousin Clarence Chase was General Manager at Temosachic, and it was at his invitation that this tenderfoot had invaded the wilds. Clarence took one look at Raymond's hat. "Say," he said, "you had better just throw that in the fireplace before somebody takes a shot at it. And that umbrella you've got there. Don't let anybody see you with that. Give it to one of those señoritas around here. You'll have a girl friend before long."[26]

So Raymond went to work as a stenographer in the office of the Greene Gold-Silver Company and eventually became Greene's personal shorthand man.

Stories about the Sierra Madre line, incidentally, multiplied over the years, particularly after Mr. Archer became the conductor. He and his train became so much a part of each other that it was known as *el tren de Archer*. The old story, told about all slow trains from Long Island to Arkansas, attached itself to this one. A worried Mexican lady comes to the smoking car, where Mr. Archer is playing cards with a few friends, and asks when the train will arrive in Juarez. The conductor says he doesn't know — that nobody knows and she should know that nobody knows. "Why," he concludes, "should you ask?"

"Because I am going to have a baby — right away!"

"Señora, you should not have got on this train in that condition."

"Señor, I was not in this condition when I got on the train."

The back country of Chihuahua was wild enough in those days, with bandits in the hills and machetes and pistols at the *bailes* on Saturday nights. Paymaster Scott White's men sometimes had to fight their way through from Temosachic to Concheño with the payroll, and White himself was in trouble in 1907 for killing three miners in a fight at a Concheño restaurant.[27]

The Sierra Madre line was not doing such business when Greene bought it, but it was not losing any money. The territory which it served was potentially rich in agriculture, timber, minerals, and wild game, and the rails could easily be extended to the heart of his holdings. The purchase price was not announced, but unofficial estimates said it was "not less than $2,000,000."[28]

Always in a hurry to get into action when he had a project on hand, Greene sent surveying crews out at once to locate a right of way. They laid out two important townsites, one at Madera[29] (which means lumber in Spanish) at the edge of a mighty virgin forest, and at Dedrick on the Aros River fifty miles beyond Madera and 125 miles from Nueva Casas Grandes, where the extension started. Madera was named San Pedro

Photos, Emadair Chase Jones

The wagon road of the Greene Gold-Silver Company.
Note wagon at top of lower photo.

before Greene moved in, but Dedrick (named for an American pioneer in the Sierra Madre) was an entirely new community.

The second round of construction would take the line to Temosachic on the flat lands at the foot of the mountains, which was to be the Mexican headquarters for Greene Gold-Silver with Greene's nephew Clarence Chase in charge. The main offices were, of course, in New York. At Temosachic the Sierra Madre would connect with the Chihuahua and Pacific with access to Chihuahua.

At first Greene said he had no plans for pushing on to the Gulf of California,[30] but his imagination could not long resist the thought of that tremendous leap across the backbone of the continent, and he let it be known that he would not stop till he reached salt water.[31] Just before the end of his active life, according to newspaper stories, he gave orders to start the work.[32]

His blueprint included a good many branches and subsidiary lines to penetrate to the corners of his empire and put his grand plan into operation. He planned to extend his Cananea-Naco connection eastward, south of the border, to Juarez–El Paso. He wanted a branch line from Dedrick southwest to the Mulatos district, which was said to be "a mountain of gold"[33] — a narrow gauge to Ocampo, still farther southwest[34] — logging roads into the wooded areas west of Madera to bring the timber to his mills.[35]

It would take time and much money to work all this out, of course, and he had another plan for immediate penetration of the high mountain country — a wagon road from Temosachic to Ocampo where only pack mules had been able to travel before. Completed in 1906,[36] this road was a real engineering feat, creeping along the sides of sheer cliffs, descending by multiple switchbacks into the valleys, rising at two points over 9,000 feet into the sky. The scenery was spectacular, and the grades were twenty percent or less — negotiable by the automobiles of that time — but the drivers at the end of the line knew they had been on a trip.

To Americans along the border, the most exciting feature of Greene's master plan was his idea of building a railroad from Naco to Juarez, across from El Paso. It was to be entirely on Mexican soil a few miles south of the line, and it would do great things for the two border communities. Greene actually had surveyors at work on the right of way in early 1905,[37] although they never got very far, and it was this project, as well as the promise of more business from the Sierra Madre extension, that raised the temperature of the first citizens of El Paso and persuaded them to arrange the testimonial dinner for Colonel Greene on Washington's birthday, 1905, described in the first chapter of this book. They could hardly do less for a man who was planning to spend fifty million dollars in devel-

Emadair Chase Jones

Hospital and commissary at Ocampo, terminus of the wagon road.

oping the resources of northern Mexico and who promised to funnel all his supplies and machinery through their home town.[38]

Greene was serious enough about the Cananea-Juarez railroad to think about the need for controlling the means of transportation between Juarez and El Paso, and in April of 1905 his agents went before the El Paso city council and secured a franchise for building a new street-railway system. The only hitch was the fact that since 1902 Stone and Webster of Boston had been operating an electric street-railway enterprise which they had no intention of abandoning. The result was a "streetcar war."

It would seem that the city council wanted to shake Stone and Webster up a bit. The company had sat on its hands since 1902, doing nothing to expand its services to keep up with an expanding city. The council felt that the least Stone and Webster could do was to extend its line down San Francisco Street to the Union Depot, but Stone and Webster never got around to it. So the city fathers granted a franchise to the new company without bothering to cancel the old one. This meant that whichever company could lay tracks to new districts in need of service would get the business — legally, since each had a franchise.

The great track-laying contest began on Saturday, April 8. Greene was no man to make a half-hearted effort, and he threw all the resources of the Sierra Madre railway into the battle. A. B. Fall directed the campaign, hiring several hundred laborers who rushed ties and rails across the river from Juarez and began laying track in all directions — on Overland Street, Second Street, Utah, and Mesa in the downtown area, and on a street not yet opened which led from the river to the Union depot across property technically belonging to the Santa Fe Railroad.[39]

There was a strong suspicion in the minds of some thoughtful people that Greene's real object was to lay rails over which his trains could cross to and from Juarez, although his franchise specifically forbade train traffic over city lines. They noted that the track laying to the station was done more carefully than the work in other sections. Apparently the Santa Fe officials noticed it too, for they sent a gang of men to tear up Greene's rails and ties and throw them in a ditch.[40]

Stone and Webster also considered the Union Station the real target, hired laborers of their own, and went to work laying rails from the station down San Francisco Street to the downtown area.

It was a wild and noisy business for several days. Greene's men, seven hundred of them, worked at night on Saturday and Sunday to an accompaniment of shouted orders, clattering wagons, clanging rails, and pounding hoofs. The guests at the Angelus and Orndorff hotels were kept awake all night and raised loud outcries in the morning.

El Paso felt a dreadful joy as the tension mounted. The police force guarded the track-laying area to prevent trouble between the rival gangs of workmen. The Santa Fe got out an injunction to keep the Greene men off their property. The old company got out an injunction to keep Greene off San Francisco Street. A delegation of citizens went to Mayor Morehead and asked to have the work stopped. Meanwhile crowds of curious people followed the workmen as they dug up the streets, unloaded rails and kept the project moving. A group called on Judge Fall and asked him where his electric plant would be located. Fall said he was not sure the new lines would use electric cars. After all, gasoline motors were doing the business in other cities and they might well succeed here.[41]

The pace never slackened till Friday morning, April 14. Then, with considerable track laid, Greene's bosses announced that wages would be cut from $1.50 a day to $1.00 for unskilled labor — and the men struck. They not merely refused to work themselves, they announced that they would prevent anybody else from working. They were "reckless and dangerous" and for several days posed a threat of mob action and violence.[42]

A compromise was reached on Monday afternoon. Laborers would still get a dollar a day but steel handlers would get a dollar and a quarter. A force of 150 men went back to work,[43] but they soon disappeared, and an alarming quiet descended where pandemonium had reigned a few days before. Something was going on behind the scenes, but nobody knew what it was. During the first week in May rumors spread throughout the town that the two street-railway companies were negotiating to see which would buy the other out. There had been a meeting in Judge Fall's office. A lot of money had changed hands. Fall, or somebody close to him, denied everything, but the wise ones shook their heads and said it was all cut and dried. When Judge Leigh Clark, attorney for Stone and Webster, made a special trip to Chihuahua to see Colonel Greene, they knew that a solution was near.[44]

It came early in July. The council, tired of looking at the cluttered streets, demanded that the new street-railway company restore the thoroughfares to "their original condition." Greene's crew of workmen immediately moved in and began taking out the tracks and ties and sending them back across the river. The council, astonished and a little appalled, issued a statement that their order had not been intended to provoke such drastic action. But by the time they had formulated the statement, the rails and ties were gone.[45]

Some sort of financial poker game was going on. Greene probably intended to do a good deal of business in El Paso. He had bought the American Smelter in northeast El Paso, inactive for four years, and had taken over an abandoned tin mine on the eastern slopes of the Franklin Mountains nearby. If he had completed his road from Cananea-Naco to El Paso and obtained rail access to the town over the traction company's tracks, he would have had an industrial complex going which might have developed into something big. His "great big game" changed somehow, however, and no part of his intention was carried out. The railroad was not built. The tin mine was not developed. The smelter was never activated, though some of the machinery was shipped to Guaymas, where the Colonel had another scheme going.[46] The millions of dollars which El Paso hoped for never did arrive and life went back to its usual leisurely pace.

Years later El Paso's most noted gossip, Owen P. White, told what he knew, or thought he knew, about the streetcar war. According to him it was all the work of Albert Bacon Fall, Greene's lawyer and confidant. Fall noted that there were great accumulations of ties and rails in the Sierra Madre yards in Juarez, "and there wasn't any reason why the Judge couldn't borrow them for a few days." He got the franchise through the city council (Owen hints that there was a payoff) and laid the tracks, blocking all the main thoroughfares. All traffic was stopped. When at last

Stone and Webster realized that they were outheld, they paid off. "Unless I am having a pipe dream," Owen said in his book *Lead and Likker,* "Judge Fall once told me with his own lips, and a contented chuckle, that this little piece of business netted him a profit of $30,000."[47]

Perhaps so. But Greene was not in the habit of letting anybody borrow his rails and ties for a month for his own private ventures. There must have been a better reason, and it had to be tied to the master plan.

Through 1905 and part of 1906 Greene continued in full flight. He was not averse to giving out information about what he intended to do, and it was understood that he meant to do everything. In April 1906 he was in El Paso with a party of directors, stockholders, reporters, and experts of various kinds and he gave an interview in which he described his objectives, particularly in his lumbering enterprise. "Within twelve months," he asserted, "we will not lose a limb of a tree which our lumbermen cut down."

Machinery will be installed for sash, door and blind manufacture, and chemical plants will be erected for treating the bark, limbs, and scraps for turpentine, lampblack, and resin.

Experiments are being undertaken with the manufacture of wood pulp preparatory to installing a paper factory in the mountains, and we expect to have this in operation within a few months.[48]

And that was not all by any means. He intended to dam the Aros river, a branch of the Yaqui, and build a power plant which would supply electricity to all of northern Mexico and the border region of the United States.

He brought Robert Brewster Stanton, a first-class civil and mining engineer, down from New York to make a complete survey of the power needs of Cananea and Nacozari, great mining centers in Mexico, and of Bisbee and Douglas in southern Arizona. Stanton completed his survey only at Cananea, on orders from Greene, but he made an impressive report on the power needs there, submitting his findings on November 30, 1906.[49]

It would have been a great feat if Greene had been allowed to work out his dream of power for all northern Mexico — the towns, the mining camps, even in time the farms and ranches. Light and heat. Pumps to draw water. Enough power to export some to the United States. The Mexican government dammed the Yaqui fifty years later, and the dynamos are humming there now, but nobody gave Colonel Greene credit for thinking of it first.

The same was true of the railroad over the Sierra Madre. The road was finally completed in 1961, a spectacular engineering feat, taking

American tourists and Mexicans going about their business through the heart of the mountains from Chihuahua to Los Mochis on the great Bay of Topolobampo, twisting and turning, flying across deep canyons on spindle-legged bridges and under the mountains through almost a hundred tunnels. It is no discredit to the Mexican engineers who completed this almost impossible task that Colonel Greene wanted to do it, intended to do it, and could have done it.[50]

The Great Hunt

IT IS POSSIBLE TO MAINTAIN that Colonel Greene's greatest talent was for entertaining. He made something of a specialty of the care and feeding of millionaires, and he loved to bring them to Mexico for special treatment.

He knew from the start that one visit was worth a million words when he had something to sell, and he brought his directors, stockholders, and friends to Cananea quite frequently. At first he brought them in his private car or sent them Pullman tickets on regular trains, but as his enterprises multiplied, his hospitality expanded proportionately. From one private car he moved onward and upward to two or three, or even four; and after he acquired the Sierra Madre line, he began to go in for special trains.

In the first years, directors and committees of stockholders were brought to Cananea, shown the mines and the works, and congratulated on their good fortune and foresight in becoming a part of "The Greene." Greene enjoyed these parties, but they took a good deal of arranging and supervision, and he considered them part of his chores. When he needed a rest or a change, he liked to go into the mountains with a few friends, or simply have the people he liked best come to visit him in the big house at Cananea. His real preferences appeared in a letter he wrote to his old acquaintance and partner W. S. Cranz of Nogales: "I shall be at Cananea all of the month of June, and I wish you could take Lola and come over and we will connubiate for a few days."[1]

As enterprises and millions and years accumulated, there was less and less time to "connubiate" and more and more occasion for entertaining actual and potential supporters by the carload and even by the trainload.

The Colonel was efficiently assisted in these projects by Henry O. Flipper, the first Negro graduate of West Point, who had been dismissed from the service after enduring a great deal of grief because of his color. Wounded but indomitable, Flipper opened engineering offices in the border town of Nogales and became a Mexican specialist. He spoke good Spanish, was at home with the Mexican people, and soon learned his way around in the mountains of northern Mexico. He was a really talented and unusual human being, and both Greene and his lieutenant A. B. Fall thought highly of him, employing him frequently in their Sierra Madre enterprises. In 1905 he became full-time member of the organization. For two years he had a special place in Greene's promotional activities, helping to pamper and provide for the Colonel's stable of millionaires. In one of the Company towns, probably Temosachic, he established a kitchen and dining room for their entertainment.

I got a Chinese cook and helper [Flipper said], fixed up a kitchen and dining room, bought chickens, sent men to scour the country for eggs, had provisions, including wines, brought out from Chihuahua, etc. Col. Greene came with the first party of millionaires from New York and Boston. At the first meal he ordered me to sit at the head of the table. We served excellent meals, the best ever served in those mountains. We had oranges, limes and *aguacates* [alligator pears] grown right there in town. For a whole year, almost every two or three weeks, sometimes oftener, there was a party of capitalists there. I had orders to feed any foreigners, particularly Americans, passing through and there were quite a number at one time and another. Flipper's restaurant became famous all over Chihuahua.[2]

During February and March of 1905 the Colonel scurried back and forth between Mexico and New York like a waterbug on a smooth pond. He was in El Paso on February 18 on his way to Cananea and back again on February 22 for the Washington's Birthday celebration in his honor, already described. He had two private cars full of guests, both ladies and gentlemen, with him at the time. He was already planning two important parties, a great hunting adventure and an automobile expedition into the Sierra Madre, which were to be talked about for many years to come.

Greene was in New York again in early March, but he was back in El Paso on March 31 with three special cars carrying another "party of capitalists." He looked over his new tin mine fourteen miles north of town, got drenched by one of El Paso's infrequent but enthusiastic rainstorms, and took off for Casas Grandes with A. B. Fall, his second-in-command, after they "had dried themselves and dined."

Next day he passed through on his way to New York for a directors' meeting, but he had already set in motion the men and materials needed

to receive the least likely corps of frontiersmen to appear in Mexico since the invasion of the Forty-niners on their way to California. Greene's idea was to bring a large group of his Wall Street acquaintances into his private wilderness for two weeks of primitive, or semi-primitive, living. Only William Cornell Greene would have thought of it. Only William Cornell Greene could have made it work.

The Colonel had other problems to occupy his mind, of course. He always did. The Streetcar War was under way in El Paso with Stone and Webster opposing A. B. Fall. Surveyors were working south from Nueva Casas Grandes on the line of the Sierra Madre Railway. E. B. Tustin, Greene's trusted friend and treasurer of Greene Consolidated Copper, was preparing to discredit the Colonel's Greene Consolidated Gold Company, and his "experts" were already in Mexico digging up evidence.[3] On the national scene the big news on April 18 was the San Francisco earthquake and fire. Through everything Colonel Greene maintained his calm and cheerful demeanor. He let it be known that he had ordered the machinery for a great tanning plant near the new town of Dedrick in Chihuahua to utilize the bark of the oak and hemlock forests which would soon be supplying his sawmills.[4] Casually he issued a bulletin about the impending invasion of Mexico by Wall Street.[5]

Joe Cannon, the salty, cigar-chewing Speaker of the House of Representatives was coming. Vice-president Fairbanks and Secretary of the Treasury Shaw had been invited. Governor Creel of Chihuahua and Governor Izábal of Sonora were included, along with assorted ex-governors,

A Covey of Capitalists: Colonel Greene and friends: (1) W. C. Greene, (2) Robert W. Goelet, (3) L. B. Baldwin, (4) James Stillman, (5) James H. Kirk, (6) Whitney Warren, (7) William G. Rockefeller, (8) J. Krutschnitt, (9) J. M. Hill (partially hidden), (10) A. B. Fall, (11) Epes Randolph, (12) Mr. Farrer, (13) J. J. Hill, Jr., (14) William V. S. Thorne, (15) native policeman, (16) Frank Hatch, (17) E. H. Harriman, (18) C. Ihlers, (19) D. R. C. Brown, (20) unknown, (21) A. S. Dwight.

Compañía Minera de Cananea

colonels, manufacturers, corporation lawyers, and general-issue millionaires from the United States. On the list also were a select group of El Paso worthies, including Mayor Charles Davis, Tom Powers (owner of a famous saloon), A. B. Fall, and ex-Sheriff Pat Garrett, who had gained fame by shooting his old friend Billy the Kid.

The Easterners would go first to Cananea to inspect the marvels there, then come back to El Paso and take the Sierra Madre into Mexico for their unprecedented penetration into "the magnificent Greene natural preserves."[6]

On April 25 the first detachment of the invaders arrived at El Paso in two private cars on the Texas and Pacific from Fort Worth and Dallas. Joe Cannon didn't make it, much to the disappointment of a number of West Texas admirers who came down to the station to greet him, but the dignitaries who *did* come more than made up for his absence. One was ex-Governor Woodbury of Vermont, a one-armed Civil War veteran who passionately supported Colonel Greene in everything he undertook. Present also were ex-Governor Charles J. Harris of North Carolina, Senator Latimer of South Carolina, Congressman Spencer Blackburn of North Carolina, Congressman John H. Stephens of Texas, Congressman W. D. Houston of Tennessee, Colonel Myron M. Parker of Washington, and many more.

The second contingent of the party arrived later that same day in the car *Sunset* over the Rock Island from Kansas City, and the entire regiment got off for Cananea that evening. Greene spent the day with

Fall and others talking business. They looked over the streetcar tracks which had been laid two weeks before. The Colonel had nothing to say about his plans for this enterprise.[7]

His visit touched off the usual chorus of panegyrics in the local papers:

Ever since Col. W. C. Greene acquired the Sierra Madre line, he has been advertising El Paso through his giant undertakings, and as they grow and develop, the city will profit. On the present trip Col. Greene is bringing some of the country's most prominent people to this section to see his properties and enjoy his hospitality on a hunt in the vast forests which he controls and to go back and tell of the wonders of the great empire of which El Paso is the center. . . .

Col. Greene is a man who undertakes big things and who has always carried them out successfully. His present undertaking, the development of the Sierra Madre country with all the attendant enterprises, such as paper mills, turpentine factory, saw mills, smelters, etc., is one of the biggest ever undertaken by one man, but he is surrounded by a corps of experienced and capable lieutenants and the work is being pushed just as fast as possible. . . . If Col. Greene does only half of what he proposes to do in the development of Northern Mexico, it will be one of the biggest things for El Paso that ever happened.[8]

After a look at Cananea and a side trip to Bisbee, Tucson, and Phoenix, the men were back in El Paso on Monday, May 4. They were still in an elevated mood, full of anticipation for the great hunt and of enthusiasm for their host. "Colonel Greene is a prince of entertainers," bubbled one of his guests. "Every cent of money we had with us was counterfeit." When the Easterners all decided to buy Western hats in Billy Brophy's store in Bisbee, the Colonel paid the bill. He provided such sumptuous food on the two private cars that the men stayed aboard for meals instead of eating at the hotels in the towns they visited.[9]

The *Sunset,* the *Olivette,* and the *Edgemere* were waiting in Juarez when the party arrived. Engine No. 22, decked with bunting and American flags, picked them up, and the great hunting party steamed off for Casas Grandes and the virgin wilderness.

As the days went by, Greene's talent for organization was fully revealed. His men had done their work well. A base camp eighty-five miles from Casas Grandes had been set up, and fifteen Mormon guides were waiting for the millionaires. Dr. I. J. Bush of El Paso, in later years chief of Villa's medical corps with the rank of colonel, was already there, as was "Captain" Bill Mayfield, bear hunter and hound-dog specialist, who had brought his pack from his ranch near Valentine, Texas. Cooking arrangements and sanitary facilities were ready. Hacks (light four-wheeled vehicles) were available for those who could not or would not ride, and horses for those who could and would.

A. Blake Brophy

Lunch Stop: Colonel Greene is on the left;
former Governor Woodbury of Vermont is on the right.

The great uncertainty was the ability of these products of civilization to stand the rigors of the trip. Clipping coupons may be medicinal
for the soul but it does not do much for the body, and clipping coupons
was about all the exercise some of the Colonel's guests ever took. Greene
did all he could, however, to make camp life endurable. He provided a
barber chair, complete with barber, for one thing, so that any slave to
custom could have his daily shave and massage out under the pines and
the sky. And report says that Colonel Greene even made sure that game
would be available by having bear and deer rounded up at a few places
and penned — to be released when the Nimrods were close at hand.[10]
This story may be a humorous invention. A. M. Tenney, one of the
guides, wrote to W. H. Brophy a month after the show was over: "Tha
party were too numerous to make hunting a success as after about the
second day the deer were all frightened away."[11] If any deer had been
penned, Tenney would have known of it. If Greene did hold a bear or

Camp Fall, or Greene Camp No. 1.

A. Blake Brophy

two in reserve, of course, he did it just for insurance. He hoped enough wild game would appear of its own volition to keep the party occupied, and besides, there were several experienced frontiersmen along, including Captain Mayfield, the bear hunter, Captain Burton Mossman of the Arizona Rangers, Tom Powers, the one-eyed El Paso saloon keeper, and Pat Garrett the man hunter, all of whom could have found game on their own.

The party disembarked at Casas Grandes and rode horses and hacks eighty-five miles down the Sierra Madre right-of-way and off into the mountains west of Colonia Chuichupa to the base of operations called Camp Fall. Fall himself was detained by business in El Paso, but Colonel Greene ordered a special train for him and his associate, lawyer Harris Walthall, and they caught up with the party a day late.[12] By May 6 everybody was present and accounted for.

On May 8 a bear-hunting party loaded up four pack mules and struggled eight miles deeper into the wilderness, set up camp, and put the dogs to work. They ran a black bear into a cave, and Mayfield followed her in and killed her. When she was dead he found that she was the mother of a little black cub, which at once became a member of the party. In a very short time this child of nature developed a taste and tolerance for whiskey which would have been a credit to any member of the hunters' fraternity.

The day following the departure of the bear hunters, a gentler and probably older group of ten men left in two hacks with a chuck wagon for the Rio Chico thirty-five miles to the south for trout fishing, mountain lion hunting, and exploration of cliff dwellings. When the bear clan came on May 11, they immediately left on the trail of the fishermen. The combined group proceeded south by easy stages to Dedrick and finally to Miñaca, western terminus of the Chihuahua and Pacific at the moment, where the private cars were waiting to take them home by way of Chihuahua and El Paso.

Those remaining at Camp Fall divided up later, one party proceeding to Casas Grandes and the railroad, eager to get back to familiar scenes and business responsibilities; the other, with pack mules and dogs, leaving for Lord Beresford's Los Ojitos ranch in the mountains west of Casas Grandes for more hunting.[13]

The days at Camp Fall were the richest part of the trip for many of the tenderfeet. There was much story telling around the campfire — so much that somebody suggested holding an election for the champion liar. There was considerable competition. Frontiersman Bill Mayfield told some of the best tales, "regaling the camp with many thrilling stories of early days in Texas." But Mayor Charles Davis of El Paso, thanks to long experience as a politician in that unconfined metropolis, qualified as president of the Ananias Club.

In spite of variant backgrounds, the men enjoyed each other. "There was never such a hunting party assembled before," said a dispatch from Camp Fall to the El Paso *Herald:* "men from every part of the Union — the old Federal and Confederate soldier, the big man of finance, the professional man, the cow man, the mining expert, all gathered about the camp fire in a free and easy democratic manner, bound together by the freemasonry of spirit found only among hunters."[14]

Greene was everywhere, supervising the cooking and packing, making sure nothing and no one was neglected, riding out with the hunting parties. "Col. Greene is the hardest rider in camp and the way he spurs his horse down steep cliffs is the wonder of his Eastern guests,"[15] the reporter said.

Back in New York he gave his own description of what happened for the benefit of curious city dwellers:

The hunting party was in the Sierras for more than a week, and we had plenty of shooting. We got three bears, between forty and fifty deer, a large number of wild turkeys, and some of our Izaak Waltons caught several hundred rainbow trout in the mountain streams. Judge Fall of El Paso killed the biggest wild turkey gobbler I ever saw. He stood 4 feet 7 inches high and with wings outstretched he measured 5 feet 8½ inches. I shot one a little heavier, but he didn't have so much spread. Our dogs chased a big silvertip bear so closely that the bear turned on them and trimmed them all up in a terrific fight. The dogs were so badly used up that we could not get them to do any work for a day or two.[16]

Not everyone in the party was bent on destruction of life. Dr. Bush was called to the bedside of a very sick woman in Colonia Chuichupa, thirty-two miles from camp. He made the round trip in fourteen hours and returned "somewhat the worse for wear."[17]

There were echoes long after all was quiet on the Rio Chico. Colonel Parker took up a collection, and the hunters showed their appreciation by presenting Mrs. Greene with a $1,500 silver tea service.[18] *Leslie's*

A. Blake Brophy

On the way to Miñaca, the hunting party stops at Dedrick.

Colonel Greene on horseback.

A. Blake Brophy

Weekly asked W. H. Brophy for a selection of the pictures he had taken of the party and its activities.[19] Greene sent some of the best prints to President Theodore Roosevelt, just back from a hunting trip of his own to the mountains of Colorado, and had in reply this letter from the White House, dated February 28, 1906:

> These are remarkable photographs. I prize them highly and am greatly indebted to you for sending them to me. What a remarkable hunt you had. . . . Do come to Washington and take lunch with me some day and give me a chance to cross examine you on all the details of your hunt. I would give pretty much anything to get out in that country on such a hunt.[20]

Even the bear cub had his innings. Greene took him back to New York to the wonder of the office boys on Wall Street and the delight of the children at the Ansonia apartment hotel, where the family was living. Remembering the bear raids on copper stocks a few months before, Greene named him Tom Lawson.[21]

The great hunt was a high point in Greene's life. It brought his two worlds together in the place he loved best. Its apparent success may have prompted him to arrange a sort of sequel a year later, in April, 1906. This time he decided to penetrate the wilds by automobile following the recently completed Greene Gold-Silver wagon road from Temosachic to Ocampo. It was hard enough for wagons to negotiate. Could an automobile possibly get through? Greene meant to find out, and he selected a special group to look into the matter with him.

He had his four cars — two Panhards and two Pope-Toledos — brought by train from Cananea to Temosachic just before two carloads of his directors, stockholders and friends arrived from the East. After a visit to Cananea the *Ahumada* and the *Cananea* carried the group to Temosachic, bringing with the rest a young writer and automobile enthusiast named Winthrop E. Scarritt who had met Greene on the New York-to-Boston train a few weeks before. Would Scarritt like to come to Mexico to observe a real test of motor cars? Of course he would. And on April 17, 1906, he was in Temosachic ready to go.

Three cars made the trip, the two Pope-Toledos and the smaller (twenty-four horsepower) Panhard. Among the passengers with Greene and Scarritt were Alfred Romer (Greene's cousin and a director of Greene Consolidated Copper) and his wife. Mrs. Romer must have been a brave woman.

A few miles out of Temosachic they were in the mountains. Up and up they went, passing over switchbacks and traversing narrow ledges a thousand feet above the valleys, walking and pushing when the grades were too steep and the cars wheezed and groaned "like a fat man out of breath." They spent the night at the Navidad mine and went on the next day, covering the last fifteen miles on muleback — and so into Ocampo, where they were honor guests at a dinner and *baile* (dance).

It was a real endurance test of flesh and metal. Scarritt thought the cars needed better brakes and improved "carburetters" for mountain work, but he was quite satisfied with Colonel Greene, "big, broad, brainy, farseeing, fearless, whatever may betide, whatever obstacles may be met, whether it be a criminal mob in Cananea or a no less criminal mob in Wall Street."[22]

Scarritt's voice was the voice of prophecy. He must have picked up a rumor of the labor troubles even then brewing in Cananea, but not even Colonel Greene could foresee that only a month after his return from his Sierra Madre adventure, armed men would be facing each other in the streets of Cananea.[23]

In Cold Blood

Estos distingos, verdaderos vejaciones, repugnantes e inhumanos, apoyados por el Regimen, servil a todo lo extranjero, fueron fecundando la semilla de la Revolución, que tuvo su primer brote, gallardo y heroico, en la Huelga de Cananea. . . .*

The Revolution, say the Mexican historians, began early on the morning of Friday, June 1, 1906, as a walkout of discontented miners employed by The Cananea Consolidated Copper Company.

The first action was scheduled for five o'clock, early enough to intercept any politically unconscious miner who might be thinking of going to work. A crowd of Mexican laborers gathered at the *portal* of the Oversight Mine, and when the seven o'clock shift appeared, ready to check in, the strikers prevented them from entering. Other parties closed down other mines immediately afterward and forced the smelter to cease operations. By noon, when the concentrating plant shut down, the camp was paralyzed.[1]

Company agents knew ahead of time what was going to happen and did their best not to be caught napping. Dr. Felipe Barroso, the mayor, was up all night trying to find out what the leaders were going to do. When Pablo Rubio, *comisario* (justice of the peace) of Ronquillo, telephoned him at 5:00 A.M. that the strike was on at the Oversight, they agreed

---

*Antonio Rivera, *La Revolución en Sonora* (Mexico: Privately printed, 1969), p. 20. "These discriminations — really oppressive, loathsome and inhumane, supported by the Regime, servile to all foreigners — nourished the seed of the Revolution, which put out its first shoot, gallant and heroic, in the Strike at Cananea."

to make a personal inspection and see what their presence and persuasion would do. They picked up Arturo Carrillo, judge at Ronquillo, and presented themselves, just as day was dawning, at the Oversight headquarters, where some four hundred excited, cheering miners greeted them with cries of *"Viva Mexico"* and demands for shorter hours and more pay. As a result of the informal conference which ensued, the workmen agreed to present their demands in writing and chose fourteen of their number to represent them at a conference which Barroso promised to arrange with the management of the Four C's.[2]

They wanted their pay raised from three pesos a day to five — with a peso-a-day increase for everybody who made more than the minimum. They wanted their ten-hour day reduced to eight. They asked that the lines of promotion be left open for qualified Mexicans and that half the foremen be of their blood. They complained of having to trade at the Company stores.

The written document which they later produced, addressed to Colonel Greene, stated with dignity and formality their dissatisfaction with the inequitable pay scale.

We the undersigned delegates designated by the Mexican miners to present our case to you, make this statement: That although injurious to our own interests and to our personal dignity, we have served the company over which you preside, although none of us has been pleased by, or found any basis in equity for, the pay offered to Mexicans.

General Manager A. S. Dwight, when he made his appearance on the scene at eight o'clock, found a message from Barroso waiting for him with the information that he was expected to attend a meeting at ten o'clock with the strikers' committee, all fourteen of them, at Doctor Barroso's offices on the main street of Ronquillo.

Dwight backed off rapidly. He said the demands were "absolutely absurd" and that he did not wish to discuss them. It would be better, he felt, for Barroso, Pablo Rubio, and Pedro Robles (the Company lawyer) to explain the Company's attitudes and discuss any Mexican laws which might apply to the situation.[3] The three Mexican officials agreed to handle the situation, probably realizing that Dwight's presence might be a drawback in view of the strong feeling against Americans which was rising like a mist all around them.

At ten o'clock the three Company men met the strikers behind closed doors. Outside in the *calle principal* of Ronquillo village, some two thousand of the unoccupied miners gathered to await the result. They were good natured — not at all hostile — more curious than concerned, it seemed. There were cries of *"Ocho horas; cinco pesos"* (eight hours; five pesos), and a few placards bearing this slogan, but the crowd seemed relaxed.[4]

At some time during this period, however, a handbill or printed broadside appeared on the street, passing from hand to hand and man to man, which showed which way the wind was blowing. It was addressed to the *Obreros Mexicanos* and called for instant and, presumably, violent action.

In the English translation which appeared in newspapers all over the Southwest, it read as follows:

MEXICAN WORKMEN!

A GOVERNMENT elected by the people to guide them and satisfy their necessities in all requirements: This Mexico does not possess.

ON THE OTHER HAND

A GOVERNMENT which is composed of ambitious persons, who criminally contemplate oppressing the people, being elected by the worst of them in order that they might assist them in enriching themselves. This MEXICO DOES NOT NEED.

PEOPLE, arouse yourselves and ACT. LEARN that which you seem to have forgotten. Congregate and discuss your rights. DEMAND the respect that is due you.

Every Mexican whom the foreigners despise is worth just as much as, or more than, those foreigners, if he will join with his brothers and CLAIM his rights.

CURSE the thought that a Mexican is worth less than a Yankee; that a Negro or Chinaman is to be compared with a Mexican. That this is a fact is the result of the very bad government which gives the advantages to adventurers rather than to the true owners of this unfortunate land.

MEXICANS, AWAKEN! The country and our dignity demand it!
Cananea, June 1, 1906.[5]

The Revolutionary historians disown this document. It could not have been produced by the leaders of the two Liberal clubs in town, they say, because they were men "of recognized prudence" determined to "preserve order at all costs." One of them (M. M. Diéguez) was not even in favor of the strike. Who, then, was responsible? Manuel Aguirre in his book *Cananea: The Claws of Imperialism in the Entrails of Mexico,* is of the opinion that Greene was responsible. Only the Company, eager to convict the strikers of rebellion and justify the bloodshed which they already had in mind, could have done it.[6]

The battle of words, however, was not conducted entirely by the workers. With Colonel Greene as spokesman, the Company had its say, too, that tense Friday morning. He replied in detail and with complete courtesy to the *comité de huelgistas* who had addressed him, listing their grievances and desires. He wrote in reply:

It is with real surprise and deep sorrow that I have examined your communication of this date — which appears to me to be without foundation or instigated by persons whose personal interest is contrary to the prosperity and well being of the workers of this mining community. You know very well that this Company has been criticized for paying high salaries and asked to reduce them but we have always refused, taking much pride and satisfaction in the well being and prosperity of Cananea.

A blanket pay raise of a peso per person, he declared, would be risky for the company in view of the great number of men employed; the hours of work expected depended on the job. As for the charge that everybody had to buy at high prices at the Company store, he assured them that the price of necessities was constantly being reduced and was in 1906 thirty percent lower than it had been two years before, much lower than in any *mineral* in Mexico. Everybody should work together, he concluded, to make Cananea the most important mining town in Mexico and to get rid of all "adventurers without conscience" whose intrigues were injuring the community.[7]

While this document was being readied for presentation, Greene came down the hill from his home on the Mesa, arriving about eleven o'clock. He looked tired, and he was tired, having been up almost all night. The evening before, when he got word of the strike, he ordered out a coach and engine and went to Bisbee to arrange for reinforcements and pick up all the firearms he could lay his hands on, returning at four in the morning. He did not seem disturbed or nervous, however. In fact, he remained calm even when the trouble was at its worst.[8]

There was no tension as he got out of his automobile and began to walk among the onlookers and bystanders, shaking hands here and there, advising the men not to let themselves be deceived by troublemakers. He reminded them that the Company paid higher wages than any mining firm in Mexico (which was true); that he had always looked out for them and their welfare (which was really the point at issue); that he wished to treat them like men and would listen to reasonable requests, but he had to follow government regulations;[9] that they ought to go home now.

They listened. They all liked the Colonel. It was not unusual for them to cheer him when he appeared on the street. *"Viva el Coronel Greene!"* they would shout. *"Viva!"* And he would smile and wave. They were inclined to take his advice, and many of them went home, as he suggested. They even cheered him as they went.[10]

Many remained, however, and their mood changed when the conference broke up. The Company had made no concessions. Barroso explained that no concessions were possible. The government had ordered

A. Blake Brophy

Hard living: workers' housing near Cananea.

not merely that wages must be kept down but that they must be reduced. Too many men were coming to the camp looking for work at three pesos a day (several times what they could expect at ranch or farm work), and employers had raised so much fuss that Governor Izábal had stepped in. The Company's hands were tied.[11]

The leaders laughed derisively and told the men that this was no answer. Greene was making excuses and must be taught a lesson. The strike would go on; injustice and discrimination must stop. Why should a Mexican workman be paid three pesos a day for ten hours work when an American got $5.00 in United States money (the peso was worth fifty

William Metcalf in his office at the lumber yard.

cents, American)? Did these invaders own the country? Posterity would remember them for what they did now. Everybody in the camp must walk off his job — everybody!

By 2:00 P.M. the crowd was back in the main street, and they had a program. They would visit every unit of the Four C's and make sure work was stopped. The march began. The move was toward the Mesa, where some of the Company business was done. They were determined but not hostile. When they met two Americans in the street, they offered no indignity.[12] There was no stopping till they reached the Company lumberyard at the extreme east end of the Mesa.

Did they have a special object in aiming for this particular spot? It would be impossible to prove that they did. The Metcalf brothers who worked there, however, were anything but popular. George, the manager of the lumber business, was also in charge of Company housing — a post which gave him ample opportunity to make himself disliked. He was impatient and arbitrary, as he had demonstrated when he was superintendent of schools at Tombstone. Greene was gradually moving the miners out of the shacks and hovels they occupied in the Ronquillo area and into Company quarters. Sometimes a man preferred his hovel among friends to a better place among strangers. It did no good to mention this fact to George. He took no backtalk and listened to no pleas.[13] Will, who worked in the office at the lumberyard, was not such a thorny character, but he stood by his brother.

The strikers behaved well up to this moment. They had on their best clothes and were quite obviously expecting to bring the Mexican employees out of the yard without any trouble. But they had reckoned without George Metcalf. He knew they were coming — somebody had telephoned him — and he had gone to his home after his rifle. Back on the scene, he unwound a four-inch fire hose and brought it out in front of the yard, closing the gates behind him.

The leaders paused when they saw him. They were carrying flags, a Mexican flag in the middle and a white one and a red one on each side.

"We want to talk to your workmen," they told him.

"If you try to go in, you will get wet," he replied.

They moved forward, and he let them have it, soaking men and banners and spoiling their Sunday suits. That blew up the powder barrel. The indignant visitors rushed him, and within five minutes three of them were lying lifeless on the ground. George and his brother were dead, stabbed to death with miner's candlesticks — iron implements with long sharp shafts for driving into crevices in mine walls.

Half a dozen variant versions tell how it happened. George did the shooting; George went down under the rush and Will did the shooting; somebody inside the yard did the shooting. One Mexican account says the shots were fired by two Americans on the "balconies" of the office building and that the unarmed Mexicans set fire to it in order to smoke them out. Two charred bodies found later in the ruins must have belonged to these unidentified riflemen. The only non-Mexican witness to these events, a hay dealer from Solomonville, Arizona, named Philo Freudenthal, ran for cover when the rush started and never saw where the bullets came from. He merely remarked, when he was interviewed, "Suddenly a shot was fired."[14]

Whoever was responsible, the damage was done. There were dead men of both races in the street, and worse trouble was coming.

To understand this terrible episode, one must begin with President

Porfirio Díaz, dictator of Mexico for thirty years, whose iron-handed rule was nearing an end. Once a rebel against the central government himself, he became a despot because he wanted to make his country a great modern nation. As a result Mexico became two nations: an elite, made up of his friends and supporters, and the workers, whose lives were too often the lives of slaves.

Díaz saw no way of bringing factories and railroads to Mexico, no way of developing Mexico's natural resources, except by encouraging foreigners with money and know-how to come in. The result was a migration of American miners, ranchers, and businessmen to Mexico, to the growing dismay of thoughtful Mexicans who were afraid the invaders could never be dislodged. Díaz' first miscalculation was his failure to realize how deeply his countrymen resented the invasion of these outsiders, particularly the Americans. His second was the assumption that the men on the bottom would remain docile and unresentful indefinitely.[15]

Before the turn of the century the inevitable reaction began. Marxists of various shades and denominations appeared in Mexico, preaching syndicalism or anarchism, publishing underground newspapers, making fiery speeches urging the workers to throw off their chains. The Flores Magón brothers — Jésus, Ricardo, and Enrique — who became revolutionary saints in Mexico, were among the leaders. They organized the Mexican Liberal Party and published *Regeneración,* the newspaper which gave the movement a voice. In 1906 the leaders of the party were living in the United States, but their agents, their influence, and their newspaper were powerful south of the border.[16]

In the United States similar radical groups were being organized, or at least the conservative people of the country considered them so. One of these was the Western Federation of Miners, which had unionized thousands of mine workers in spite of determined opposition from mine owners and investors. In the spring of 1906 the miners' union had its annual convention in Denver, where Librado Rivera and Antonio I. Villareal were publishing *Regeneración.* Both the Mexican liberals and the Federation of Miners were interested in promoting discontent among the miners in Mexico, and their agents were active in Cananea.

They had help on the local level. Enrique Bermúdez, a young Mexican journalist who for some time had made Douglas, Arizona, his headquarters, moved his radical newspaper *El Centenario* to Cananea in April 1906, thereby adding to the impact of smuggled copies of *Regeneración* which had been circulating for some time among a small group of miners and office workers.[17]

These men were already organized. On January 6, 1906, fifteen of them gathered at the house of Cosme Aldana and formed a secret revolutionary society which they called *Unión Liberal Humanidad.* Manuel Diéguez was the first president; Francisco M. Ibarra vice-president; Esteban Baca Calderón, secretary. Diéguez, a man of superior capabilities who spoke English and had learned his syndicalism in the United States, was an assistant timekeeper at the Oversight mine. Eventually he became a general in Madero's revolutionary army and later still governor of the State of Jalisco. Baca Calderón, whose great talent was a gift for making impassioned speeches, was also a timekeeper at the Oversight, and he too became a general. These prime movers attracted a group of about twenty like-minded men.[18]

From the first, they were in touch with the leaders of the Liberal Party, exchanging letters with Antonio I. Villareal and even with Ricardo Flores Magón, reading smuggled copies of *Regeneración,* and talking about the great day when the means of production would be in the hands of the workers.

Their activities might have remained on the level of discussion if the Company, under governmental pressure, had not been obliged early in May to reduce the scale of pay for Mexicans by fifty centavos. Porfirio Díaz himself is said to have confirmed the order, sending word that Greene's high wages were upsetting the economy and they would have to be lowered.[19]

This happened just before one of the great Mexican holidays, the Fifth of May, and the Liberals in Cananea saw at once that here was their great opportunity. There would be a place in the patriotic oratory for some admonitions of their own. A young socialist lawyer named Lázaro Gutiérrez de Lara organized another radical club about this time, and the two groups combined as *La Junta Patriotica,* pointing toward the May 5 celebration.

They had their say. The newly arrived newspaper *El Centenario* reported Esteban Baca Calderón's speech:

Señores Mineros: Now is the time to open your eyes to the light of reason and to leave off vain lamentations. If the situation is bad, it is yours to remedy it. To resolve to do so — that is all. A people which goes to sleep in timidity awakens in conquest. . . . Forward, mighty champions of Labor! Your sons will enjoy the fruit of your loyal, honorable, and energetic struggle. Do not vacillate. The laurels of triumph will adorn your brows. Long live the Republic! . . . Teach the capitalist that you are not beasts of burden — the capitalist who in every way and everywhere has displaced us with his legion of blue-eyed blonds.[20]

Company officials had some idea of what was going on, but they could do little but set up a curfew after the speechmaking to keep people off the streets.[21]

American miners were under pressure too. Raymond Reid found out about that. Clarence Chase, his cousin, sent him to Cananea from Temosachic. "You spend about a year around those different mines," he said, "and then come back here and I'll put you in charge of a hole in the ground."

Raymond went underground at Cananea and in time became a foreman, but the old miners from Leadville and the Comstock were always after him to join the union. He asked Jim Kirk about it. Kirk said, "Stay out."

I didn't join the union and the next thing I knew they were blowing my timbers out and doing a lot of damage to the work I was doing, and things just weren't going right. It took me a little while to get down to what was going on. Then I saw that they were just making trouble for me, and I thought, "By golly, I know these fellows can be pretty tough. The first thing I know, they are going to blow the ground out from under me." So I quit and went up to Michigan.[22]

Greene was watchful. When the Western Federation of Miners met in Denver in May 1906 he arranged to have copies of the proceedings sent to him.[23] In one of his reports on the Cananea disorders he said:

I was informed by a man working in the Cobre Grande . . . that agitators of the Western Federation had been through the mines inciting the Mexicans, and that they had been furnishing money for the socialist club that had been established at Cananea.[24]

Even so, he could not believe that real trouble would occur. "It looked ridiculous," he said afterward, "that anything of that kind would be done." When one man told him about it, he was sure it was just a rumor. When another one "in whom I had confidence" told him the same story, he began to be alarmed.

Their program, according to the reports which came to him, included "dynamiting the bank, where it was reported we had $1,000,000, breaking open the store and getting firearms and ammunition, and with them starting a revolution against the Díaz government."[25]

Kirk, Dwight (the general manager), and Galbraith (the U. S. consul) were skeptical until they learned that several boxes of dynamite were reported to be missing from the Oversight, where the leaders of the Liberal club worked. Then they got nervous too.

Did they have real cause for worry? All the Mexican sources say no. The strikers had planned no violence whatever and intended only to present their grievances in an orderly and respectful manner. No dynamite was involved. The strikers had no arms. They even had their best clothes on when they approached the lumber yard.[26] They were only exercising their rights as men and citizens to demand fair treatment and equal pay for equal work.

Greene was sure they meant mischief, and he never changed his mind. Under the circumstances, he had no choice but to prepare for the worst. It was better to take unnecessary precautions than to laugh at the reports and get blown up. He was no man to dally when he had made up his mind to act, so he had an engine and a passenger car brought around to the station, and at ten o'clock at night he left at full speed for Bisbee. Ignacio Macmanus, in charge of the bank, went with him. Greene telegraphed ahead for a special train to take Macmanus to Hermosillo to impress on Governor Izábal the seriousness of the situation.

Greene himself went directly to W. H. Brophy's Copper Queen store at Bisbee, kept open in response to his telegraphic message, and collected all the guns in the place — 98 rifles and twenty pistols, with 5,000 rounds of ammunition. At 1:30 in the morning he passed through Naco on the return trip, got off the train at 4:00, distributed his arms to "our most reliable men," and "returned to the house thinking I had made a fool of myself, as everything was quiet."[27]

In Hot Blood

Voy a dar un pormenor
de lo que a mi me ha pasado:
que me han agarrado preso,
siendo un gallo tan jugado.*

LEAVING THE DEAD GRINGOS lying in their blood, the strikers picked up
their own casualties and left the burning lumber yard, from which a great
plume of black smoke was beginning to rise.

Greene was some distance away when the trouble at the lumber yard
started. Kirk had come down from the Veta Grande just after noon to
report to him at the Company offices that the mine was closed down and
that work had stopped at the concentrators. A group of strikers had forced
the Mexican workmen to leave.

"They looked ugly and vicious," Kirk said.

"Let's go and see if we can do anything with them," Greene suggested.

They found a horse and buggy they could borrow and started up
the road.

"Between Ronquillo and the concentrator," Greene recalled later,
"we passed through large mobs of them who were being marshaled evi-

---

* First stanza of the famous revolutionary *corrido,* "La cárcel de Cananea," from
Vicente Mendoza's *El Romance Español y el Corrido Mexicano* (Mexico: Imprenta
Universitaria, 1939), p. 588.

I will give you a complete account
of what happened to me:
they took me prisoner —
me the rooster that knew it all!

[188]

Veta Grande, one of Greene's copper mines.

dently by experienced agitators. I tried to talk to them and stop them, but to no avail."

At the concentrators they left orders with the American workmen still on duty to post guards and watch out for fires.

Dynamite and fire were the great worries at this point. Greene and Dwight had heard repeatedly that the offices and works were to be blown up and that what the dynamiters missed would be fired. Since no dynamite was used by the strikers, the rumors were false, but the Americans could not know how much danger they and their families might be in. The fate

Burned Out: the lumber yard after the fire, June, 1906.

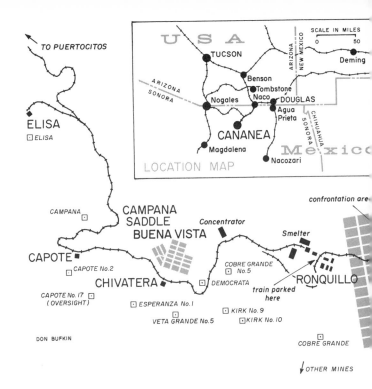

of the Metcalf brothers convinced them that the situation was serious if not desperate.

Greene feared the worst as he saw the black smoke billowing sky- ward on the mesa as he left the concentrators. Making what speed he could, he hurried back down the hill and found General Manager Dwight at the Company offices.

"How many men have we got?" he asked.

"About thirty. I asked for extra policemen and there weren't any so I told Castañedo we would use our own men if he approved. He said there was nobody else he could call on and they have been deputized."[1]

"Well, we may need them. I'm going up on the mesa and see what's going on."

His own account tells what happened next:

On crossing the railroad track, the broad-gauge locomotive was there. I jumped in, requesting the engineer to run to the Cananea depot as quickly as possible. Before arriving there, I found that the mob had already arrived at the Mesa Lumber Yard, killed the Metcalfs and set fire to the lumber yard. I saw 2,000 or more Mexicans, being marshaled by leaders waving red flags and shouting "To the bank," "To the store." I immediately ordered the engineer to run full speed to the store and bank where I had two automobiles waiting, and getting Kirk and one or two other men in the automobiles, I told Mr. Dwight to col- lect the entire force from the bank and store and get to the Mesa as quickly as possible, for, if we encountered the mob, that was the place to do it. We ran those automobiles at the rate of 50 miles an hour through the thick crowds,

The Cananea neighborhood at the time of the strike.

(Robert Brewster Stanton's map revised by Don Bufkin)

scattering them in all directions, arriving at my house, where I got my rifle and a few boys who were there with arms, by which time Mr. Dwight and about 40 of the employees from the store, bank, etc., with the hose cart had gotten on the mesa. The mob had returned as far as the jail, the police being absolutely unable to do anything with them, there being about 25 policemen as against the entire rioters. I ran down by the Sonora hotel, thinking that I could cross the bridge and head them off, but before I got to the bridge, the outfit had passed above it. I whirled the autos and returned to the two vacant blocks, located just in front of my house, where we met the mob as they were arriving at the empty block going up the Avenida Principal, the entire street being filled with them. I gave strict orders to all the boys not to shoot unless absolutely necessary, then at the leaders.

From this point on the Mexican and American accounts do not seem to be describing the same set of events. Leon Díaz Cárdenas gives the official Mexican version:

The workers, carrying their wounded and dead at the head of the column, continued their demonstration . . . directing their course to the town hall in order to demand justice.

They were near the hall when, at the crossing of Chihuahua Street and Third Street, a discharge of firearms opened bloody wounds in the flesh of the proletarians. Six men fell dead, among them a child of less than eleven years. The massacre, cold blooded and premeditated, had begun. . . . The workers, indignant as they were, could not repel the aggression. Unarmed, they replied to the shots with curses and stones, sustaining a desperate and unequal contest.[2]

To compound their crimes, say other Mexican accounts, the Americans used dum-dum bullets (provided by Greene) which "carry away bone and flesh, leaving an enormous hole."[3]

Colonel Greene, as would be expected, told a different story:

> After passing the jail and coming up the principal street, Mr. Dwight endeavored to stop one of the ringleaders, who was at the head carrying a red flag and turn him back when one of the men who carried a red flag shot at him, at a distance of only a few feet, evidently shooting over his head. I immediately shot, which was the signal to shoot, and the four leaders of the mob fell. The mob scattered in all directions. I immediately ordered all the boys to retire to my house and not shoot any more under any circumstances, and for all to get together and keep together to avoid individual collisions.

A. S. Dwight tells a similar tale. He says that Greene and his men turned back one group of strikers leaving the lumber yard and hoped to do the same with the main body. When the confrontation came, Dwight grappled with the leaders.

> While struggling with one man who resisted, my shotgun fell to the ground. At this moment a large man with a black shirt rushed out from between two houses on the side and discharged his revolver at me at a range of about eight feet. This was the first shot fired and immediately shooting commenced on both sides.

The marchers had numbers on their side but not much else. One group of them, after the encounter with Greene and his men, hurried to the city offices, where they found Judge Isidoro Castañedo, in charge of the police force and the jail, and demanded arms. Castañedo responded by putting a number of them behind bars, including some who were not involved with the *huelgistas*.[4] A second and larger group proceeded to Ronquillo, where there were several pawnshops which they broke into in search of weapons. Greene said they got hold of "about 300 guns and a miscellaneous lot of ammunition."[5]

This concentration of strikers now became the main object of official interest. Greene sent a detachment of men from his house to the jail to guard the newly installed prisoners, thus freeing the regular police force for duty in disarming the strikers and "scattering the mob below." In the collision that followed, according to information which came back to Greene, "about 20 Mexicans were killed and about 45 were arrested and immediately put in jail. This was the last serious collision that day."

There were plenty of collisions that could have been serious as trigger-happy riflemen on both sides opened up. Fred Walker, an American office worker who had never seen anything like this before, found himself in danger from his own people. He recorded in his notebook:

A lot of drunken cowboys got on top of the Los Angeles Hotel and shot at everything that moved — Chinamen, chickens, Mexicans and gringos all got shot at. And then we had to make war on the Los Angeles outfit. Braced up by their booze they sure put up a scrap, but one by one they were captured from behind.[6]

Walker, with three others, set off late that night with an engine and three freight cars for Puertecitos on the west slope of the Cananea Mountains, hoping to pick up a squad of Mexican *rurales* (ranger force) who were reported to be coming in from the railroad at Imuris. He wrote:

I knew we would never reach our destination, and I was along for the excitement (which I got). We left Ronquillo at 11 p.m. There was some moon and the sky was lighted up by the burning lumber yard. We wound up the mountain road till we reached Buena Vista. Here the Mexicans had turned the switch and the front wheels of our engine derailed — and then from two sides they let us have it. Mexicans were all over, on both sides of the canyon. That's the first time I ever heard bullets whistle and zip past my head. I knew my time had come. After half an hour the Mexicans let up and we got back to Ronquillo — alive!

Greene sent his three automobiles to the Capote mine and back several times during the night, "to maintain confidence and order." He estimated that one hundred shots were fired at them, but there were no hits. Automobiles were something new and strange in Cananea in 1906, and "the men who did the firing were evidently too badly rattled for fear the things would jump at them to take aim."

The American employees were afraid for their women and children as shooting continued into the night, and about ten o'clock a train load of refugees departed for Naco. Those who remained gathered at Greene's house.

Meanwhile the telegraph wires were humming with activity. Dr. W. J. Galbraith, the U.S. consular official, was close to panic and sent off a barrage of messages to important people all the way up to the president of the United States. He telegraphed first to Elihu Root, secretary of state, in Washington: "Send assistance immediately to Cananea, Sonora, Mexico. American citizens are being murdered and property dynamited. We must have help." Root got in touch with Ambassador David E. Thompson in Mexico City, and Thompson went to President Díaz. Díaz was worried but said the Mexican authorities could handle the situation.[7]

Dr. Galbraith also wired the commanding officer at Fort Huachuca in southern Arizona. As a result four troops of cavalry proceeded to Naco, ready to cross the border. Galbraith telegraphed President Roosevelt, "This is the time for action."[8] Fortunately, however, heads were cooler in Washington than in Cananea, and no irresponsible moves were made.[9]

Other telegrams were exchanged by Greene and the municipal authorities on the one hand and the military and civil leaders of Sonora on the other. The most urgent of all were from Greene to Governor Izábal, urging him to come to Cananea. The last one read: "URGENT. Bring troops with you. Don't stop at Imuris. Take special train. Situation serious. About forty killed. I will meet you at Naco with train to bring you here." [10]

Izábal had been alerted the night before in the course of Greene's journey by midnight special to Bisbee, and Ignacio Macmanus was already at Hermosillo explaining the situation to the governor. The trouble was geography. Izábal could not possibly reach Cananea until Saturday. General Luis E. Torres, military commander of Sonora with headquarters at Magdalena, could not bring his troops in through the United States and would have to march his men forty miles across country from Imuris west of Cananea. He would get there even later. Emilio Kosterlitzky, whose *rurales* were also based at Magdalena, would need two days of hard riding to arrive. If help was to come, it would have to come from some place near at hand, and near at hand meant the United States. Greene got on the phone and called Walter Douglas at Bisbee.

As general manager of the Copper Queen mine, Douglas had to be knowledgeable and resourceful, and he came up at once with an idea. He knew that Captain Tom Rynning of the Arizona Rangers was in town, and he sent a message to Tom to call Greene at Cananea. As Rynning reported this conversation later, Greene said, "Hell is popping here and every American's life is in danger." [11]

While Rynning was on the telephone talking to Greene, Douglas got hold of Marshal Biddy Doyle of Bisbee and suggested that he put out a call for two hundred volunteers.

Bisbee was already on the alert as messages and reports and rumors came boiling up from the center of unrest. Two thousand excited people were gathered in the Bisbee plaza that Thursday evening waiting for bulletins from Cananea. Every word that came in excited them more: "Forty Americans killed." "George Metcalf and brother dead." "Troops sent for from Fort Huachuca."

The saloons began to do a land-office business as more and more men repaired their shattered nerves at these oases. The mayor was worried about it and finally ordered the saloons closed. What happened thereafter was done without benefit of alcohol.

Considerably more than the two hundred volunteers called for assembled in front of the Copper Queen store early in the evening. Rynning took them in hand and told them that he had had a wire from Governor Izábal, who would meet them at Naco. "You can't cross the border as an armed body," he reminded them. "That would be an invasion of Mexico. We'll see how the Governor handles it."

Bisbee volunteers en route to the smelter, June 3, 1906.

In order to clear himself of any active connection with American law-enforcement bodies, Rynning wired Governor Joseph H. Kibbey of Arizona asking for a leave of absence from his post with the Rangers. The governor wired back, "I cannot permit any officer or man in the territorial service to go into Mexico at this time."[12] Rynning was already in Mexico when the message reached Naco.

The excitement threatened to last all night. There was difficulty in arranging for a train to take the volunteers from Bisbee to Naco, and the men waited impatiently. About eleven o'clock the first trainload of refugees arrived from Cananea, and more wild stories and exaggerated reports hit the street. When their special train left for Naco about midnight, the men were convinced that everything in northern Mexico was about to go up in flames.

It is only eight miles from Bisbee to Naco, and the train came in about 12:30. The governor did not arrive until 7:30 in the morning after an all-night trip from Hermosillo, but even then the men could not get started. The Mexican constitution expressly forbade the intrusion of an armed force from a foreign country on the soil of the fatherland, and

Izábal well knew what a hornet's nest he would run into if he did not find some way to make the expedition of the Bisbee volunteers look good.

Rynning found it for him. He suggested that the men could cross the line as individuals and reassemble on the other side. Any private citizen had the right to cross for his own private purposes. Izábal accepted the suggestion. The volunteers were marched to the line, drawn up in military formation, and asked to listen while Rynning explained what was about to happen. The Mexican officials on the other side, perhaps ten feet away, relayed instructions to let the men cross. They did so, and reformed on the Mexican side. Rynning offered their services to Izábal, who accepted. General Torres then swore them into the Mexican army, and Izábal addressed his new troops. "I am deeply grateful," he assured them "for the offer of your services." He insisted, at the same time, that every man was "absolutely under my orders and in addition is subject to the laws of Mexico."[13]

Rynning accepted the conditions in the name of all the men, and in a matter of minutes the Bisbee volunteers were on their way.

Cananea knew they were coming. Several thousand people filled the street near the station when the train pulled in at mid-morning. Greene

Short-Order Police Force: Armed employees guarding the Company store.

Arizona Historical Society

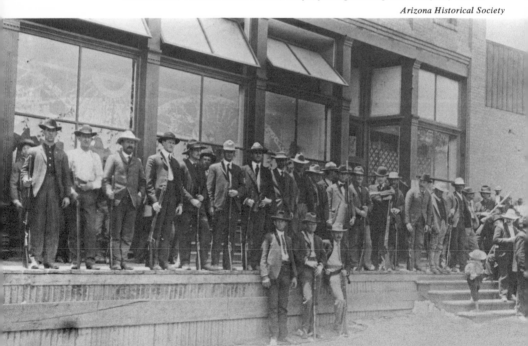

Colin Rickards

Colonel Greene, from his automobile, addresses the strikers at Cananea on June 3, 1906. Deputized Company employees are in the background. Governor Izábal is seated behind Greene to his left; Frank Moson, bareheaded, is on the running board.

was there with his three automobiles and met the governor at the steps of his coach. He even proposed a cheer for him: *"Viva el gobernador."*[14] The mood of the townspeople, however, was such that they were willing to let Greene have the cheering all to himself.

The volunteers put on a show of force, marching from the train to the smelter and concentrators. Greene and Izábal made a brief tour of inspection in the automobiles. About noon they returned to Ronquillo.

The crowd was bigger than ever now. Word had spread that the governor was in town, and a great many people wanted to hear what he had to say — wanted, perhaps to make him listen to what *they* had to say.

The Company police force, which had been sworn in the day before, was grouped in front of the Company store, rifles at their sides. Frank Moson, Colonel Greene's stepson, stood on the running board of the Panhard in which Greene and Izábal were riding. The crowd flowed around them and enclosed them like a human sea.

There was silence when Izábal rose to speak, his heavy features dark and grim, but it did not last long. When he started talking about law and order and said that "killing and looting cannot find a place in this camp so long as I am governor," he got a quick reaction. He was interrupted often by men who wanted to talk about their grievances. Finally he sat down, not at all happy with the situation.

Then it was Greene's turn, and he made the speech of his life, standing in his car with one foot on the back seat, gesturing with his right hand, his big voice carrying to the outer edges of the huge crowd. He spoke in Spanish, with a smile on his face, as if to his friends. W. B. Kelly of the Bisbee *Review* summarized the speech for his readers:

> You Mexican people all know me. I have been a poor man myself. Some of you were my friends then, and all of you know that I have acted always honestly and fairly with you. When I have been able to pay you $3.50 for your work, I have gladly paid it. But a man cannot pay more than he makes. I cannot pay you five dollars at this time. The revenue from the mines would not permit it. I have tramped over these hills for a long time. I have spent millions of dollars in building up here among you the most thriving mining camp in Mexico. I have always been fair and candid with you and I ask you to do the same by me. . . .

Kelly listened with both ears during the speaking — one for the Colonel and one for the crowd. He reported:

> Often they ridiculed certain statements. . . . But the meat of the cocoanut, and the bone of contention, was contained in the remark of a Mexican laborer to another, who said, "Yes, all that is true, but why don't the company pay the Mexicans the same wages they pay the Americans?" [15]

It was the great question to which the Company never gave an answer satisfactory to the miners. They were thinking about Justice. Greene was talking about Necessity. He needed experienced American miners and had to pay American wages to get them.

Having made an appearance and emphasized the point that they had arrived, ready for business, the Bisbee volunteers were marched back to the train and put on board. There they remained all afternoon and on into the evening, restless and frustrated, but taking no part in what followed.

Kosterlitzky's *rurales* arrive at Cananea.   *F. R. Walker*

Just before sunset of that same day, Saturday, June 2, Colonel Kosterlitzky, at the head of a column of his *rurales,* rode down the main street of Ronquillo, and the trouble was all but over. Kosterlitzky was known among the *peones* as The Butcher, and they were not about to take any liberties with him. With the *rurales* in control, the Bisbee men were obviously superfluous. It was time for them to go home. It is said that Kosterlitzky told them so. With darkened windows so as to provide no target for snipers, the special train pulled out about ten at night and the "invasion" was over.

Not a shot had been fired by the invaders. Not a shot had been fired at them. They had behaved with complete discretion and followed orders to the letter. Greene felt that their arrival had prevented "the most serious outbreak on the second day." Their mere presence, however, touched off tremendous repercussions in Mexico. No matter how well they behaved, they had no business being there.

During the afternoon, before the *rurales* arrived, there was a good deal of shooting, some of it by American "cowboys" who should have known better than to make trouble.[16] Most of the casualties were Mexican, and they included one simple citizen from Naco, who, according to the Mexican chroniclers, arrived on foot in complete ignorance of what was going on. When he passed the Greene residence, somebody shot him dead on the supposition that he was getting ready to dynamite the house.[17]

Arizona Historical Society

Guarding the Big House, Cananea, June 1, 1906.

There was not much firing after those tough *rurales* rode in. With the proclamation of martial law, a death-like calm settled down. Word went out to all quarters of the town: "All persons, Mexican and American, are to remain in their houses. Anybody found on foot in the streets after dark will be shot."

Greene issued orders of his own:

> There must be no more shooting for any cause tonight. All Americans will obey strictly the orders issued. We are going to have law and order in this camp and we are going to have it quick. . . . There is no cause for alarm any longer. Go to your homes and go to bed. Myself, in company with Col. Kosterlitzky and the Governor, will be on patrol duty with the *rurales* for the remainder of the night.[18]

In the morning one hundred soldiers arrived and went into camp near town. Twice as many came in the following day, the fourth of June.[19] They were not needed. Kosterlitzky had everything well in hand.

There are stories about Kosterlitzky's rounding up and shooting everybody he suspected of complicity in the riot, but they are without foundation. He did bring in about twenty of the strikers who were known as ringleaders. Diéguez, Ibarra, and Baca Calderón were among them. Gutiérrez de Lara escaped to Tucson. For some time the *carcel de Cananea* continued to be crowded with *huelgistas* of all grades and degrees, some, like the one in the ballad quoted at the head of this chapter, in custody because they happened to be in the wrong place at the wrong time. Diéguez and Baca Calderón, future generals in the Revolutionary army, were sentenced to fifteen years in prison and were sent to the dungeons of San Juan de Ulúa, the most notorious of the Mexican political bastilles.[20] Others went elsewhere. The rank and file went back to work.

Their return to their jobs was partly due to Greene, who went among them, as was his way, and urged them to get busy. "I started out at daylight," he said (this was Sunday morning, and he had been up Thursday, Friday, and Saturday nights) "and rode through all the outside Mexican camps, talking with them and urging them to go on and resume work. A few went to work that day. The next morning all resumed work."

As important as Greene's urging, undoubtedly, was a little talk made to about 2,000 of the men by General Torres, also on Sunday. "Anyone not back at work in two days," he promised, "will be drafted into the army and sent to fight the Yaqui Indians."[21]

So it was over. There were no more dead men in the streets.[22] But the repercussions went on and on. The leftist press, seeing a priceless opportunity for propaganda, went into action at once. Two things played into the hands of the radicals. One was injustice — the discrimination in wages, the appropriation of the wealth of the country by foreigners, the assumption of superiority, the proprietary air assumed by these outsiders. Even if the outsiders tried, like Greene, to better the lives of the workmen, they were giving evidence of a *patron* mentality: "The laborer was an essential ingredient in productivity," as one writer put it, "but the owner knew what was best for his worker and, in his infinite wisdom and kindness, distributed his beneficence to his peons."[23]

The other made-to-order issue was the "invasion." An armed group from a foreign country had been not merely allowed but actually invited to set foot on Mexican soil with the object of subduing — or killing — Mexican citizens.

"Our territory," shrieked *Regeneración,* "was invaded by foreign troops brought in by Izábal, and no charge has been brought against this traitor."[24]

The hardest morsel of all for some to swallow was the fact that Izábal had come when summoned by Greene, whose "arrogant messages"[25] showed, supposedly, that he considered the governor of a Mexican state his servant and lackey. Injured national pride caused much of the bad feeling.

As a result of these outcries the legend of Cananea has become one of Mexico's favorite horror stories. The cruelty of Greene and his Janissaries becomes more loathsome with each retelling; the heaps of dead mount skyward; the saintliness of the strikers is magnified. One example will stand for many:

> The director, Colonel Greene, surrounded by a band of assassins armed with rifles, responded to the just demands of the petitioners, ordering his servants to shoot the workers without pity, and gave the example by firing himself on the *peones*. The first volley was terrible. About a hundred corpses and several hundred wounded fell to the earth. The miners tried to defend themselves with knives and stones and attempted to seize Colonel Greene, but they were massacred after a heroic resistance during which a number of the director's assassins were killed.[26]

People who were nowhere near Cananea on June 1, 1906, heard this story so often that they felt they had been there and seen the brutal slaughter for themselves. John Kenneth Turner, the American socialist who did so much to expose the inhumanities of the Díaz regime in the United States, was never in Cananea in his life but had "talked with so many persons who were in one way or another connected with the affair . . . that I cannot but believe that I have a fairly clear idea of what happened." In his version the strikers "never assumed the aggressive" and were shot down as they ran by Greene's men, who drove about in automobiles, "shooting right and left." Greene offered a hundred dollars a man to the Bisbee volunteers and by "grossly misrepresenting the situation" he persuaded them to come to his aid. The Mexican forces under Torres and Kosterlitzky behaved with complete barbarity. "Miners were taken from the jail and hanged. Miners were taken to the cemetery, made to dig their own graves and were shot. Several hundred of them were marched away to Hermosillo, where they were impressed into the Mexican army. Others were sent away to the penal colony on the islands of Tres Marias."[27]

History, in the long run, is what we agree to believe, as these stories quite clearly show. Every Mexican schoolboy who walks through the New Museum of History in Mexico City's Chapultepec Park is sure they are true and historical when he sees near the end of his tour a diorama and a cartoon, supposedly faithful representations of the encounter at Cananea in 1906. The diorama shows a group of unarmed, refined-looking *obreros* under attack by a squad of uniformed Americans directed by Greene from the doorway of the commissary building. The drawing pictures a wild melée in which the workers are being blown to ribbons by cannon

Diorama and cartoon from the Gallery of History, Mexico, D.F.

Arizona Historical Society
A Mexican victim of the strike.

and by pistols as big as cannon, while a commander who looks like General Torres waves his sword in frenzy and bellows commands.

In Cananea some sixty years later it seems quite natural that the strikers who fell should be the Martyrs of 1906. The Cananea *secundaria* school is named for them, and their bodies rest under the monument at the west side of the plaza.[28] They are the heroes of the Mexican Revolution just as the embattled farmers of Concord are the heroes of the American Revolution.

It must be admitted, if the truth is to be told, that American legend-makers have gone even farther than the Mexicans in revising the facts about the unfortunate events under discussion. Perhaps the most imaginative of the revisers is Jack Ganzhorn, who says he was holed up in the servants' quarters behind Greene's house during the rioting. Another group of defenders fought from behind the stone fence which surrounded the big house.

When the Mexicans got organized and drunk enough to fight, the circus opened in full blast. About a thousand of them, all bunched, charged the wall in front of Greene's house. Allison held his men's fire till the Mexicans were within seventy yards — then let them have it. Meanwhile, we in the adobe cracked .45's as fast as we could trigger and load. A man couldn't miss that packed mob. They piled up in twos and threes. . . . Now the dead and wounded out in front were too thick to count with any accuracy, but the dead alone numbered well over 130.

The dynamiters who failed to show up during the two-day engagement appear in Ganzhorn's pseudo-history, disappearing in a yellow cloud of their own smoke when the defenders put a couple of bullets into their supply of explosives.[29]

If there is a kernel of truth in this story, it may lie in the fate of the unsuspecting Mexican who came in from Naco, walked past the Greene house, and was shot on suspicion that he was carrying dynamite. Great oak trees grow from these small acorns.

Greene was bitter for the rest of his life against all red-flaggers, revolutionaries, and socialist agitators. He blamed the Western Federation of Miners as much as he did the Mexican revolutionaries for what had happened to him, and he was certain that a substantial number of them had infiltrated his organization and encouraged the strike. On Sunday, when work was resumed in the mines, he let the word get around that the Company knew who these men were and that they would be picked up very shortly. It is said that some three hundred American workmen did not show up at the works on Monday morning and were presumed to have found means to reenter the United States.[30]

Not content with eliminating the infection from his camp, Greene attacked it at its source. He sent one of his top policemen, named Rowan, to St. Louis to set up a spy organization of his own. Rowan transmitted confidential reports indicating that he had planted a contact inside the miners' headquarters who dug up some remarkable — if true — bits of information. New campaigns were under way to make trouble in Cananea financed by none other than Greene's old enemy John W. Gates. A dynamiter had been sent to Bisbee to blow up "certain people."[31] And so on. In September, Greene went in person to St. Louis and helped to break up the headquarters of the Mexican revolutionists. His partner and agent A. B. Fall said later in a letter to the president of the United States that Greene had helped to "seize their printing presses, etc., including private papers, lists of agents, and those acting with them in the United States," which he turned over to U.S. agents.[32]

There can be no doubt that the strike gave Greene a major shakeup, and as a result, he was implacable against the agitators afterward, willing to go to almost any lengths to bring them to book. Lázaro Gutiérrez de Lara, for instance, got away to Tucson and then Los Angeles, but Greene had him picked up on a charge of stealing wood in Cananea. Gutiérrez De Lara explained that in 1903 he had served as legal representative of a widow who owned the timber and had authorized the cutting in her name. He was released on a plea that the Statute of Limitations protected him and that the value of the wood had not been shown to exceed twenty-five dollars. The object of the suit was to have him extradited to Mexico, where his fate undoubtedly would have been hard.[33]

Sixty years after, we still wonder about many aspects of the riot. Could it have been avoided? If the Metcalf brothers had not overreacted, would the demonstration have been peaceful? Was it just a strike for higher wages, or was it an abortive attempt to start the Revolution?

President Díaz told Ambassador Thompson that it was an uprising against his government.[34] Ricardo Flores Magón and his men actually crossed the Rio Grande in September, three months after the strike, and tried unsuccessfully to overthrow Díaz by force of arms.[35] If the strikers had been successful in Cananea, the movement might have spread to other communities. As it turned out, the day of reckoning had to be postponed until 1910.

The Descent Begins

JUNE CONTINUED WARM AND SUNNY, and peace of a sort descended on Cananea. The great black plumes of smelter smoke rose skyward once more. The timekeepers checked the men in at the mines. Their women came to the Company stores as usual for flour and beans. Colonel Greene, portly but neat in his business suit and Stetson, mounted the steps of his new private car, which he had named the *Verde* after himself,[1] and rattled away on his endless journeys.

He seemed normal and cheerful. An outsider could not have suspected how much was wrong with him and his enterprises; what constant worry he lived with; how close to desperation he sometimes came. He was still able to master his inner tensions. His energy seemed to be unlimited. It was part of his business to be always cheerful and confident, and cheerful and confident he was.

He had to be extra careful not to show his concern now, for the *huelga,* the strike, had set in motion a chain reaction of difficulties. Nothing really serious. But bad enough! Production and marketing were thrown out of step and the Company's ability to pay its bills, always delicately balanced, was impaired. Treasurer John Campbell had to ask for an extension of time from a number of firms who were requesting payment for overdue accounts. The losses in property and production occasioned by the strike, he explained, "places us in a position which necessitates our making this request."[2] Greene always fretted over this sort of thing.

Along with financial embarrassment came worry and some dissension within his business family. The newspapers and magazines were alarmed

[207]

by the strike, fearful of revolution in Mexico, afraid that there was some imperialistic fire in Cananea to produce all this revolutionary smoke. He could stand disapprobation from outsiders — he was used to it — but even a hint of dissatisfaction among his close associates was hard for him to bear. He was badly stung when two of the directors of Greene Cananea resigned: Judge W. D. Cornish, vice-president of the Union Pacific, and Thomas F. Wilson, a capitalist from Minneapolis. Both were supposed to be "Harriman people," loyal to E. H. Harriman of the Southern Pacific, the magnate with whom Greene had repeatedly skirmished and repeatedly made up. Greene's railroad operations were sometimes thorns in Harriman's tender flesh since he was involved in railroading in Mexico. Did these men want out because Harriman was irritated about something? Did the strike have something to do with it? One of them mentioned "the pressure of other business interests." The other said nothing at all.[3]

The rising pressure was felt by every Company official. The gossip mills of New York ground out their daily quotas of rumor and insinuation, provoking Greene to telegraph that "the report that many employees have resigned is false."[4] And Secretary George Robbins turned a cheerful face to the lowering heavens when he promised George Young that the Company "would go right on doing business in spite of no longer having the support of the Harriman people."[5]

At Cananea some straws in the wind pointed in the wrong direction also. The Norwich Union Fire Insurance Company explained, convincingly, that it was not liable for the loss of the lumber yard, and there went about $350,000![6] On the first of July General Manager Dwight resigned and was replaced by David Cole, no official reason given.

The signs of trouble were there, but to his own people Greene had never seemed more impregnable and indestructible than he did in the summer of 1906. They could not say too much in praise of him and his triumph. He had saved the enterprise from destruction. He was "a giant in physical and moral courage." He "towered above all others."[7]

This incense burning seemed justified by the apparent prosperity of everything the Colonel touched. All his enterprises were on the verge — the very verge — of wonderful developments. The high whine of the saws was sounding louder in the lumber mills at Madera. Those mills, the key to success for the Sierra Madre Land and Lumber Company, had started operations on a small scale, and machinery had been ordered which would increase capacity to half a million feet of lumber a day — making Madera the biggest producer on the North American continent.[8] The subsidiary enterprises — turpentine plant, tannery, paper pulp plant, furniture factory, planing mill — would begin to produce as soon as equipment could be brought in.

Emadair Chase Jones

Sixty-stamp mill at Concheño, with construction under way for forty stamps more.

In the meantime, just as soon as the railroad was finished from Temosachic to Madera, mine timbers and lumber could be brought to Cananea by way of Chihuahua, El Paso, and Naco. Completion was only a few weeks away, and Greene spoke of it as if it were already accomplished.[9]

Greene Gold-Silver was likewise just poised on the brink of big production. A 300-ton mill was in operation at Concheño in 1905, and Greene had plans for enlarging this plant and building a smelter at Dedrick.[10] Mountains of rich ore were ready for the miners, and concentrates were on their way to Cananea for refining.[11] In October Greene opened a bank at Temosachic with F. E. Beecher in charge. To encourage the workers at Ocampo, sixty miles from Temosachic at the end of the new wagon road, he contributed $5,000 toward the building of a new school, added $1,500 for books and furniture, and gave $1,000 for a church.[12]

At Cananea, in spite of the troublesome straws in the wind, there was cause for optimism. The mercantile department was doing so much business that additional space had to be provided, and prices were going down.[13] Electric power reached the Mesa in August.[14] A station for the branch line of the Southern Pacific, building from Nogales to Cananea, was under construction.[15] Plans for a soap factory, a packing plant, and a lard-rendering plant were announced.[16] A bandstand (gift of Colonel Greene) and other improvements were added to the central plaza.[17] His stable of racehorses at Phoenix was concrete evidence of the master's prosperity,[18] and a dividend of two million dollars for stockholders of Greene Consolidated should have been the final reassurance.[19]

It all fitted together so beautifully in Greene's mind, each part of the great whole contributing to every other part, everything working together yet making its own contribution — the railroads, the mines, the lumber — with electric power and agriculture just around the corner! The Greene empire! It was so close to becoming a reality. The narrow margin by which he missed made the collapse of the mighty structure, when it finally came, all the harder for him to bear.

He was so confident of success that he even prepared to leave behind him, as a sort of legacy to posterity, an institution for carrying on his work. He planned to found and endow a College of Mining at Cananea where bright young men could learn metallurgy and contribute to the development of northern Mexico after Greene himself had retired from the field. In November of 1906 he submitted his plan to the government in Mexico City for approval, and he had no reason to fear that it would be rejected.[20]

It pleased him to think that although he had not been to college himself, he could provide educational facilities for the W. C. Greenes of the future, bright boys with energy and ambition who needed only a chance. Staff would be no problem. There were plenty of trained mining men working for the Company, and the exceptional ones like Dr. Ricketts, who had a Ph.D. from Princeton, could provide the links between the practical and academic approaches to mining science. Such a school would be a monument worthy of his struggles and successes — almost the best he could have, next to the smelter stacks at Cananea. He liked to think of it in the rare moments when business let him choose his own thoughts.

Yes, there was much to encourage him in the summer and fall of 1906, but he had constant reminders that no man lives forever and no man sees all his dreams come true. There was a pain in his chest that told him so, more and more often. At first he refused to think much about it, refusing to slow down or give in to the cries of his body for rest. He was pleased when he could outride and outshoot everybody on the great hunt, but a year later it caught up with him and he had to go to Hot Springs, Arkansas, for treatment. The El Paso papers said he was suffering from an attack of rheumatism—so painful he had cut short a trip to Guaymas with Epes Randolph of the Southern Pacific.[21] The news stories kept reassuring the public that he was in excellent health[22] — a good way of convincing them that he probably was not. His exertions during the Cananea riots certainly did him no good and reminded him again that he did not have forever. In November, returning from California, he was taken sick on the train again.[23]

The fact was never mentioned outside the family,[24] but his heart was going bad. He suffered from angina pectoris, and angina is something one does not ignore. Anxiety and exhaustion are bad for an angina patient, and even before the riots Greene was anxious and exhausted.

Money was always a worry. He had to have it for his enormous payrolls, for the hundreds of men working on his railroad, in his mines, in his sawmills, on his ranches. He had to have it to pay the avalanche of bills which poured into his offices every month. He had to have it when the bear raiders attacked him in New York and he needed to protect his stock. Most of all he had to have it because conditions were changing in the Cananea mines. He explained to the stockholders: "During the past few months, our development has shown a large increase in the amount of sulphur contents of our ores and has accentuated the need for roasters and additional reverberatory capacity as recommended by Mr. Dwight and Mr. Lloyd in our last report."[25]

This actually meant that as it became necessary to work lower-grade ores, the reduction plant had to be revised to handle them profitably. Greene was not exaggerating when he said that there was ore in sight to keep the plant busy for many years, but it averaged out around three and a half percent copper — and the Cananea furnaces were not built to handle it efficiently.[26] The cost of production was going up all the time.

There was no great need for worry at the moment. The price of copper was high, the margin of profit was satisfactory, and until conditions changed, the Company could make money and pay dividends (Greene was paying 24% in 1906). But sooner or later the price had to go down, and what then?

Greene found a way to tell his stockholders the truth and yet keep them happy. He reported that the Company policy was to work low-grade ore while prices were high. He did not stress the fact that the Company had only low-grade ores to work at the moment, but in his defense it must be admitted that some good-grade deposits had been located by his exploration crews. George Young described the situation in a letter to Secretary Robbins back in New York:

> To sum the matter up, the efficiency of all the operating departments is greater today than ever before in the history of the Company, and the sole reason for the high copper costs is the grade of ore which is being treated, and this also is the only reason in the world why we are not producing more copper. The grade of ore is up to the Lord, and there seems to be a good prospect of his doing something for us in that direction before long. Just how soon we will begin to reap benefit from the bodies of direct smelting ores now being blocked out is a question which I cannot undertake to answer. Meantime you may rest assured that every man in the service of the Company in Cananea is doing his level best to make the maximum production at the minimum cost.[27]

Green was very much concerned about production and profit — so much so that he asked George Young, his auditor, for a breakdown. He learned that during the fiscal year ending July 31, 1906, the Company's profits on copper were $2,836,629.66.

Dividends amounted to $2,182,400.

The net profit was $654,229.66.

Subtracting the cost of development work and exploration — half a million dollars — the remainder was $70,515.34.

In view of the millions needed for reconstructing the plant, this was a drop in the bucket. The funds required to replace the blast furnaces, rebuild the converters, and reclaim the flue dust were not going to come from such tiny leftovers.

Still, the Company was making money. The net profit on a pound of copper was a little over half a cent a pound. George Young did not quote the price per pound of production, but it was somewhere between twelve and fifteen cents.[28] In October of 1906 it was down to less than eleven cents, the lowest in several months.[29]

George noted with indignation:

> A statement has been made that the dividends declared and paid by the Company during the past year were not earned. This is absolutely wrong as the . . . analysis of the deductions from income in the published Income Statement will show.

A long succession of "authorities" have repeated this charge since 1906, most of them without any real knowledge of the situation. A contemporary scholar, without a blush, says that Greene's dividends came "out of later receipts from sales of stock — one of the oldest tricks in the portfolio of the shady promoter. Greene kept his books so badly that none of his figures was really reliable. It later appeared that the Company had never produced copper as cheaply as it claimed, and it is doubtful whether Greene ever knew what his copper cost him."[30]

Greene's accountants turned over in their graves, en masse, when that statement was made, but they could not have denied that Greene was operating on a very close margin of profit.

In former years when Greene had to raise money to enlarge and improve his plant, he followed a well-established routine. First he acquired more mining claims and increased production in the ones he already had. He could then show a need for plant enlargement and persuade his stockholders to authorize the issue of more shares. He did this for the last time in February 1906, increasing the capitalization by 864,000 shares — making the total an even million. The stockholders approved the issue with considerable hesitation, and Greene knew that he could not hope to raise money again in this fashion for some time.[31] He had three million dollars in the treasury, but he needed five, and he was afraid he could not hope to finish providing what was needed: the new smelter on San Pedro Creek; the slimes treatment plant; the roasters for high-sulphide ores; a bigger chamber for reclaiming flue dust.[32] Well, maybe the Lord would provide, though he was more inclined to trust himself than to call on any outside agency. He could at least start. So he began tearing out the old furnaces in the smelter and getting ready to install new ones which would operate more efficiently and could be charged automatically instead of by hand.

He also sent Kirk and Massey to look into a report that there was a better way to mine low-grade copper ore than the system of "square sets" that had been employed up to that moment. He reported to the stockholders in October:

During the past year, the Company has been gradually preparing for the installation of the caving system of mining. We are now operating the system upon the Esperanza and Henrietta mines and will in a few months have the system installed on the Veta Grande, Oversight, and Massey bodies. The change into the caving system has naturally entailed a large amount of expense. . . .[33]

There was one other thing he could do. Since 1904 he had held an exploration concession from the Mexican government authorizing him to prospect a large tract of land south and east of his Cananea properties. Through 1904 and 1905 he had not made any serious attempt to explore this new ground, but in 1906 he went vigorously to work to look into its possibilities. This too cost money — but it had to be done if production was to be maintained.[34]

It turned out that other people were doing development work too in the same general area. One was Greene's old rival Lycurgus Lindsay.

Stories began to circulate that he had located rich new ore bodies on his America claim. Not far away from the America was another mine called the Cananea-Duluth, which also began to make noises which sounded like money. Both properties had been optioned by the Lewisohn brothers of New York, but when they allowed their claims to lapse, Greene stepped in and tied them up himself.

Between the two was a wide strip of unclaimed land which the Colonel denounced in his own name.[35]

At this point he found himself in communication with Thomas F. Cole, one of the shrewdest and most successful operators in the copper business. Behind Cole was John D. Ryan, his friend and associate, who had been made president of Anaconda the year before. They were both heavily interested in mines at Butte, Montana, which meant that they were part of the Amalgamated Copper complex. Ryan was, in fact, on his way to the presidency of Amalgamated.[36]

With typical diplomacy the historian of Anaconda remarks that Ryan and Cole "had eyed the Cananea district for some time." As a matter of fact Greene had complained for years that men connected with Amalgamated were always trying to beat him at his "great big game." He had always managed to avoid the snares that were laid for him, however, and he was on friendly terms with the men in charge. Tom Lawson, in fact, had lumped him with them as part of THE SYSTEM, and Greene had defended Rockefeller and Rogers at the time of Lawson's attack. There was no reason why they could not talk business, and apparently Cole made the first move. When he heard in July that something new was being added to the mineral prospects at Cananea, he sent his engineers to look into it and made his contact with Colonel Greene.

There was nothing really novel in this approach. Cole and Ryan liked to infiltrate the edges of an established mining district and try to pick up something others had overlooked. They had done this in the Bisbee District, where they were developing the profitable Calumet and Arizona at Warren and giving the venerable Copper Queen plenty of competition. Now they were ready to move into Cananea.

The partners in what was to be for Greene a dance of death took their places about the middle of July. Unannounced and without any fanfare whatever, Thomas F. Cole came to Cananea accompanied by Captain James Hoatson, a copper magnate from Michigan. Ostensibly, they wanted to inspect the America, Copper Belt, and Cananea-Duluth mines. Greene knew they were coming and had brought L. L. Lindsay (owner of the America) in the *Verde* from Chihuahua to take his part in the financial minuet.

The story broke in the newspapers on July 21: Greene and Cole had gone into partnership. They took up Greene's options and were said to have paid $2,225,000 for the America and $500,000 for the Cananea-Duluth.[37] It is entirely possible that these figures were highly exaggerated.

A week later announcement was made that the partnership had been formalized as a new corporation, the Cananea Central Copper Company, with headquarters at Duluth, Minnesota, where Cole and a number of the major stockholders lived. For his option on the America and the Cananea-Duluth, plus his claim to the vacant land between the two and title to the Bryan, Seguro, Square, and Massey No. 2 mines, Greene received two million dollars in Cananea Central Stock.[38]

Greene's friends regarded the deal as a great coup for him and spoke of the two million dollars as a "handsome present" to the Greene Consolidated stockholders.[39] Like the Greeks, however, the Amalgamated men were most to be feared when they came bearing gifts. Business historians have been inclined to assume that Greene was outplayed by a pair of clever operators who joined him when they could not lick him and then froze him out. Since his company was taken away from him, in toto, less than six months later, this theory is easy to accept. On the other hand it is quite certain that Greene knew he had to have help, and these were powerful allies who could put the company back on its feet. Always a gambler, Greene may have taken a calculated risk, hoping that he would be able to stay in control of his company. At this late date the truth cannot be certainly known.

The Cole-Ryan people, as one historian says, had plenty of money but no really good mines, whereas Greene had plenty of good mines but not enough money.[40] Before anything further could be done, it seemed necessary that the properties of the new partnership should be given a better image. At once newspaper stories began playing up the America as a great potential producer. Huge new bodies of ore were said to have been located. New shafts had been, or were about to be, sunk. The poor old tired America suddenly became the belle of the mining ball. The stories declared that 14,000 acres of mineral land were being added to the company's holdings, and all the mines controlled by Cananea Central were promising. The campaign was managed so expertly that all interested citizens in Cananea were convinced that the town was on the eve of a period of unparalleled prosperity with copper ore pouring into the smelters from all sides and a potential population of 100,000 happy people.[41]

The reason for all this promotion became obvious at the end of December when Greene Consolidated and Cananea Central merged. A new holding company, known as Greene Cananea Copper Company, was organized at Duluth with T. F. Cole as president and Greene as vice-president. It looked as if the America build-up had been for the purpose of making the two merging companies seem more like equals and providing a base for an enormous stock issue.

Greene's directors approved the merger on December 17, and on that same day Greene got out a circular letter to the stockholders informing them — not asking them — about the deals that had been made.

In view of the very large ore bodies that have been developed during the past few months, the necessity of increased reduction capacity, spoken of in my last Annual Report, became more apparent. . . . The estimated cost of these improvements, together with the necessary transportation facilities, will be about $5,000,000. Several plans were discussed by the directors of your Company of the best means of raising this additional capital, among which was a proposed increase of 250,000 shares of capital stock . . . at a price of $25.00 per share. In view of the present financial conditions, this was considered inadvisable.

A proposition was then considered by the stockholders of the two companies looking to a merger of the Cananea Central Copper Company and the Greene Consolidated Copper Company. A plan has been formulated by which a holding company, to be known as the Greene Cananea Copper Company, a corporation under the laws of Minnesota with main offices at Duluth, would take over the stock of the two companies.[42]

It was intended that the new holding company would absorb the stock of its two component units. It was obviously impossible to tell the stockholders that they had to make the exchange, but the deal was made attractive by offering 1½ shares of the new company for each share of Greene Consolidated. A million and a half shares of the new company out of 2,500,000 were to be held for Greene Consolidated stockholders; 1,000,000 for those in Cananea Central at 1⅔ for one. Par value of Greene Cananea was $20 a share.

The deal sounded like a replay of the organization of Amalgamated in 1899 when the incorporators voted themselves a lot of money by issuing a huge block of stock. Fifty years after the event of 1906, historians describe the $50,000,000 stock issue as "unbelievable" and a "fantastic watered figure"[43] — though they admit it might be justified by later production figures.

The New Yorkers made it worth Greene's while to go along.

Stockholders of the Cananea Central Copper Company will take over and pay for in cash to the Treasurer of the Greene Consolidated Copper Company the 200,000 shares of the Cananea Central stock held by the Greene Consolidated Copper Company. The price of $4,000,000 cash has been paid in escrow to the Wells Fargo & Company's bank in this city to be delivered to the Treasurer of the Greene Consolidated Copper Company upon the completion of the organization of the Greene Cananea Copper Company, and legal details necessary.[44]

No stock was offered to the public, although Greene managed to find some for Billy Brophy and the "boys" at Bisbee and Cananea.[45]

It was neatly and efficiently done. Cole and Ryan, says Isaac Marcosson, "provided the $6,000,000 necessary to clean up Greene's financial situation."[46] Immediately plans were announced for expansion and revision of the works — doubling the capacity of the concentrators, building a new slimes treatment plant, overhauling the smelters. The business was said to be in "splendid condition."

The result was a dramatic shift in attitude toward Greene stocks. The stories about reorganization had set up a nervous reaction among stockholders and in November there was a wave of selling. "Greene is being heavily sold from New York," the stories said. "Stock prices are sagging"; "the action of Greene is at present very disappointing."[47] A week later the tendency had reversed itself. In Boston Greene was "the most active stock, selling up to 29⅝." The next day it went up to 33.

There was always a correlation between Greene's public image and the price of his stock. As news of the merger spread and the stock began to rise, Greene was once again a hero, a "benefactor to his fellow man,"[48] a superior being who operated on a plane far above the activities of ordinary mortals.

To Greene's ears these plaudits must have begun to sound extraordinarily hollow and meaningless. He was close to ruin, and he knew it.

For the last time he played host to the copper giants when late in December they came to Cananea for another "inspection." Led by Thomas F. Cole and John D. Ryan, they arrived on December 31 in two special cars at the El Paso station on their way to Cananea. Colonel Greene, coming in from New York, had arrived at Chicago behind schedule, hired an engine to pull the *Verde,* and overtaken the main party at Bucklin, Kansas. Mayor Charles Davis and a group of El Paso notables entertained the group at lunch at the St. Regis Hotel. El Paso, for the moment, was still Colonel Greene's town.[49]

The capitalists spent ten days at Cananea deliberating and laying plans. One important result was the appointment of Dr. Louis D. Ricketts as general manager. He had been in control at Globe for Phelps Dodge but had served since 1903 as a consultant for the Four C's.[50] Now he was in charge of the entire plant, ready to continue the reconstruction program which Greene had already begun, and great was the rejoicing among stockholders, officers, and directors. With the Doctor in command, everybody felt safe and able to relax. Even Greene was pleased,

Compañía Minera de Cananea
The converter floor as it appeared in 1908.

for he shared their confidence in Ricketts, but he was already on the side-lines in the decision-making department and foresaw, with deep depression, what was about to happen to him.

He left a day before the rest and on January 11, 1907, was on board the *Verde* headed for New York.[51]

It is said in the border country that Cole and Ryan had an interesting experience en route to Naco the following day. A poker game got started in their private car in which one of the participants was a local man who operated under local rules. When the game did not go to suit him, he pulled a pistol and was barely prevented from killing another of the players. It gave Cole and Ryan, as the phrase used to go, "a turn." As they paced the platform at Naco waiting for another engine, Ryan, an extremely correct and dignified gentleman, turned to Cole and said,

"I wonder how the story would look in the New York papers if that man had pulled the trigger."[52]

To a top man from Wall Street, firearms seemed brutal and in bad taste, but he had weapons in his armory which were just as deadly. They were brought out and used at a meeting of the Greene Consolidated Copper Company held in New York two weeks later, on February 15, 1907. The exchange of Greene Consolidated shares for Greene Cananea shares had put the Cole-Ryan combination in the driver's seat. They had the votes to take the Company away from Greene and they did so. W. D. Thornton was elected president. George S. Robbins, who had served so long and faithfully as secretary, was replaced by J. W. Allen. Alfred Romer, the treasurer, gave way to C. D. Fraser. Since there was no remedy, the entire board of directors resigned and were immediately replaced.[53] It was a complete housecleaning. The operating corporation in Mexico, the Four C's, continued more or less as before, but Greene and all his New York staff were gone — without a word; without a chance to fight. They must have left the meeting a stunned and speechless little group.

Cole and Ryan, since they had undertaken to set the Cananea enterprise on its feet, naturally wanted to do the job their own way. Greene understood that. But he was still crushed and defeated. The Copper Skyrocket, which had carried him so high, had brought him down again, all the way to the earth.

Back to Earth

COLONEL GREENE'S RIGHT-HAND MAN in Mexico in 1906 was Albert Bacon Fall, a forty-six-year-old lawyer who later became a senator and later still Secretary of the Interior in the administration of his friend Warren G. Harding. Fall's brilliant career was brought to an unhappy conclusion by the Teapot Dome affair and other scandals of the Harding era.

Slender, erect, hawk-eyed and keen witted, Fall was an unusually attractive and forceful personality. As a lawyer and businessman he was aggressive and sometimes pugnacious, rough on his rivals and opponents, but completely loyal to his friends. His efficiency and loyalty made him Greene's most important ally during the final phase of the Colonel's spectacular flight through the financial firmament.

Son of a Kentucky family reduced in circumstances by the Civil War, Fall scrambled for a living in Kentucky, Texas, and the plains country, working as a teacher, cowboy, farm hand, cook, and real-estate agent, reading good books and studying at night. In 1883, still in his early twenties, he began a long love affair with Mexico.[1] Traveling on horseback, he crossed the country from east to west, acquired mining property in the state of Zacatecas, learned Spanish, and developed a real affection for the Mexicans, whom he described as the most "charitable, hospitable, naturally kindly and courteous" people he had ever encountered.[2] He knew them all, from the *peon* all the way up to President Porfirio Díaz.

In 1884 he came back to the United States, swung a hammer in the mines at Hillsboro, New Mexico, and finally opened a law office in Las Cruces, where he went into politics. He retained some of his interests in Mexico, however, and remained for many years deeply involved in Mexican affairs. When he became a senator he thought of himself as a spokesman for and defender of the humble Mexicans on both sides of the border who could not speak for themselves, and he was called on to testify as an expert on Mexican affairs when his senatorial colleagues needed to tap his special experience.[3]

Fall's association with Greene resulted from their ventures in Mexico. Fall says that he spent much time prospecting in the Sierra Madre country "along the line of Sonora and Chihuahua" in 1899. He also grubstaked other searchers, including one Sam Dedrick, who sold Fall some promising claims in order to raise money to see what was on the other side of the mountain. In the course of a trip to New York, Fall met the Colonel, and they talked of Sam Dedrick's claims, among other things. Greene wanted to have them appraised, and they talked some more. The acquaintance quickly ripened, and, in a matter of days, Greene retained Fall as his personal lawyer. Fall told his family that Greene "made him dizzy with the rapidity of his decisions"; that he was fascinated and "found himself constantly hanging onto Greene's coattails to keep him down to earth." The two men complemented each other, respected each other, and developed a sincere affection for each other.[4]

They became partners in the Sierra Madre Land and Lumber Company in 1904. Fall had a Mexican associate, Senator Roman Alcazar of Guanajuato, who joined him in taking an option on a large tract of timber land in the Sierra Madre belonging to Telesforo García of Mexico City. "This land," Fall said, "I turned over to Col. W. C. Greene, who formed a lumber company for handling same."[5]

Fall had a hand in all of Greene's major enterprises. He was the top legal adviser for both Greene Gold-Silver and the Land and Lumber Company, with an office in New York. He was vice-president and general counsel of the Rio Grande, Sierra Madre, and Pacific Railroad, the line from El Paso-Juarez to Nueva Casas Grandes, and president of the Sierra Madre and Pacific, organized in 1907 to build from Nueva Casas Grandes south to Madera. He was Greene's second in command for all the Mexican enterprises outside the Cananea area. The relationship between them could not have been more warm and friendly. They had absorbed the same frontier philosophy whose first principle was: "You never let your partner down."

In view of this basic premise, Fall's course of conduct in the summer of 1906 may need a little explanation. Even before the tragic events of June 1, he had become uneasy about the future of Greene's empire. So had a great many other people. One of them, a "New York copper man," remarked in August:

If Colonel Greene ever comes to grief, it will be because he has tried to do too much without adequate capital. He has many enemies in Wall Street who take advantage of his weakness. He has always won out in the past although at a great financial loss to himself at many times, but unless he is very careful, Harriman and other Wall Street interests will lasso him and if they ever get him down, they will never let him up.[6]

Fall was nothing if not perceptive, and from his strategic position in the very center of Greene's web of corporations, he could see the signs of approaching change long before the public, or even Greene's local managers, could possibly do so. He knew that Cole and Ryan were moving into a position of strength. He knew that Greene planned to pay out another big dividend in October. He knew that the Mexican ventures were close to the edge financially. Besides, he was not in good health[7]; he was having to live away from his family most of the time; and he wanted to get into the mainstream of New Mexico politics. Statehood was coming up; it could mean high position for Albert B. Fall. He made up his mind to sever all ties — get out of Mexico once and for all.

Fall stated in 1919:

When it became evident to me that the affairs of the company were being conducted recklessly, I sold to my associates in the company or companies, everything that had a sales value for anything I could get for it and resigned all association with the companies.[8]

He came out on July 14, 1906. All his life he remembered that date. Undoubtedly he had very mixed feelings about doing it, but he had a wife and a family and a flock of political ambitions. There was no break with Greene. Fall kept the power of attorney Greene had given him in case he should need it — and before long he did.

In the meantime, he took the money he brought out of Mexico, plus what he had made in his New Mexican ventures as lawyer, miner, and land owner, and became the sole possessor of the great Three Rivers Ranch just north of Tularosa, New Mexico, in the shadow of 12,000-foot Sierra Blanca Peak and within sight of the gleaming White Sands — a lovely spot which was to be his home for the rest of his life, and his nemesis.[9] He also had a fine Georgian house on a hilltop in El Paso, which was his home away from home.[10]

Through the first half of 1907 it looked as if Fall's withdrawal had been a mistake. Business had never been better. The price of copper kept rising and reached a good plateau in March. Greene seemed confident and secure, and was reaching out, as always, for new things. He bought land for a home in Redlands, California, where he planned to spend the winters, and there was talk about his going into the oil business. The house at

Redlands never rose above the foundations, but he did buy a residence in the old West Adams section of Los Angeles, where his son Charles was born, and made it his second home.[11]

For a time all publicity was favorable. "Greene Erects New Mill at Concheño";[12] "Pushing Work on Greene Gold-Silver Property"; "A Big Chihuahua Concession for Colonel Greene"[13] — so ran the headlines. The Colonel, in his old magisterial manner, issued reassuring pronouncements: "I can confidently assert that . . . within a few years the Greene Gold-Silver Company will alone produce more gold values from the mines owned by it than the entire amount of gold now produced in the Republic of Mexico."[14] To show that he was still moving onward and upward, he formed a new corporation, the Sierra Madre and Pacific, to complete the rail link between Nueva Casas Grandes and Madera.[15]

The Colonel never talked about his feelings, at least for publication, and it is impossible after all these years to know what was going on in his mind, but he probably never acknowledged, even to himself, that the situation was really critical. He had pulled his chestnuts out of the fire so many times when nobody thought he could do it. He was always sure he could do it again. This time, however, things were different. The Gold-Silver Company was by no means ready to begin big production. The Land and Lumber Company was likewise at a stage where much money must be spent to get into really profitable activity. The railroad from Temosachic to Madera was well under way, but it was not finished; and the great sawmills were among the things hoped for but not seen. The payrolls of these two potentially profitable companies were enormous, and the sums owing for new machinery, housing, roads, stores, equipment, and supplies were astronomical likewise. With luck, the Colonel might make it. But could his fantastic good fortune hold out much longer? That was the real question.

The danger lay in the fact that all his companies were interlocked and dependent on each other. There was sometimes a good practical reason for the relationship. For instance, the Four C's owned a good many tracts of land outside the town of Cananea which it leased to the Cananea Cattle Company, owned by Colonel W. C. Greene. The reason was that the Copper Company wanted to retain title to the areas where there was a chance of finding minerals. The Company also wanted to control the ranch land immediately adjacent to the town as a sort of buffer zone between its business and the outside world. The Four C's, which was making money and expanding, was really the heart of all Greene's promotion. Almost everything started with the Four C's and came back to the Four C's. The Yaqui River dam and power project was intended to bring electric power to Cananea and cut costs there. The Cananea Cattle Company had a contract to supply beef to the Four C's. The Greene railroads were conceived in the first place as a means of getting supplies into and products out of Cananea. The Land and Lumber Company was intended to supply the Four C's with mine timbers and Cananea with lumber for construction. The Four C's owned 51 percent of the Land and Lumber Company. When the Cole-Ryan combination took over the Four C's, all of Greene's projects were placed in jeopardy.

Greene realized that he was vulnerable, and on October 25, 1906, he tried to strengthen his hand by negotiating a contract between Cananea Consolidated Copper (which, at least on paper, he still controlled) and the lumber company. It obligated the copper company to absorb at least a million dollars worth of the lumber company's product every year, "at current prices." One of the first acts of the Greene Cananea management, after the takeover, was to cancel this contract made between Greene and Greene and substitute a more reasonable one which committed the Company to buy only what timber products it needed — "at current prices."[16]

Not even George Young, general auditor for the Four C's, could follow all the ins and outs of the financing outside his own special area. When Dr. Ricketts, at the beginning of his time as general manager, asked about the ownership and financing of the railroad from Temosachic to Madera, Young replied:

> It seems to me likely that the money for construction has been advanced to the Cananea Consolidated Copper Company's railway so called by the Sierra Madre Land & Lumber Company. The only charges which our books show against the latter company are $650,000 gold, being the purchase price of 51% of its capital stock. The books of the Greene Company at July 31st showed a loan to the Sierra Madre Land and Lumber Company secured by their bonds of $400,316.67. I believe there have been some additional loans since that date, but the only statement which I had, which would show this, namely, Balance Sheet of the Greene Company's books as of November 30th, 1906, was taken away by the public accountants.[17]

The one certain fact among these financial uncertainties was the danger to other parts of the structure if one part were removed. The Copper Company, the Lumber Company and the Gold-Silver Company were like a three-legged stool. Take away one leg, the other two must fall together. The new management took away one leg. W. D. Thornton, who replaced Greene as president of Greene Consolidated, made this clear in his first report to the stockholders:

> Referring to the 51 percent of the stock of the Sierra Madre Land and Lumber Company owned by the Cananea Consolidated Copper Company, your company had advanced large sums to the lumber company, and as to carry on that enterprise still further large advances would be necessary, it was deemed

wise to retire from this enterprise. The 51 percent of the lumber company stock was sold for $2,000,000 on deferred payments secured by deposit of 75 percent of the lumber company stock as collateral.[18]

Mr. Thornton did not mention the fact that the buyer of this block of stock, costing $2,000,000, was W. C. Greene. In order to get everything straight, the Lumber Company (meaning W. C. Greene) repaid to the Copper Company "its cash advances aggregating about $1,000,000 and has also paid off notes for $150,000 which had been guaranteed by us."[19]

So Greene gave up over $3,000,000 to get his lumber company out of hock, and he had six years to make good on two of those millions. It was a backbreaking load, but Greene might have managed it if the panic of 1907 had not come along. He could not foresee it, of course — nobody could — and he went on doing business, and spending money, as usual. When Eduardo Arnold of Cananea made a copper strike in the Santa Cruz Mountains between Nogales and Cananea, Greene rushed over and got his share, denouncing four thousand *pertenencias* of potentially rich ground,[20] and he bought into another field near Patagonia in southern Arizona.[21] In April he tossed away $51,000 in a gesture which was, in its way, magnificent and showed a side of his character which would have puzzled his New York friends.

A year before, he had encouraged his employees to invest in Greene Gold-Silver stock at par value — $10 a share. Although it was selling below that figure, he assured them that in a year or less it would sell for more. His prediction did not come true. In April 1907 it was selling for $1.50. Greene announced that he would make the losses good. The investors brought in their stock and he gave them their money back.[22] It was this sort of generosity which gave Greene his heroic stature and brought him closer to ruin.

Ruin was just around the corner for a good many people, but through the spring and summer of 1907 the economy was apparently in the best of health. Copper was at its peak. On May 17 market reports placed it at 25 cents a pound.[23] The price slumped temporarily in March, but nobody worried. In June it dropped again, and this time it stayed down. By June 17, "not a pound of copper is selling at any price."[24] The market went lower and lower. On September 20 copper was down to 15½, and the Cananea mines began to curtail production. The downward trend persisted, and by mid-October the metal market was "thoroughly demoralized."[25] Dr. Ricketts announced that the Cananea mines would shut down in November. The panic of 1907 had gripped the country.

Some people thought of it as a "copper scare"[26] brought on by a bear raid on United Copper.[27] Others blamed the outmoded banking laws which prevented the country from enjoying an "elastic currency."[28] Almost everybody gave President Theodore Roosevelt a good deal of credit as he went after the "trusts" and "malefactors of great wealth." It was noted that "foreign wars, the Baltimore fire, the San Francisco earthquake and fire, had absorbed $2,000,000 of liquid capital, tying up four times that amount of credit."[29] Banks called in their loans. The stock market dried up. The railroads could not find enough money to pay for operations. Banks and businesses began to fail, and all commerce slowed to a standstill.

Copper was heavily involved. As the channels of credit constricted, the demand for copper fell off, and the great producers were left with enormous stocks on hand — as much as 225,000,000 pounds.[30] Overproduction, according to some economists, was actually nation-wide and even world-wide,[31] but "manipulative campaigns in the stock market" pulled the trigger and brought on the "Bankers' Panic."[32]

Greene, of course, was more or less out of copper, and at first his other enterprises did not seem to be affected at all. Although all work stopped at Cananea and everyone was nervous about more riots when the men were laid off,[33] Greene had no such worries. "GOOD REPORTS COME IN FROM COLONEL GREENE," said the newspaper accounts. "Colonel W. C. Greene is the only big promoter who is not seriously affected by the panic."

"We are doing practically no development work," said General Manager Clarence Chase of Greene Gold-Silver, "as we are producing far more ore now than we can handle."[34]

The stockholders apparently shared Clarence's confidence, for at the annual meeting in October they endorsed Greene's management 1,300,-000 shares to 135 and accorded him "one of the greatest ovations ever given to a man at the head of a great project."[35]

Two developments cast a shadow over these hopeful bulletins. One was the fact that Colonel Greene always took a physician with him now on his trips to New York and into Mexico. Dr. W. J. Galbraith attended him in the *Verde* when he went East for the October meeting. The other was his transfer of almost eight million dollars of Greene Gold-Silver stock to the company treasury. Speculators deduced that "the mining concern is in need of ready money to continue operations in the 120 or more properties which have been acquired in Mexico in recent years."[36]

The speculators were as right as they could be. The depression had finally caught up with Greene, and he was struggling to keep his head above water. Early in October he sent a letter to Thomas F. Cole which must have cost him many a pang to write:

THE SIERRA MADRE LAND AND LUMBER CO.

New York, October 5, 1907

Mr. Thomas F. Cole
Duluth, Minnesota.
Dear Mr. Cole: —

At the annual meeting of the Sierra Madre Land & Lumber Company, held at Stamford, Conn., on the 3rd day of October, 1907, Mr. L. D. Ricketts, General Manager of the Cananea Consolidated Copper Company, S. A., was elected a director, this in accordance with the agreement between the Cananea Consolidated Copper Company, S.A., and myself in regard to the sale of stock to me by the Cananea Consolidated Copper Company, S.A.

I am now making negotiations with view of interesting capital in the Land & Lumber Company. You will remember that certain moneys are to be paid to the Cananea Consolidated Copper Company, S.A., under the contract of purchase made with me, for 51% of the Sierra Madre Land and Lumber Company stock, these payments to be made, running over a period of six years.

Will you kindly make me a price as to what the Copper Company will take, in cash, for the deferred payment due, as I think that I can make a deal on a reasonable figure. As you will remember, the Copper Company has been entirely reimbursed, with the exception of $150,000 note due September 20th, 1907, which they paid, and which, of course, will be repaid by the Land & Lumber Co. Consequently their stock in the Land & Lumber Company is clear profit.

I think that I could obtain for you $500,000.00 in cash if you will release the contract. It is absolutely necessary that we have some outside money in the Land & Lumber Company immediately, to meet pressing obligations, or the Land and Lumber Company will be forced into bankruptcy, without you can advance through the Copper Company to the Land & Lumber Company, sufficient money to meet its pressing obligations.

Personally, obligations of the Land & Lumber Company guaranteed by me, have exhausted my cash resources, and I am unable to advance further money, as I explained to you in Chicago. If an equitable arrangement, in the line I have mentioned, in regard to the sale of stock, can be made, I think that I can make a turn that will relieve me and enable me to meet all my outstanding obligations at once.

Will you kindly give this matter your immediate consideration?

Sincerely yours,
W. C. Greene[37]

Cole's answer to this plea has not been preserved, but there can be no doubt about its content. When President Thornton reported to the stockholders of Greene Consolidated on March 10, 1908, he said that "it was deemed wise to retire from the enterprise." He added, "Payments under this contract with Greene have been defaulted upon; and with 75 percent of the stock in their possession, your officers are considering what course to pursue."[38]

With three-quarters of his stock in the Land and Lumber Company forfeited, Greene was already washed out, but he probably still hoped he could retrieve the loss. Possibly because there was nothing else he *could* do, he went about his business as usual and sometimes found ways to put his predicament out of his mind.

E. J. Gates, treasurer of the Gold-Silver Company, liked to tell of a visit he paid the Colonel at the Ansonia Apartments in New York when an important cablegram came in from London. Gates remembered:

> I tried for half an hour to get to the Colonels' room, but the bellboy absolutely refused to allow anyone near the door. At last, growing desperate, I brushed the boy aside and walked unceremoniously into the parlor of the apartment. Everything was topsy-turvy, chairs were lying on the floor, pillows were strewn about, things looking as if a Kansas cyclone had struck the place. In the center of the room Colonel Greene was seated on the floor instructing William, Jr., how to rope a chair.
>
> I handed the Colonel the cablegram which he put in his pocket, and taking the lariat himself, he gave a few whirls, but it missed fire; instead of roping a tabourette, it knocked a valuable piece of French bric a brac off the mantel. William, Jr., went hurrying for the paste, and the Colonel spent an hour in trying to patch it together so it wouldn't be discovered by Mrs. Greene. Over an hour and a half elapsed after I entered the room before the Colonel opened the cablegram.[39]

It seems not to have occurred to Mr. Gates that Greene put off opening the cablegram because he did not want to know what was in it.

Through the spring and summer of 1908 Greene lived from day to day, facing his problems as they arose. In January he discovered that some skulduggery had been going on in the Land and Lumber enterprise, fired E. C. Hargrave, the man in control, and a number of his subordinates, and took charge of operations himself. He complained that many thousands of dollars' worth of unnecessary equipment had been ordered and that former employees had cleaned up $50,000 by doing the ordering.[40] Two carloads of material consigned to Madera were held up at the border. A Chicago firm sued for $19,000.[41] In February eight more suits were filed.[42]

Undaunted, Greene told interviewers that he believed "times will be considerably better within a few weeks." Businesses producing $2,000,000 a year, he said, "cannot be other than prosperous for a long period. When a man is climbing a hill, he is compelled to stop now and then to get his breath, and that is just what the country is doing now. We have been climbing up constantly and are now merely resting for a brief spell preparatory to another climb."[43]

He was not nearly as optimistic as he sounded. By now his health was so badly shattered that he and his doctors decided that it was absolutely necessary for him to get away from business — as far away as he could. He decided that a trip to Japan would just about fill the prescription, and on June 30, 1908, he left San Francisco,[44] taking his daughter Eva with him. There was talk that he went to raise capital for the benefit of his Mexican enterprises, but this could hardly have been true. Japan, of all places, was not a good hunting ground for an American capitalist in search of a new stake; and besides Greene was in no shape to put on a campaign of any kind. He was really in serious danger of a breakdown.

He and Eva visited all the interesting places and bought some furniture and porcelain to take home to Mary and the children.[45] He may have achieved some peace of mind, but it did not last long. Before the summer was over he came home, summoned by a cablegram from his step-daughter Virginia. There was trouble brewing in his cattle business and he was needed in Mexico at once. Mary was so concerned for his health that she took a stateroom on the *San Francisco* and met him in Hawaii.

He returned to find everything in a state of collapse. There was no more money. He could not pay his workers or run his mills and smelters or keep his sawmills going at Madera. The work stopped. Drivers did not bother to bring in the great ore wagons from Navidad and Concheño to Temosachic, and some of them could still be seen, sixty-five years later, where they were abandoned beside Greene's famous mountain highway.[46]

In September, sick and discouraged, Greene had to admit that his companies were gone — bankrupt — finished.[47] No man can plumb the depths of despair like a congenital optimist, and the bitter waters now rolled over his head. He suffered something like a nervous breakdown, gave up all attempts to look after his business, lapsed into inactivity and gloom.[48]

There was only one man he could turn to — his former partner and faithful friend A. B. Fall. When Fall heard what had happened, he got up off a sick bed and hurried back to Mexico. He recalled some years later:

I again took up Mexican business through interest in my partner, in attempting to save something for his family out of the wreck of a fortune which was tangled up in the investments and operations in which I had been interested, and with which I was more familiar than anyone else.[49]

It was Fall who released the news that Greene was "broken in health and with his own private fortune greatly depleted" — that he had "jeopardized every private interest to aid the companies, and his losses, through advances made, will aggregate over $3,500,000 in addition to his interest in some of the companies which are bankrupt."[50]

The affairs of the interlocked companies were in a monumental mess. Greene seemed to be in debt to everybody in the United States and Mexico.

In El Paso alone, Fall estimated, he owed $130,000. He had given his personal notes to cover Company debts for machinery and supplies, which made it possible for creditors to sue Greene personally, and they did so in droves. His medical adviser told him to stay out of it and spend six months as "a recluse in the mountains of Sonora."[51]

Fall worked without compensation for the better part of a year to dispose of the Greene properties and pay off as many creditors as he possibly could. His first effort was to satisfy the debts incurred in Mexico, because under Mexican law Greene's ranch property could have been seized for nonpayment of these obligations, leaving the Greene family without means of support. Fall was almost as devoted to Mrs. Greene as he was to the Colonel — called her "Sister Mary" and was always her trusted adviser.[52]

Fall actually did a remarkable job of handling the bankrupt companies. The lumber enterprise at Madera, with the blessing of the Copper Company (owner of 75 percent of the stock through Greene's default), was sold to Weetman Pearson, a British entrepreneur who had a big lumber enterprise of his own at a town in the Sierra Madre named for him. The unfinished railroad from Nueva Casas Grandes to Madera, as well as the established line from El Paso-Juarez to Nueva Casas Grandes, went to a corporation headed by Dr. F. S. Pearson of Canada (no relation to Weetman Pearson)[53] and became the *Noroeste de México* line when the link from Casas Grandes to Madera was completed in 1910.

By selling everything he could for anything he could get, Fall raised an amazing amount of money. In 1910, in connection with a payment of $11,000 to General Luis Terrazas of Chihuahua, he wrote:

I am sorry that no creditors whatsoever or whomsoever of Colonel Greene's companies will receive in full every cent due to them. It has been my effort to pay the majority of them or to secure their money for them through a deal with the Pearson Syndicate, all amounts due creditors of the Land and Lumber Company, who are now very nearly paid up. I hope within a short time to be able to complete payments to the creditors of the Greene Gold-Silver Company, S.A.[54]

In order to get the most out of the major mines of Greene Gold-Silver, Fall organized a new corporation, the Sierra Mines Company, Ltd., issued stock, and paid off most of the creditors. He took $75,000 in the stock of the company. He says he paid for it himself, asking and accepting nothing in payment for his services.[55] Resentful and disappointed creditors accused him of profiting by the Greene catastrophe.[56] He threatened suit, however, and apparently heard no more about it. In 1919 he stated that he still had the Sierra Company stock, would take $7,500 for it, and would "entertain any bid under that sum."[57]

His great regret was his inability to pay off the Mexican workmen to whom wages were owing at the time of the collapse. The Pearson Syndicate insisted, he said, that judgments against the lumber company should be paid off first, and there was nothing left for the workers.[58]

In the long run, it was the poor people who lost the most, and sad pictures have been painted of the "unemployed families who sat in their drafty cabins wondering what lay ahead. Where was the prosperity now, with no cornmeal or beans, even those to be bought on credit from the tienda de raya?"[59]

In spite of the resentment in Mexico against Greene and his kind, it was worse for the Mexicans when he could no longer operate.

The last traces of the Gold-Silver principality were erased when Greene's mineral concessions expired on January 31, 1910, and his locations were open to new denunciations.[60] It was reported that John W. "Bet-a-Million" Gates, long hungry for a share of Greene's holdings, hurried to Mexico City as the empire began to crumble to see if he could get his hands on some of the spoils. So far as is known, he did not succeed.[61]

At this point Greene's career touched bottom, but one man did not count him out. A. B. Fall told the world in his announcement of the Colonel's failure: "If he regains his health, a great many people who think he is down and out will be surprised. Men like Colonel Greene are never down and out."[62]

Cowman's Heaven

THE CATTLE RANGES of northern Sonora are as good as any in the world, and the pasture lands around Cananea are the best in Sonora. Eastward the great grama-grass plain rolls gently toward the Ajo mountains. North and west toward Nogales on the Arizona border, the hills grow steeper and the valleys deeper, but it is all first-class cattle range. In Apache times this bovine Eden lay untenanted and unused, and when Colonel Greene came to Mexico it was virgin country, all its resources of grass and water intact.

After fifteen years on the San Pedro, the Colonel was first of all a cowman, and his eye glistened as he surveyed that enormous, unfenced, grass-rich expanse; and of course he wanted it, just as he wanted everything else that he could make something out of. Within a year after his first big plunge as a mining promoter, he was ready to organize his two cattle corporations — the Greene Cattle Company in Arizona and the Cananea Cattle Company in Mexico — and when in 1908 his other enterprises crashed in ruins, he still had his cattle on a thousand hills and about 800,000 acres of ranch land on both sides of the border. He was back where he started, only he was operating on a much larger scale.

For two years he managed his ranch property as a good ranchman should, trusting his foremen but looking over his land and livestock in person at every opportunity. While he was living in New York, he could not get out on the range very often, but he kept in close touch with the work and the workmen.

In the summer of 1902 he wrote to his friend and partner B. A. Packard, vacationing in Chicago:

We are rounding up all of the River and Ojo de Agua pastures and throwing all strays out this week, which is making a big fuss again. By next year I am going to keep all the strays off our pastures or break a leg.[1]

When he came home to Cananea to live in 1906, Greene could do a little better by his ranch enterprises, and after the crash his cattle became his major concern. He spent much of his time on the range. Sometimes he parked the *Verde* on a siding and spread out from there, but most of the time he went out in his buggy behind two fast horses, his rifle beside him, checking the cattle, the grass, the water, the supplies. At meal time he sat cross legged in his business suit with his cowboys by the cooking fire, switching from Spanish to English and back again.

Everything else he put out of his mind. A. B. Fall wrote to Governor Luis Terrazas of Chihuahua in 1910, "Since Colonel Greene's trip to Japan, now over two years ago, he has not been able to attend to any business whatsoever except around his ranches in Sonora and Arizona."[2]

The outdoor life and the routine of familiar duties were good for him. His face grew suntanned and wind-reddened. He slept and ate better. When his daughter Eva wrote to him in October 1909 from her home in New York state about his health ("I pray it is much better and you are again your own self"), he replied:

Yours of Wednesday the sixth duly to hand; and I was very glad to hear from you and that you and Harry are both well. Am gradually getting better, and in another year hope to be all right again. My head bothers me a good deal but, outside of that and occasional attacks of my old trouble, I am getting along very well. Mary and the children are enjoying good health; the babies are growing very fast. Mary says you owe her a couple of letters, and that she has been expecting to hear from you. . . .

We have had a fairly prosperous year with the cattle. About your wedding anniversary you will probably get your dividend of $3,000 on your Greene cattle stock. . . .[3]

The Mexican ranches were more than enough for one man to oversee. In Greene's time the irregularly shaped area controlled by the Cananea Cattle Company was forty-two miles north and south and sixty-eight miles east and west. It was two hundred miles all the way around the outside, and inside it was broken up into pastures with something like six thousand miles of fence.[4] There were fifteen mountain ranges within the boundaries. Three rivers — the San Pedro, the Santa Cruz, and the Sonora — headed inside the fences. Greene developed additional water from springs and wells. Eventually he had ninety windmills working for him.[5]

The Cananea Cattle Company was really a collection of ranches. Mexican law forbade that any one man should own more than 10,000 hectares (24,700 acres) of land. To get around this regulation, big operators broke their holdings up into smaller units. Greene divided his into seven divisions of about 100,000 acres, each with a separate headquarters, a separate management, and a separate set of books and officers: The Nogales, Martínez, Turkey Track, Cananea, San Fernando, San Lázaro, and Cuitaca. They did not form a solid block of land. José Elías, Rafael Elías, the Bringas family, and Miguel Molina owned large tracts north and west of Cananea, somewhat west of center of the Cattle Company's holdings, and on the west side, the Santa Cruz community occupied considerable land just inside of what should have been the western boundary. Two large leased tracts, the Bacanuchi and the Cocospera, joined the southern boundary, the first on the east side of the Cananea Mountains, the second on the west. Two farms, one in the Santa Cruz Valley on the San Lázaro Division and the other on the San Pedro in the Cananea Division eight miles below the boundary, were part of the holdings.[6]

An important percentage of the land in use belonged to the Cananea Consolidated Copper Company and was held by the Cattle Company under lease. When Greene saw in 1908 that he was going to lose his copper mines, he made sure of continued use of the Copper Company lands by making out a long-term lease at nominal rental[7] — a lease which continued in effect until 1929, when the Copper Company got tired of paying the taxes and sold its grasslands to the Cattle Company.

The great ranch was not born all at once. It was a product of gradual expansion as Greene found money to invest and places to invest it. The beginning was the purchase already noted of a large tract of timber and range land in 1901 from the California Land and Cattle Company headed by Senator George C. Perkins and the Gird brothers — Richard, W. K. and L. J. This group is said to have owned some three million acres surrounding the infant settlement of Cananea.[8] Greene did not acquire anything like that much land from them, but he secured a very satisfactory nucleus to start with.[9]

The story of how these divisions grew would take a long time to tell. Each one was made up of as many as a dozen separate holdings, each with a history of transferred titles. The easternmost division, the Turkey Track, was at first held in partnership with Greene's old friend and backer B. A. Packard, the shrewd and crochety old banker from Douglas. There was a partnership deal and some swapping around with the patriarch of the region, Don Rafael Elías.[10] And Greene was always picking up tracts owned by one or another of the old families. He was always dealing, to the end of his life.

There was nothing monotonous about the great expanse of territory brought together under Greene's name. It ranged from the high pineclad Ajo Mountains, on the Turkey Track, to the soggy swamps at the head of the San Pedro — from the irrigated farm lands by the Sonora River on the south to the rugged hills of the Cuitaca and San Lázaro divisions on the west — country so rough that when Greene traversed it in his buggy, he took a couple of cowboys along, their lariat ropes attached to his rear axle so they could hold him back when he drove down the precipitous slopes.[11] It was all beautiful and unspoiled, and Greene could not have loved it more.

He organized the Cananea Cattle Company at Nogales, Sonora, on May 10, 1901. The first meeting of stockholders and officers was held at Cananea on the following July 10. Greene was not present — he was holding the fort in New York — but since he owned 980 shares of stock out of 1,000, he was the logical choice for president.[12] At the second meeting on August 4, 1902 (Greene was present this time), the first arrangement between the cattle and copper companies was recorded — a good example of how Greene's enterprises intermeshed. The Cattle Company agreed to pay $6,000 annual rent to the Four C's and in return was given the right to supply meat to the Cananea community at an average cost of no more than twelve cents a pound. Ten per cent of the meat profits went to the Copper Company.

At the third meeting, September 20, 1902, Greene's father-in-law, Frank Proctor, was elected general manager.[13]

The Mexican divisions were only part of Greene's cattle kingdom. Two weeks before he put them together as a Mexican corporation, he set up an Arizona company to control his range land north of the line. The Greene Cattle Company was organized on April 21, 1901, two months after his second marriage. The incorporators were Greene, his stepson Frank Moson, and Benjamin Sneed, husband of his stepdaughter Virginia. Frank was manager of the Company and remained so for ten years. Virginia received 20,000 shares of stock, worth at par two dollars a share, and presumably Frank received the same.[14] Eva was given fifty thousand shares as a wedding present when she married in 1908.

On the following July 22, Greene transferred the OR iron (brand) to the Greene Cattle Company.

This was the brand which belonged during her lifetime to Ella Roberts Greene, his first wife. She died without leaving a will, and Greene took possession of her property as surviving spouse without making a division, since the children were all very young.

By 1899, the year of Ella's death, there was considerable property to divide since her cattle herd had grown by natural increase to five thousand head. Greene took care of the matter in characteristic fashion. He asked the two Moson children, Frank and Mary Virginia (according to a statement he made in 1909), to evaluate these cattle. Their estimate

R. F. Torrance

Charles E. Wiswall, a special human being.

was $30,000, $10,000 each for them and their half sister Eva. He paid $10,000 each to the first two and, as he said, "much more than that" to Eva.[15] He thought he had done what was needed, but his informal method of settling the claims of his stepchildren was to cause trouble later as the herds bearing the OR brand increased and multiplied. Mary Virginia, who was always very close to her stepfather and very dear to him, was satisfied. But Frank was not happy about the settlement, and Greene made a final transfer of stock and land to him after the expedition to Japan.[16]

The ranch holdings north of the line grew piece by piece, like the Mexican ranches. Greene began putting together the San Rafael del Valle (including his old Hereford "homestead") in 1902 and spent the next three years settling the claims of the widely scattered heirs to this old Spanish grant. In 1903 he bought part of what was to become the Palominas ranch, which lay along the border astride the San Pedro. Eventually he controlled a corridor of land beginning in Mexico and following the San Pedro Valley to a point some distance beyond Hereford, Arizona.

In 1903 also Greene acquired for $1,500,000 the jewel of them all, the other San Rafael — San Rafael de la Zanja — west of the San Pedro with the Huachuca Mountains in between. Beautiful and isolated, this oasis had been developed by Colin Cameron and his two brothers. They had made it a show place and had built up a fine herd of blooded Hereford cattle.[17]

The San Rafael was Greene's pride. To begin with, it was home base for his magnificent herd of purebred Herefords. He ran his grade herd in Mexico, but he brought fine bulls across the line to improve his Mexican livestock, and in time most of the old blood was bred out.[18] There was, incidentally, a good deal of the old blood to eliminate. In 1904 Greene's men branded 35,000 calves on his Mexican ranches.[19]

Passionate as he was about fine horses, the Colonel had to have a

W. H. Holmes

Beef, beans, and coffee: lunch is served in an RO cow camp.
Elsie Holmes is the lady; Red Fox is on the right.

Greene cowboys: Bronco buster
Archie Smith and top hand
Tommy Farrell.

W. H. Holmes

stable of thoroughbreds on the San Rafael also. Some, with once-famous names like Arizona and Florence Wilton and Cobre Grande, he shipped to New York during his time there and often drove them around the track himself. Later on he raced them at Phoenix. He even had a herd of Shetland ponies, partly because he loved anything that looked like a horse and partly because he liked to give them as gifts to his friends and business associates.[20]

In the early years Greene cattle from Mexico went to feed lots and markets all over the United States — livestock in his own brand and steers that his buyers brought to Cananea or Naco for shipping. In 1904 the Colonel began to consider setting up his own feeding arrangements and by 1905 had leased many sections of grazing land on the Rosebud in South Dakota and another ample area near Tulare, California. The business of moving these cattle was planned like a military campaign. They

San Simon Jack,
the greatest character of all.

F. R. Walker

were assembled and dipped at corrals near Naco, taken across the line to the Palominas for rest, and then loaded for shipment to the point where they would put on the most weight or bring in the most money.[21]

Greene was ahead of his time in his ideas about stock raising, as he was in many other fields. He was already worrying about the environment in 1905. He cross-fenced his ranches so he could take his pastures entirely out of circulation and let them rest for a whole year. He stopped wood cutting on his property. On one of his first visits to the San Rafael, which he managed for many years, Tom Heady was standing beside Greene when a wagon load of oak and juniper went by. "That will have to be stopped," Greene remarked, "or the land will eventually go with it."[22] He experimented with arid-land grasses from Russia and Turkestan and paid attention to developments in the Department of Agriculture in Washington.[23] Not many ranchmen had that much vision in the early 1900s.

He had time to be progressive because he had good men working for him. From Charlie Wiswall, his second in command, down to the newest and lowliest cowboy, they were a remarkably loyal and efficient group. The Cananea Cattle Company was known all over the West as a sort of ultimate — the place where every cowpoke wished he could be. Once hired, he felt himself a step closer to the ranks of cow-country aristocracy.

Part of the reason was Greene himself, who was respected and liked by his men, but another large part was Charlie Wiswall. From the time Greene took Charlie out of the Naco business office and began to groom him for ultimate command, he became the contact man, the shock absorber, the man in charge. The cowboys called him "The Big Noise," and they loved him.

Although he was a kind and gentle man, he was never soft. His mind was decisive; his manner was firm. He had a sharp eye and a direct gaze which commanded attention and respect. The toughest cowboy listened when he talked and said, "Yes, Sir!" At the same time this same cowboy knew that Wiswall thought of him as an important and useful human being, regardless of where he came from or how much he knew besides cows.

His dominant trait was conscientiousness — an unwavering intention to do what was right. The Mexicans called him *Jesu Cristo*. It was characteristic of him that when he caught a man bringing merchandise across the line without paying duty, he made him go back and settle up.[24] The Mexican officials trusted him as they trusted no other American except Colonel Greene himself.

The Colonel was well aware of Charlie's fine qualifications and picked him as his successor. His failing health reminded him that somebody would have to take charge before long, and Wiswall seemed to be the man to do it. He said to Mary, "The ranch is for you and the children. You trust Charlie Wiswall and you'll always have a roof over your head."[25]

Charlie provided more than a roof. He kept on building up the property after the Colonel was gone, until it included better than a million acres. In its day it was perhaps the biggest ranching enterprise in the world. Thanks to his high rating with the Mexican government, he kept it going when other great ranches were being expropriated and broken up.

Next to Charlie, the Colonel's greatest reliance was on his foremen — a tough and rugged lot but absolutely dependable. Tom Turner had put a herd across the desert from Tucson to California in 1889, they said, and he was as good as any in the business. Tom Lasseter, called Red Fox because of his flaming hair and freckled face, was as crochety as an old woman, especially about the way his cattle were handled. If a hand in a hurry showed any signs of "chousing" the stock, he was in bad with Red

Bill Adams, who went to work
on the ranch at age 16.
W. H. Holmes

Fox right away. Everything had to be done to suit him. "I rode off and
left him more than once," Tommy Farrell says. Sherman Rinehart of the
Nogales Division was as much interested in cowboys as he was in cows
— watched out for them and took care of them and was loved accordingly.
And Tom Heady started with small jobs, became manager of the Cuitaca
Division, and took charge of the San Rafael in 1908.[26]

They were all good men, and they had to be to handle the boys who
did the work. These were "big ranch" cowboys, a breed which has almost
disappeared. They were used to solitude and content to live with the cows
and the sky and the landscape. The world outside their fence lines meant
little to them, but in their own small universe, nothing much got past them,
and they were highly educated in the skills and mysteries of their business.
They got up while it was still dark and went to bed the same way, did
what needed to be done without counting the hours or the cost in horse
or human flesh. The welfare of the outfit was their religion, and they didn't

Captain George Burbank,
man of many talents.

F. R. Walker

much care who owned it. For weeks at a time they were mostly by themselves with no amusements and few comforts, and naturally when they came to Cananea they made up for lost time. Tim Cohane's saloon, or John Donlevy's, served as headquarters, and they looked for girls where they could find them. In the morning it was back to the Nogales or the Cuitaca headquarters with empty pockets and lead in the head. And they would not have changed it for any other life.

There was no place for conformity on the cattle ranges. Each man was different from all the rest and built to his own specifications. Fiercely proud and quick to resent a slight or an insult, they frequently came to Mexico on the run and sometimes left the same way. There was a grim humor in the stories told by and about them.

There was Dan McKinley, for instance (McKinley is not his right name) who made it across the border and did not go back — ever. He was living near San Angelo, Texas, and found that some men were stealing his stock. He went over to see about it. They asked him in and served coffee. He took a sip and it tasted bitter. In a minute he started shaking all over and he knew what had been done to him.

"They never poisoned anybody else," he told his friends.

Dan went out to California with Tom Heady when the Cattle Company started its ranch out there. Mr. Wiswall came out to check on things and found a big Holstein steer in the herd branded RO, the Greene brand in Mexico. "How did he get in here?" Mr. Wiswall inquired.

"He got here the way Columbus discovered America," Dan said. "He kept jumping the fence, so I cut him and branded him."

Tom Lerner (not his right name, either) was another one. When he left Mexico, he went to Colorado and was sentenced to the penitentiary for rustling. "I thought all the cattle in that valley were mine," he said.

San Simon Jack Lassiter was another one. He had been a country school teacher and read a lot, even subscribed to the *Literary Digest*. That was enough to make him unusual. To add to his individual difference, he

W. H. Holmes

Cowboys and would-be cowboys: *Top row:* Tex McCulloch, RO Cattle Company Manager; T. S. Patrick (Pat), cowpuncher and poker player; Tommy Farrell (Irish), RO top hand; Lee Hardin, Assistant General Manager, Cananea Cattle Company; Bill Holmes, a would-be. *Bottom row:* Sherman (Rhiney) Rinehart, boss of the Nogales Division; G. T. (Daddy) Green, resident of Cananea; Archie (Yaqui) Smith, bronco buster, Nogales Division; D. T. Green, Jr., another would-be.

was cross-eyed. He explained that he had once worked for the San Simon Cattle Company at Rodeo and in an encounter with a bucking horse he was thrown so high and far that he hit the Chiricahua Mountains. The shock crossed his eyes.

Back in the States a couple of cowboys who were not good at reading and writing asked Jack to close a deal of some kind. He managed to get their X's on a power of attorney and walked off with their money. That was when he came to Mexico.

He was not much good around a ranch, but Colonel Greene liked him and enjoyed him and even bought a mining prospect from him — for cash. With the money that was left over after he finished celebrating, Jack bought a small pack of hounds and went in for hunting and trapping. For a while he kept a saloon.

Wiswall was disgusted with Jack's shiftless ways and often told him so. "Jack," he once inquired, "why are you so useless? You had everything going for you and you threw it away."

"Charlie, I wasn't to blame."

"Why weren't you to blame?"

"I had a saloon up on the hill, a red-headed woman, and a race-horse. Any one of them would break a man."

He spent his declining years at Hot Springs, New Mexico, and lived to be well over ninety. His old-age pension, plus cash provided by Charlie Wiswall and Lem Shattuck of Bisbee, brought in more money every month than he really knew how to spend, but he did his best. He got drunk every day. A taxi driver took him to town in the mornings and brought him back when he had made enough progress, and Jack no doubt felt that he was a happy man. When it was time to die, he came back to Bisbee and breathed his last at the Copper Queen Hotel.[27]

They all knew Colonel Greene and had stories to tell about him. Bill Adams, sixteen years old, went to work on the ranch in 1906. He was the only Anglo in his crew. His first meeting with the Colonel threatened to be his last. Greene had brought two fine horses down from the San Rafael — thoroughbreds. Bill remembers:

One of them was a little on the skinny side, but I could see the muscles all the way down his legs. His mane and tail were not bushy like the Mexican horses. I broke him and he made a hell of a good horse. But when Greene came to the camp and saw what I had done, he got furious. He was one of the kindest men I ever knew, but he had a violent temper. I guess he was mad because a cowboy was using his fancy horse. He cussed a little and told them to take the horse back to headquarters. I didn't say anything, but I went back to camp and started packing my stuff.

Tom Ewing, a Company policeman.

F. R. Walker

"What are you doing?" the boss asked.

"I'm gone. If he thinks more of that horse than he does of me, I'm quitting." I was proud too, and wouldn't stand for that sort of thing.

So they told Greene, and he didn't send for me. He came down to where I was and said, "I hear you're quitting."

"Yes, I am," I told him.

"I hear you think a lot of that horse."

"Yes, I do."

"Well, you are worth more to me than any horse, so I guess I'll just let you have him."

So I didn't quit.[28]

In 1956 Bill was called back after many years as an independent rancher to become general manager of the Cananea Enterprises.

They are almost all gone now, in 1973. Bill Adams at El Paso is

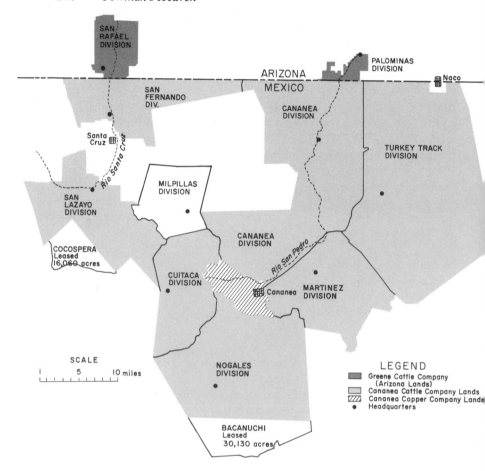

The Greene cattle empire in 1911. (Adapted from map by Sidney Hatch)

still around, but where are Charlie Wright and Joe Rhodes, corral bosses for Greene — Archie Smith, the bronco buster, and Bob Harding, who proudly claimed an outlaw for a brother? Where is George Spindles, who used a pile of stones to help his arithmetic when he was buying his cattle; Jim Stevens, who once a year would take a remuda of old mares south into Mexico and come out (thanks to his gifts as a trader) with a fine bunch of steers; Charlie Montgomery the lion hunter, with his dogs, and his hair down to his shoulders; Captain Burbank, Greene's friend since the 1870s and the days at the Tiger Mine, who built the wagon road from Temosachic to Ocampo; Bill Kennon, Frank Davis, and all the rest? All gone — to the pastures, we hope, of Heaven. But their names were familiar in that long-ago time and that forgotten country when Colonel Greene was still the mighty man of northern Mexico.[29]

They were so authentic, so completely suited to their special place, so proud and free, that men without horses envied them and dreamed of being a part of the cowboy's world. One such was Fred Walker, a timekeeper in the mines at Cananea who liked to wear cowboy clothes and watch the boys at work. He took pictures with his Brownie Kodak and filled notebooks with his experiences and the stories he heard. It nearly broke his heart when the Company let him go and didn't tell him why.[30]

Another interested observer was Billy Holmes, who worked in the Electrical Department for the Copper Company in 1911, wore a big hat, and looked with some envy at Tommy Farrell and Bill Adams. Eventually he and Adams became partners in a cattle business of their own and, at the end of twenty-three years, came out better friends than when they went in.

Cowboys and bystanders alike felt that they knew Colonel Greene, but they seldom had much conversation with him. He was not ordinarily talkative and was usually intent on business, but when there was occasion for friendliness, he was always friendly. Ira Joralemon, a geologist with Calumet and Arizona Copper Company at Warren-Bisbee, spent three days with Greene on the *Verde* in 1909 when the Colonel was hoping to uncover new copper prospects in the Santa Cruz Mountains. The private car was parked on a siding twenty-five miles from Cananea, and the foremen would come in to report.

In the daytime I would go out and look at this mine and take some samples, and he would ride over his ranch, and in the evening the Mexican ranch foremen would come in to talk with him and it was most interesting to see the deep respect and affection that they had for Colonel Greene. They all called him "Meester Greene" — never called him Colonel at all — just "Meester Greene" — and they thought he was wonderful. And he knew exactly how to treat them and he liked them. And so every evening after I came in from looking at the mines, he would have them in the *Verde* and would keep them for dinner, which would be something they had never seen. He had a very good colored cook on the *Verde* and would give them a meal that they had never heard of before.[31]

It was not all steaks and syrup, of course. Ranch life is seldom placid, and everything from screw worms to low beef prices is always about to break loose. The Colonel had his share: rustling, for instance. On a big ranch somebody is always trying to make a modest living by branding Company calves or butchering Company beef. Greene lost a few, but he kept a little group of Company police led by such men as Tom Ewing and Gus Gildea, and there was really very little trouble. The great difficulty was that the ranch property was heavily encumbered during the Colonel's last years, and it took Mr. Wiswall until 1927 to get it all paid off.[32]

Meanwhile Colonel Greene was getting his feet under him again. As A. B. Fall had said in 1908, "A man like Colonel Greene is never down and out." As his health improved, he began to dream once more, and, knowing from bitter experience what this might involve, in 1910 he put the ranches in Mary's name. If in any new venture he followed his gambler's instinct and laid everything on the line, he didn't want the land and cattle to go too. In his mind was the echo of his own words:

"This is for you. Trust Charlie Wiswall. . . ."

Two Fast Horses

THE BIG HOUSE AT CANANEA was a warm and hospitable place, and many people came there when the Greenes were in Mexico. The family spent most of the year at their Los Angeles house after the Revolution started in 1910, but Cananea was still home, and in the summer of 1911 they had taken up the old familiar routine. They enjoyed having visitors. Mary did not make new friends easily, but she valued her small group of intimates above rubies and liked to have them come to see her. Her husband was hospitable too, and he had a much wider range of acquaintances to draw on: old companions from Tiger and Tombstone days, business associates from a dozen corporations, relatives from back East. Amy Chase, his niece, had been there a year before and recorded the experience with her Eastman Kodak.[1] Mr. and Mrs. Alfred Romer (Alfred was his cousin) were frequent guests. Mexican dignitaries from Hermosillo and Mexico City came in a steady stream and were entertained at dinner in the big oak-paneled dining room.

Mary marshaled her household with unobtrusive skill. She had a good staff of servants trained and directed by herself, and in the kitchen she kept several cooks, Chinese or Mexican.[2] The Colonel was fond of *menudo* (tripe, Mexican style), and Mary's Mexican cook always had it ready for him when he came back after a trip.[3]

The children were still small but full of energy and growing fast. Their father could be with them now. He had tutors for the older ones (Frank learned French before he learned English, somewhat to the Colonel's astonishment), but he was able to contribute something to their education himself now and then. William, for instance, was terrified of

[249]

thunder until one time during a thunderstorm the Colonel took him outside and explained what was happening up in the sky. After that William
was not afraid any more.[4]

Along with his own children, Greene looked out for Vida Burns,
stepdaughter of his old friend Frank King, who was reared and educated
with the little Greenes.

In this busy but relaxed household Greene found what peace he had.
Although his thick hair never turned gray, one saw lines in his face which
had not been there before his world collapsed. The pain in his chest
bothered him less, but his heart sent him stern reminders if he worked
too hard or too long. He tried to slow down — tried to stay calm and
cheerful, and little by little he was making his way back out of the shadows
and into the sunlight. It was a help to be at home in his own house with
his family and his friends coming and going. The story that he became
a "recluse" after 1908[5] has to be wrong. In that bustling house it would
have been like setting up as a hermit in Grand Central Station.

As his health improved, the Colonel found himself able to concentrate better on his business. He still had the Cananea Realty Company
which controlled his real estate holdings, and for a while held title to some
of his mines. He still owned the slaughter house and was getting ready to
make it into a packing house, and he was responsible for a number of
business subsidiaries in Cananea. His days were full — sometimes too
full; but when the Colonel had to rest, Charlie Wiswall, firm and faithful,
was always there to pick up the reins.

Most mornings Greene's buggy, pulled by two of his blooded horses,
would be brought round from the stables to the carriage step on the east
side of the house, and he would drive off to his daily duties. He usually
went first to the barber shop in the Alexandria Hotel, two blocks south,
for a shave, and after that wherever business called him — to his office
in the Cattle Company headquarters; to the Cananea Club for a conference; to the *palacio municipal* to see the mayor. If he had business out of
town, his driver took him to the station in his snubnosed Franklin automobile. He boarded the *Verde,* still reserved for his use though the Copper Company owned it,[6] and he was off to Naco or Tucson or Los Angeles.
When he came back from a long trip, he still liked to bring presents for
everybody. One of his last gifts to his children was a pony cart. His herd
of Shetland ponies provided plenty of motive power, and the young ones
got much enjoyment from this new toy.

With returning health Greene felt the stirrings of reviving ambition.
The wheels began to turn again; new ideas began to come. In 1910 he
was moving ahead with several projects, the big one being the Santa Cruz
Reservoir scheme.

This venture was actually the brain child of a group of his close friends, headed by Epes Randolph, who managed the Southern Pacific railways in Mexico, and General Levi H. Manning of Tucson. Their idea was to use the flood waters of the Santa Cruz and Santa Rosa Rivers to irrigate an expanse of desert land near Toltec, Arizona, between Tucson and Phoenix, and sell the land with accompanying water rights to farmers. Most of the year the Santa Cruz and the Santa Rosa were likely to be as dry as the Gobi Desert, but when the rains came, thousands of square miles of barren hills and naked mountain slopes sent the runoff roaring through the river channels to the Gila and the Gulf of California. Diversion dams across the two rivers would channel these waste waters into the Santa Cruz Reservoir for storage and eventual distribution to the fields, which would be leveled and ready.[7]

There was no reason in the world why the enterprise should not succeed. With know-how and salesmanship, and of course money, a great tract of useless country could be made productive, and the promoters could reap rich rewards. The Colonel saw at once, when Randolph and Manning talked to him, that this was a great promotional opportunity which had bogged down for lack of enthusiastic leadership — exactly what Greene was equipped to provide. He called Raymond Reid, his stenographer, into the office and began sorting it all out in his mind. Reid remembers:

He put his feet up on the desk and started dictating. He built the dam, caught the rains, filled that reservoir, planted the crops, irrigated them, brought them to maturity, harvested them, put them on the market, sold them, put the money in the bank and paid off the debt — the money he was going to borrow on this — all in one afternoon in about three hours and a half of constant dictation to me. He was writing this letter to a financial firm in England, and they were going to sell the stock. He was going to borrow money from them, but he never did.[8]

As always, Greene thought big, and he persuaded the original developers that the only thing wrong with their idea was its failure to realize the immense possibilities of the project. The dam they had constructed was too low. It would have to be raised to impound more water. What about tapping the Gila River for its flood waters also? The acreage to be served was insignificant compared to what might be opened up. The old Master Planner was back in business, and the old persuasiveness was there too. Randolph and Manning agreed that he was right and took fire themselves. They signed the papers for the new corporation on December 15, 1908, and capitalized it at $10,000,000. Their plans included a second impounding lake to be called the Black Mountain Reservoir, and a diversion dam on the Gila. The total capacity of the two reservoirs was to be 2,000,000 acre feet, and the area ultimately to be reclaimed was 400,000 acres.

Some time in 1909, when he felt able, Greene took charge, started moving in machinery, including four big traction engines, and began to level and ditch the land. The original dam was raised to a height of twenty-four feet. A great mound of earth, it was twelve feet wide at the top and 7,800 feet — a mile and a half — in length. The Company planned to put 3,000 acres into cultivation initially. Greene set up a base camp at a place he called Santa Cruz and got off to a thundering start. The project was nothing like as stupendous as Greene Gold-Silver or the Sierra Madre Land and Lumber Company, but it was big enough, and it was going to succeed. It had to. Once more Greene felt the old determination and confidence and found that the resources of energy he needed were available. In three years he and his associates spent $300,000,[9] and apparently it was carefully used.[10]

Late in 1910 Greene took ship for Europe, undoubtedly to promote the Santa Cruz Reservoir project. The newspapers reported in November that he had had some success:

Nogales, Ariz., Nov. 22 — Col. W. C. Greene, accompanied by R. L. Hows and Willis Wilkey of Cananea, passed through in Col. Greene's car "Verde" en route to Sonora points. Statements are that Col. Greene secured a big sum of money on his recent European trip for his Santa Cruz project.[11]

While the dust clouds followed his traction engines clearing the land southwest of Toltec, Greene found time for other matters. He never gave up his hopes for the copper deposits in the Santa Cruz district near Cananea, for one thing. Geologist Ira Joralemon gave him a mixed report when he came down to make an examination in 1909,[12] but Greene relied, as in the old days, on his own judgment, and his judgment told him that he might have a second Cananea in the Santa Cruz Mountains.

"Mr. Greene had a plan," George Young revealed in 1911, "to consolidate the principal holdings of the district under one company, but failed in this on account of the high price asked by different owners."[13]

Meanwhile the seeds sown at Cananea by the miners' strike of 1906 were beginning to sprout, and the revolution which Greene said could never happen was now becoming a bloody and bitter reality. In 1910 a mystical little liberal named Francisco Madero brought the opposition to Díaz into focus with a cheaply produced book on the presidential succession. Little brush fires of insurrection began breaking out everywhere, especially in northern Mexico — in Chihuahua and Sonora. The vested interests — the establishment — were still incredulous. Emilio Kosterlitzky, head of the *rurales,* wrote to George Young at Cananea in June:

I myself most earnestly hope that there may be no trouble, while I personally take no stock in the so called Free Ticket, for it certainly is the most ridiculous "TICKET" this Madero thing, still there is a certain unrest in many parts and we must be prepared, for it needs only a spark to start a hell of a blaze. . . .[14]

Late in the month Colonel Kosterlitzky was in camp on the ranch watching "every trail and road"[15] into Cananea, convinced that the whole thing was "a huge joke" but still dangerous.[16] It was no joke, however, and though there was no big trouble in the Cananea vicinity through the fall and winter of 1910–11 (Kosterlitzky called the calm "monotonous"),[17] the whole country blew up in March and April, 1911. Madero and his irregulars lost a pitched battle to the Federals at Casas Grandes on March 6. The United States concentrated troops in Texas for "maneuvers" — which to many Mexicans spelled "intervention." There was skirmishing all over Chihuahua and Sonora.

Active in the region was a former Cananea boy named Juan G. Cabral, son of well-to-do parents who had sent him to be educated in the United States. Influenced by such persuasive Liberals as Lázaro Gutiérrez de Lara, he joined the proletarians, became *persona non grata* to the rulers of Cananea, and was invited to leave the community. He left, but said as he took his departure,

"I will be back. And then it will be *my* turn."[18]

A few Cananeans remembered this when Cabral moved into the country southward with about two hundred men and occupied the village of Bacanuchi. He had wiped out a detachment of Federals on patrol from Cananea a few days before, shot the officers, it was said, and told the men they could join him or suffer the same fate.[19] They joined. Five years before, at the end of the famous strike, the miners had been offered a similar choice — go back to work or join the army. Now the revolutionaries were giving the orders and not a word was said about injustice.

Cananea began preparing for an invasion. The city hall and the jail were fortified and were surmounted by machine guns, possibly brought in by Colonel Greene.[20] The tiny garrison of Federal troops gripped their rifles and feared for the future. Trouble held off, however, until May, when the *Maderistas* were badly mauled in a battle at a village called San Rafael and headed for the border for rest and recuperation. A camp near the line gave them a chance to import supplies and to seek safety in the United States if necessary.

Captain (soon to be Colonel) Cabral stationed himself in the Ajo Mountains twenty miles east of Cananea at the edge of Colonel Greene's ranch property where there was plenty of wood, water, and Cattle Company beef. A messenger arrived with an ultimatum for the mayor and city officials: Cabral was coming in and they were to leave. If they did not go, he was coming anyway, and it would be the worse for them.[21]

There was great consternation among the élite of Cananea — all Díaz supporters, of course. No one knew what to do. Cabral's strength was unknown. He might have fifty men, and he might have five hundred. It seemed that this was a time to turn to Colonel Greene. "Why, yes," he told them, "I would be willing to go and talk to Cabral." And he sent for his horses and buggy.

They had their interview. Cabral was firm. He had a large force of well-armed men and he was coming in. There would be blood in the streets if he was opposed. Greene could go back and tell the military leaders and city officials that it was their last chance.

Greene went back and told them. "He has a good-sized force," he reported. "There were heads popping up from behind every rock. It looked as if he had 500 men, and they seemed to have good weapons." After his conference with the mayor, he dashed off a telegram to Governor Torres at Hermosillo.

Have just returned from interview with Cabral. He says he is resolved to take Cananea, that he has men enough to capture the place even if it takes two or three days of fighting and the loss of many men. Now that you have evacuated Agua Prieta strongly advise that you order the evacuation of Cananea and save needless loss of life and property. If the fight starts, all miners will join Cabral as soon as fighting begins and battle in Cananea will result in needless loss of life and destruction of property without any chance of your holding town more than two or three days.

W. C. Greene[22]

The *porfirista* officials and army officers thought they saw the hand-writing on the adobe wall and decided to take no chances. They made arrangements with the Copper Company to have some boxcars and a gondola placed on a side track for them. They loaded all their possessions aboard, and late in the afternoon of May 11, 1911, the train pulled out for Naco and safety.[23]

Two days later, Captain Cabral appeared with his little army—about a hundred men armed with a startling miscellany of weapons, including clubs. His bluff had worked, and there was a big celebration for him that night. The hometown boy had made good.[24]

From this time on the *insurrectos* ruled Cananea and the country at large, though the Federals were not yet entirely beaten and there was much factional fighting ahead among the rebels themselves. Kosterlitzky wrote to George Young, "They wanted liberty. . . . now they got it and don't know what to do with the thing."[25]

Young was cautious in his statements:

Conditions here are quiet. There has been very little disorder, practically none from the time that the *insurrectos* came in. Naturally there is some ill feeling between the old crowd and the new. . . . I believe this feature of the situation is being overcome now. We all hope to see the time of peace and prosperity. For our own part we only ask that we may be let alone in the peaceful occupation of turning out copper.[26]

It was too much to hope. Years of trouble were ahead before conditions became stable in Sonora. In 1913 a pitched battle was fought in and around Cananea, though Greene was not there to see it.

The Colonel's time was already short, but he was doing business as usual to the very end. Near the end of August his trusted cowboy Tommy Farrell happened to meet him near the slaughter house. Tommy was getting ready to go back to the Nogales Division headquarters. He was in a bad state of mind because the revolutionaries, in addition to confiscating Company beef,[27] had taken most of the *remuda* on the Nogales. Only four horses were left in Tommy's string, and they were, as he tells it, "give out."[28]

"Why," Greene asked him, "do you think we are not getting any more steers down there?"

"Well," Tommy replied, "there are steers up in them mountains but the people down there ain't got nothing to ride, and all them steers and wild cattle is getting away from them. They're all on foot."

"All right. I'll see Fox and Rinehart and make them get a bunch of horses together and a bunch of men. I'll send them down there and we'll work out that whole country. There's a big demand for beef in Europe, and anything that can walk across that line, I'm going to ship to California and put them on feed."

"So I went back to the Nogales," Tommy says, "and told them what was going to happen. It was the last time I ever saw him. Two days later he had the accident, and a week after that, he was dead."

It happened on Monday, July 31. The day at first seemed like any other. Breakfast was served as usual. The buggy was brought around. Greene crossed the wide veranda, buttoning his coat, and got in. He noticed that the team was different. One of the two sleek brown horses that he usually drove had been kept in the stable for some reason, and another had been substituted. The two were not used to each other and danced around a little. The Colonel was not bothered. He took a firm grip on the reins and drove them over to the Alexandria, tied them up, and went in for his shave. Half an hour later when he came out, they were still restive.

"Can I hold them for you, Colonel?" a man in the street asked.

"No, don't worry, I can handle them," he replied, and got into the buggy. Before he could sit down, they jumped ahead. He lost one of the reins and fell to the bottom of the vehicle. Running wild, the team swung around the corner and smashed the buggy against a telephone pole. Greene was thrown out, falling heavily against the wooden fence in front of the Catholic church. He lay on the ground for a minute; then got up under his own power and walked into the street. A Mexican carriage was passing. It stopped for him and he got in, still without help, and was driven to his house, where he went to bed.

Raymond Reid, his stenographer, was standing in front of a shop a block and a half away talking to the proprietor and saw it happen. "Why that looks like Colonel Greene's team," he said, and started for the scene, arriving too late to be of any help.

The Colonel had broken his collar bone and several ribs, and a lung was punctured, but at first nobody imagined that he could be in serious danger. His vitality and courage were as strong as ever, and it seemed that he must survive this peril too. Within two days, however, Dr. W. P. Haney, the Copper Company physician, called Mary aside and told her that pneumonia was setting in.[29] She put Raymond Reid on the telephone and kept him there almost night and day trying to get help. A special train was made up at El Paso and sent off with doctors, nurses, and a supply of oxygen aboard. At Naco they were met by the Colonel's automobiles and whisked off to Cananea as fast as they could travel. They arrived too late.

He knew that he had to go. He talked at length to Charlie Wiswall about business matters, and he was able to say goodbye to Mary and the children. Only Eva was missing. She lived too far away to get there in time. At five o'clock on the morning of August fifth he left them. Headlines all over the Southwest carried the message: "Bill Greene Crosses Over."[30]

The funeral was the biggest Cananea had ever seen. Mary decided to have the religious ceremony at the house, and on August 7 the place was crowded with great and humble people. Some had come from far away. After the simple service the procession formed which was to take him to the crepe-festooned *Verde* at the railroad station to begin his last ride to Los Angeles. All his cowboys were there, mounted on black horses, and every carriage in Cananea followed Mr. Hillman's hearse in solemn procession.[31] People on foot numbered in the hundreds, all gathered to say goodbye to an extraordinary human being whom all of them had admired and many of them had loved.

He went out, as always, to a sound of trumpets. The tone was muted, but it was there. News releases everywhere — in mining journals, financial organs, and daily papers — carried stories, full of the usual errors, about his origin, early life, struggles, and success. They celebrated his courage and resourcefulness, his optimism, his power of vision. They remembered his kindness and generosity, his unfailing gratitude to the men who stood by him. They praised him as a dreamer of dreams and a doer of deeds — a man of power and stature whose like would not be seen again in the places of his triumph and defeat.

The editor of his hometown newspaper had said it for all of them five years before, when the evil days came not: "... when he does go beyond the Styx, there will be a lot of old timers from the Pyramid builders on up who will take notice and get active."[32]

The trumpets were still sounding as the *Verde* pulled into the celestial station to be met by the Colonel's peers, the dreamers and doers of all the ages.

The Distorted Image

MEN LIKE COLONEL GREENE do not die entirely when their physical life is over. They live on in legend and anecdote and folklore, and the image which remains often bears little resemblance to the real human being. Long before his death, the Colonel's image began to be distorted, and after his failure in 1908 a good deal of vicious gossip distorted it still further.

Mary knew that something like this was happening, and after the funeral she began making contact with his closest friends, asking them not to say anything about him for publication.[1] She was afraid that someone who never knew or understood him would paint his portrait in the lurid colors which seemed to be in demand, cheapening him and his achievements, making him ridiculous. Mary, it must be admitted, was hypersensitive about slanted newspaper stories and overanxious to avoid publicity, but in this case she was right. Journalists, novelists, and historians have done exactly what she thought they would do and made her husband over according to their desires and illusions.

We can begin with what has happened to him in Mexico. When he died, one Mexican newspaper editorialized: "Surely there is not a single person in the whole state who does not profoundly lament his tragic death" and described him as "a man of generous principles with a noble heart."[2] A few years later the revolutionary historians were calling him "a man without scruples and with unrestrained and illimitable ambitions" — "an adventurer, a filibuster of major proportions, a man with the soul of a pirate."[3]

In a nutshell, Greene thought he was a developer and his Mexican critics called him an exploiter. To them he was a tool of the *porfirista* government, a symbol of domination by foreigners. He had to go. So they threw the baby out with the bath water.

There should have been a way to use his special skills and experience. After their grim struggle was over, the revolutionary leaders found out that if the people were really to have better lives, a material revolution would have to follow the political and social one. At this point they began to think like capitalists, organizing and concentrating capital in order to carry forward great projects like the Sierra Madre Raiload and the Mexican City subway system, the border-improvement enterprise and the workers' housing developments. The government planners were dreaming and doing just as Greene did, but the Greenes of this world are better than a bureaucracy at getting the job done.

Greene's image in Mexico has indeed been twisted, but the one which has developed in his own country has been distorted just as cruelly. In the first place, he has been remodeled to fit a well-known stereotype — the Wolf of Wall Street.

This creature appeared often in the cartoons of a few years ago — a bulbous, fat-faced sensualist in a cutaway coat, striped pants, spats, and a top hat, with greed in his eyes and money dribbling from his pockets. He was assumed to have no conscience and no regard for anything but money. Anyone who made millions in the market was credited with these characteristics. Some people thought that Colonel Greene epitomized them.

Greene, however, did not really fit the pattern, for the stereotype was complicated by his supposed Western origin. The result was a hybrid: the Cowboy Capitalist. The contrast between his small beginnings and his spectacular climax was good copy, and his biographers have tended to make him as poor and ignorant as possible at the beginning and as extravagant and self-indulgent as possible at the peak. In between are numerous variations — the happy-go-lucky drifter, the irresponsible wastrel, the charming moocher, the habitual cheat and liar. Ira Joralemon in *Romantic Copper* calls him a "ragged-tail gambler'" and adds: "Bill had spent forty-seven years being just as worthless and ornery as the Lord would let him."[4] Ernest J. Hopkins sees him as a "penniless prospector" and tells us that "his is a rags to riches story."[5]

The rags-to-riches emphasis has tempted some writers to reconstruct the Colonel's character entirely and make him out to be a sort of happy hobo. "He rambled all over Sonora," declares Dane Coolidge (father of a good deal of the folklore), "always broke, always happy, always in debt to his friends, still following that mysterious will-o'-the-wisp."[6]

Coolidge goes on to portray him as an irresponsible hobo as well as a happy one, cajoling B. A. Packard out of loans that the banker could not afford to make in order to develop mines that Greene never went near, cheating the miners working for him, always preferring a lie when the truth would have served him better, charming his critics out of their wrath with a disarming smile.

Coolidge proceeded to add insult to injury by writing a novel called *Rawhide Johnny*[7] based on what he believed to be Greene's character and career. It is a travesty which would be laughable if irreparable damage to another human being were not the result.

The principle involved here is that a little folklore, like a little learning, is a dangerous thing. Writers could not let Greene be what he was. How could a man who rose from obscurity to great riches be a quiet fellow who loved his fellow creatures and kept his word? He could not possibly be as simple as that. He had to be a swaggering, boastful, temperamental extrovert, a "buckaroo of Wall Street."[8] No professional journalist could conceive him otherwise. It is almost impossible for one of them to refer to him without using the adjectives "flamboyant" and "swashbuckling." To Isaac Marcosson, historian of the Anaconda Corporation, he is "a swashbuckler, gambler, extrovert" with an "ingratiating, if blustering, personality."[9] Dane Coolidge goes even farther with this sort of nonsense:

> Rawhide Johnny Meadows was a giant, even for the West — a man's man. A courageous, fearless hot-head — ruthless and daring. A gambler with a smile no one could resist — as bold a swashbuckler of high finance as ever trod the street.[10]

Even scholars fall victim to such infectious folklore, and they serve it up garnished with footnotes. "By far the most swashbuckling figure in the history of the Mexican mining industry," writes Marvin D. Bernstein, "was 'Colonel' William C. Greene."[11] The *Dictionary of American Biography* declares that Greene "carried over into Wall Street the Wild-West characteristics of bluff heartiness, braggadocio, and gun toting which he had found effective in Arizona." Economic historian David M. Pletcher remarks that Greene was one of the American promoters who "carried south of the border the grandiose designs, the drawling braggadocio, and the slap-dash energy of the Wild West . . . relying on his native talent for bluff and none too careful about his business methods."[12]

The innuendo about Greene's business ethics reminds us that since he was a promoter he must be not merely a fire-eater but a crooked one as well. The pattern called for a shrewd operator who was primarily interested in money and unscrupulous about how he got it, a Bet-a-Million Gates or a Diamond Jim Brady, a sleight-of-hand performer whose real business was deceiving the public. Marvin Bernstein says:

The wonder of it is, that in spite of its inefficiency the Greene Consolidated Copper Company managed to declare dividends of $2,812,000 between 1900 and 1903 on a total capital (in 1905) of $8,640,000. The explanation seems to be that Greene paid many of them out of later receipts from sales of stock — one of the oldest tricks in the portfolio of the shady promoter. . . . Greene kept his books so badly that none of his figures was really reliable.[13]

These stories, as we have seen, were current in Greene's time to the great indignation of Auditor George Young and the staff of Greene's business office. It is too bad that such loose and unfounded charges should be perpetuated by business historians.

In commenting on Greene's business morality two factors need to be taken into account. First of all, business was not regulated as carefully in his day as it was later on. It was much easier, for instance, to set up a corporation. Greene could put together his interlocking organizations without violating any law. Furthermore, rumors, half-truths, exaggerations, and outright lies were weapons habitually used by the titans of finance to destroy public confidence in their rivals and force them as close to the wall as possible. Thomas W. Lawson did it in *Frenzied Finance* and then complained that he was being assassinated in "the war of mud-slinging and vilification directed by the New York *Commercial,* Henry H. Rogers' own paper, which printed the ridiculous statement that I was crazy."[14]

In such an atmosphere, it was probably inevitable that any man who got rich during this era had his detractors who charged him with every sin from watering his stocks to neglecting his poor old mother. Some of this pitch was bound to stick, and in the case of W. C. Greene, a great deal of it has clung to him down through the decades.

The folklore about Colonel Greene's "shady" dealings begins with his first trip to New York to get financial support for his Cananea venture. In its simplest form the tale picks him up as he sits with pencil in hand writing his first prospectus. He reads it over after he has finished and remarks thoughtfully, "By God, I believe that's true." He was thus the first victim of his own salesmanship. J. Evetts Haley, an ordinarily scrupulous Texas historian, tells it with elaborations:

After thirty years of mining from the Bradshaws to Bisbee and beyond, he knew the high-sounding technical terms and sat down with pencil and paper to write a prospectus that would charm the cash from the pockets of the skeptical financiers on Wall Street.

The story is told that Bill scratched his head, pulled his mustache and scribbled all day at top speed. In the evening his practical partners dropped in to hear the results. Bill threw down the script, thanked the Lord he was finished, and admitted that it was "a daisy." With proper pride he picked it up to read it again to himself. As he read he began to fidget in his chair. He bit off a healthy chew of tobacco, he ran his hand through his hair, and grew more nervous by the minute. At last he tore the script in two and threw it upon the floor while his partners gaped and wanted to know if he was crazy.

"No, by God," Bill shouted. "That mine's too good to sell. I'm going to keep her." [15]

This interesting bit of folklore, too, has passed in somewhat chastened form into the files of the scholars. David Pletcher retails it thus:

Greene, realizing the opportunities which lay before him, began to talk grandly of making Cananea a second Butte, Montana, and he called in friends to help him secure capital and begin operations. One of them, Jim Kirk, reputedly the best miner in Tombstone, went to work as foreman at Bisbee to supply the informal partnership with a little cash, while a second crony, Ed Massey, recruited a few Indians to begin reconnaissance operations at Cananea, hoping to cajole them into accepting promises instead of wages until Greene could find more money. At first the three planned to sell off the mines outright to the highest bidder, and Greene dashed off a tempting prospectus. Early in 1899 he organized the Cobre Grande Company. . . .[16]

Once in New York, according to the story tellers, Greene really let himself go:

He washed off the desert dusts, formed the Cananea Consolidated Copper Company, and headed for New York City to raise a million. He hit the Waldorf like a Western breeze, took a sumptuous suite, registered with a flourish as "Colonel" Greene, rigged himself out in a black frock coat and big black hat, strewed five dollar tips about the place, kept the passing brokers entertained at the bar, and within one month's time actually was "Colonel William C. Greene, the great and new copper magnate." [17]

The idea that the Colonel was actually a bluffer and a fake, not really understanding his business and staying ahead of the game by fast foot-work, was the product of the agencies that were always trying to force him out of control of his companies. If he had been able to stay in command, these charges might have died a natural death; but when he lost his mines, the new management quite understandably sought to improve its own position by downgrading Greene. Any business which posts a sign, "UNDER NEW MANGAGEMENT," has automatically accused the old management of inefficiency. Every communiqué issued by the president and board of directors of the new copper company stated, in one way or another, that things would be better now.

Mining publications went along with this view. When Greene died, the *Engineering and Mining Journal* commented:

The mines were valuable, but of their early management perhaps the less said the better. Colonel Greene was not a miner and under his charge a large amount of money was spent on unsystematic mining and expensive and unsuitable machinery. It was not until later, when a competent management was substituted, that success was really attained.[18]

In view of the fact that in 1906 Greene was turning out 50,000,000 pounds of copper a year,[19] it is hardly fair to say that it was not until 1912 that "Cananea became a sturdy member of the fraternity of great copper mines," or that "Greene's great corporate structure rested on jerry-built foundations," and his operations "were shot through with waste and inefficiency."[20]

Greene's old friends all say that he was honest — that his word was good and that he paid his debts, eventually. He considered himself a professional mining man who knew his business. A retired officer of the *Compañía Minera de Cananea, S. A. de C. V.,* which took over the Colonel's mines, draws what is probably the proper conclusion: "Greene may have expanded too fast, but he was feeling his way." The image of Greene as an amateur in both finance and mining, basically incompetent and actually a high-class confidence man, is unjust and untrue.

Almost as unjust and untrue is the image of Greene the waster, which occurs in close combination with the image of Greene the crook. In this case, however, there is some fire under the smoke. He did spend a lot of money. He spent it on his mines and on his living and on his friends. He liked spending it, and he had been poor long enough to enjoy his financial freedom thoroughly. It is true that none of his old acquaintances ever called on him in vain and that he went far out of his way to take care of men who had stood by him when he needed help. He put many an old buddy on his payroll — Scott White, Jim Kirk, George Burbank, Ed Massey, George Mitchell and many, many more. He expected them to pull their weight, however, and if they didn't, he let them go or moved them to some job that they could handle. The number of these "cronies" who spun off from the organization is quite impressive, and not all of them were happy when they left. Sometimes they sued him, or threatened to.

He took the same attitude toward young people, whom he was always ready to encourage. He would help the sons of his relatives and friends to get through college and would find them a place in his enterprises, but they knew they had to prove their right to stay there.

He was always generous to people in need, whether they were his close friends or not. Morris Parker, a mining man who left a record of his experiences in Mexico, tells of a typical episode:

In Juarez one morning, at the station to take the train to Casas Grandes, I met Mr. Greene, who invited me to ride in his private car. With several of his New York associates, we had a pleasant journey. At Guzman, a station about half way, the train stopped and we got off for a stroll on the platform. Presently we saw, among the second-class passengers, a man we both knew — Charlie Smith, the prospector. . . . In reply to our questions Smith told us he had been prospecting out beyond Casas Grandes and was on his way back. Greene asked him, "How are you fixed for money, Charlie?"

"Oh, all right," Charlie said. "Had a little hard luck last time. Lost one of my mules, but I'm all right now."

Fumbling in his left vest pocket, Greene pulled out several new, folded bills, calmly pulled one off and handed it to Smith. "Here, maybe this will help," he said. "When that's gone, let me know."

It was a $500 bill, U.S. money. Flabbergasted, Smith endeavored to protest, but to no avail.

"O.K. now, Charlie, we're partners. Write to me and keep me posted. If you find anything worth while, maybe I can help you swing it."

When the train started, Greene insisted that Charlie, overalls, battered hat, worn-out shoes, and all, come along and ride in the private car with us.[21]

He loved to make such generous gestures, but when the legend makers got through with him, he was carrying ten-thousand-dollar bills in that vest pocket; standing around on the streets of Bisbee handing out money to the passersby; borrowing from his friends to make a poor man happy when the vest pocket was empty and never paying the lenders back. In time he might have evolved into an Arizona-style Haroun-al-Raschid amusing himself on the streets of his desert Baghdad.

Such tales, plus his suite at the Waldorf, his private railroad cars, and his lavish entertaining of actual and potential stockholders laid him open to a charge of extravagance which he never could, and probably never will, live down. The capitalists who wanted to take over his mines kept these stories going month after month and year after year, though good men disagreed.

In 1902 Walter Harvey Weed, a first-class mining man, made a casual visit to Cananea in the course of other investigations in Mexico. He wrote an unsolicited letter, already quoted, to George Robbins in New York in which he said, in part:

My first impression of your property, railroad, townsite, smelting plant and mines was one of amazement that so much has been accomplished in so short a space of time, my second at the harmonious and systematic way in which the development of so large a district has been carried out.[22]

A year later, when Gates, Hawley and the rest were trying to get Greene into a corner, they sent an engineer to Cananea to make an unfavorable report. He came back with the familiar charges of waste, mismanagement, and extravagance. So Greene sent Robert T. Hill, an eminent geologist, to make a second report — an honest one, supposedly.

Hill's opinion, as Greene transmitted it to the stockholders, said: "The allegations of mismanagement and wasteful expenditure faded before the expansion of system and plan. . . . Cananea today stands as the most remarkable mining achievement of modern years. . . ."[23]

Since there are two sides to this question, a modern historian would seem to be going pretty far out on a limb when he says that at the time of Greene's death, his name was "a synonym for extravagance and waste."[24]

Greene did spend a lot of money, but much of his flourishing of greenbacks was done in connection with his occupation. His old friends and employees say that he was "all business." Over and over his acquaintances made this statement. A certain amount of ostentation was expected of him in the position to which he had attained, but he didn't waste an inordinate amount of time and attention on providing it. His wealth was to him what artillery was to Napoleon, a means to an end — and the end was always development. He wanted to see his ideas bloom and bear fruit.

About the only place where he spent money because he really loved to was in the Equine Department. He did love horses — fast horses, beautiful horses, spirited horses. Anything resembling a horse delighted his soul. He even had a soft spot in his heart for a fine mule. Once on the road from Naco to Cananea with his nephew Clarence Chase, he overtook a man driving a ten-mule team with a brand new wagon and trailer.

"Fine outfit you have there," Greene called out.

"Yes, it is," the man agreed.

"How much do you want for it?"

"Five thousand dollars."

"Get down off that seat and give me those lines."

And Greene handed the reins of his own team to Clarence, wrote a check for $5,000, climbed on the seat of the wagon and drove his mules to Cananea.[25]

And then finally, in talking about Greene's extravagance, we have to admit that he was a gambler — a big one and a good one. As a rancher he had to be something of a gambler. As a promoter he had to be a super-gambler. At the same time he enjoyed and practiced the more sociable and intimate forms of gambling: poker, blackjack, roulette, faro. According to the folklore, he would gamble on anything and once offered to match coins with E. H. Harriman, the railroad magnate, for a million dollars.[26]

On his prolonged and frequent trips by train, he liked to play poker with his friends, and sometimes the stakes were high. Once, coming back from Los Angeles with his friend and partner B. A. Packard of Douglas,

Greene was fifty thousand dollars ahead when they got to Tucson. Instead of getting off, as originally planned, Packard stayed aboard; by the time the train reached El Paso, he had his money back.

The stakes may have been high, but the players were deceptively calm about them. One story tells of a kibitzer who watched Greene, Fall, Burton Mossman, and one or two others in a poker game and decided that it was cautious enough to give him a chance. He asked to sit in and was welcomed. He presented a ten-dollar bill for chips, and Greene said to Mossman, "Captain, will you break up a white one and fix the gentleman up with a fourth?"[27]

At times his poker-playing talents were useful in the conduct of his business. Frank Brophy tells about the time the *Verde* was en route to Naco and points north bearing some important Mexican officials along with the usual assortment of American capitalists and businessmen. Greene lost consistently while the Mexicans were aboard. They got off at Naco, however, and when the game was resumed without them, Greene's poker improved amazingly. Before long he was ahead.[28]

These tales may or may not be true. They have the ring of folklore. Apparently Greene could take care of himself in a poker game, however, and if he consistently won, his gambling can hardly be called extravagance.

Still a third image was added as time went on to the figures of Greene the confidence man and Greene the waster. This was Greene the man of violence, the pistoleer. The father of this *persona* was, in a way, Greene himself. When a bullet from his pistol killed Jim Burnett in the entryway of the O. K. Corral at Tombstone, Greene became a man with notches on his gun, a man who would not let a human life stand between him and his desires. Although we know that Greene did not carry weapons after this tragedy, except for the rifle which he always took along when he drove out in his buggy to inspect his cow pastures, the popular mind pictured him as a Wyatt Earp of Wall Street.

The picture was perpetuated by generation after generation of popular chroniclers, including "Colonel" James H. McClintock who in 1916 turned out a two-volume history of Arizona and its founders. McClintock told how Greene had fallen out with Jim Burnett and "hunted him down on the streets of Tombstone."[29] He went on to recount how Greene, a man of "tremendous pluck and known willingness to kill saved, on one occasion, stock valued at several millions of dollars taken by him from a desk which he had broken open in the office of one of his associates whom he then awaited, revolver in hand. This wild-western way of playing the game was the only one known to him and for a time succeeded."[30]

It would be interesting to know where McClintock got this little jewel. It cannot be documented. Nobody else mentions it until after the

Colonel's death. It was picked up by the New York *Tribune*[31] and made a part of the Colonel's obituary notice. It has been retold over and over since then. Something must have happened to start the story, but what it was, nobody now can say.

The great opportunity for the manufacturers of lethal legends came when Greene had his encounter with Tom Lawson in December 1904. This bloodless battle, already described in detail, has appealed to several generations of inventive journalists. All their stories agree, mistakenly, that the news of Lawson's raid on Greene's Copper Company came to him in the form of a telegram while he was passing some time in Bisbee, and that he then and there determined to get rid of Lawson. "'I'm going to kill him!' the hard-rock miner said, coldly and simply." In one account he gives up the idea when "Jim Burnett's terrorized face" comes before him as he sits in the train. "Greene let the gun drop to the floor. He buried his face in his huge hands."[32]

A more fantastic version takes it from there:

"Don't do it," the priest said. William E. Greene, fingers already touching the .45 beneath his coat, looked up in surprise. The man he intended to murder was in front of him, riding past in a carriage.

"Don't do it," the priest sitting beside him on a bench opposite New York's Central Park, repeated.

The former financial baron of the Arizona-Sonora copper fields let his hand slide down the front of his coat and fall limp in his lap. The revenge he had hoped for was never to be his. Once again Lawson had escaped his wrath. . . .

Greene told this version of his "salvation" after his return to Bisbee and it is supposd to have been corroborated by a Father Carney there.

That Greene went to New York in September, 1907, has been verified. . . . The rest the writer cannot completely vouch for, but passes along as Greene himself passed it along when telling how he "regained his soul." After learning Lawson's habits, Greene decided the best place to assassinate him was near the Seventy-ninth Street entrance to Central Park.[33]

In view of the fact that Greene's visit with Lawson happened on December 18, 1904, in a Boston hotel and that it was perfectly peaceful, there is a certain artless charm in the author's statement that he "can't completely vouch for" a part of the story.

And so, in the popular mind, Colonel Greene became a crooked promoter, a big spender and a pistol-toting man of violence. In the later years of his life another set of stories began to circulate — stories which made him out to be a man who spent an appreciable part of his time in debauchery — drinking, wenching, and gambling. The truth is, Greene was not a heavy drinker, though he was by no means a teetotaler. He took little whiskey at home — a drink or two before dinner — and he did not frequent bars. Mary said she had never in her life seen him under the influence of liquor. Raymond Reid, his stenographer, asserts positively that "Mr. Greene was not a drinking man."[34] He was certainly not the alcoholic which gossip in 1910 and 1911 made him out to be.

His relationships with women were likewise talked about. There can be no doubt that he liked women and had several close friendships with them. At this late date it would be impossible to say, with certainty, how close these friendships were.

Two men who claim to have special knowledge of the Colonel present him as a playboy who spent his nights and a good part of his days in loose living. Dan de Lara Hughes in his scarce book *South From Tombstone* tells how his father Harry Hughes acted as Greene's bodyguard and confidant, aiding and abetting him in his progress through the dives of Naco and other sinful communities on both sides of the border.[35] An old Tombstone citizen who calls himself Niño Cochise is another who claims to have watched out for the Colonel when he was living it up.[36] Neither of these men sounds convincing.

After so many years, and in the absence of almost any contemporary testimony, not much can be known about Colonel Greene's private life. Whatever mistakes he made — and, being a man, he must have made some — there is not much point now in trying to find the kernel of truth in the bushel of gossip.

Mary was sure that the gossip was all vicious and malicious. She became so sensitive to anything that would smirch her husband's reputation that she assumed anything printed about him to be a lie, and she wouldn't look at it. When Frank Brophy's *Arizona Characters,* not at all anti-Greene, came out in 1952, she said, "Lies, lies, all lies," and refused to open it.

She knew what he was to her and to his family and friends — kind and generous, grateful for any token of love or respect, a man of great courage and imagination, great energy and determination, great personal charm and human warmth. She was always proud to be his wife.

To us he is a man typical of his era with its ideals and attitudes firmly riveted in his mind and heart. He was a frontiersman to the end — a man looking for new country and new challenges, a lone fighter pitting his strength against nature and hostile human beings. He was in some ways a New York state Quaker to the end, too, even if he didn't go to church. He believed in success — financial success — as the measure of achievement, and thought hard and constant work was what a man was for. He put it all into words for James Freeman when he turned in his biographical sketch for *Prose and Poetry of the Livestock Industry* in 1905:

The opportunities for becoming financially independent or even very wealthy were never as great as they are today. What the country needs and what it is constantly calling for, are young men of energy and industry who are capable of taking the initiative. . . . The man who recognizes the natural resources that are lying about unnoticed by the ordinary observer — he is the one who rightfully bears off the prize. Any young man who will have confidence in himself and watch for the unknown value, has a foundation that ought to carry him to success.[37]

It was his own prescription, and it describes his own career. In 1905 it sounded right and sensible. It is our misfortune that in our time, when the old Quaker notions of honesty, responsibility, independence, labor, and dedication seem to be vanishing from the earth, his ideas no longer seem — in today's language — "relevant."

Postscript

IT TOOK ALMOST FIFTY YEARS to pull down the house that Greene built.

The first thing to go was the Santa Cruz irrigation project. After his death the whole enterprise ground to a halt. He was the driving force, the motive power, and when he was gone, nobody could or would contribute the time and the skill to keep it going. In 1913 an attempt was made to reactivate it, but before any real effort could be exerted, a flood washed everything away. For several years a prolonged drouth had prevented more than a trickle of water from entering the reservoir. Then came unusually heavy rains, and the dam went.

Sidney Hatch, who did much of the engineering work on the project, thinks one lone gopher may have brought on the catastrophe. The smallest seep of water through the dam would have opened the way for a washout in no time.

In the years that followed, the Colonel's dream was partly realized, though not as he dreamed it. The dam was never restored, but irrigation from wells took its place, and the desert bore fruit, as Greene knew it would.

Under Charlie Wiswall's guidance, the ranch empire survived and even expanded. By the end of the 1920s he had, through care and economy, put the operation in the black for the first time since the Colonel's death. Then came the depression, and the struggle began again.

When the children grew old enough, they took part in the management in various capacities, and the Cattle Company in Mexico continued to exist until 1958, when the Mexican government finally expropriated it. The heirs were compensated, though not to their entire satisfaction.

Mary and Mr. Wiswall were married in 1918. Characteristically, he stipulated that he would continue to draw his salary but would have no part of the estate. He died in 1953; Mary in 1955. She sleeps now in the Cananea cemetery with her first and second husbands beside her.

Within a year after Mary's death a rash of lawsuits broke out among her children and between her children and Eva Day, Greene's daughter by his first wife. As a result of this litigation the ties in a once closely knit family have been seriously and sadly weakened.

Only one of Greene's children, in 1973, retained a part of his empire — Florence (Bebe) on the San Rafael. Until it was sold in 1973, Charles, the youngest, managed the Baca Float fifty miles out of Prescott, Arizona, a ranch acquired by Mary and her children in 1936. Virginia and William had followed their mother and father in death. Eva and Frank were living in the San Francisco Bay area. Kirk was a resident of Nevada.

Time has chipped away most of what Colonel Greene created and held dear. His ranch holdings in the United States have been decimated, and his Mexican enterprises have all passed into other hands. Time, however, has not been able to erase the trail he left across the continent, all the way from the lonely deserts and grasslands of Mexico and the American Southwest to the strenuous streets of New York and Boston.

Chapter Notes

Pages ix–7

THE COPPER SKYROCKET

1. Ira B. Joralemon, *Romantic Copper* (New York: Appleton-Century, 1934), p. 198.
2. Isaac Marcosson, *Anaconda* (New York: Dodd, Mead, 1957), p. 2.
3. Edward Kirkland Chase, *Dream and Thought in the Business Community 1860–1900* (Ithaca: Cornell University Press, 1956), p. 8: "Contemporary observers were prone to assert that 95 percent of all capitalists, 'men carrying on business,' failed. Since successful business talent was a rarity, the bulk of capitalists were in just as 'precarious a position' as other classes in the community."

WITH A SOUND OF TRUMPETS.

1. El Paso *Times,* February 18, 1905.
2. El Paso *Herald,* February 18, 1905.
3. The other members were Mayor C. R. Morehead, Richard Caples, J. A. Smith, Charles De Groff, W. W. Turney, H. J. Simmons, H. B. Stevens, B. F. Hammett, James Magoffin, and Adolf Krakauer.
4. Judge Raymond Reid, Burbank, California, June 30, 1969; Mrs. Charles Greene, Prescott, Arizona, July 4, 1969.
5. El Paso *Times,* February 23, 1905.
6. *Ibid.*
7. El Paso *Herald,* February 18, 1905.

THE MAKING OF A WESTERNER

1. Arizona Census, 1880, part 2 (Pinal, Yavapai, etc.), p. 417.
2. Richard J. Hinton, *The Handbook of Arizona* (San Francisco: Payot, Upham, & Co., 1878), p. 99.
3. Patrick D. Henderson, "Bradshaw Bonanza" *New Mexico Historical Review* 38 (April, 1963): 158, quoting the *Weekly Arizona Miner,* February 21, 1879.
4. El Paso *Herald,* February 23, 1905.
5. Deposition of Mrs. Cicero Martin (Greene's stepdaughter, nee Virginia Moson), Nogales, Arizona, February 25, 1959, filed in the Cochise County Courthouse, Bisbee, Arizona: "He was reserved about a lot of things, and other times he would be most impulsive."

6. Greene family Bible, in possession of Charles H. Greene, Prescott, Arizona.
7. Frank T. Greene to C. L. S., November 16, 1969.
8. The Greenes (the final "e" seems to have been optional) descended from "Surgeon John" Greene, who migrated from England to Rhode Island in 1635 (Harriet Stryker-Rodda, "Ancestry of William C. Greene," Work Chart, 1970–71, MS, in possession of Mrs. Charles H. Greene). Fifth in line of descent from Surgeon John was Dr. Israel Greene, 1792–1886, physician and school inspector of Orange County, New York. The Rhode Island Greenes moved about freely. Some went to Massachusetts — later to New York state when a "Western fever" struck them (Lora S. La Mance, *The Greene Family and Its Branches from A.D. 861 to A.D. 1904,* Floral Park, New York: Mayfield Publishing Company, 1904; Samuel W. Eager, *An Outline History of Orange County,* Newburgh, New York: S. T. Callahan, 1846–1847; Principal Frank L. Greene, *Descendants of Joseph Greene of Westerly, R. I.,* Albany: Joel Munsell's Sons, 1894). More members of the Greene family came to Orange County in the migrations that followed the Revolutionary War.
9. The Quaker records show that Israel Greene, Townsend's father, attended a Quaker meeting at Green Bay, Wisconsin, in 1848. Townsend may have settled there by that date. W. W. Hinshaw, *Encyclopedia of American Quaker Genealogy* (Ann Arbor, Michigan: Edwards Brothers, 1936), (New York Monthly Meeting), vol. 3, p. 138.
10. The Cornell story is told by the Rev. John Cornell in *Genealogy of the Cornell Family* (New York: T. A. Wright, 1902). Thomas Cornell was born in 1595 in Essex, England. He came to the New World in 1638 and left Massachusetts in 1640 to escape persecution, settling in Portsmouth, Rhode Island. Samuel Cornell (1761–1812), father of Haydock and grandfather of Eleanor, was a resident of Orange County and a neighbor of the Greenes and the Townsends in Monroe Township, but he had many relatives across the Hudson in Westchester County — one reason, perhaps, for Haydock's settling in Newcastle Township at or near the village of Chappaqua. Large families were the rule with the Greenes and the Cornells (Haydock Hunt Cornell had ten children; Israel Greene had seven), and there were cousins and uncles and aunts in every direction.
11. Eleanor Greene was somehow related to the Truman Chase family of Kasson (Emadair Chase Jones to C. L. S., February 2, 1970).
12. Mary Ann was still part of her grandfather's household in 1870 (U.S. Census, Newcastle Township, Westchester County, New York, 389).
13. Mary Romer (Charlotte's granddaughter) of Pleasantville, New York, to John W. Ackley of Rahway, New Jersey, December 6, 1954, letter in possession of Mrs. John W. Ackley.
14. *The Cananea Herald,* April 4, 1903, says William attended "Chappaqua College." According to Mrs. Douglas Grafflin, Director, Chappaqua Public Library (letter to C. L. S., September 17, 1969), Chappaqua Mountain Institute was founded in 1870 by a Quaker group. Greene could have attended briefly, but Mrs. Phoebe Whitney, President, Chappaqua Historical Society, reports that Greene's name is not found in the "partial list" of students for 1870.
15. Judge Raymond Reid, Burbank, California, June 30, 1969.
16. John P. Baker, New York Public Library, in letters to C. L. S., July 18, November 19, 1969, reports on notices in the New York Directory for 1868 and 1871–72 regarding Onderdonk Angevine and W. C. Greene. His wife Mary and his friends understood that he was seventeen when he left home (Frank T. Greene to C. L. S., November 20, 1969).
17. Mrs. Charles H. Greene, Prescott, Arizona, June 24, 1970.
18. Judge Raymond L. Reid, Burbank, California, June 30, 1969.
19. El Paso *Herald,* November 15, 1905; Cananea *Herald,* April 4, 1903; *Fads and Fancies of Representative Americans at the Beginning of the Twentieth Century* (New York: Town Topics Publishing Company, 1905), pp. 170–71.
20. E. V. Smalley, *History of the Northern Pacific* (New York: Putnam, 1883) p. 187.
21. Historians of the Northern Pacific Railroad and of Fargo, North Dakota, have found no mention of Greene's name in their records (Frank H. Coyne, Vice President, Northern Pacific Railroad, to C. L. S., September 19, 1969; Ralph

W. Hidy, Isidor Straus Professor of Business History, Harvard University, to C. L. S., October 28, 1969; Robert L. Peterson, Hill Professor of Business History, University of Montana, to C. L. S., January 19, 1970; W. C. Hunter, Archivist, Cass County Historical Society, Fargo, North Dakota, to C. L. S., August 20, 1969).

22. *Dictionary of National Biography,* vol. 7, p. 577; Ralph A. Donham, "Buckaroo of Wall Street," *Arizona Republic,* November 24, 1957.
23. Little Mineral is listed in *Southern and Western Texas Guide for 1878,* by J. L. Rock and W. I. Smith (St. Louis: H. Granger, 1878).
24. The envelope is missing. Charles Greene, who has preserved this and the following letter, conjectures that Will's correspondent was a Romer, one of a family of cousins living in Tarrytown, New York.
25. Frank T. Greene to C. L. S., December 1, 1969.
26. *Prose and Poetry of the Livestock Industry* (New York: Antiquarian Press, 1932), p. 621.
27. Greene's stepdaughter, Mrs. C. H. Martin, and his stepson Frank Moson in several interviews gave 1877 as the date of his arrival in Arizona. See "Dark Postscript Looms for Greene," Tucson *Daily Citizen,* July 29, 1958.
28. Edward H. Peplow, Jr., *History of Arizona* (New York: Lewis Publishing Company, 1958), vol. 2, p. 505.
29. *Ibid.*
30. Harshaw had an unusually brief period of prosperity. By 1882 it was becoming a ghost town (Tombstone *Weekly Epitaph,* January 16, 1882; Georgia Wehrman, "Harshaw: Mining Camp of the Patagonias," *Journal of Arizona History* 6 (Spring, 1965): 21–36.
31. Joe Chisholm, *Brewery Gulch* (San Antonio: Naylor, 1949), p. 152; Edward H. Peplow, *History of Arizona,* vol. 2, p. 505; Carl Hays, interview, El Paso, Texas, January 30, 1970.

TOMBSTONE DAYS

1. Frank C. Lockwood, *Pioneer Days in Arizona* (New York: Macmillan, 1932), pp. 206–211; John Myers Myers, *The Tombstone Story* (New York: Grosset & Dunlap, 1950), pp. 21–33.
2. Odie B. Faulk, *Tombstone: Myth and Reality* (New York: Oxford, 1972), p. 87.
3. Myers, *The Tombstone Story,* p. 42.
4. *The Private Journal of George Whitwell Parsons,* vol. 3, Sunday, April 4, 1880 (Phoenix: Statewide Archival and Records Project, 1939).
5. Walter Noble Burns, *Tombstone* (New York: Penguin, 1942), pp. 18–22.
6. C. L. Sonnichsen, *Billy King's Tombstone* (Tucson: University of Arizona Press, 1972), pp. 93–116.
7. Mack Axford, interview, Tombstone, Arizona, June 24, 1969.
8. Judge Raymond L. Reid, interview, Burbank, California, June 30, 1969.
9. Tombstone *Weekly Epitaph,* March 13, 1882.
10. Ben Williams, Sr., interview, Douglas, Arizona, June 23, 1969.
11. Myers, *The Tombstone Story,* p. 38.
12. Greene to George Mitchell, August 1, 1901, files of Compañía Minera, Cananea, Sonora, Mexico (hereafter referred to as CM files).
13. Dane Coolidge, *Fighting Men of the West* (New York: E. P. Dutton, 1932), p. 195.
14. Joe Chisholm, *Brewery Gulch* (San Antonio: Naylor, 1949), p. 152.
15. Myers, *The Tombstone Story,* p. 57.
16. George W. Chambers to C. L. S., July 31, 1969, quoting an interview with Columbus Giragi, former co-owner of the Tombstone *Epitaph* and *Prospector:* "Bill Greene never did work in the Tough Nut, let alone as a hardrock miner."
17. National Archives, Record Group 123, Claim No. 2278.
18. Paul I. Wellman, *The Indian Wars of the West* (New York: Doubleday, 1954), pp. 424–25.
19. The date of the last raid is given as December 26, 1866 — obviously a mistake since Greene was a schoolboy of thirteen in that year. Although Geronimo and his Chiricahuas were sent to Florida in September of 1886, raiding continued. John Gray's horse herd was raided in Rucker Canyon in the Chiricahua

Mountains in June, 1890, and a man named Hardie was killed (Tombstone *Epitaph,* June 14, 1890).

20. Ralph Donham, "Buckaroo of Wall Street," *Arizona Republic,* November 24, 1957.
21. Cananea *Herald,* April 4, 1903.
22. James M. Barney, "W. C. Greene, Paul Revere of Arizona." Prescott *Evening Courier,* March 26, 1951; *Dictionary of American Biography,* vol. 7, p. 577.
23. Los Angeles *Daily Times,* October 17, 1901; *Prose and Poetry of the Livestock Industry* (New York: Antiquarian Press, 1960), p. 622.
24. *Fads and Fancies of Representative Americans* (New York: Town Topics Publishing Company, 1905), pp. 170–71.
25. El Paso *Herald,* November 15, 1905; Mack Axford, *Around Western Campfires,* pp. 185–86.
26. Frank T. Greene, Tucson, November 29, 1970.
27. No claims are registered in Greene's name. Four, owned by Sam Barrow, in the Dos Cabezas Mountains fifty miles east of Tombstone, were located in 1880 and could have been registered by Greene in Barrow's name. Transcribed Mining Record, Index of Names of Locators of Mines, vol. 5, pp. 670, 671, 680, 681, Cochise County Courthouse, Bisbee, Arizona.
28. Sam G. Barrow to C. L. S., September 19, 1969.
29. Sam G. Barrow to C. L. S., September 19, 1969, November 14, 1969; interview, St. David's, Arizona, June 27, 1970.
30. Interview, August 24, 1969.
31. Frank T. Greene, Tucson, April 6, 1970.
32. Probate Records, Santa Clara County, San Jose, California. John G. Roberts' will, dated July 18, 1874, was probated after his death in 1878. A printed form added to the will on July 25, 1874, values his real estate at $125,000, profits from real estate at $10,000, and personal property at $150,000. Half of the estate was to go to the widow. The rest, $142,500, was to be divided among eight heirs. The Decree of Partial Distribution shows that Ella had borrowed $3,000 from her father on September 14, 1878. The sum of $5,000 "advance" had been given her at the time the will was made, the same amount having been given to the other children. The papers do not contain a record of what she received in the final settlement, but it should have been either $14,812 or $9,812, depending on whether the $5,000 advance payment was subtracted. Colonel Greene's statement that she had $8,500 to invest must be nearly correct.
33. Unsigned statement of Frank B. Moson, MS, John B. Tittmann files.
34. Parish records, St. Paul's Church, Tombstone.
35. Eva Moson Bradshaw to C. L. S., September 4, 1969.
36. Deposition of Mrs. Cicero Martin.
37. John B. Tittmann files. The letter is dated October 15, 1909. Frank Moson in his statement, made during the litigation over the Greene inheritance, said, "... we were always told that the amount she had was very large and ran around $100,000." The value of Ella's property was a major point of difference among the heirs.
38. Copies of the affidavits are in the John B. Tittmann files.
39. Statement of Frank B. Moson, John B. Tittmann files.
40. Minutes of the Cochise County Board of Equalization, meeting at Tombstone on July 8, 1899, Brophy papers in possession of A. Blake Brophy, Phoenix, Arizona.
41. Final Decree in the Case of the San Rafael del Valle Grant, Arizona, no. 30, National Archives, Record Group 9, Case no. 3. The file is no longer available.
42. In the J. B. Tittmann files is a letter from J. B. Tittmann to Norman S. Sterry (an associate) dated March 31, 1961, containing a review of exhibits in the case of Day vs. Greene: "Included in that exhibit is a deed of trust executed by W. C. Greene and his wife Ella on December 27, 1887, to the Cochise Hardware & Trading Company to secure an indebtedness of $1,664.14 for a period of one year. The . . . deed of trust offers as security for this account land on both sides of the San Pedro River containing 168 acres 'now occupied by the first parties' [Col. Greene and Ella], together with a water right. The deed of trust quotes the filing of the water right which was sworn to by Col. Greene and recites that he had by that notice located and claims that ditch and water

right in connection with 'the homestead located by me in October, 1883.' The above instrument is the only record which discloses the source of Col. Greene's claim to the ranch on which he and Ella lived and which is referred to as the Hereford Ranch."

43. Greene employed Tucson attorney Eugene Ives in the matter of clearing title to the San Rafael del Valle property. The Ives letter books in the Special Collections of the University of Arizona Library, particularly for the year 1905, show how complicated the whole proceeding was.

44. Frank C. Brophy, Elgin, Arizona, August 23, 1969; *Arizona Sketchbook* (Phoenix: Arizona Messenger Ptg. Co., 1952), p. 241.

45. Mrs. Burton Devere, Tombstone, June 23, 1969.

46. Copy in John B. Tittmann files.

47. Deed Record, Cochise County, copy in John B. Tittmann files. He described the property as follows: "An undivided one third (⅓) in of and to that certain Dam and Ditch situated on the San Pedro River just below Hereford and now supplies my ranch and the ranch of Peter Moore with water. Said ditch was first used by one Tanner in 1877 and known as the 'Tanner ditch' and later has been and now is known as the 'Greene and Moore ditch,' and is of record in Cochise County which record is hereby referred to."

48. Miscellaneous Records, Cochise County, vol. 3, pp. 315–17.

49. Civil Actions, Cochise County, Book I, Nos. 1993, 2015 (Greene sued two citizens named Warnekros and Dake in 1895); No. 1169 (Allen English). Greene paid in three installments: on July 16, August 24, and September 4. 1895. In the middle nineties Greene borrowed twice from William Brophy's bank in Bisbee: $450 in July, 1893, which was repaid in April, 1895; $150 in April, 1895, repaid in December (Frank C. Brophy to C. L. S., June 1, 1970).

50. Civil Actions, Cochise County, Book I, Case No. 1970, January 7, 1898. Judgment rendered May 20, 1898 (Register of Actions and Fees, Book 5). Papers in this case have not been located.

51. Greene to Mitchell, August 21, 1901, CM files.

52. Greene to W. H. Brophy, August 1, 1904, Brophy papers.

53. Robert Lenon, interview, Patagonia, Arizona, June 29, 1970.

54. Statement of Frank B. Moson, MS, John B. Tittmann files.

55. Deposition of Mrs. Cicero Martin, Nogales, February 25, 1959: "We financed him for three years before he made a go of Cananea."

56. Frank T. Greene, interview, Tucson, April 6, 1970.

57. The issue of January 16 reported a horse-stealing raid on the Helm ranch. On February 8 the murder of Jacob Whitsel at Willow Springs was reported. The Indians had beaten him to death with stones. Their trail led to Cochise Stronghold and passed within eight miles of town.

58. Mack Axford, interview, Tombstone, Arizona, June 24, 1969.

TROUBLE ON THE SAN PEDRO

1. Hal Mitchell, "Justice Jim," *Arizona Highways* 21 (July, 1945): 32.

2. Richard W. Fulton and Conrad J. Bahre, "Charleston, Arizona, a Documentary Reconstruction," *Arizona and the West* 9 (Spring, 1967): 53–54.

3. The census of 1880 noted his origin and said he was a widower forty-eight years old. In 1897 he had a wife and two daughters who came to his funeral (Tombstone *Prospector,* July 2, 1897).

4. F. R. Walker, *Stamping Grounds,* MS in possession of W. H. Holmes of Berkeley, California. Frank C. Lockwood (*Pioneer Days in Arizona,* p. 266) confirms Walker's story of the "self-sustaining court."

5. Lockwood, *Pioneer Days,* p. 266.

6. *Ibid.* p. 267.

7. *Arizona Weekly Citizen* (Tucson), October 29, 1882.

8. Allen A. Erwin, *The Southwest of John Horton Slaughter* (Glendale: Arthur H. Clark, 1965), p. 209.

9. Fulton and Bahre, "Charleston," p. 44.

10. Mack Axford in *Around Western Campfires* (Tucson: University of Arizona Press, 1969), p. 20, notes that as long as Burnett stuck to cattle raising, there was no trouble. When he decided to farm his acres, the difficulty began.

11. July 8, 1897.

12. Tombstone *Prospector,* December 17, 1897; Nogales *Border Vidette,* July 17, 1897. For Packard, see *Arizona, the Youngest State* (Chicago: S. J. Clarke, 1916), pp. 30–33.
13. The *Border Vidette* for July 17, 1897, quoting the Bisbee *Lyre,* notes that at the habeas corpus proceedings a Mrs. Hart testified to hearing Burnett say that he "would kill Greene on sight or at the first chance he had."
14. Dane Coolidge, *Fighting Men of the West,* p. 199: Greene threatened Burnett "before several witnesses." Sutton Menard, interviewed for the University of Arizona Tape Collection in July, 1969, says "He sent word to Burnett to always carry a gun because Greene had come to kill him."
15. July 1, 1897.
16. Their names were Ah On, On Lum, On Sam, Sam On, and Ah Quay. Greene sued them later on (Civil Actions, Cochise County, Book I, Cases no. 1969, 1970).
17. Nogales *Border Vidette,* July 17, 1897; Axford, *Around Western Campfires,* p. 21.
18. Stephen E. Aguirre, retired U.S. Consul General, undated letter to C. L. S.: "Another time I remember having seen Colonel Greene was when Mother took me to the funeral of his oldest daughter, Ella, in Bisbee, Arizona."
19. Tucson *Daily Citizen,* July 3, 1897.
20. Tombstone *Prospector,* July 1, 1897.
21. *Ibid.,* December 17, 1897. There may be some significance in the fact that Greene brought suit against Ah On about this time (Civil Actions, Cochise County, Book 2, numbers 1969, 1970, *W. C. Greene* vs. *Ah On et al,* Register of Actions, vol. 5, pp. 317, 318). The Chinese farmers had become indebted for goods and services to A. H. Emanuel, who was clerk of the District Court. He assigned his account to Greene, who instituted action on June 29, 1897. Sheriff Scott White took possession of "wagons, horses, mules, harness and growing crop on the Games ranch on the San Pedro . . . the property of Ah Lum Company." This was five days after the dam was blown out.
22. The Tucson *Daily Citizen* for July 3 says Burnett's dam had been blown out and he was on his way to see about it.
23. Testimony of witnesses at the coroner's inquest, July 1, 1897, testimony of John Montgomery.
24. Jerry Beller, a specialist in Charleston and Tombstone history, provides the information about Tombstone geography (Beller to C. L. S., December 11, 1969).
25. This statement does not agree with Greene's later testimony that he learned about what had happened after his return from Mexico, or the newspaper story that the news reached him in Nogales.
26. Tombstone *Epitaph,* July 2, 1897.
27. Testimony of witnesses at the coroner's inquest, July 1, 1897.
28. Mrs. Burton Devere, Tombstone, June 23, 1969; Dane Coolidge, *Fighting Men of the West,* p. 199.
29. Tombstone *Prospector,* July 6, 1897.
30. *Ibid.,* July 8, 1897.
31. Robert E. Ladd, "Vengeance at the O. K. Corral," *Arizoniana* 4 (Summer, 1963), pp. 6–7.
32. Dane Coolidge, *Fighting Men of the West,* p. 199.
33. Frank King and his brother Sam were lifelong friends and employees of Colonel Greene. Frank became well known as a writer of reminiscent and biographical articles about the West.
34. Robert E. Ladd, "Vengeance at the O. K. Corral," p. 8.
35. Tombstone *Prospector,* December 17, 1897.
36. *Ibid.,* December 20, 1897. The *Daily Star* for December 19 says there was "an uproar of applause."
37. Mack Axford, Tombstone, June 24, 1969.

CANANEA

1. Jerry Beller, "Helltown, Arizona," MS (a history of Charleston).
2. George Young, "Greene Cananea Copper Company and Subsidiaries: Histori-

cal Sketch," MS, Cananea, Sonora, August, 1920, p. 11: "A legend exists that perhaps a century and a half ago a woman called La Cananea — the Canaanite Woman — lived in the original settlement. But the experts say that if she were really a woman of Canaan, she would have been called La Canaanense. The word Canaan is spelled the same in both Spanish and English."

3. Ernest J. Burrus, *Kino and the Cartography of New Spain* (Tucson: Arizona Pioneers' Historical Society, 1965), Plate IX.
4. J. N. Bowman and Robert F. Heizer, *Anza and the Northwest Frontier of New Spain* (Los Angeles: Southwestern Museum, 1967), p. 45.
5. Ignaz Pfefferkorn, *Sonora, A Description of the Province,* trans. Theodore Treutlein (Albuquerque: University of New Mexico Press, 1949), pp. 42–43, 89.
6. Francisco Almada, *Diccionario de historia, geografía y biografía Sonorenses* (Chihuahua: n.p., n.d.), pp. 5–6.
7. George Young, *Greene Cananea Copper Company,* p. 11; Almada, *Diccionario,* p. 140; Cananea *Herald,* April 4, 1903.
8. William F. Nye, *Sonora: Its Extent, Population, Natural Productions, Indian Tribes, Mines, Mineral Lands, Etc.* (San Francisco: H. H. Bancroft and Company, 1861), pp. 148–149 (trans. from the Spanish of José F. Velasco).
9. Sylvester Mowry, *Geography and Resources of Arizona and Sonora: An Address Before the American Geographical and Statistical Society, New York, February 3, 1859* (Washington: Henry Polkinghorn, 1859), p. 25.
10. Leonidas Hamilton, *Border States of Mexico,* New York, 1883, quoted by George Young in "Historical Data About the Mines at Cananea," MS, 1921, pp. 1–4, CM files.
11. Rudolph F. Acuña, "Ignacio Pesqueira: Sonoran Caudillo." *Arizona and the West* 12 (Summer, 1970), pp. 139–72.
12. Eduardo W. Villa, *Compendio de la historia del estado de Sonora* (Mexico: Editorial "Patria Nueva," 1937), p. 304.
13. Ramón Corral, *El General Ignacio Pesqueira* (Hermosillo: Imprenta del Estado, 1900), pp. 131–32.
14. George Young, *Greene Cananea Copper Company,* MS, p. 12.
15. Fernando Pesqueira to C. L. S., June 3, 1970.
16. George Young, *Greene Cananea Copper Company,* MS, pp. 12–13; George Young, *Historical Data Concerning the Mines of Cananea,* MS, pp. 4–5.
17. George Young, *Historical Data,* MS, pp. 4–5.
18. *Memoria de la administración publica del estado de Sonora, presentada a la legislatura del mismo por el gobernador Ramón Corral,* II, Hermosillo, 1891 (transcript provided by Sr. Fernando Pesqueira of Hermosillo).
19. George Young, *Greene Cananea,* p. 13.
20. J. R. Southworth, *The Mines of Mexico.* (Liverpool: Blake and Mackenzie, 1905), p. 230. George Young's account differs from Southworth's in a number of details.
21. Corral, *Memoria.*
22. Charles Wise, Nogales, Arizona, June 29, 1970.
23. J. D. Southworth, *The Mines of Mexico,* vol. 9, p. 231.
24. Brophy papers.
25. Press Reference Library, vol. 1, p. 193.
26. The Sonora Mining Company, G. A. Harmes, President, was based in Newport, Kentucky (Cananea *Herald,* April 14, 1903).
27. Mrs. Gladys Lindsay Splane to C. L. S., January 6, 1970.
28. Southworth, *The Mines of Mexico,* p. 231.
29. Mrs. Lena Des Saulles, Tucson, June 25, 1970.
30. A clipping from the Boston News Bureau, mailed by Harrison and Wyckoff to W. H. Brophy on February 2, 1903, mentions some potent names: "At least twenty people had examined and turned down the Greene property before it was taken up by Mr. Greene. Phelps Dodge & Co. examined it, found the title defective, and dropped it. Weir, the Mexican copper mining man, could find no proper title and abandoned it. Heinze of Montana looked at it and like all the others turned it down. Then along comes Colonel Greene, who never before saw a copper mine, picks it up, wades through litigation, straightens out the title and brings forth a 'whale' in the copper world" (Brophy papers).
31. A copy of the indenture is in the Tittmann files.

32. George Young, *Greene Cananea Copper Company,* MS, pp. 7–8.
33. Deeds were exchanged on May 19, but apparently these were not protocolized (recorded). On January 19, 1901, in Arizpe, Storman and Iruretagoyena took the final steps. By this time Greene had deeded all the mines to the Cananea Consolidated Copper Company (George Young to D. J. Haff, June 26, 1909, CM files.
34. The company was never dissolved, but Greene destroyed all stock certificates and it died a natural death (George Young, *Greene Cananea,* p. 8).
35. Federico García y Alva, *México y sus progresos: Album directorio, Estado de Sonora* (Hermosillo: Imprenta Oficial, 1905–1907), no pagination.
36. Frank T. Greene, Tucson, November 29, 1969.
37. According to Frank T. Greene, the Colonel's son, W. C. Greene was in jail in Hermosillo at the time of his wife's death, "the Justice Burnett heirs having had him arrested or detained in Mexico, after the trial." (Frank T. Greene to C. L. S., December 3, 1970).
38. Greene was in Arizpe on September 7, 1898, when the concessions were granted by the *Agencia de la Secretaria de Fomento en Ramo de Minería,* Expedientes no. 372, 373, and 374. The transaction was reported in *La Constitución,* official periodical of the State of Sonora, on October 12.

COBRE GRANDE

1. Cananea *Herald,* April 4, 1903, biographical sketch of George Mitchell.
2. *Ibid.*
3. Litigation in the Cobre Grande suits went on until 1906. Greene and his associates put together all the material bearing on the final suit, including records of previous litigation, and presented it to the Supreme Court of the State of New York, where the case was heard, on December 20, 1906, as *Answer to the Amended Complaint.* The Answer included twenty-five exhibits, the last one being a transcript of the decision of the U.S. Supreme Court rendered on appeal from the Supreme Court of the Territory of Arizona, No. 87, argued November 29 through December 1, 1905, and decided on January 6, 1906. The Greene-Mitchell agreement is rehearsed several times. The entire file exists in a bound volume in the Special Collections division of the University of Arizona Library.
4. Cananea *Herald*, April 4, 1903.
5. The Mines deeded in this agreement, with Mexican registry numbers, were as follows:

Group I		Group II	
Mina Grande No. 2	370	San Ignacio	2401
Cobre Grande No. 2	371	La Chivatera	2402
El Ronquillo No. 2	373	Cobre Grande	2403
La Chivatera No. 2	374	El Ronquillo	2469
Pavo Real No. 3	375		
La Suerte No. 3	376		
Veta Grande	379		
Perdida	377		
La Esperanza	6117		

6. Cananea *Herald,* April 4, 1903.
7. *Answer to Amended Complaint,* Defendant's Exhibit II (George Mitchell's Answer to Amended Complaint), p. 3.
8. *History of the Counties of McKean, Elk, Cameron and Potter, Pa.* (Chicago: J. H. Beers & Co., 1890), pp. 1104–09, 1209–12.
9. Nogales *Oasis,* August 19, 1899.
10. Buffalo *Daily Courier,* May 5, 1903. On May 4 Costello's wife shot him but did not kill him. She had written to Mitchell on September 4, 1901, "I firmly believe that he is crazy." (CM files.)
11. *Arizona Republican,* September 25, 1899.
12. *Ibid.,* September 23, 1899.
13. *Answer to Amended Complaint,* p. 53.
14. Jerome *Reporter,* December 28, 1899.

15. Nogales *Oasis,* July 29, 1899, quoting the *Arizona Republican.*
16. *Statement of J. Henry Wood,* John B. Tittmann collection (list of letters, papers, and telegrams retained by him as secretary of the Cobre Grande Corporation), letters of September 2, 6, 7, 20.
17. Brophy papers, undated.
18. *Answer to Amended Complaint,* pp. 26, 113–14; *Arizona Republican,* September 29, 1899.
19. Brewery Gulch, Bisbee's street of sin, was named for Muheim's brewery.
20. George Young, *Greene Cananea Copper Company and Subsidiaries: Historical Sketch,* MS, Cananea, Sonora, August, 1920, p. 9, CM files.
21. *Statement of J. Henry Wood,* MS, telegram, Costello to Wood, August 4, 1899; letter, August 5, 1899, regarding shipments to Aguas Calientes.
22. *Arizona Republican,* October 14, 1899.
23. *Statement of J. Henry Wood,* J. Henry Wood to J. H. Costello, September 2, 1899 (Chase wants to examine the books).
24. Dane Coolidge, *Fighting Men of the West* (New York: C. P. Dutton, 1932), p. 202.
25. Mrs. Burton Devere, Tombstone, June 23, 1969.
26. *Arizona Republican,* October 14, 1899.
27. *Ibid.,* October 22, 1899.
28. *Dictionary of American Biography,* vol. 7, p. 577.
29. The exact relationship between the Greenes and the Chases has not been established, but Greene's mother went to live with the Chases in Minnesota after the death of her husband. Greene's sister Phoebe married a Chase, and her son Clarence found a place in the Colonel's organization.
30. Nogales *Oasis,* September 2, 1899.
31. *Ibid.,* September 25, 1899. Chase was representing "various mining parties."
32. Logan was a famous clubman and civic worker. Member of an old Connecticut family, he knew everybody worth knowing. He died suddenly of a heart attack on July 19, 1906 (New York *Times,* July 20, 1906).
33. Descendants of the first Mrs. Greene believe that a major part of the money came from her (Frank B. Moson, *Statement,* MS, Tittmann files: "Where else would he get it?"). See page 275, note 32.
34. Nogales *Oasis,* August 12, 1899, quoting the Prescott *Courier;* El Paso *Herald,* October 31, 1907.
35. J. A. Campbell to J. C. Kirk, September 8, 1906, CM files.
36. Thomas W. Lawson, *Frenzied Finance,* New York: Ridgway-Thayer, 1905, pp. 2–3.
37. J. Evetts Haley, "Bill Greene of Cananea Copper," *The Shamrock* (Summer, 1962), p. 6.
38. Nogales *Oasis,* September 9, 1899.
39. *Answer to Amended Complaint,* Supplemental Petition in Texas Suit, Exhibit D., p. 33.
40. *Answer to Amended Complaint,* pp. 54–57; *ibid.,* Greene's Answer to Amended Complaint in Maricopa Suit, Exhibit 8, pp. 9–10.
41. *Arizona Republican,* October 19, 1899.
42. *Answer to Amended Complaint,* Defendant's Exhibit I, pp. 11–12; *Arizona Republican,* September 23, October 13, 1899.
43. *Answer to Amended Complaint,* Defendant's Exhibit B (W. C. Greene's answer to original complaint in Maricopa suit), p. 6.
44. *Answer to Amended Complaint,* Exhibit B, Statement of Aurelio Melgarejo to Judge of First Instance, pp. 22–24.
45. *Arizona Republican,* October 8, 10, 13, 14, 19, 1899.
46. Frank M. King, *Pioneer Western Empire Builders* (Los Angeles: Trail's End Publishing Co., 1946), pp. 164–68. There is material on Sam King in *Western Livestock Journal,* vol. 24 (November 15, 1945). The *Jerome Mining News,* June 29, 1903, says Greene has given Sam "a mine, fully equipped, in Sonora."
47. Nogales *Oasis,* October 7, 1899.
48. Haff to Young, June 13, 1909 (list of mines with dates of acquisition).
49. It cost the Company $5,000 in 1909 to get the books (F. E. Searle to Dr. L. D. Ricketts, February 26, 1909, CM files).

50. Nogales *Oasis,* October 21, 1899. Costello wires from New York that all has been settled amicably. The *Arizona Republican* for October 10 covers Wood's arrest.
51. Arizona *Republican,* October 19, 1899.
52. George Young, *Greene Cananea Copper Company,* MS, CM files.
53. *Arizona Republican,* September 23, 1899.
54. Letter to Cobre Grande stockholders, November 1, 1899, unsigned copy, Brophy Papers.
55. George Mitchell, Letter to Cobre Grande stockholders, November 3, *Ibid.*
56. *Statement of J. Henry Wood,* Judge's order suspending order for Greene's arrest, dated December 12, 1899, CM files.
57. El Paso *Herald,* October 30, 1900.
58. The case was filed on September 21, 1899. *Answer to Amended Complaint,* Defendant's Exhibit 12; *Arizona Republican,* October 22, 1899.
59. *Arizona Republican,* October 19, 1899.
60. W. H. Brophy of Bisbee was one who took the stock — 250 shares of Greene Consolidated for 500 shares of Cobre Grande (Walter S. Logan to W. H. Brophy, October 2, 1900, Brophy papers).
61. *Answer to Amended Complaint,* Defendant's Exhibit I, p. 11.
62. Shirley vs. Mitchell and the Cobre Grande Copper Company is mentioned in the *Engineering and Mining Journal* 74 (March 30, 1901): 414; the Bisbee *Daily Review,* January 27, 1904; New York *Times,* March 19, 1901.
63. *Answer to Amended Complaint,* Defendant's Exhibit 25. J. E. Addicks was a party to the complaint.
64. *Answer to Amended Complaint,* pp. 104, 112–13.
65. Greene to Gage, July 8, 1902, CM files.
66. L. H. Chalmers was one of Greene's lawyers during this period, and his papers in the Arizona Collection, Arizona State University, Tempe, Arizona, are enlightening.
67. J. D. Dort to L. H. Chalmers, May 16, 1902, Arizona Collection, Arizona State University, Tempe. Greene won the suit when it came to trial (Bisbee *Review,* January 27, 1904).
68. Greene arranged to have men of his selection replace him and Barnes. Telegrams, Greene and Barnes to Chalmers, August 21, 1901, Arizona Collection, Arizona State University, Tempe.
69. Franklin E. Searle to L. D. Ricketts, February 26, 1909. Searle included with his letter the *Statement of J. Henry Wood* listing the documents he had retained. He concluded his letter, "I am writing you this letter as counsel for the Cananea Consolidated Copper Co. as well as the Cobre Grande Copper Co. and request that you treat it as a confidential communication and file it among papers that come under your own control" (CM files).
70. Kosterlitzky to Greene, January 17, 1901, CM files.

THE ASCENT BEGINS

1. *Remarks of General T. H. Anderson and W. C. Greene, President, at the Stockholders Meeting, July 22, 1901,* Brophy Papers.
2. *Engineering and Mining Journal* 92 (August 19, 1911): 347.
3. *Engineering and Mining Journal* 67 (April 29, 1899): 512: A 500-ton smelter will be erected "without sinking a shaft, as there is said to be sufficient ore near the surface. . . ." Mining geologists note that major desert copper deposits often showed surface deposits of gold nuggets and silver chlorides on top of high-grade copper chlorides and carbonates; beneath these, copper oxides; below the oxidized zone, low-grade copper sulfides. In Greene's time the oxidized zone could be profitably mined, given adequate water, cheap labor, and railroad transportation. The low-tenor copper porphyries are being open-pitted at Cananea in 1973.
4. Greene to Mitchell, August 16, 1901, CM files.
5. Walter S. Logan to George Mitchell, December 31, 1900, CM files.
6. Greene to Mitchell, August 16, 1901, CM files.

7. Logan to Mitchell, December 11, 1900, CM files.
8. J. H. McClintock, *Arizona* (Chicago: S. J. Clarke, 1916), vol. 2, p. 604. The story is quoted by many modern writers including Marvin D. Bernstein in "Colonel William C. Greene and the Cananea Copper Bubble," *Bulletin of the Business Historical Society* 26 (December, 1952): 183.
9. Frank Mason, "The Baron of Cananea," *Frontier Times* 38 (December-January, 1963): 21. Cf. Joe Chisholm, *Brewery Gulch* (San Antonio: Naylor, 1949), p. 157.
10. San Francisco *Call,* April 29, 1901. Perkins was much impressed by the mines: "The ore in sight is something beyond comprehension . . . there is a ledge 800 feet long, 20 feet thick, and goodness knows how deep." The Greene Consolidated office broadcast the story as part of its advertising.
11. The advertisement, undated, exists in the Tittmann papers.
12. The Cananea *Herald* records some of the dates. The bank opened in January, 1902; the new hospital and the Hotel Sonora in September, 1902; the Fire Department, November 9, 1902; the slaughterhouse, December, 1902. Plans for the pumping plant were announced on December 11, 1902. Development of the *plaza municipal* (city park) did not get under way until 1906. Greene built a bandstand and then furnished uniforms and instruments for a band to play in it. Fernando Pesqueira, director of the Historical Museum at Hermosillo, was one of the musicians (Pesqueira to C. L. S., December 9, 1969).
13. Frank T. Greene, Tucson, April 6, 1970.
14. *La Constitución,* Hermosillo, November 10, 1901.
15. M. P. Freeman of the Tucson Consolidated National Bank reporting in the *Arizona Daily Star,* January 31, 1901; Report of the Second Vice President and Comptroller, July 31, 1902, CM files; George Young to Greene, February 12, 1904, CM files (Greene gave half the money for the Library).
16. Cananea *Herald,* April 4, 1903.
17. Mitchell to Greene, December 1, 1900, CM files.
18. O. O. Kelly Co., to GCCC Company, November 6, 1900, CM files.
19. Circular letter signed by W. C. Greene, President, La Cananea, July 16, 1902, announcing the sale; a similar announcement by Epes Randolph, Los Angeles, July 18, 1902 — both in the CM files.
20. Mitchell had applied for a patent on his Economic Hot Air Blast Furnace but the patent had not been granted and the Colorado Iron Works, among other firms, was building furnaces to his specifications. Logan, Demond and Harby wired him, "Until your patent is granted, I fear we will not be able to intercede in the matter." (Clausen to Mitchell, September 17, 1900, CM files).
21. Clausen to Mitchell, August 20, 1900, CM files.
22. Mitchell to Clausen, October 14, 1900, CM files.
23. Mitchell to Clausen, November 25, 1900, CM files.
24. *Ibid.*
25. W. G. Dodd to George Mitchell, December 1, 1900, CM files.
26. Berolzheimer to Scott White, March 14, 1901, CM files.
27. Von Petersdorff to Aguirre, July 19, 1901, CM files.
28. Greene to Aguirre, July 27, 1901, CM files.
29. Greene to Mitchell, August 16, 1901, CM files.
30. *Ibid.*
31. *Press Reference Library,* vol. 1, p. 193; Young, *Greene Cananea,* MS, pp. 3–5.
32. In October 1902 the Copper Queen acquired the Sierra de Cobre. Lindsay claimed it. "We are likely to hear of big lawsuits to follow" (Cananea *Herald,* October 19, 1902).
33. Cananea *Herald,* September 28, October 19, 1902.
34. George Young to J. S. Douglas, May 31, 1913, CM files.
35. *Ibid.*
36. The America Mining Company was incorporated on November 30, 1902, with title to the America and Copper Belt mines. In 1907 the shareholders authorized transfer to the San Pedro Copper Company which became part of the Greene Cananea Copper Company — successor to the Four C's (George Young, *Greene Cananea,* MS, p. 5).
37. Sidney Hatch, Douglas, Arizona, June 18, 1970.

38. Cananea *Herald,* July 21, 1906.
39. Mrs. Gladys Lindsay Splane, to C. L. S., January 6, 1970; Charles Greene, Prescott, Arizona, June 24, 1970.
40. The litigation was initiated at Duluth, Minnesota, in March 1907 and was settled out of court in Los Angeles in October "at no cost to Colonel Greene" (El Paso *Herald,* March 13, October 10, 1907; Los Angeles *Times,* October 9, 1907).
41. W. J. Galbraith to George Young, April 19, 1904, CM files.

ENTER MARY

1. Frank T. Greene, Tucson, November 30, 1969; letter to C. L. S., December 3, 1970.
2. Proctor's advertisements appeared regularly in the Cananea *Herald.* The liquor concession was granted on August 1, 1902 (the agreement is in the CM files).
3. The first Benedict came to Long Island in 1617, but Connecticut was the family home until the adventurous ones moved west (Mrs. Charles H. Greene, September 17, 1971); Aurora Hunt, *Kirby Benedict* (Glendale: Arthur H. Clark, 1961), pp. 16, 84–88; Henry Marvin Benedict, *The Genealogy of the Benedicts in America* (Albany: Joel Munsell, 1870), pp. 126–27.
4. Frank T. Greene to C. L. S., December 3, 1970.
5. Gertrude M. Case to Albert Benedict, May 28, 1873, Benedict file, Arizona Historical Society, Tucson, Arizona.
6. Benedict file, Arizona Historical Society, Tucson.
7. *Arizona Weekly Star,* April 1, 1880.
8. Frank T. Greene to C. L. S., December 3, 1970; Mrs. Charles Greene, February 13, 1971.
9. Adoption papers are dated January 19, 1885. Guardianship was approved on January 26 (Albert Case Benedict file, Arizona Historical Society, Tucson.
10. Frank T. Greene, Tucson, November 29, 30, 1969.
11. Byron Ivancovich to C. L. S., August 22, 1970. His mother was a classmate of Mary's.
12. Mrs. Charles Greene, Prescott, June 24, 1970.
13. *Arizona Daily Citizen,* February 28, 1901.
14. Frank T. Greene, Tucson, November 30, 1970.
15. Frank T. Greene to C. L. S., December 3, 1970.
16. *Arizona Daily Citizen,* February 28, 1901.
17. George Smalley, *My Adventures in Arizona: Leaves From A Reporter's Notebook,* Yndia Smalley Moore, ed., (Tucson: Arizona Pioneers' Historical Society, 1966), pp. 92–93. Cf. Don Schellie, *The Tucson Citizen* (Tucson: Tucson *Citizen,* 1970), pp. 69–70. In 1901 Greene became co-owner of the newspaper.
18. Frank T. Greene, Tucson, Arizona, April 6, 1970.
19. Bisbee *Daily Review,* December 19, 1901: Greene sues L. C. Hughes, editor of the *Star,* for libel. Smalley did not get the full treatment.
20. Mary Virginia, December 11, 1901; William Cornell, January 25, 1903.
21. Cananea *Herald,* January 11, 1903. The Greenes moved permanently to Cananea in 1906.
22. Kirk Greene, Berkeley, California, July 27, 1969.
23. *Ibid.,* Mrs. Anita Greene, Douglas, Arizona, June 23, 1969.
24. Mary Lou Howe, Bisbee, Arizona, December 2, 1969; Charles Greene, September 17, 1971.
25. A copy is in the Tittmann papers.

THE FINANCIAL STRATOSPHERE

1. Tombstone *Epitaph,* December 17, 1900.
2. Robert Sobel, *The Curbstone Brokers* (New York: Macmillan, 1970), p. 99.
3. M. D. Bernstein, "Col. William C. Greene and the Cananea Copper Bubble," *Bulletin of the Business Historical Society* 26 (December, 1952): 185.
4. Sobel, *The Curbstone Brokers,* p. 100.

5. Isaac Marcosson (*Anaconda*, 96–97) says, "The implication was that Amalgamated was out to trim the public when . . . the major purpose was constructive."
6. *Ibid.*, p. 95.
7. *Dictionary of American Biography*, vol. 7, p. 577.
8. Marcosson, *Anaconda*, p. 95.
9. The names of John W. Gates, Edwin Hawley, and Bernard M. Baruch appear for the first time as directors in the *Annual Report* for 1902–1903. Henry E. Huntington preceded them by one year. See Chapter 12 for Lawson's version of what happened.
10. Henry Clews & Co., *Weekly Financial Review*, May 4, 1901, Brophy papers.
11. Brophy papers.
12. W. C. Greene to Bank of Bisbee, July 5, 1901, Brophy papers.
13. Cunningham to Brophy, September 16, 18, 1901, Brophy papers.
14. Kirk Greene, Berkeley, California, July 27, 1969.
15. New York: Town Topics Publishing Company, 1905, pp. 170–71.
16. Cananea *Herald*, July 28, 1906.
17. Greene to Mitchell, June 17, 1901, CM files.
18. *Report of the Stockholders* of the Greene Consolidated Copper Co., La Cananea, January 27, 1901. Brophy papers.
19. Frank T. Greene, Tucson, November 30, 1969.
20. Helen L. McL. Kimball to George S. Robbins, July 18, 1902; Robbins to Greene, July 19, 1902, CM files.
21. Greene to Berolzheimer, July 8, 1902, CM files.
22. *To the Stockholders*, March 8, 1901. Brophy papers.
23. *Ibid.*, quoting C. B. Lewis to Wm. Reichman, March 8, 1901.
24. Announcement signed by George S. Robbins, Treasurer, for Greene Consolidated Copper Company, New York. March 19, 1901, Brophy papers.
25. W. C. Greene *To the Stockholders*, June 19, 1901; George S. Robbins for GCCC *To the Stockholders*, April 1, 1901 — both in Blake Collection, Yale University Library.
26. W. C. Greene *To the Stockholders*, June 19, 1901, Blake Collection, Yale University Library.
27. Ben Williams, Douglas, June 23, 1969.
28. Report signed by Wm. C. Greene on April 17, 1901, on "Actual Smelter Returns, April 1st to April 12th, 1901," Brophy papers. Later historians have said that Greene probably never really knew how much it cost him to produce his copper and that he could have bought it cheaper in New York than he could produce it in Cananea (Marvin D. Bernstein, *The Mexican Mining Industry*, State University of New York, 1964, p. 58). The company records, carefully kept and submitted quarterly to the New York office, refute this charge.
29. W. C. Greene *To the Stockholders*, June 19, 1901, CM files.
30. W. C. Greene *To the Stockholders*, August 10, 1901, CM files.
31. *Ibid.*; Secretary Robbins reported to George Mitchell on August 12 that payment had been received for over 40,000 shares of stock, one quarter of them paid for in full (Tittmann papers).
32. *Remarks of General T. H. Anderson and W. C. Greene, President. at the Stockholders' Meeting, July 22, 1901*, CM files.
33. Greene to Mitchell, August 24, 1901, CM files.
34. Walter S. Logan *To the Stockholders*, August 2, 1902, CM files.
35. W. C. Greene *To the Stockholders*, March 8, 1901, Brophy papers.
36. *Annual Report for the Year Ending July 31, 1902*, Balance Sheet of the Greene Consolidated Copper Company, p. 13, Brophy papers.
37. George Young to Jim Kirk, March 21, 1903.
38. Greene Chronology, Tittmann papers.
39. Bisbee *Daily Review*, December 29, 1901.
40. Judge Raymond L. Reid, Burbank, California, June 30, 1969; Greene to Young, March 31, 1903, CM files.
41. Cananea Cattle Company, S. A., Book I; "Statement of Admitted Facts," Pre-trial Conference, Eva Greene Day, Plaintiff, Case no. 666,006, Superior Court of California, County of Los Angeles, October 6, 1960, p. 11, Tittmann papers.

42. Lawson, Arnold, & Co., *Market Letter,* December 11, 1901, Brophy papers.
43. Unidentified clipping, December 16, 1901, Brophy papers.
44. Greene to Mitchell, October 4, 1901, CM files.
45. Reports of Sales, Outside Securities Market, compiled by Frank Bennett, December 19–31, 1901, Brophy papers.
46. Block to Mitchell, November 15, 1901. Greene indicated in a talk with Block that he thought there might be a connection between Treadwell and James Shirley, who had tried unsuccessfully to collect a million dollars in commissions from him (Block to Mitchell, November 26, 1901), CM files.
47. Helen L. McL. Kimball to George S. Robbins, July 18, 1902, CM files. According to the *Copper Handbook* for 1905, Treadwell was the treasurer of the San Luis Mining Company of Tayoltita, Durango. He was also president of the Treadwell Mining Company of Mayer, Arizona — a corporation with "1854 shareholders — mostly fools."
48. Greene to Mitchell, November 29, 1901, CM files.
49. Harrison and Wyckoff to W. H. Brophy, May 21, 1902, Brophy papers.
50. Marvin D. Bernstein, *The Mexican Mining Industry 1890–1950* (State University of New York, 1964), p. 58: "... Cananea's methods were woefully inefficient. By forcing 5 or 6 years development into one, too much was unplanned and uneconomical."

THE SHORT BUSY REIGN OF ANSON W. BURCHARD

1. Much of Burchard's correspondence is preserved in a letter book (*General Correspondence,* January 25, 1902 to June 11, 1902), hereafter referred to as LB. This, along with other correspondence in the CM files, makes 1902 one of Greene's best-documented years.
2. New York *Times,* January 23, 1927 (obituary notice). According to this source Burchard went to work for Greene in 1900.
3. *To the Stockholders.* Report of a committee sent to inspect the mines, dated at Naco, January 4, 1901, CM files.
4. Burchard's first letter appears in the letter book on March 21, 1902 (LB 48).
5. Mitchell to F. Marion Wigmore, March 8, 1902 (LB 445).
6. Mitchell to Greene, March 10, 1902, CM files.
7. George S. Robbins to Anson W. Burchard, June 27, 1902, CM files: "Mr. Mitchell has been in the office several times within the last week or so during his visit to Washington. He says you have greatly relieved him in many ways, for which he is very thankful."
8. Kirk to Greene, January 6, 1902, CM files.
9. Kirk to Greene, January 2, 1902, CM files.
10. Jimmy Kirk McClure to C. L. S., December 30, 1970.
11. The Bisbee *Daily Review,* June 23, 1903, reported that George was in Alaska. By August of that year he had resigned from the Four C's and had gone to Los Angeles to live, according to the Jerome *Mining News,* August 10, 1903. His multiple interests are described in *"Mexico y Sus Progresos": Album Directorio del Estado de Sonora.* Ed. Federico García y Alva (Hermosillo: Imprenta oficial, 1905, 1907), n.p.
12. *Wall Street Journal,* December 15, 1904. Greene was always borrowing stock from his friends and associates for use in his Wall Street activities. He always paid it back, of course. This sort of thing was part of the financial game. Harrison and Wyckoff, for instance, wrote to W. H. Brophy on March 10, 1902, "Our previous reference to $50 per 100 shares was in regard to a premium which we could probably secure if you wished to loan your stock to someone who was short. ... It would be very much to your advantage to loan your stock to the shorts, as thereby you would not only have the use of the money without paying interest on it, but would receive a premium of $50 per 100 shares, or $250 for the use of 500 shares for sixty days. At the end of that time you would return the money and get your stock back. This operation would take only 200 shares to raise about $5,000 (Brophy papers).
13. Notice of appointment issued by the Company, May 5, 1903, CM files.
14. T. A. Rickard, "Louis Davidson Ricketts, an Interview." *Mining and Scientific*

Press, vol. 123 (October 1, 1921): 463–473; W. R. Bimson, *Louis D. Ricketts* (New York: Newcomer Society, 1949), pp. 17–18.

15. AWB (Burchard) to Robbins, March 25, 1902, CM files.
16. AWB to Pacific Hardware Co., San Francisco, May 22, 1902 (LB 437).
17. Kirk to Greene, January 2, 1902, CM files.
18. Robert Mitchell to Hardinge, February 2, 1902, CM files.
19. Cananea *Herald,* April 4, 1903.
20. Greene to Berolzheimer, March 28, 1902, CM files.
21. The converters were in operation on May 28 (Cananea *Herald,* May 29, 1902).
22. AWB to Nichols Chemical Company, May 1, 1902 (LB 242).
23. AWB to George S. Robbins, May 2, 1902 (LB 265).
24. AWB to C. S. Cass, March 23, 1902 (LB 48).
25. AWB to T. Evans, April 2, 1902, CM files.
26. AWB to C. M. Burkhalter, May 28, 1902 (LB 495).
27. AWB to George Robbins, June 1, 1902; AWB to Paul Morton, April 23, 1902 (LB 591).
28. AWB to I. Macmanus, June 1, 1902; AWB to S. M. Aguirre, May 5, 1902; AWB to T. Evans, May 15, 1902 (LB 541, 292, 370).
29. AWB to C. S. Cass, March 24, 1902 (LB 50).
30. AWB to James Douglas, March 24, 1902 (LB 152).
31. AWB to Colorado Fuel and Iron Company, April 26, 1902 (LB 204).
32. AWB to J. F. Welborn, May 7, 1902 (LB 304).
33. AWB to Cochise Lumber Company, May 15, 1902 (LB 372).
34. Memorandum of Agreement, May 29, 1902 (LB 519).
35. AWB to H. C. Rolfe et al., May 1, 1902 (LB 237).
36. AWB to George E. Roe, May 25, 1902 (LB 464).
37. AWB to I. J. Spence, April 5, 1902 (LB 135).
38. AWB to Trost & Rust, May 19, 1902 (LB 395).
39. AWB to H. C. Clark, June 1, 1902 (LB 540).
40. Robert Mitchell to Hardware and Supply Department, May 10, 1902 (LB 330).
41. AWB to Mr. Rolfe, June 7, 1902 (LB 622).
42. AWB to A. C. Bernard, April 28, 1902 (LB 219–221).
43. AWB to Tomas Macmanus, May 5, 1902 (LB 297).
44. AWB to Philip Berolzheimer, May 19, 1902 (LB 413).
45. AWB to T. Evans, April 28, 1901 (LB 222): "I return herewith papers in reference to the annual report regarding the railroad for the Federal Government, together with a pro-forma of the report made in accordance with the several paragraphs of Article 182 of the Railroad Law."

    In June a new patent on the mining claims had to be processed in Mexico City in order to clear the Company's claims as a result of the Cobre Grande business. Burchard sent titles of thirty-one claims to Macmanus with instructions to cancel the old titles (AWB to T. Macmanus, June 10, 1902, CM files) and the Company had to submit periodically a list of employees with occupations, wages, etc. (AWB to T. Evans, April 26, 1902, LB 183).
46. Greene to Mitchell, April 20, 1902, CM files.
47. AWB to Trost and Rust, May 19, 1902 (LB 345).
48. The directors came to Cananea for meetings on July 1, 1901, April 20, 1902, and September 21, 1902.
49. AWB to George Mitchell, June 1, 1902 (LB 245).
50. AWB to Dr. Van Dorn, May 2, 1902 (LB 203).
51. Greene's comment: AWB to Philip Berolzheimer, March 28, 1902 (LB 63–64).
52. AWB to Roy and Titcomb, May 10, 1902 (LB 340).
53. AWB to Carl Clausen, April 26, 1902 (LB 209).
54. AWB to S. M. Aguirre, May 5, 1902 (LB 209).
55. LB 320.
56. AWB to Dr. R. C. Van Dorn, May 27, 1902 (LB 488).
57. Robert Mitchell to Thomas Wiggins, May 24, 1902 (LB 442).
58. AWB to Sr. Doctor Don Filiberto Barroso, May 16, 1902 (LB 371).
59. AWB to Los Angeles *Herald,* Los Angeles *Times,* May 24, 1902 (LB 421).
60. May 21, 1902 (LB 422).
61. AWB to Los Angeles *Times,* May 30, 1902 (LB 511).
62. AWB to W. H. Hardinge, May 19, 1902 (LB 409).

63. AWB to A. B. Wadleigh, May 1, 1902 (LB 252).
64. AWB to Paul Morton, May 3, 1902 (LB 289).
65. AWB to Paul Morton, May 8, 1902 (LB 318).
66. AWB to Walter Douglas, May 2, 1902 (LB 286).
67. AWB to C. C. Sroufe, May 19, 1902 (LB 494).
68. AWB to Barnes and Martin, May 24, 1902 (LB 450).
69. AWB to C. C. Sroufe, May 28, 1902 (LB 494–495).
70. AWB to H. J. Temple, June 3, 1902 (LB 565).
71. AWB to J. H. Kuhns, April 2, 1902; AWB to Philip Berolzheimer, April 8, 1902 (LB 114, 142).
72. AWB to H. C. Rolfe, May 10, 1902 (LB 353).
73. AWB to T. Evans, June 1, 1902 (LB 533).
74. Ira Joralemon, *Romantic Copper* (New York: Appleton-Century, 1934), p. 148.
75. Greene to Aguirre, July 8, 1902, CM files.
76. Greene to Barroso, July 11, 1902, CM files.
77. AWB to James H. Kirk, June 3, 1903, CM files.
78. W. J. Galbraith to J. T. Morrow, December 7, 1903, CM files.
79. Announcement of organization, July 16, 1902; Macmanus to Burchard, June 18, 1902; Chase to Greene, July 9, 1902; Greene to Bernard, July 10, 1902, CM files. For Randolph's career see *Arizona, the Youngest State* (Chicago: S. J. Clarke, 1916), pp. 26–27.
80. Judge Raymond L. Reid, Burbank, California, June 30, 1969. Wiswall was a veteran of the Spanish-American War, though he never saw Cuba, and came to the Southwest with a spot on his lungs (Frank T. Greene, Tucson, June 26, 1970).
81. C. E. Wiswall to J. T. Morrow, September 16, 1903, CM files.
82. Berolzheimer to Greene, June 30, 1902, CM files.
83. Greene to Berolzheimer, July 8, 1902 (LB 629).
84. *Engineering and Mining Journal* 75 (March 28, 1903): 469.
85. Secretary John Campbell reported to Burchard from Cananea on that date.
86. *The Wall Street Journal,* February 11, 1904.
87. J. M. Morrow to I. Macmanus, February 16, 1904, CM files.
88. Bisbee *Daily Review,* February 25, 1904.
89. Greene to Young, February 19, 1904, CM files.
90. New York *Times,* January 23, 1927.

THUNDER AND LIGHTNING

1. Leslie Dorsey and Janice Devine, *Fare Thee Well* (New York: Crown, 1964), pp. 107–31.
2. Lloyd Morris, *Incredible New York* (New York: Random House, 1951), pp. 243–45.
3. Wilford J. Eiteman, Charles A. Dice, David K. Eiteman, *The Stock Market* (New York: McGraw-Hill, 1966), quoting A. G. Gardiner, *New Republic,* August 19, 1920.
4. Mary Virginia was born on December 11, 1901; William Cornell on January 25, 1903; Frank Townsend on October 4, 1904; Florence Louise on September 18, 1906. Clarence Kirk was born in Cananea on June 3, 1909, and Charles Harrison in Los Angeles on October 2, 1910.
5. New York *Times,* January 1, 1903.
6. Robbins to Burchard, June 27, 1902, CM files.
7. Cananea *Herald,* January 18, 1903.
8. Kirk to Greene, March 6, 1902, CM files.
9. Weed to Robbins, April 12, 1902, CM files.
10. Greene to Brophy, January 28, 1903, Brophy papers.
11. *Engineering and Mining Journal* 74 (December 6, 1902): 773.
12. Brophy papers.
13. Greene said the decline was the result of "manipulation" (Greene to Brophy, December 20, 1901); Cf. Horace Stevens, *The Copper Handbook* 4 (1903): 321.
14. N. L. Amster & Co., *Copper and Copper Shares* (newsletter), January 25, February 8, 1902, Brophy papers.

15. President's Report, *Annual Report* for 1903, p. 4, William H. Brown Collection, Yale University.
16. Dwight E. Woodbridge, "Ore Dressing at Cananea," *Engineering and Mining Journal* 76 (June 30, 1904): 1044–45.
17. T. E. Newlin to Hibbard, Spencer, Bartlett & Co., December 30, 1903, CM files.
18. This rumor started early in 1902. Harrison & Wyckoff to W. H. Brophy, March 1, 1902, Brophy papers.
19. Mallett & Wyckoff to W. H. Brophy, May 12, 1903, Brophy papers.
20. For example, Bisbee *Review,* March 29, 1902, March 18, July 11, 1903, January 10, 1904.
21. *The Copper Handbook* 4 (1903): 415.
22. *Engineering and Mining Journal* 75 (March 14, 1903): 415–16.
23. *Ibid.,* March 28, 1903, p. 469.
24. Undated clipping, Boston dateline, Brophy papers: ". . . present low prices are believed to have resulted from knowledge of his report."
25. Greene to Dwight, February 15, 1904, CM files.
26. Undated clipping, Boston dateline, Brophy papers.
27. *Wall Street Journal,* February 18, 1904.
28. Walter R. Bimson, *Louis D. Ricketts* (New York: The Newcomer Society, 1949), pp. 17–18.
29. *Wall Street Journal,* February 18, 1904.
30. *Ibid.,* February 11, December 14, 1904.
31. W. C. Greene, *To the Stockholders,* April 4, 1904, Brophy papers.
32. Copy in CM files.
33. Greene to Dwight, February 15, 1904, CM files.
34. Greene to Young, February 23, 1904, CM files.
35. Robbins to Campbell, March 8, 1904, CM files.
36. Greene *To the Stockholders.* April 4, 1904, Brophy papers.
37. El Paso *Herald,* October 14, 1903.

THE LAWSON COMEDY

1. Production through 1904 was well over 5,000,000 pounds per month (W. C. Greene *To the Stockholders,* April 4, May 2, June 14, July 22, October 8, 1904, Brophy papers). Copper prices held at 14 cents in November. *Walker's Weekly Copper Letter,* November 4, 1904, Brophy papers, reported, "There has been good buying of Greene stock lately." A ninth dividend of 4% was announced in December (New York *Times,* December 9, 1904).
2. The Bisbee *Daily Review* reported that Greene had "recently returned from a trip to Liverpool, London and Paris." An unidentified "intimate friend" revealed to a reporter for the *Wall Street Journal* in December, issue of December 17, that Greene was "the owner of the Franco-American Bank of Paris, which owns 20,000 shares of Greene Copper and 85,000 shares of Greene Gold."
3. *Wall Street Journal,* December 16, 1904.
4. El Paso *Herald,* December 16, 1904.
5. Thomas W. Lawson, *Frenzied Finance* (Boston: The Ridgway-Thayer Company, 1905), p. 26.
6. *Ibid.,* p. 24.
7. Cedric B. Cowing, *Populists, Plungers, and Progressives* (Princeton University Press, 1965), p. 34: "The Pujo Money Trust Investigation of 1912 confirmed the general validity of Lawson's charges."
8. New York *Times,* December 9, 1904.
9. Boston *Herald,* December 17, 1904.
10. *The Wall Street Journal* printed it on December 14.
11. Lawson quotes the letter in *Frenzied Finance,* pp. 522–24.
12. New York *Times,* December 14, 1904; *Wall Street Journal,* December 14, 1904.
13. *Wall Street Journal,* December 15, 1904, an article entitled "Firearms in Finance."
14. Boston *Herald,* December 17, 1904.
15. New York *Times,* December 15, 1904.
16. *Ibid.,* December 16, 1904.
17. Undated clipping, Boston dateline, Brophy papers.

18. Unidentified clipping, Boston, December 14, 1904, Brophy papers.
19. Undated clipping, Boston dateline, Brophy papers.
20. New York *Times,* December 15, 16, 1904; *Wall Street Journal,* December 16, 1904. Goodman was released from the Tombs on December 19 (New York *Times,* December 20, 1904), and disappears from the record.
21. New York *Times,* December 14, 1904; *Wall Street Journal,* December 14, 1904.
22. New York *Times,* December 14, 1904.
23. *Ibid.,* December 16, 1904.
24. *Ibid.,* December 19, 1904.
25. Boston *Herald,* December 17, 1904.
26. *Ibid.*
27. *Frenzied Finance,* p. 525.
28. El Paso *Herald,* August 8, 1905, quoting the *Examiner.*
29. *Wall Street Journal,* February 14, 1904.

FLYING HIGH

1. Greene to Max Muller, July 8, 1902, CM files.
2. Richard D. Wyckoff, *Wall Street Ventures and Adventures* (New York: Harper & Brothers, 1930), p. 149.
3. Eugene Ives, Letter Books, MS, University of Arizona: Ives to Greene, April 20, 1906 (Hereford will sue); October 10, 1906 (Hereford refuses to settle); October 27, 1906 (Hereford's duties; the break becomes final).
4. Civil Actions, Book 1, Cochise County, Arizona, Case 4394, order filed December 1, 1906; Book 2, Case 4394-b, order filed March 12, 1906.
5. The slaughter house was built in 1902 (Cananea *Herald,* November 17). A packing plant, started in 1906, went into full and successful operation forty years later, producing canned meat for Europe under the Marshall plan (Kirk Greene, Berkeley, California, July 27, 1969).
6. Greene *To My Friends of the Greene Consolidated Copper Company,* August 1, 1904, Brophy papers. A *Libro de Actas,* in possession of Mrs. Anita Greene, Douglas, lists three meetings, 1903–1905.
7. Greene to Storman, June 9, 1902, Letter Book p. 639, CM files.
8. On May 18, 1903, at Magdalena, Sonora, Ed Massey transferred two claims, Pure Gold and Pure Gold No. 2, to Greene's Gold Company (copy of *traspaso de derecho* dated May 18, 1903, in possession of Charles Greene, Prescott, Arizona. This document mentions Storman's suit).
9. Greene *To My Friends,* August 1, 1904, Brophy papers.
10. El Paso *Herald,* July 10, 1905.
11. Greene to Massey, May 19, 1910; Massey to Greene, October 9, 1910, Charles H. Greene files.
12. Bisbee *Review,* January 2, 1903.
13. Eugene Ives handled the negotiations. See Letter Books, October 30, November 13, 1905.
14. Ives worked on this case too: Letter Books, October 29, November 12, 1905, March 15, 21, 26, 31, 1906. Greene came to own two San Rafael ranches. In 1904 he acquired San Rafael de la Zanja from Colin Cameron and his brothers (Bisbee *Review,* June 8, 1904).
15. Ives, Letter Books, February 17, June 4, 1905.
16. Cananea *Herald,* September 17, 1906.
17. Ives, Letter Books, October 27, 1906.
18. Cananea *Herald,* December 22, 1906, March 23, 1907; El Paso *Herald,* March 23, April 22, 1907; Don Schellie, *The Tucson Citizen,* Tucson, 1970, p. 69.
19. El Paso *Herald,* December 30, 1904, February 10, 1905.
20. J. R. Southworth, *The Mines of Mexico* (Liverpool: Blake and Mackenzie, 1905), p. 224; Greene *To the Investing Public,* October 18, 1905, CM files, reporting new concessions dated December 14, 1904.
21. R. J. Hartman (Greene's chief assistant at the moment), in the El Paso *Herald,* February 10, 1905.
22. Jorge Griggs, *The Mines of Chihuahua* (Chihuahua: privately published, 1907), pp. 74–77, 206–09; Southworth, *The Mines of Mexico,* p. 224.
23. The suffix *chic* means village. The final *c* is not pronounced.

24. El Paso *Herald,* November 1, 1904.
25. Greene *To the Stockholders of Greene Gold-Silver,* September 28, 1905, CM files, announcing plans for the Chihuahua and Pacific extension.
26. Judge Raymond L. Reid, Burbank, California, June 30, 1969.
27. El Paso *Herald,* March 8, 1906; *Arizona Journal-Miner,* December 14, 1907. What happened to Scott White is not clear, but it was probably at this time that he left Mexico. Dan de L. Hughes, *South From Tombstone,* pp. 274–75, mentions the affair.
28. El Paso *Herald,* November 3, 1904. The cost of building the road to Terrazas (which was left at the end of a branch line) was $1,700,000.
29. Sawmills were being installed at Madera in the spring of 1907 (El Paso *Herald,* April 29, 1907).
30. El Paso *Herald,* November 3, 1904: "There is at present no intention of building through to the Pacific coast."
31. *Ibid.,* December 6, 1904: "The terms of the concession provide for the construction of a line from the port of Guaymas." On February 22, 1905, at the banquet in his honor in El Paso, Greene promised: "I have started to build a railroad . . . and I will run it to the Pacific."
32. *Ibid.,* April 25, 1907.
33. *Ibid.,* December 27, 1904.
34. *Ibid.,* November 3, 1904, February 18, 1905.
35. *Ibid.,* December 13, 1906.
36. *Ibid.,* July 15, 1905, March 8, 1906.
37. El Paso *Herald,* May 4, 1904.
38. *Ibid.,* February 10, 1905.
39. *Ibid.,* April 10, 1905.
40. *Ibid.*
41. *Ibid.*
42. *Ibid.,* April 11, 12, 17, 1905.
43. *Ibid.,* April 18, 1905.
44. *Ibid.,* May 8, 9, 15, 1905.
45. *Ibid.,* July 4, 5, 1905.
46. The Federal Smelter and the tin mine were in the news off and on for a long time; El Paso *Herald,* March 31, April 1, October 10, 1905; March 12, 19, 28, April 10, 21, November 14, 15, 1906. The Cananea *Herald,* July 26, 1906, mentions the Guaymas smelter.
47. Owen P. White, *Lead and Likker* (New York: Minton, Balch & Company, 1932), pp. 15–16.
48. El Paso *Herald,* April 11, 1906. Greene announced plans for a tannery in 1905 (El Paso *Herald,* May 13, 1905).
49. The report is in the files of the Compañía Minera at Cananea.
50. There was another dreamer besides Greene. Arthur E. Stilwell incorporated the Kansas City, Mexico, and Orient Railway on April 30, 1900, and built eastward from Chihuahua toward Presidio, Texas, and westward toward the Pacific Coast. In 1905 the westward extension had reached a point fifty kilometers west of Miñaca, where the branch line turned north up the Guerrero Valley to Temosachic (El Paso *Herald,* September 2, 1905). Financial troubles intervened to prevent full extension of the line westward and the company failed in 1912.

THE GREAT HUNT

1. Greene to Cranz, May 27, 1902, Letter Book, CM files, p. 487.
2. Theodore D. Harris, *Negro Frontiersman: The Western Memoirs of Henry O. Flipper, First Negro Graduate of West Point* (El Paso: Texas Western Press, 1963), pp. 42–43.
3. The story of Tustin's revolt did not reach the public for three months (El Paso *Herald,* July 10, 1905).
4. *Ibid.,* April 18, 19, May 13, 1905.
5. *Ibid.,* April 21, 1905.
6. *Ibid.*
7. *Ibid.,* April 26, 1905.

8. *Ibid.,* April 25, 1905.
9. *Ibid.,* May 4, 1905.
10. Frank Brophy, Elgin, Arizona, August 23, 1969.
11. A. M. Tenney to W. H. Brophy, July 20, 1905, Brophy papers.
12. El Paso *Herald,* May 4, 1905.
13. Lord Beresford was a bona fide Irish peer who was famous in the Southwest and Mexico as a connoisseur of cows and whiskey. He lived with a common-law wife, a black woman whom he and everyone else called "Lady Flo." (See Eugene O. Porter, *Lord Beresford and Lady Flo,* El Paso: Texas Western Press, 1970).
14. El Paso *Herald,* May 16, 20, 1905.
15. *Ibid.,* May 20, 1905.
16. *Ibid.,* May 31, 1905.
17. *Ibid.,* May 20, 1905.
18. Myron M. Parker to W. H. Brophy, May 26, June 5, 1905, Brophy papers.
19. Humphries Photo Company (El Paso) to W. H. Brophy, May 19, 1905, Brophy papers.
20. Letter in possession of Charles H. Greene, Prescott, Arizona.
21. El Paso *Herald,* May 31, 1905.
22. *Ibid.,* May 4, 1905.
23. Winthrop E. Scarritt, "On the Road to Ocampo," typed copy of an unidentified article in CM files. The trip was noticed in area newspapers, for instance El Paso *Herald,* April 27, 1906, "Greene Party Returns from Temosachic."

IN COLD BLOOD

1. Both Colonel Greene and Arthur S. Dwight, the general manager, made detailed statements which are preserved in the files of Compañía Minera de Cananea, S. A. de C. V., at Cananea, Sonora, Mexico. Greene's statement is dated June 11, 1906; Dwight's, June 8, 1906. Greene's was printed in the Douglas *Daily Dispatch,* issue of June 19, 1906. A brief extract is quoted by Herbert O. Brayer, "The Cananea Incident," *New Mexico Historical Review* 13 (October, 1938): 394.
2. Felipe Barroso to Señor Juez 2do de Primer Instancia en Cananea (equivalent to district judge in the United States), June 1, 1906, reproduced in Manuel González Ramírez, *La huelga de Cananea* (Mexico: Fondo de Cultura Economica, 1956), p. 33.
3. *Ibid.,* p. 20.
4. Statement of Colonel W. C. Greene, MS, CM files.
5. Brayer, "The Cananea Incident," p. 390 (English translation); González Ramírez, *La huelga de Cananea,* pp. 19–20 (in Spanish).
6. Manuel J. Aguirre, *Cananea: Las garras del imperialismo en las entrañas de México* (Mexico: Editorial B. Costa-Amic, 1958), pp. 100–01. González Ramírez merely says that Greene "exploited" this exhortation.
7. A. B. Fall papers, Henry E. Huntington Library, San Marino, California. This copy bears the notation that the letter never reached the committee, the outbreak occurring before it could be delivered. Greene ordered 2,000 copies from the Cananea *Herald* (letter, June 14, 1906, Fall papers), and it was widely disseminated. The Mexican Revolutionary historians have attacked it bitterly, for example Leon Díaz Cardenas, *Cananea, Primer brote del sindicalismo en México* (Publicaciones del departamento de bibliotecas de la secretaría de Educación Publica, 1956), p. 37 ff.; Cesar Tapia Quijada, *Apuntes sobre la huelga de Cananea* (Hermosillo: Editada por la Universidad de Sonora, 1956), pp. 25–27.
8. Statement of A. S. Dwight, MS, CM files.
9. Greene prided himself on following regulations. He wrote to General Manager John T. Morrow on October 15, 1903 (CM files): "... any petty savings that may be made through evasion of stamp duties we do not want."
10. Statement of W. C. Greene, MS, CM files; Kirk Greene, interview, Berkeley, California, July 27, 1969.
11. Reports disagree about the wage reduction. Ethel Duffy Turner (*Ricardo Flores Magón y el partido liberal Méxicano,* tr. Eduardo Limon G. Morelia: Editorial

"Erandi," 1960), p. 86, says the base pay for miners was cut from three pesos to two-fifty. There is confirmation in records kept by the Company which give miners three pesos per day; pick-and-shovel workers outside the mines, two-fifty (Fall papers). American newspapers stated that the Mexicans had not been reduced but that wages of American miners had been raised (Brayer, p. 395, quoting the Bisbee *Daily Review*).

12. Brayer, p. 395.
13. Kirk Greene (interview, Berkeley, California, July 27, 1969) says that the Colonel was trying to upgrade workers' housing and that George Metcalf forced the workmen to move. Mr. and Mrs. Burton Devere (interview, Tombstone, Arizona, June 23, 1960) gave information about Metcalf's career in Tombstone. Matia McClelland Burk, Metcalf's daughter, emphasizes his "integrity and courage" in "The Beginnings of the Tombstone School, 1879–1893," *Arizona and the West* 1 (Autumn, 1959): 256, n. 44.
14. "Testimonio de Esteban Baca Calderón" and "Informe" of Governor Rafael Izábal in González Ramírez, *La huelga,* pp. 95, 121; Statement of P. Freudenthal, *Arizona Silver Belt,* June 14, 1906 (reprinted from the Solomonville *Bulletin*). Freudenthal escaped because he spoke good Spanish.
15. James Morton Callahan, *American Foreign Policy in Mexican Relations* (New York: Macmillan, 1932), p. 475 ff.
16. A huge literature exists in Mexico on the Flores Magón brothers and their contribution to the Revolution, for instance: Samuel Kaplan, *Peleamos contra la injusticia: la epopeya de los hermanos Flores Magón* (Mexico: Libro Mex editores, 1960), 2 vols.; Ethel Duffy Turner, *Ricardo Flores Magón y el partido liberal Méxicano* (already cited); Diego Abad de Santillán, *Ricardo Flores Magón: el apostol de la revolución social Méxicana* (México: Grupo-cultural "Ricardo Flores Magón," 1925).
17. Brayer, "The Cananea Incident," p. 390; Aguirre, *Cananea,* p. 53.
18. González Ramírez, *La huelga,* pp. 7–9; Aguirre, *Cananea,* p. 53; Turner, *Ricardo Flores Magón,* p. 85; Myra Ellen Jenkins, *Ricardo Flores Magón and the Mexican Liberal Party,* unpublished doctoral dissertation (The University of New Mexico, 1953), pp. 210–18.
19. Greene, *Al comite de huelgistas,* Fall papers.
20. Aguirre, *Cananea,* p. 59.
21. Brayer, "The Cananea Incident," p. 389.
22. Judge Raymond L. Reid, interview, Burbank, California, June 29, 1969.
23. M. G. Turner, Director, Manufacturers' Information Bureau to H. J. Temple, Superintendent of the C. Y. & P. R. R., Naco, Arizona, June 19, 1906. Temple forwarded the letter to Greene (Fall papers).
24. Statement of W. C. Greene, MS, CM files.
25. *Ibid.*
26. *Regeneración,* July 1, 1906 (copies of the newspaper are in the Fall papers): "Nobody puts on his best clothes to throw himself into a riot."
27. Statement of W. C. Greene, MS, CM files.

IN HOT BLOOD

1. Statements of Greene and Dwight, MSS, CM files.
2. Leon Díaz Cárdenas, *Cananea: primer brote del sindicalismo en México* (Publicaciones del departamento de bibliotecas de la secretaría de educación pública, 1956), p. 52 ff. Esteban B. Calderón in his "Testimonio" (in Manuel González Ramírez, *La huelga de Cananea* (Mexico: Fondo de Cultura Economica, 1956), p. 122, quotes this account in full. Manuel J. Aguirre, *Cananea: garras del imperialismo en las entranas de México* (Mexico: Libro Mex Editores, 1958), p. 122, quotes it likewise.
3. Aguirre, *Cananea,* p. 124.
4. Manuel González Ramírez, *La huelga de Cananea,* p. 122.
5. Greene, *Statement,* CM files.
6. F. R. Walker, *Stamping Grounds,* MS. Compare the "Testimonio of Placido Ríos" in González Ramírez, *La huelga de Cananea,* p. 139.
7. James Morton Callahan, *American Foreign Policy in Mexican Relations* (New York: Macmillan, 1932), p. 523.

8. Herbert O. Brayer, "The Cananea Incident," *New Mexico Historical Review* 13 (October, 1938), 411, 413. Brayer's account is based almost entirely on contemporary Southwestern newspapers.

9. *Ibid.,* p. 413. Word came from the War Department to the cavalry commander, "Absolutely and under no conditions was he to pass beyond the border without instructions."

10. González Ramírez, *La huelga de Cananea,* p. 28.

11. Brayer, "The Cananea Incident," p. 399, quoting personal letter from Rynning to Brayer, January 21, 1938.

12. *Ibid.,* p. 402.

13. *Ibid.,* p. 404; Rynning, *Gun Notches* (New York: A. L. Burt, 1931), p. 290 ff.

14. Brayer, "The Cananea Incident," p. 405, quoting the Bisbee *Daily Review* for Saturday, June 2, 1906.

15. Brayer, "The Cananea Incident," p. 405.

16. *Ibid.,* p. 407.

17. González Ramírez, *La huelga de Cananea,* p. 25.

18. Brayer, p. 409.

19. González Ramírez, p. xxvi.

20. Manuel J. Aguirre, *Cananea,* pp. 144–47; John Kenneth Turner, *Barbarous Mexico* (Austin: University of Texas Press, 1969), p. 185; Leon Díaz Cárdenas, *Cananea,* pp. 71–72, says fifteen were taken out of jail and executed.

21. González Ramírez, *La huelga de Cananea,* p. 69.

22. According to Francisco Medina Hoyos (*Cananea, cuna de la Revolución Méxicana,* Mexico: privately printed, 1956), the total casualties were twenty-three dead (including two unidentified) and twenty-two wounded.

23. Charles C. Cumberland, *Mexico, the Struggle for Modernity* (New York: Oxford, 1968), p. 226.

24. *Regeneración,* July 1, 1906, Fall papers.

25. Manuel J. Aguirre, *Cananea,* p. 97.

26. Diego Abad de Santillán, *Ricardo Flores Magón: el apostol de la Revolución Social Méxicana* (Mexico: Grupo-cultural "Ricardo Flores Magón," 1925), p. 17. Francisco I. Madero in his famous book *La sucesión presidencial* (Mexico, 1910), p. 168, makes capital of the *huelga,* accusing the "copper trust" in the United States of suspending work because of low copper prices and leaving the workers hungry. Members of the Greene family have heard that a man on horseback tried to rope the Colonel and drag him out of his automobile (Kirk Greene, Berkeley, California, July 27, 1969). Perhaps some such attempt was made to seize Greene, but none of the other accounts mention it.

27. Turner, *Barbarous Mexico,* pp. 184–85.

28. They were first buried in the old Cananea cemetery, but in 1952 they were moved to the new Pantheon on the Mesa. When Greene's body was brought back from Los Angeles in 1956 by his son Charles for final interment in the family plot where Charles Wiswall and Mary Greene Wiswall were already resting, his grave was thought to be too close to those of the martyrs, and they were moved to a new location on the west side of the plaza (Charles Greene, El Paso, September 17, 1971).

29. Jack Ganzhorn, *I've Killed Men* (New York: Devin-Adair, 1959), p. 227. The only other mention of dynamite is in Wm. Liggett's book of reminiscences, *My Seventy-Five Years Along the Mexican Border* (New York: Exposition Press, 1964), p. 68: "... completing my last trip of the night, I was dropping off my passengers in the little mining town of Chivatera. I was about to head back home when the night shift of the Chivatera mine came out throwing bombs and dynamite."

    About as far from the truth as Ganzhorn is Captain Thomas H. Rynning's *Gun Notches,* pp. 290–315. Rynning was there but his memory was bad, or else his editors embroidered his text. Ganzhorn's account of the pitched battle in front of Greene's house seems to have been lifted from Rynning.

30. Brayer, "The Cananea Incident," p. 414.

31. David Cole to Greene, December 12, 1906, Fall papers. Greene believed that Gates had helped to foment the strike. In a message to his stockholders on August 11, 1906, he said, "The money for fomenting and inciting the riots

was furnished from New York and was part of a deliberate attempt to depreci-
ate, by the destruction of its property, the securities of the Company, and has
been supplemented by the usual crop of malicious and misleading rumors"
(Greene *To the Stockholders of the Greene Consolidated Copper Company,*
W. H. Brown Collection, Yale University).
32. Fall to President Wilson, July 30, 1913, Fall papers; Cananea *Herald,* September 29, 1906: ". . . W. C. Greene last week took steps which put out of business
the St. Louis office of the anarchistic journal published there. . . ."
33. El Paso *Herald,* January 15, 1908. In 1913 Gutiérrez de Lara was back and
threatening to sue the Company for "libel, false imprisonment, injury to his
character, malicious persecution and a few other things." He offered to settle
for $5,000 but threatened to sue for $50,000. George Young wrote to J. S.
Douglas, then general manager, "I am inclined to think he has some sort of a
case against us," but the record does not show what followed (George Young to
J. S. Douglas, August 21, 1913) (CM files).
34. James Morton Callahan, *American Foreign Policy in Mexican Relations,* p. 523.
35. When Flores Magón and his group were on trial in San Antonio in January,
1907, the newspapers reported that captured documents indicated that Cananea
had been selected as a starting point for the revolt (El Paso *Herald,* January
22, 1907).

THE DESCENT BEGINS

1. El Paso *Herald,* November 9, 1900. The *Verde* "was recently built for him by
the Pullman Company of Chicago." It was company property.
2. Campbell to Hibbard, Spencer, Bartlett Company, July 26, 1906, CM files.
3. "Copper Directors Resign," undated clipping from a New York or Boston paper
sent to Cananea by the Argus Press Clipping Bureau, received July 18, 1906,
CM files.
4. *Ibid.*
5. Robbins to Young, July 16, 1906, CM files.
6. George Young to Lancashire and London Fire Insurance Co., August 21, 1907,
CM files.
7. Cananea *Herald,* September 29, 1906.
8. *Ibid.,* March 11, 1907.
9. El Paso *Herald,* March 7, 1907: the railroad is completed.
10. *The Copper Handbook* 6 (1906): 547.
11. George Young to Ignacio Macmanus, October 17, 1906, CM files.
12. El Paso *Herald,* April 28, 1906.
13. George Young to David Cole, July 5, 1906, CM files.
14. Cananea *Herald,* August 4, 1906.
15. *Ibid.,* September 29, November 17, 1906.
16. *Ibid.,* August 16, November 17, 1907.
17. *Ibid.,* October 6, 1906.
18. *Ibid.,* July 28, 1906.
19. *Ibid.,* August 18, 1906.
20. *Ibid.,* November 17, 1906.
21. El Paso *Herald,* May 9, 1906.
22. *Ibid.,* March 7, 1907.
23. *Ibid.,* November 9, 1906.
24. Frank T. Greene, Tucson, November 30, 1969.
25. Greene *To the Stockholders,* January 25, 1906, Wm. H. Brown Collection,
Yale University.
26. *The Copper Handbook* for 1906, p. 545, gives the average as 3.74.
27. Young to Robbins, November 27, 1906, CM files.
28. *The Copper Handbook* 6 (1906): 545, says the average cost of production in
1905 was 11¢ and that little change was expected for 1906. Marvin D. Bernstein in *The Mexican Mining Industry* (State University of New York, 1964),
p. 58, makes Greene's copper cost 25¢ per pound.
29. Young to Greene, October 16, 1906, CM files.
30. Bernstein, *The Mexican Mining Industry,* p. 58.

31. *Remarks of President W. C. Greene at the Meeting of the Stockholders of the Greene Consolidated Copper Company Held at 24 Broad Street, New York, February 10, 1906,* Brophy papers; Hayden, Stone & Co., *Weekly Market Letter,* February 16, 1906, Brophy papers.
32. Greene *To the Stockholders,* December 17, 1906, W. H. Brown Collection, Yale University.
33. Cananea *Herald,* August 11, 1906.
34. *Ibid.*
35. *Ibid.,* August 25, 1906.
36. Isaac Marcosson, *Anaconda* (New York: Dodd, Mead, 1957), p. 255.
37. Cananea *Herald,* July 21, 1906. The Chihuahua *Enterprise* for August 4, 1906, quoted the figures as $2,250,000 and $500,000.
38. Cananea *Herald,* August 25, 1906.
39. *Ibid.,* August 11, 1906.
40. Ira B. Joralemon, *Romantic Copper* (New York: Appleton-Century, 1934), p. 163.
41. Cananea *Herald,* July 21, August 11, 1906.
42. Greene *To the Stockholders,* December 17, 1906, Wm. H. Brown Collection, Yale University.
43. Marvin D. Bernstein, "Col. William C. Greene and the Cananea Copper Bubble," *Bulletin of the Business Historical Society* 26 (December, 1952): 196.
44. Greene *To the Stockholders,* December 17, 1906, William H. Brown Collection, Yale University.
45. Greene to Brophy, October 26, 1906, Brophy papers.
46. *Anaconda,* p. 255.
47. Cananea *Herald,* October 13, 20, 27, November 10, 1906.
48. *Ibid.,* December 22, 1906. The Chihuahua *Enterprise,* August 18, 1906, commented that Greene's friends "took advantage of the market and bought everything offered with the result the bears are out of the market for the time, while Greene's position is greatly strengthened."
49. El Paso *Herald,* December 31, 1906.
50. Cananea *Herald,* January 5, 1907.
51. El Paso *Herald,* January 12, 1907.
52. Frank C. Brophy, San Ignacio del Babocomari Ranch, August 23, 1969. Actually Ryan left "some days" before the rest of his party (El Paso *Herald,* January 12, 1907).
53. New York *Times,* February 15, 1907.

BACK TO EARTH

1. David H. Stratton (ed.), *The Memoirs of A. B. Fall* (El Paso: Texas Western Press, 1966). Fall's recollections of his life up to 1931.
2. Press statement by Fall dated August 23, 1912, Fall papers, Henry E. Huntington Library, San Marino, California.
3. For instance, he was called to testify in 1920 in a senate investigation of Mexican affairs. U.S. Senate, *Investigation of Mexican Affairs.* Preliminary Report and Hearings of the Committee on Foreign Relations, 66th Congress, Second Session. (Washington: Government Printing Office, 1920), vol. I, pp. 1130–34.
4. *Ibid.,* p. 1131. Alexina Fall Chase, in a letter to Mrs. Mary Lee dated May 24, 1957, described her father's early association with Greene.
5. Press Statement, August 23, 1912, Fall papers.
6. El Paso *Herald,* August 1, 1906.
7. At the time of his trial in 1925, he was shown to have a history of tuberculosis, chronic bronchitis, pleurisy, arthritis, and heart trouble.
8. Fall to Senator Medill McCormick, August 16, 1919, Fall papers.
9. The elusive $100,000 which Edward Doheny loaned Fall for improving the ranch figured prominently in Fall's troubles in 1925 (David S. Stratton, *Albert Fall and the Teapot Dome Affair,* Ph.D. Dissertation, University of Colorado, 1955, p. 99).
10. A. B. Fall, *Memoirs,* p. 57.

11. El Paso *Herald,* January 17, 1907; Cananea *Herald,* January 19, 1907.
12. El Paso *Herald,* January 26, 1907.
13. *Ibid.,* April 23, 1907. The concession was for mines, stores and smelters.
14. *Ibid.,* March 7, 1907.
15. *Ibid.,* January 18, 1907.
16. George Young to James H. Kirk, February 8, 1907 (CM files). The Board of Directors have ratified an "amended lumber contract, by which certain features of the original contract are eliminated." Cf. the El Paso *Herald,* January 29, 1907: "Greene Buys Timber from Greene."
17. Young to Ricketts, February 2, 1907, CM files.
18. *Sixth Report of the Greene Consolidated Copper Company.* Report of W. D. Thornton, President, March 10, 1908, to the stockholders. Arizona Historical Society, Tucson, Arizona.
19. *Ibid.*
20. F. J. H. Merrill, "Santa Cruz, a New Copper Camp in Sonora," *Engineering and Mining Journal* 83 (June 1, 1907): 1043.
21. El Paso *Herald,* March 21, June 1, 1907.
22. *Ibid.,* April 2, 1907.
23. Hayden, Stone, *Weekly Market Letter,* May 17, 1907, Brophy papers.
24. *Ibid.*
25. El Paso *Herald,* October 20, 1907.
26. *Ibid.,* October 26, 1907.
27. *Ibid.,* October 3, 1907.
28. Thomas A. Cochran and William Miller, *The Age of Enterprise* (New York: Macmillan, 1942), p. 190.
29. Richard Wyckoff, *Wall Street Ventures and Adventures* (New York: Harper, 1930), pp. 141–42.
30. E. J. Hopkins, *Financing the Frontier* (Phoenix: Arizona Printers, 1950), p. 89.
31. Eugene Meyer, Jr., "The New York Stock Exchange and the Panic of 1907," *Yale Review* 18 (May, 1909): 34.
32. Cedric B. Cowing, *Populists, Plungers, and Progressives: A Social History of Stock and Commodity Speculation 1890–1930* (Princeton University Press, 1965), p. 30.
33. El Paso *Herald,* October 23, 26, 28, 30, 1907.
34. *Ibid.,* October 26, 27, 1907.
35. *Ibid.*
36. *Ibid.,* November 2, 1907. The stock was "very low."
37. CM files.
38. *Sixth Report of the Greene Consolidated Copper Company,* Report of President W. D. Thornton, March 10, 1908, William H. Brown Collection, Yale University.
39. El Paso *Herald,* November 5, 1907.
40. *Ibid.,* February 5, 1908.
41. *Ibid.,* February 19, 1908.
42. *Ibid.,* February 20, 1908.
43. *Ibid.,* April 30, 1908.
44. Fall to Charles A. Spiess, July 9, 1908, Fall papers.
45. Some of these pieces are still in possession of his children.
46. Sidney Hatch, Douglas, Arizona, December 2, 1969.
47. El Paso *Herald,* September 26, 1908.
48. *Ibid.*
49. Fall to Senator Medill McCormick, August 16, 1919, Fall papers.
50. El Paso *Herald,* September 26, 1908.
51. *Ibid.*
52. Fall to "My Dear Sister Mary," May 23, 1917. Fall papers.
53. El Paso *Herald,* March 29, 1909.
54. Fall to Luis Terrazas, June 30, 1910, Fall papers.
55. United States Senate, *Investigation of Mexican Affairs,* 1920, vol. I, p. 1132.
56. In 1914 B. F. Darbyshire of El Paso made such accusations: Darbyshire to Fall, June 25, 1914; Fall to Darbyshire, August 21, 1914, Fall papers.
57. Fall to Senator Medill McCormick, August 16, 1919, Fall papers.

58. Fall to Mrs. W. M. Veley, November 12, 1915, Fall papers.
59. Florence C. Lister and Robert H. Lister, *Chihuahua, Storehouse of Storms* (University of New Mexico Press, 1966), p. 178.
60. El Paso *Herald,* December 12, 1908, February 1, 1909.
61. *Ibid.,* January 22, 1909.
62. *Ibid.,* September 26, 1908.

COWMAN'S HEAVEN

1. Greene to Packard, July 8, 1902, CM files.
2. Fall to Terrazas, June 30, 1910, Fall papers, Huntington Library.
3. Both letters are in the John B. Tittmann Collection, Albuquerque, N.M. Harry Langslow was Eva's husband.
4. Sidney Hatch, Douglas, Arizona, August 26, 1969.
5. R. F. Sharp, University of Arizona Tape Collection, July, 1967.
6. Sidney Hatch, Douglas, Arizona, June 18, 1970. Mr. Hatch was employed by both the Cattle Company and the Copper Company, off and on, from 1920 to 1953. He has a collection of 6,000 maps and a tremendous fund of information about Cattle Company history. He is one of the few Americans to be certified as an engineer by the Mexican government.
7. A contract was made on December 1, 1907, to become effective, for some reason, in 1910. In October 1908 officials of the two companies agreed to put this agreement into effect immediately (George Young to C. E. Wiswall, October 7, 1908; C. E. Wiswall to George Young, October 23, 1908, CM files).
8. San Francisco *Call,* April 29, 1901 (reprint by the Four C's for advertising purposes, CM files).
9. In the files of John B. Tittmann, Albuquerque, is a compendium of the dates of registry of titles of the ranch lands, dated June 25, 1958. Sixteen parcels were transferred by the California Land and Cattle Company on April 24, 1901.
10. In May 1909 Elías was trying to exchange valley land for mountain land "to furnish his cattle with sheltering canyons in winter" (George Young to L. D. Ricketts, May 17, 1909; George Young to David Cole, September 24, 1909. CM files).
11. Tom Farrell, Harshaw, Arizona, November 29, 1969.
12. *Libro de Actas,* vol. I, Cananea Cattle Company, S. A., in possession of Mrs. Anita Greene, Douglas, Arizona. The other shareholders (one share each) were B. A. Packard, A. C. Bernard, Scott White, Egbert Gates, and S. M. Aguirre.
13. *Ibid.*
14. Statement of Admitted Facts, Cases No. 666,006, 692,673, 714,004, Superior Court of California, County of Los Angeles, filed October 11, 1960. The number of shares issued to Frank "cannot be determined from any records now existing."
15. Greene to Eva Greene Langslow, October 15, 1909, Tittmann papers.
16. Frank T. Greene, Tucson, November 30, 1969; Bill Adams, El Paso, April 13, 1971.
17. Jane Abigail Wayland, *Experiment on the Santa Cruz: Colin Cameron's San Rafael Cattle Company,* Master's Thesis (University of Arizona, 1964), p. 110.
18. Sidney Hatch, Douglas, Arizona, December 2, 1969.
19. National Livestock Association, *Prose and Poetry of the Livestock Industry of the United States* (New York: Antiquarian Press, 1959; original copyright 1905), p. 625.
20. Judge Raymond Reid, Burbank, California, June 30, 1969.
21. Sidney Hatch, November 27, 1969.
22. Matt Culley, "Tom Heady," *American Hereford Journal* 43 (January, 1953): 113.
23. *Prose and Poetry of the Livestock Industry,* p. 625.
24. Sidney Hatch, November 27, 1969.
25. Kirk Greene, Berkeley, California, June 27, 1969.
26. Tom Farrell, Harshaw, Arizona, November 29, 1969; Bill Kennon, Deming, New Mexico, August 24, 1969; Bill Adams, El Paso, Texas, April 13, 1971.
27. Information about San Simon Jack is from Sidney Hatch, Bill Adams, and Bill Kennon.

28. Bill Adams, El Paso, Texas, June 18, 1969.
29. W. A. Holmes to C. L. S., February 17, 1971; interview, Berkeley, California, June 28, 1969.
30. Fred wrote from Estes Park, Colorado, to ask why he had been discharged. A letter signed BW, Treasurer, told him, "You were known to be closely affiliated with men in this camp who were regarded by the Company as trouble makers. One instance which came to our attention was your participation in a dinner given in celebration of Mr. Douglas's forcible expulsion from Cananea." (B. W. to Fred R. Walker, July 1, 1913, CM files).
31. Ira Joralemon, interview with Leon C. Metz, Berkeley, California, February 20, 1969. Mr. Joralemon is the author of *Romantic Copper* (New York: Appleton-Century, 1934), reissued as *Copper* (Berkeley: Howell-North, 1973).
32. Sidney Hatch, August 26, 1969.

TWO FAST HORSES

1. Amy's son, Robert T. Jesson of Sepulveda, California, still has the snapshots (letter to C. L. S., March 29, 1970).
2. Mrs. Charles H. Greene, Prescott, Arizona, June 24, 1970.
3. Judge Raymond H. Reid, Burbank, California, June 30, 1969.
4. Mrs. Anita Greene, Douglas, Arizona, June 23, 1969.
5. Marvin D. Bernstein, "Colonel William C. Greene and the Cananea Copper Bubble," *Bulletin of the Business Historical Society* 26 (December, 1952): 197.
6. John V. Montague, Auditor, to W. V. Ingram, Assistant Auditor, Southern Pacific Railway, October 25, 1910: "... all charges against this car should be billed against the Cananea Realty Company.... This car is in the service of Mr. W. C. Greene, who has no connection with the Cananea Consolidated Copper Company." After the Colonel's death the *Verde* was sold to the Pullman Company for $10,000 in 1912 (John V. Montague, KNOW ALL MEN BY THESE PRESENTS, January 27, 1912, CM files).
7. P. E. Fuller wrote and printed a *Report Upon the Santa Cruz Reservoir Project,* dated June 11, 1913, which outlines the history of the enterprise. After the Colonel's death development came to a halt and this report was part of an effort to get it going again.
8. Judge Raymond Reid.
9. P. E. Fuller, *Report.*
10. P. E. Fuller's report indicates that in 1912 the installations were still solid and serviceable. But cf. Will C. Barnes, *Arizona Place Names,* revised, (Tucson: University of Arizona Press, 1960), pp. 295–96.
11. El Paso *Herald,* November 22, 1910.
12. Ira Joralemon, telephone interview, February 17, 1969: "The mine turned out to be a 'teaser' with some good ore but not enough to be a good risk."
13. Young to John O. Campbell, April 3, 1911, CM files.
14. Kosterlitzky to George Young, June 8, 1910. CM files.
15. Kosterlitzky to Young, June 20, 1910, CM files.
16. Kosterlitzky to John A. Campbell, June 30, 1910, CM files.
17. Kosterlitzky to Young, February 12, 1911, CM files.
18. Judge Raymond Reid. Cabral, born in La Colorada, Sonora, was the son of a Portuguese father and a Mexican mother.
19. El Paso *Herald,* March 17, 18, 21, 1911.
20. Judge Raymond Reid.
21. *Ibid.*
22. The pencil draft, undated, is in the manuscript collection of Charles H. Greene at Prescott, Arizona.
23. Judge Raymond Reid.
24. Antonio G. Rivera, *La Revolución en Sonora* (Mexico: Privately printed, 1969), p. 226; Eduardo Villa, *Historia del estado de Sonora* (Hermosillo, Editorial Sonora, 1951), p. 416.
25. Kosterlitzky to Young, July 5, 1911, CM files.
26. Young to Kosterlitzky, June 6, 1911, CM files.
27. Mr. Wiswall kept track of livestock appropriated by rebel forces and the estate finally collected (CM files; Charles Greene, Prescott, July 4, 1969).

28. Tom Farrell, Harshaw, Arizona, November 29, 1960.
29. Dr. W. P. Haney to M. E. Harby, August 29, 1911, CM files.
30. El Paso *Herald,* August 7, 1911; Tucson *Citizen,* August 7, 1911; Los Angeles *Tribune,* August 6, 1911; New York *Tribune,* New York *Times,* August 6, 1911; *Engineering and Mining Journal,* vol. 92, August 19, 1911.
31. H. H. Hillman to C. L. S., April 26, 1971.
32. Cananea *Herald,* July 28, 1906.

THE DISTORTED IMAGE

1. Ben Williams, Douglas, Arizona, August 26, 1969.
2. Translation of an editorial in *El Cuarto Poder,* Cananea, August 10, 1911, CM files.
3. Manuel J. Aguirre, *Cananea: las garras del imperialismo en las entrañas de Mexico* (Mexico: Editora B. Costa-Amic, 1958), pp. 30, 161.
4. Ira S. Joralemon, *Romantic Copper* (New York: Appleton-Century, 1934), p. 136.
5. *Financing the Frontier* (Phoenix: Arizona Printers, 1950), p. 88.
6. *Fighting Men of the West* (New York: Dutton, 1932), pp. 196–97.
7. New York: Dutton, 1936.
8. Ralph A. Donham, "Buckaroo of Wall Street," *Arizona Republic,* November 24, 1957, pp. 42, 44–46.
9. *Anaconda* (New York: Dodd, Mead, 1957), pp. 251, 254.
10. *Rawhide Johnny,* title page.
11. *The Mexican Mining Industry* (Albany: New York State University Press, 1964), p. 56.
12. *Rails, Mines and Progress* (Ithaca: Cornell University Press, 1958), p. 219.
13. *The Mexican Mining Industry,* p. 58.
14. *Frenzied Finance* (New York: The Ridgway-Thayer Co., 1905), p. 525.
15. J. Evetts Haley, "Bill Greene of Cananea Copper," *The Shamrock,* Summer, 1962, p. 5.
16. Pletcher, *Rails, Mines, and Progress,* pp. 223–24.
17. J. Evetts Haley, "Bill Greene of Cananea Copper," p. 6.
18. Vol. 92 (August, 1911), p. 347.
19. Hayden, Stone and Co., *Weekly Market Letter,* November 16, 1906, Brophy papers.
20. Bernstein, "Colonel William C. Greene and the Cananea Copper Bubble," pp. 194–95; Pletcher, *Rails, Mines and Progress,* p. 132.
21. Morris Parker, *Men, Mules and Me in Mexico,* MS.
22. Walter Harvey Weed to George F. Robbins, April 12, 1902, CM files.
23. Robert T. Hill, *Cananea Revisited,* December, 1903, p. 15, CM files.
24. Pletcher, *Rails, Mines and Progress,* p. 258.
25. Judge Raymond Reid, Burbank, California, June 30, 1969.
26. Sidney Hatch, Douglas, Arizona, December 2, 1969. The story is often told.
27. Ben Williams, Douglas, Arizona, June 23, 1969; M. T. Everhart to C. L. S., May 1, 1970.
28. Frank Brophy, *Arizona Sketchbook,* p. 242.
29. James H. McClintock, *Arizona* (Chicago: S. J. Clarke, 1916), vol. 2, pp. 603–04.
30. *Ibid.,* p. 604. Mahlon T. Everhart (A. B. Fall's son-in-law) has heard that Fall was the gunslinger: "Greene was induced by an Eastern operator to sign some documents which turned out to imperil his interests seriously. Fall, as his attorney, went to New York to try to straighten out the matter. Legal approaches failing, he pulled a gun on the holder, demanded and got the instruments, and returned successful" (M. T. E. to C. L. S., May 1, 1970).
31. August 6, 1911.
32. George Jones, "Fightingest Man of the West," *True West,* September-October, 1959, p. 14.
33. Frank Mason, "The Baron of Cananea," *Frontier Times,* December-January, 1963, pp. 21, 52.
34. Judge Raymond T. Reid, Burbank, California, June 30, 1969.

35. Dan de Lara Hughes, *South From Tombstone* (London: Methuen, 1938), pp. 223–24.
36. Niño Cochise, with A. Kenney Griffith, "Apache Tears." *Old West* 4 (Winter, 1967): 13. Niño Cochise, whose authenticity is seriously questioned by Arizona Indians and old-timers, collaborated with Mr. Griffith in 1971 in the production of a full-length autobiography, *The First Hundred Years of Niño Cochise* (New York: Abelard-Schuman). Although he claims to have been with Greene as bodyguard and confidant during the years of his success, the accounts of Greene's loose living are completely omitted.
37. National Livestock Association, *Prose and Poetry of the Livestock Industry of the United States* (New York: Antiquarian Press, 1959), p. 626.

Acknowledgments

According to Bob Lenon, engineer and philosopher of Patagonia, Arizona, Colonel Greene's biographer must follow "a cold trail." A surprising number of people, however, were able and willing to supply special help and information.

The book owes its greatest debt to Mr. and Mrs. Charles Greene, who, because they were convinced that the Colonel's life could and should be written, were tireless in providing information and encouragement. Charles had a file of his father's papers and a good collection of photographs. His wife, Margarethe Tittmann Greene, was close to Mary, the Colonel's second wife, and proved to be a storehouse of information. Frank Greene, deeply interested in the genealogy and early history of all branches of his family, read the manuscript and provided much data. Kirk Greene and Florence Greene Sharp likewise filled in many gaps.

An indispenable collection of original documents was the archive of letters, papers, and photographs preserved by the Compañía Minera de Cananea, S. A. de C. V., of Cananea, Sonora, Mexico, made available through the courtesy of Robert C. Weed, general manager, and Robert F. Torrance, retired treasurer of the company. Bob and Minnie Torrance, specialists in Cananea history, did much to preserve its records. Minnie indexed the surviving files of the Cananea *Herald;* Bob sorted and classified correspondence and accumulated maps, books, pictures, and documents. Both of them read the manuscript and supplied aid and comfort to the writer.

Luckily for Greene's biographer, the Colonel's friend W. H. Brophy, storekeeper and banker, was a man who never threw anything away. The

Brophy papers, made available by Frank Brophy and A. Blake Brophy (son and grandson), helped to make this book possible.

Another important resource was the John B. Tittmann file of legal and family documents used by his courtesy.

In Mexico special help was provided by Fernando Pesqueira, Director of the *Instituto Sonorense de Historia e Geografía* at Hermosillo, who furnished records, extracts from *La Constitución* (official newspaper of Sonora), and recollections of his boyhood in Cananea.

Many libraries and many librarians have put a shoulder to the wheel, especially the Arizona Historical Society (Sidney B. Brinckerhoff, director; Margaret Sparks Bret Harte, librarian); University of Arizona (Phyllis Ball, in Special Collections; Harwood Hinton, editor of *Arizona and the West* and ramrod of the Oral History project; John Gilchriese, former field historian); the Arizona Collection of Arizona State University (with the genial and helpful Bert Fireman in charge); the Henry E. Huntington Library at San Marino, California, with special thanks to Mary Isabel Fry and to Virginia M. Rust, assistant in manuscripts; the Department of Library and Archives in the Arizona State Capitol at Phoenix (Marguerite B. Cooley, director, and Grayce Owen, state archivist); the Bancroft Library of the University of California at Berkeley (John Barr Tompkins); the El Paso Public Library and its Southwest Collection (Lisabeth Lovelace and Shirley Watson; former librarians Mrs. Vaughn Evans and Virginia Hoke); Library of the University of Texas at El Paso (James Cleveland, microfilms; Leon C. Metz, archivist; Jeanne Reynolds, interlibrary loans); the Library of Congress (John B. Broderick, acting chief, Manuscript Division); the Buffalo and Erie County Public Library (Ridgway McNallie); the Chappaqua, New York, Public Library (Mrs. Douglas Grafflin, director); the New York Public Library (John P. Baker).

Individuals who have gone out of their way to be helpful include Jerry and Charlotte Beller, specialists in the history of Charleston, Arizona; W. H. Holmes, an old Mexico hand with a good collection of Greene material; Maybel H. Swanson, secretary, Potter County Historical Society, Coudersport, Pa. (who looked up John H. Costello); Ira Joralemon, author of *Romantic Copper;* P. W. Newbury, once a resident of Cananea and an authority on Cochise County history; Mary Lou Howe, formerly librarian of the Copper Queen Library at Bisbee; M. E. McPherson, clerk of the Superior Court, Bisbee; McPherson's secretary, Linda Appelt; Carl Hays, deeply versed in the history of the Mexican border; Ben Williams, whose father was a close friend of Colonel Greene's; Anita Greene, widow of William C. Greene, Jr., who retained possession of many records of Greene business ventures; Henry P. Ehrlinger, who helped locate issues of *The Copper Handbook;* Mrs. Robert Cunningham, who dug deeply into the El Paso newspapers for me; Charles S. Wise, past president of the Pimería Alta Historical Society, and Lupe E. Scooler, former secretary; Robert Lenon, mining engineer, raconteur, and friend; Fred Benedict, a cousin of the second Mrs. Greene; Ella Culin, who provided the picture of her grandmother, the first Mrs. Greene; Mrs. J. W. Ackley, who put me in touch with Romer descendants; David Myrick, railroad historian with fruitful connections everywhere in the Southwest; Colonel Cornelius Smith, biographer of Emilio Kosterlitzky; George E. Fowles, who found the probate record of John G. Roberts; Colin Rickards, with files of notes and pictures; Mary Lee, closely connected with the Fall family; Emadair Chase Jones, who lent her copy of the Greene Gold-Silver prospectus of the mines in Chihuahua; Bill McGaw, who lent his unique volume of the Chihuahua enterprise; George Chambers, who interviewed Columbus Giragi for me; George Eckhart, specialist in the mission history of northern Mexico; Glenn Hay, who made available his Greene index to the *Bisbee Daily Review;* Byron Ivancovich, who shared family recollections and archival material; Lena Des Saulles, with recollections of early days in the Bisbee region.

Special thank you's go to David S. Stratton, a specialist in the life and career of Albert B. Fall, who held back none of his treasures; Leon C. Metz, who interviewed Ira Joralemon for me; Arthur Campa, folklore specialist, who dug up the *corrido, La Carcel de Cananea*; Mr. and Mrs. Burton Devere, who love books and people and have roots in pioneer times; Sidney Hatch and Don Bufkin, who made the maps; Jay Wagoner, who photographed exhibits in the Gallery of History in Mexico City.

A final salute is due four of Greene's old cowboys — Mack Axford, Bill Adams, Tommy Farrell, and Bill Kennon — and to Judge Raymond L. Reid, Greene's one-time stenographer. Their recollections were firsthand and indispensable.

Special recognition is due Alice Carbajal, who worked long and hard on the manuscript.

To all these, and to those listed in the following pages under Interviews and Letters, thanks — and again, thanks.

Finally, a word of appreciation is extended to the University of Arizona Press for effecting publication of the book under its imprint.

C. L. S.

Sources

Interviews

Bill Adams, El Paso, Texas, June 18, 1969; April 13, 1971
Mack Axford, Tombstone, Arizona, June 24, 1969
Sam G. Barrow, St. David's, Arizona, June 27, 1970
Frank C. Brophy, Elgin, Arizona, August 23, 1969
Mrs. Lena Des Saulles, Tucson, August 24, 1969; June 25, 1970
Mr. and Mrs. Burton Devere, Tombstone, Arizona, June 23, 1969
Tom Farrell, Harshaw, Arizona, November 29, 1969
Mrs. Anita Greene, Douglas, Arizona, June 23, 1969
Mr. and Mrs. Charles H. Greene, July 4, 1969; June 24, 25, 1970;
    February 13, 1971 (telephone interview); September 17, 1971
Frank T. Greene, Tucson, Arizona, November 29, 30, December 2, 1969;
    April 6, June 22, 1970
Kirk Greene, Berkeley, California, June 27, 1969
Sidney Hatch, Douglas, Arizona, August 26, November 27,
    December 2, 1969; June 18, 1970
Carl Hays, El Paso, Texas, January 30, 1970;
    Deming, New Mexico, August 24, 1969
W. A. Holmes, Berkeley, California, June 28, 1969
Mary Lou Howe, Bisbee, Arizona, December 2, 1969
Ira Joralemon, Berkeley, California, February 17, 1969 (telephone interview);
    February 20, 1969 (with Leon C. Metz); June 29, 1969
Bill Kennon, Deming, New Mexico, August 24, 1969
Robert Lenon, Patagonia, Arizona, June 29, 1970
Mrs. George Millar, El Paso, Texas, May 6, 1969
Judge Raymond Reid, Burbank, California, June 29, 1969
Mrs. Florence Greene Sharp, San Rafael Ranch, August 24, 1969
Mr. and Mrs. Robert F. Torrance, Cananea, Sonora, Mexico,
    November 28, 1969
Robert C. Weed, Cananea, Sonora, Mexico, November 28, 1969
Ben Williams, Douglas, Arizona, June 23, August 26, 1969
Charles Wise, Nogales, Arizona, June 29, 1970

Letters

Aguirre, Stephen E., to C. L. S., undated (1970).
Baker, John P., to C. L. S., July 18, November 18, 1969.
Barrow, Sam G., to C. L. S., September 19, November 14, 1969.
Beller, Jerry, to C. L. S., December 11, 1969.
Bradshaw, Eva Moson, to C. L. S., September 4, 1969.
Brophy, Frank C., to C. L. S., June 1, 1970.
Chambers, George W., to C. L. S., July 31, 1969.
Chase, Alexina Fall, to Mary Lee, May 24, 1957.
Coyne, Frank H., to C. L. S., September 19, 1969.
Everhart, Mahlon T., to C. L. S., May 1, 1970.
Grafflin, Mrs. Douglas, to C. L. S., September 17, 1969.
Greene, Mrs. Charles H., to C. L. S., February 13, 1971.
Greene, Frank T., to C. L. S., November 16, 20, December 1, 1969,
    November 20, December 3, 1970.
Hidy, Ralph W., to C. L. S., October 28, 1969.
Hillman, Harold H., to C. L. S., April 26, 1970.
Holmes, W. A., to C. L. S., February 17, 1971.
Hunter, W. C., to C. L. S., August 20, 1969.
Ivancovich, Byron, to C. L. S., August 22, 1970.
Jesson, Robert T., to C. L. S., March 29, 1970.
Jones, Emadair Chase, to C. L. S., February 2, 1970.
McClure, Jimmy Kirk, to C. L. S., December 30, 1970.
Pesqueira, Fernando, to C. L. S., December 9, 1969, June 3, 1970.
Peterson, Robert L., to C. L. S., January 19, 1970.
Romer, Mary, to John W. Ackley, December 6, 1954.
Splane, Mrs. Gladys Lindsay, to C. L. S., January 6, 1970.
Whitney, Mrs. Phoebe, to C. L. S., February 1, 1970.

Newspapers and Periodicals

Arizona Daily Citizen (Tucson)
Arizona Daily Star (Tucson)
Arizona Republican (later, *Arizona Republic*) (Phoenix)
Arizona Silver Belt (Globe)
Arizona Weekly Citizen (Tucson)
Bisbee *Daily Review*
Boston *Herald*
Buffalo *Daily Courier*
Cananea *Herald*
Chihuahua *Enterprise*
La Constitución (official periodical of the state of Sonora)
The Copper Handbook, annual publication edited by Horace Stevens,
    Houghton, Michigan, 1899 ff.
Douglas *Dispatch*
El Paso *Herald*
El Paso *Times*
Engineering and Mining Journal
Jerome *Mining News*
Jerome *Reporter*
Los Angeles *Herald*

Los Angeles *Times*
Los Angeles *Tribune*
Mining and Scientific Press (San Francisco)
Mining World (Chicago)
New York *Times*
New York *Tribune*
Nogales *Border Vidette*
Nogales *Oasis*
Prescott *Evening Courier*
Regeneración (St. Louis)
San Francisco *Call*
Tombstone *Prospector*
Tombstone *Weekly Epitaph*
Wall Street Journal (New York)

Manuscript Collections

Albert Case Benedict File. Arizona Historical Society, Tucson, Arizona.
William P. Blake and William H. Brown Collections (Annual Reports of
Greene companies, letters to stockholders). Yale University Library,
New Haven, Connecticut.
W. H. Brophy Papers (letters, telegrams, financial and stockmarket reports,
newspaper clippings), in the collection of A. Blake Brophy, Phoenix, Ariz.
L. H. Chalmers Papers, Arizona Collection. Arizona State University,
Tempe, Arizona.
Files of Compañía Minera de Cananea, S. A. de C. V. (business and personal
correspondence, reports, letters to stockholders, telegrams, statements of
Company officials, miscellaneous material relating to the affairs of the
Greene Consolidated Copper Company, Cananea Consolidated Copper
Company, Cananea Cattle Company, and related companies).
Cananea, Sonora, Mexico.
Albert Bacon Fall Papers (correspondence and miscellaneous material from
the files of Albert B. Fall). Henry E. Huntington Library,
San Marino, California.
Charles H. Greene Papers (letters, documents and miscellaneous manuscript
material), Prescott, Arizona.
Eugene Ives Letter Books. Special Collections, University of Arizona,
Tucson, Arizona.
Harriet Stryker-Rodda. "Ancestry of W. C. Greene, Work Chart, 1970–71,"
MS.
John B. Tittmann files (letters, legal records, and miscellaneous material
mostly related to litigation between and among members of the Greene
family). Albuquerque, New Mexico.

Individual Manuscripts

Beller, Jerry. *Helltown, Arizona,* MS.
Bryson, Conrey. *History of the El Paso Tin Mine,* History Seminar Paper.
Texas Western College, 1957.
Cananea Cattle Company, S. A. *Libro de Actas y Acuerdos,* vol. 1.
In possession of Mrs. Anita Greene, Douglas, Arizona.

Cananea Consolidated Copper Company. *Letters, General Correspondence,*
1902 (Bound volume, files of Compañía Minera de Cananea, S.A. de C.V.,
Cananea, Sonora, Mexico).

Corral, Ramón. *Memoria de la administración publica del Estado de Sonora*
presentada a la legislatura del mismo por el gobernador Ramón Corral,
Tomo II. Hermosillo, 1891 (transcript provided by Sr. Fernando Pesqueira,
Hermosillo).

Fuller, P. E., *Report Upon the Santa Cruz Reservoir Project,* June 11, 1913
(privately printed).

Greene Consolidated Gold Company. *Libro de Actas y Acuerdos.*
In possession of Mrs. Anita Greene, Douglas, Arizona.

Jenkins, Myra Ellen. *Ricardo Flores Magón and the Mexican Liberal Party,*
Unpublished Doctoral Dissertation, University of New Mexico, 1953.

Martin, Mrs. Cicero. Deposition, Nogales, Arizona, February 25, 1959,
(Eva Greene Day vs. the Estate of Mary Greene Wiswall, Civil Action
No. 17003), filed in Cochise County, Arizona, Courthouse.

Parker, Morris. *Men, Mules and Me in Mexico.* MS, in possession of
Lina Parker Mathews, Hermosa Beach, California.

Stanton, Robert Brewster. *Report Upon the Cananea Consolidated Copper*
Company at Cananea, Sonora, Mexico, with Reference to a proposal to
build a Water Power and Electrical Plant upon the Yaqui River in Mexico.
Typescript. Report submitted November 30, 1906.

Stratton, David S. *Albert Fall and the Teapot Dome Affair.* Unpublished
Ph.D. Dissertation, University of Colorado, 1955.

Supreme Court of the State of New York. Axel Hallenborg, Plaintiff,
against William C. Greene et al. Answer to Amended Complaint, filed
December 20, 1906 (Bound volume in Special Collections,
University of Arizona, Tucson, Arizona).

United States Senate. *Investigation of Mexican Affairs, Preliminary Report*
and Hearings of the Committee on Foreign Relations, vol. 1, 66th Congress.
Second Session (Washington: Government Printing Office, 1920),
Statement of Albert B. Fall.

Walker, Fred R. *Stamping Grounds,* MS. Notebooks in collection of
W. H. Holmes, Berkeley, California.

Wayland, Jane Abigail. *Experiment on the Santa Cruz: Colin Cameron's San*
Rafael Cattle Company, 1882–1893. Unpublished M.A. thesis,
University of Arizona, 1964.

Young, George. *Greene Cananea Copper Company and Subsidiaries:*
Historical Sketch, MS. Files of Compañía Minera de Cananea.
Cananea, Sonora, Mexico, August, 1920.

Books and Journal Articles

Abad de Santillán, Diego. *Ricardo Flores Magón: el apostol de la Revolución*
Social Méxicana. Mexico: Grupo Cultural "Ricardo Flores Magón,"
1925, p. 17.

Acuña, Rudolph F. "Ignacio Pesqueira: Sonoran Caudillo."
Arizona and the West 12 (Summer, 1970): 139–72.

Aguirre, Manuel J. *Cananea, garras del imperialismo en las entrañas de*
Mexico. Mexico: Editora B. Costa-Amic, Mexico, 1958.

Almada, Francisco. *Diccionario de historia, geografía y biografía Sonorenses.*
Chihuahua, n.d., n.p.

Arizona, the Youngest State. Chicago: S. J. Clarke, 1916.

Axford, Joseph "Mack." *Around Western Campfires*. Tucson:
University of Arizona Press, 1969.

The Bank of Douglas. *The Bank of Douglas, Arizona, 1887–1950*, 2nd ed.
Phoenix: Privately printed, 1954.

Barnes, Will C. *Arizona Place Names*, Revised and Enlarged by Byrd H.
Granger. Tucson: University of Arizona Press, 1960.

Barney, James H. "W. C. Greene, Paul Revere of Arizona." Prescott
Evening Courier, March 26, 1951.

Benedict, Henry Marvin. *Genealogy of the Benedicts in America*.
Albany: Joel Munsell, 1870.

Bernstein, Marvin D. "Col. William C. Greene and the Cananea Copper
Bubble." *Bulletin of the Business Historical Society* 26 (December, 1952):
179–98.

————. *The History and Economic Organization of the Mexican Mining
Industry, 1890–1940*. Albany: State University of New York, 1964.

Bimson, Walter Reed. *Louis D. Ricketts (1859–1940)*.
New York: Newcomer Society, 1949.

Bowman, J. N., and Robert F. Heizer. *Anza and the Northwest Frontier of
New Spain*. Los Angeles: Southwest Museum, 1967.

Brandes, Ray. *Frontier Military Posts of Arizona*.
Globe, Arizona: Dale Stuart King, 1960.

Brayer, Herbert O. "The Cananea Incident." *New Mexico Historical Review*
13 (October, 1938): 387–415.

Brophy, Frank Cullen. *Arizona Sketchbook*.
Phoenix: Arizona-Messenger Printing Company, 1952.

Burk, Matia McClelland. "The Beginnings of the Tombstone School,
1879–1893." *Arizona and the West* 1 (Autumn, 1959): 248–57.

Burns, Walter Noble. *Tombstone*. New York: Penguin Books, 1942.

Burrus, Ernest J. *Kino and the Cartography of New Spain*. Tucson: Arizona
Pioneers' Historical Society, 1965.

Callahan, James Morton. *American Foreign Policy in Mexican Relations*.
New York: Macmillan, 1932.

Chase, Edward Kirkland. *Dream and Thought in the Business Community
1860–1900*. Ithaca: Cornell University Press, 1956.

Chisholm, Joe. *Brewery Gulch: Frontier Days of Old Arizona*.
San Antonio: Naylor, 1949.

Cleland, Robert Glass. *A History of Phelps Dodge 1834–1950*.
New York: Alfred A. Knopf, 1952.

Cochran, Thomas A., and William Miller. *The Age of Enterprise*.
New York: Macmillan, 1942.

Coolidge, Dane. *Fighting Men of the West*. New York: E. P. Dutton, 1932.

————. *Rawhide Johnny*. New York: E. P. Dutton, 1936.

Cornell, (Rev.) John. *Genealogy of the Cornell Family, Being An Account of
the Descendants of Thomas Cornell of Portsmouth, Rhode Island*.
New York: T. A. Wright, 1902.

Corral, Ramón. *El General Ignacio Pesqueira*.
Hermosillo: Imprenta del Estado, 1900.

Cowing, Cedric B. *Populists, Plungers and Progressives: A Social History of
Stock and Commodity Speculation, 1890–1930*. Princeton University Press,
1965.

Culley, Matt. "Tom Heady." *American Hereford Journal*
43 (January, 1953): 112–13, 116–17, 120.

Cumberland, Charles C. *Mexico: The Struggle for Modernity.*
New York: Oxford, 1968.

Díaz Cárdenas, Leon. *Cananea, primer brote del syndicalismo en Mexico.*
Mexico: Publicaciones del departamento de bibliotecas de la secretaría de
Educación Publica, 1956.

Donham, Ralph. "Buckaroo of Wall Street." *Arizona Republic,*
November 24, 1957, pp. 42, 44–46.

Dorsey, Leslie, and Janice Devine. *Fare Thee Well.* New York: Crown, 1964.

Eager, Samuel W. *An Outline History of Orange County with . . . Short
Biographical Sketches of Early Settlers, etc.*
Newburgh, New York: S. T. Callahan, 1846–1847.

Eiteman, Wilford J., Charles A. Dice, and David K. Eiteman. *The Stock
Market.* New York: McGraw-Hill, 1966.

Erwin, Allen A. *The Southwest of John Horton Slaughter.*
Glendale: Arthur H. Clark, 1965.

Fall, Albert Bacon. *The Memoirs of A. B. Fall,* ed. David S. Stratton.
(Southwestern Studies, vol. 4, no. 3) El Paso: Texas Western Press, 1966.

Farish, Thomas Edwin. *History of Arizona,* vol. II.
Phoenix: Privately printed, 1915.

Fuller, P. E. *Report Upon the Santa Cruz Reservoir Project.*
Privately printed, 1913. n.p.

Fulton, Richard W., and Conrad J. Bahre. "Charleston, Arizona:
"A Documentary Reconstruction." *Arizona and the West* 9 (Spring, 1967):
41–64.

Ganzhorn, Jack. *I've Killed Men.* New York: Devin-Adair, 1959.

Garcia, Janet. "Cochise's Grandson Recalls Historic Past."
Douglas *Dispatch,* October 8, 1969.

García y Alva, Federico. *"México y sus progresos." Album directorio del
Estado de Sonora.* Hermosillo: Imprenta oficial, 1905–1907.

González Ramírez, Manuel. *La huelga de Cananea.*
Mexico: Fondo de Cultura Economica, 1956.

Greene, Principal Frank L. *Descendants of Joseph Greene of Westerly,
R. I., Also Other Branches of the Greenes of Quidnesset, or Kingston, R. I.,
and Other Lines of Greenes in America.* Albany: Joel Munsell's Sons, 1894.

Griggs, Jorge. *The Mines of Chihuahua.* Chihuahua: Privately printed, 1907.

Haley, J. Evetts. "Bill Greene of Cananea Copper." *The Shamrock,*
Summer, 1962, pp. 4–7.

Hamilton, Leonidas. *Border States of Mexico: Sonora, Sinaloa, Chihuahua,
and Durango.* San Francisco: Bacon & Co., 1881; 4th edition, revised
and enlarged, New York, 1883.

Harris, Theodore D. (ed.). *Negro Frontiersman: The Western Memoirs of
Henry O. Flipper, First Negro Graduate of West Point.*
El Paso: Texas Western Press, 1963.

Hinshaw, William Wade. *Encyclopedia of American Quaker Genealogy,*
3 vols. Ann Arbor: Edwards Bros., 1936.

Hinton, Richard J. *The Handbook to Arizona and Its Resources, History,
Towns, Mines, Ruins, and Scenery.* San Francisco: Payot, Upham & Co.,
1878. Republished by Arizona Silhouettes, Tucson, 1954.

Hopkins, Ernest J. *Financing the Frontier: A Fifty Year History of the
Valley National Bank.* Phoenix: Arizona Printers, 1950.

Hughes, Dan de Lara. *South From Tombstone*. London: Methuen, 1938.

Hunt, Aurora. *Kirby Benedict: Frontier Federal Judge*.
Glendale: Arthur H. Clark, 1961.

Jones, George. "Fightingest Man of the West," *True West,* September-October, 1959.

Joralemon, Ira. *Romantic Copper*. New York: Appleton-Century, 1934.
Reissued as *Copper*. Berkeley: Howell-North, 1973.

Kaplan, Samuel. *Peleamos contra la injusticia: la epopeya de los hermanos Flores Magón,* 2 vols. Mexico: Libro Mex Editores, 1960.

King, Frank M. *Pioneer Western Empire Builders*.
Los Angeles: Trail's End Publishing Co., 1946.

Ladd, Robert E. "Vengeance at the O. K. Corral." *Arizoniana* 4 (Summer, 1963): 1–10.

Lawson, Thomas W. *Frenzied Finance*.
New York: The Ridgway-Thayer Co., 1905.

Liggett, William (Bill), Sr. *My Seventy-Five Years Along the Mexican Border*. New York: Exposition Press, 1964.

Lister, Florence C., and Robert H. Lister. *Chihuahua, Storehouse of Storms*.
Albuquerque: University of New Mexico Press, 1966.

Lockwood, Frank C. *Pioneer Days in Arizona*. New York: Macmillan, 1932.

McClintock, James H. *Arizona,* 3 vols. Chicago: S. J. Clarke, 1916.

Madero, Francisco I. *La sucesión presidencial en 1910*. Mexico: 1910, n.p.

Marcosson, Isaac F. *Anaconda*. New York: Dodd, Mead, 1957.

Mason, Frank. "The Baron of Cananea." *Frontier Times* 38 (December-January, 1963): 20–21, 50–51.

Medina Hoyos, Francisco. *Cananea: cuna de la Revolución Méxicana*.
Mexico: Privately printed, 1956.

Merrill, F. J. H. "Santa Cruz, a New Copper Camp in Sonora."
Engineering and Mining Journal 83 (June 1, 1907): 1043.

Meyer, Eugene. "The New York Stock Exchange and the Panic of 1907."
Yale Review 18 (May, 1909): 34–46.

Mignone, A. Frederick. "A Fief for Mexico: Colonel Greene's Empire Ends."
Southwest Review (Autumn, 1959): 332–39.

Mitchell, Hal. "Justice Jim." *Arizona Highways* 21 (July, 1945): 32–37.

Morris, Lloyd. *Incredible New York*. New York: Random House, 1951.

Mowry, Sylvester. *Geography and Resources of Arizona and Sonora: An Address Before the American Geographical and Statistical Society*.
Washington: Henry Polkinghorn, 1859.

Myers, John Myers. *The Tombstone Story*. New York: Grosset and Dunlap, 1950.

National Livestock Association. *Prose and Poetry of the Livestock Industry of the United States*. New York: Antiquarian Press, 1959.

Niño Cochise, with A. Kenney Griffith. "Apache Tears."
Old West 4 (Winter, 1967).

Niño Cochise, Ciyé. *The First Hundred Years of Niño Cochise,* as told to A. Kenney Griffith. New York: Abelard-Schuman, 1971.

Nye, William F., translator. *Sonora: Its Extent, Population, Natural Productions, Indian Tribes, Mines, Mineral Lands, etc., etc. Translated from the Spanish of Francisco Velasco*. San Francisco: H. H. Bancroft and Company, 1861.

Paré, Madeline Ferrin, with the collaboration of Bert Fireman, *Arizona Pageant: A Short History of the 48th State.*
Tempe: Arizona Historical Foundation, 1967.
Parsons, George Whitwell. *The Private Journal of George Whitwell Parsons.*
Phoenix: Arizona Statewide Archival and Records Project, 1939.
Peplow, Edward H. *History of Arizona,* vol. 2.
New York: Lewis Historical Publishing Co., 1958.
Pfefferkorn, Ignaz. *Sonora: A Description of the Province,* Translated and Annotated by Theodore E. Treutlein. Albuquerque: University of New Mexico Press, 1949.
Pletcher, David M. *Rails, Mines and Progress: Seven American Promoters in Mexico.* Ithaca: Cornell University Press, 1958.
Porter, Eugene O. *Lord Beresford and Lady Flo.*
El Paso: Texas Western Press, 1970.
Rickard, T .A. "Louis Davidson Ricketts, an Interview."
Mining and Scientific Press 123 (October 1, 1921) : 463–73.
Rivera, Antonio G. *La Revolución en Sonora.* Mexico: Privately printed, 1969.
Rock, J. L., and W. I. Smith. *Southern and Western Texas Guide for 1878.*
St. Louis: H. Granger, 1878.
Ruttenber, E. M., and L. H. Clark. *History of Orange County, N.Y., with Illustrations and Biographical Sketches of Many of Its Pioneers and Prominent Men.* Philadelphia: Everts & Peck, 1881.
Rynning, (Captain) Thomas H. *Gun Notches.* New York: A. L. Burt, 1931.
Schellie, Don. *The Tucson Citizen: A Century of Arizona Journalism.*
Tucson: Tucson *Daily Citizen,* 1970.
Smalley, Eugene V. *History of the Northern Pacific Railroad.*
New York: Putnam, 1883.
Smalley, George Herbert. *My Adventures in Arizona: Leaves from a Reporter's Notebook.* Edited by Yndia Smalley Moore.
Tucson: Arizona Historical Society, 1966.
Sobel, Robert. *The Curbstone Brokers.* New York: Macmillan, 1970.
Sonnichsen, C. L. *Billy King's Tombstone.* Tucson: University of Arizona Press, 1972.
Southworth, J. R. *The Mines of Mexico,* vol. 9.
Liverpool: Blake and Mackenzie, 1905.
Tapia Quijada, Cesar. *Apuntes sobre la huelga de Cananea.*
Hermosillo: Editada por la Universidad de Sonora, 1956.
Thompson, Benjamin F. *The History of Long Island from Its Discovery and Settlement to the Present Time.* 2nd ed., 2 vols.
New York: Gould, Banks, & Co., 1843.
Turner, Ethel Duffy. *Ricardo Flores Magón y el partido liberal Méxicano.*
Tr. de Eduardo Limon G. Morelia: Editorial "Erandi," 1960.
Turner, John Kenneth. *Barbarous Mexico.* Austin: University of Texas Press, 1969.
Villa, Eduardo W. *Historia del Estado de Sonora.*
Hermosillo: Editorial Sonora, 1951.
Wehrman, Georgia. "Harshaw: Mining Camp of the Patagonias."
Journal of Arizona History 6 (Spring, 1965) : 21–36.
Wellman, Paul I. *The Indian Wars of the West.* New York: Doubleday, 1954.

Wendt, Lloyd, and Herman Kogan. *Bet A Million: The Story of John W. Gates*. Indianapolis: Bobbs, Merrill Co., 1948.

White, Owen P. *Lead and Likker*. New York: Minton, Balch & Co., 1932.

Woodbridge, Dwight E. "Ore Dressing at Cananea." *Engineering and Mining Journal* 76 (June 30, 1904): 1044–45.

Wyckoff, Richard. *Wall Street Ventures and Adventures Through Forty Years*. New York: Harper, 1930.

Index